You Know They're Here

Paul J. Kenyon

"You Know They're Here," by Paul J. Kenyon. ISBN 978-1-60264-464-9.

Published 2009 by Virtualbookworm.com Publishing Inc., P.O. Box 9949, College Station, TX 77842, US. ©2009, Paul J. Kenyon. All rights reserved. No part of this publication may be reproduced, stored in a retrieval system, or transmitted in any form or by any means, electronic, mechanical, recording or otherwise, without the prior written permission of Paul J. Kenyon.

Manufactured in the United States of America.

PROLOGUE

AN INTRODUCTION TO THE HINSDALE HOUSE
AKA THE DANDY HOUSE

I was twenty one years old when I heard about the haunted house in Hinsdale, NY, better known as, "The house near Hinsdale," aka "The Dandy House." The date was August 17, 1973. For more than a year from that day, I would be involved in something most people only hear, or read about, and generally wouldn't want to be involved with. At first, it was just noises or movement seen from the corner of the eye, or hearing the voice of a young lady when there were no females present. You might observe one of the family's pets, playfully catching a tossed ball, and moments later, see that same pet cowering in a corner, tail tucked between its legs. Alternatively, you might hear the story of a boy being struck by a car, a boy whose description fit that of someone seen on many occasions on or near the property, who would suddenly disappear before your eyes. Many of the usual signs were present, from cold spots appearing out of nowhere, and the sudden turning on of burners on the kitchen stove with no human intervention, to the jiggling of doorknobs by unseen hands, and the insertion of a letter opener into a picture of a family member. From overpowering odors and unusual vehicle breakdowns that made mechanics shake their heads in amazement, to chanting heard coming from the hillside and a picture taken on the property and authenticated by the American Psychic Society as being that of a spirit.

When one breaks all of this down and examines the reality of it all, there is one thing missing—a definitive explanation. What was the reason for all of these things happening was the question most who were involved asked at one time or another. There were many explanations offered by psychics, mediums, ghost hunters, and clergy not to mention those who wanted a piece of the paranormal action surrounding this quaint, rural farmhouse. Some offered stones to bury in the yard for protection from the spirits. Some offered God and spiritual

1

help. Others offered home remedies, those used to ward off vampires and witches. Nonetheless, something was very wrong—maybe sinister or evil. The situation was most likely supernatural. The family members were not kooks or attention getters. They were not out to make a fast buck on their story. They were just like you and me, with the same worries about finance, health, family, and their future. The parents worked hard to raise their children and their children worked hard at school to make their parents proud. They conformed to the usual standard: playing games, enjoying picnics and visiting relatives. They initially moved to this quiet, country location because they had grown tired of the hustle and bustle of the city. When their story hit the newsstands, they were scoffed at by some, supported by others and harassed by many. People by the score searched the Hinsdale countryside looking for the house. Within hours of the story's surfacing, there was an uncountable number of vehicles congesting the winding country roads for many days to come. Some made the drive from as far as 100 miles away. Neither the address nor the name of the family was given in newspaper accounts, yet people, persistent and determined to see a ghost, found their way to this off-the-beaten-path farmhouse. I was given explicit directions and it still took my driving twice up a back country road to locate it. It probably would have been easier if I had followed the flow of traffic!

It seems we, as a society, become defensive against something we do not understand. We become judges; oftentimes judging harshly, even to the point of being cruel. Several curious people went out of their way to find the hidden farmhouse, tucked deep into the countryside from the main roads only to harass and curse the family. The Dandy family soon became my very dear friends and I had become one of their willing protectors from those who were hell-bent on making their lives miserable by harassing and threatening. There were even some who had an altogether altered agenda— to frighten the family beyond anyone's comprehension. At first, my reasons for visiting the house were no different than most....curiosity, wanting to know if what they were saying were true, maybe to see some proof of life after death. In short time, I became so involved with the house and with Father Alphonsus Trabold O.F.M, a Franciscan Friar, that I all but took up residence.

What happened surrounding the Hinsdale, NY farmhouse remains to be definitively explained. The conclusion of these disturbances has not yet been fully determined although many have given several opinions. While reading, I hope you will keep an open mind—I imagine you have if you have read this far!

This book is lovingly dedicated to my dear and missed friend: Father Alphonsus Trabold O.F.M 1925–2005

CHAPTER I

It was a sultry afternoon and the cartons of ice cream were in jeopardy of melting. The building where The Fountain of Youth, my first business venture, was located was condemned due to old and faulty wiring. I had purchased the business from a local business owner on my twenty-first birthday, April 14, 1973. I was the third owner of the old soda bar. It was formerly Questa's Soda Bar, a business that dated back to the early '30s. Prior to that, it had been a mercantile store. I had only been in business a short four months when a fire broke out in the wall of the adjoining barbershop. Upon inspection of the basement, firefighters who were investigating to see if the fire had spread through the joists, found the wiring of the building to be frayed, cracked and unsafe. At the end of the investigation, it was determined that the same deteriorating wiring in the building next door caused the fire. The Fire Marshall ordered that the business be closed, the occupant of the upper apartment moved and the building be rewired. The Olean Savings and Loan owned the building and they opted to have the building razed rather than pay to have it rewired. I had offered to pay the estimated cost of the first floor of the historical landmark, but they refused to have the work done. The roof was in dire need of repair even though it didn't leak, and there were foundation issues, not to mention that most of the plumbing and wiring was as old as the building. The fire was all the Savings and Loan needed to make their decision and I, as well as the tenant on the second floor, was to vacate as soon as possible. It was a shame that we could not work together to keep the grand old building from becoming rubble.

While preparing the cartons of ice cream to be loaded into the Perry's ice cream delivery truck, the paper carrier brought in the afternoon paper and set it on the bar as he did every day.

"What happened, Mr. Kenyon?" he asked.

"There was a fire in the wall between the Fountain and the barber shop next door," I said.

"Oh, man, this is the only place we can play pinball and hang out!" Jimmy exclaimed. I told him what the bank's decision had been and that the Fountain would be closed permanently. "I'm sorry to hear that, Mr. Kenyon. Hey, look at the front page of the paper, there's a haunted house in Hinsdale. Oooooooohhhhh. Hahahaha. Maybe the bank will change its minds and we can still come here after school," he said as he walked out the front door to continue on his route.

Three of the regular kids dropped in and asked if they could help with anything. "Sure," I told them, "help me carry these cartons to the truck before they melt."

There were many cartons as an order was delivered at the beginning of the week. "Do we get paid like when we helped with the other junk?" one of the kids asked.

I grinned. "Tell ya what; I'll give you five bucks each as soon as the last carton is on the truck."

"Come on, guys, let's get this ice cream outta here!" One of the boys said.

"Be careful, don't drop them! I won't get credit if the ice cream is running down the sidewalk!" I said.

It was upsetting to see my first business venture *go up in smoke*; no pun intended. It was a grand old building, built in 1852. The walls were lined with beveled glass mirrors reflecting the beauty of the Italian marbled topped tables and chairs. So many kids and families had relaxed at those tables while enjoying their favorite floats, sundaes, chocolate and cherry cokes and banana splits. The top, sides and front of the main bar were also constructed of Italian marble. Behind the bar was an exquisitely hand-carved back bar of solid oak, standing over 10 feet high and 28 feet wide. In the center was a beveled oval mirror some 8 feet high by 16 wide. From the tinned ceiling hung four, still working fans circa 1920. They still spun silently, keeping patrons cool during the afternoon heat. It seemed a crime that all of this was going to be gone to create a parking lot for a bank!

"Hi," I heard one of the boys say out front while I was in the back room gathering my paper work. I looked to see George Stephan, one of the greatest guitarists in the area, walking in.

"Hey, Paul, did you see the paper?" George asked.

"The story about the haunted house? Yeah, I didn't read it but the paperboy mentioned it when he brought it in."

George has been my best friend since we were 14. He was the co-founder of G&G Music store that was directly across the street from the Fountain. George and I had formed a rock band in eighth grade and have played together for over 7 years. Those years undoubtedly yielded some on the best memories of my life.

"Everything okay? You okay?" he asked.

"Best as can be expected I suppose; under the circumstances," I replied.

"Well, if there's anything I can do, just stand at the front window and pat your head or throw your hand at me," George said as he turned to leave.

George and I have had our own form of communication since we met. Even to the present, we can have a conversation about someone in the same room and they would be none the wiser. He has been my closest and truest friend for over 40 years. He left and I continued gathering the rest of the paperwork and bills from the back room. One of the kids came in and told me that all of the cartons had been put on the Perry's truck. The two other boys were close behind him.

"Thanks, guys, I really appreciate the help." I told them as I pulled out three five-dollar bills from my wallet.

"Thanks, Mr. Kenyon! Can we play some games?" one boy asked.

"Well, normally I'd say yes, but hadn't you noticed....the power is out?"

"Oh yeah, duh!" He responded.

They all seemed a bit disappointed but ran out the front door double time with their booty. I placed all the papers in a box and took them to the front bar. I picked up small odds and ends and threw them in the box as well. I had a lot of fun those short four months serving up sodas, floats, cherry cokes and other refreshing favorites.

"Paul, the ice cream is on the truck and I'm ready to roll," Bill, the driver for Perry's ice cream, told me.

"Thanks, Bill. I'll call Monday and get the adjustment for the full returns," I replied with a pang of regret I couldn't quite hide.

"OK, kid, good luck," he said as he walked out to his truck.

I looked out the front window and saw that the last fire truck was pulling away from the curb. The Fire Marshal was leaving as well. There were still people standing across the street watching and talking among themselves. I was happy no one else came in to ask what happened. I double-checked to be sure the kids got all the cartons out of the coolers: they were empty. There were still a lot of toppings in smaller containers so I moved them to the refrigerator in the back room. I still had to call Debbie and tell her what had happened but I wasn't in a real hurry to do that or to leave the building. I made myself one last chocolate coke, sat at the bar and picked up the paper to read the article about the haunted house.

I don't know if I really believed in ghosts, but I had always been interested in stories I'd heard from some of my family members and friends who supposedly experienced paranormal activity. I had quite a scary experience when I was 8 years old. My aunt Mame had passed away and I accompanied my parents and brother to her visitation. It was the first time I had ever seen someone in a coffin. I found it kind of scary, seeing my aunt lying in a coffin. I had just visited her the week before when my parents and I went to my grandmother's. We visited almost every Sunday because my parents, grandmother and a few aunts and uncles played cards. My aunt lived in one of the second floor apartments in a large apartment house that was owned by my grandmother. No sooner had we arrived at my grandma's than I was out the back door and up the stairs to my aunt's. We had a game we played every time I visited. There was a basket on a rope and she would tell me to go downstairs and get something to place in it. She'd pull the basket up with the desired article and lower it back to me with a bright new shiny dime for my efforts! Once she asked me to place a harmonica in it. I had no idea where I was going to find a harmonica! I told my grandmother of my dilemma and she told me,

"Go and check on your uncle's dresser."

I ran into his room, and sure enough, there it was! I ran back outside and placed it in the basket. I waited for Aunt Mame to lower it, and to my surprise, I was rewarded with a quarter! Wow, jackpot!

It had been three weeks after my aunt passed away before we visited my grandmother's again. As always, I ran out the back door and up the stairs to visit my aunt. As soon as I reached her door, I remembered she had passed away. I felt such a cold dread come over me and I turned and began running down the stairs. I was frightened. You had to pass the basement door that usually stood open at the bottom of the stairs. To this day I don't understand why I was so scared coming down those stairs and passing the basement but, when I passed the door, I remember the hair standing up on the back of my neck. I felt as if something sinister was lurking in the darkness—a child's imagination. When I went back into my grandmother's apartment, my mom had asked where I had been. She could see that I was visibly shaken as I told her I went to visit aunt Mame. She immediately pulled me to her, which caused me to sob uncontrollably. Later that evening my mom came in to tuck my brother and me in. As she sat on the side of my bed, I told her I was really scared when I came down the stairs from aunt Mame's apartment. I told her I felt so alone when I left her door because she wasn't there looking over the railing, making sure I had gotten down okay. I explained how scared I had become when I looked into the basement. It felt as though there was something waiting to grab me, to pull me in and close the door behind me. She assured me it was because I had forgotten aunt Mame had passed away and that maybe I was thinking of how it upset me seeing her in the coffin. Mom told me to ask God to take care of my aunt and tell her that I loved and missed her very much. She gave me a hug and a kiss, tucked my brother Mark and me into bed, and said goodnight. Mark said I was being a baby and I was afraid of the boogeyman. I asked him to stop picking on me and rolled over to say my prayers. Later that night, I woke up from what felt like someone rubbing my hair. I turned over and saw my aunt Mame standing at the side of my bed. My scream not only woke my brother but my mom was up the stairs and at my side in no time. Was it a dream, or did my aunt visit me? Mom believed the prior—I honestly believe the latter.

I read the complete story of the haunted house reported by Bob Schnettler of the Olean Times Herald. His account told of the family, Phil and Clara Dandy and their four children, Mike, Beth Ann, Laura and Mary and some of the "troubles" they had experienced in their house. One item mentioned in the article was odd noises, as if someone had been dragging furniture across the floor upstairs, but upon inspection, nothing appeared to have been moved. The story began on the front page of the paper and continued on almost half of page three. It was probably one of the more interesting articles that had been in the news for some time. I called my fiancée Debbie to tell her about the fire and that the business was going to be closed permanently. She sided with my dad when he was against my purchasing the business and I really dreaded having to tell her the unfortunate incident. I still had my income from playing in the band and we were booked most weekends. Nonetheless, I was beside myself because I had built up the idea of owning my own business and I had assured my parents and Debbie that it would be okay.

"How much of the building was damaged?" She asked.

"There really wasn't any damage to the Fountain; the fire was in the wall of the barber shop next door. When the investigator, who had been inspecting the damage, spotted the frayed wiring, and ordered the building be closed. I've still got at least $175 a week from the playing and I have the income from my students." I explained.

I heard a woman talking to Debbie and it sounded as though others were gasping at what the woman was saying.

"What's all the ruckus, is everything okay?" I asked.

"Yeah, I don't know if you saw today's paper but there's a story about a haunted house on the front page. Clara, the woman who lives there, just told some of the people in the data processing area that her husband called and told her there was a line of cars coming up their road. She…"

"You work with the woman who lives there?" I interrupted.

"Yeah," she said. "Why?"

"Hey, ask her if we can come up tonight. I could use a good laugh after what happened today," I said.

"I'm not sure I'd want to go after hearing some of the stuff she's talked about. It's almost quitting time. I'll let you know when I get home," Debbie said.

"Okay, see you in a bit."

I hung up and went behind the bar to pack some of the smaller items into boxes. I had tons of silverware, and the only items that were ever really used were the spoons. There must have been 75 knives and forks but we never had any use for them. I think Hank had plans of serving lunches in the future. Now, after today's incident, I didn't know what the future held. There were probably three dozen sundae and float dishes and over 30 coke glasses. In the four months I'd been serving ice cream, I must have made at least 200 floats and twice as many various sundaes. People sure liked their cherry and chocolate cokes. It's odd it took so many years before Coca Cola actually bottled cherry cokes. Why is it they never offered chocolate cokes, or did they?

I was one of only two tenants who rented space in the building. I rented the downstairs, and there was an apartment upstairs rented by Ms. Questa, Olean High's music teacher. She was also the daughter of Mr. and Mrs. Questa who were the original owners of Questa's Soda Bar. The rents were very reasonable. If the bank had chosen to have the work done that was needed, I'm sure our rents would have increased considerably. In my four months of operation, I had profited approximately $800 in ice cream sales and an additional $1200, which had been my split of the vending machines. Not a fortune by any means, considering I worked 10 hours a day five, sometimes six, days a week. I also had to pay a part time employee at least 4 hours a night on the weekends because I left early to play.

"Holy Christ, what happened?" Shouted Hank K. as he threw the front door open. "Hi, Hank," I said. "There was a fire in the wall next door. The good news is, there wasn't any

10

damage to this building, but the bad news is, I'm not in business anymore."

Hank stood, nodding his head in acknowledgment. "Yeah, the wiring in this building isn't in the best of shape," he said.

"You knew that and yet you didn't say anything to me?" I asked.

"Hell, the wiring in more than half the buildings and homes in Olean is as bad if not worse than in this building. Besides, you and your old man looked the building over before you bought the business. It's just crappy luck that a fire broke out. No one would have even noticed the wiring if it hadn't happened," he insisted

I didn't know if I should be mad or agree with what he was saying. I know my dad had replaced one of those old 'twist' switches in his basement recently. I remember him saying how old and frayed the wires were, and many others in the house were just as bad.

"Well, I still think you could have brought it to our attention," I insisted.

Hank repeated himself and said it was just a freak accident. Maybe he was right; it wasn't even the wires in this building that caused the fire.

"What are you going to do?" He asked.

"What is there to do? I've already started packing up the small items," I replied.

"Well, don't forget, you can make a few bucks selling the fixtures in this building. Remember that when you purchased the business it included the mirrors, the fans, all the coolers and freezers, the marble that the bar is made of and even that clunky old safe. And don't forget this big bastard of a back bar," Hank told me.

Looking around, I wondered what anyone would want with all this stuff. Obviously, I had a puzzled look on my face.

"Antiques, Paul!" exclaimed Hank. "Those mirrors are beveled and beautiful. They'd make a great addition to some of the Victorian homes in the area."

It hadn't crossed my mind because I was thinking of staying in business not selling everything inside the building.

"I'll help you in any way I can," he said. "I've got to get to the diner. Keep me informed as to what's happening, Paul."

I assured him I would, and continued packing. It was becoming quite warm inside and the smell of smoke was getting much stronger now. I finished packing all the silverware and began placing the glasses on the front bar when the phone rang. I walked to the back of the room and answered, "Hello?" It was Debbie. She told me Clara said it was okay to come up. She had to tell her what kind and color car we would be driving. She also said it was a good idea to call before we got there so her husband could estimate the time of our arrival. Clara suggested calling from Crosby's because it was only a couple of miles from the house.

"Clara said the paper's only been out for a few hours and already there are a lot of cars driving to the house," Debbie said.

Debbie went on to tell me that Clara's husband was standing vigil at the edge of the driveway with a .22 rifle to ward off the 'lookie-loos.'

"We have to worry about being shot when we pull up?" I asked nervously.

Laughing, she said, "No, she said it wasn't loaded, it's just for show."

"Loaded or not, I'm not looking forward to someone pointing a gun at me! I'll see you when you get home. I have a few things I want to take to the house, so I have to pack the car," I told her.

"Okay, see you soon; love you," she said.

I didn't really know why I wanted to go to the house. I didn't totally believed in ghosts but the paranormal always interested me. Maybe my vision of my aunt really was her visiting me that night. Perhaps it was her way of telling me everything was okay.

I took a few small boxes out to the car and put the key in the lock of the front door. As I was locking the door, I noticed the box of assorted potato chip bags on one of the marble tables. I unlocked the door and grabbed it. I thought to myself, *they have four kids; this might be just the thing to take up as a peace offering.* Debbie had also told me that Clara wrote down the directions to the house because it would be difficult to locate the house without them. How were all of these other people able to find it? There was no address given in the story. It just said the house was located in the hills of Hinsdale. There are a lot of hills and winding dirt roads in the Hinsdale area. I guess if you want to find something badly enough, you'll find it. My curiosity was piqued now; I was looking forward to driving up. I wasn't looking forward to the family "sentinel!"

Debbie arrived home about half an hour after I did. I met her at the door and immediately she started talking about some of the things Clara told her and their co-workers.

"There's a woman who was seen looking in her daughter's window! Everyone keeps hearing footsteps but there's never anyone walking around! And there's a woman who dances around their pond in circles; her husband calls her the dizzy bitch." Debbie said excitedly.

"Dizzy bitch?" I asked.

"Clara said her husband and her two youngest daughters are the only ones who have seen her."

"Come on, a woman dancing around the pond? How long has this stuff been going on?" I asked, my skepticism showing.

"Well, I don't know exactly—I guess a while. I'm gonna change, why don't you make us a couple of sandwiches we can eat on the way. I want to get up there as soon as we can," she said.

Before making the sandwiches, I went out to the car and brought in the boxes I had packed at the Fountain but I left the box of potato chips in the back seat. I placed the boxes in the kitchen next to the table, washed my hands, and proceeded to make three roast beef sandwiches. I knew she would want two but I didn't have much of an appetite. I spread a generous amount of mustard on Debbie's and mayonnaise on mine. I grabbed a couple of Pepsi's from the fridge and tore off a few paper towels. Debbie had returned to the kitchen just as I picked up the phone to call my mom.

"Who you calling?" she asked.

"I want to call my mom and tell her we're going up to the house," I said.

13

"Okay, while you're doing that, I'll check the mail," Debbie said as she opened the front door.

My mom was my best friend. She was a stay at home mom until I was 16 when she then took a job as housekeeping supervisor at Saint Bonaventure University. She only worked for a few years before suffering a heart attack in 1970. Life had been tough living with my dad until that frightening day. From that day on, she was his queen.

"Hello?" she answered

"Hi, mom, what're you doing?" I asked.

"I was doing dishes but you got me out of that job for the time being," she said.

"Did you see today's paper?" I asked her.

"The story about the haunted house?" She asked.

"Yeah, Debbie and I are going up to see it tonight," I told her.

There was silence for about 10 seconds. "Mom?"

After a few more moments of silence, she said, "Yeah, I'm here."

"You okay?" I asked.

"Why do you want to go to a house that's supposedly haunted?" She asked.

It wasn't the question, but the inflection in her voice as she said it.

"Just curious, I guess. Debbie works with the mom and I've always been interested in stuff like that."

"You need to call me as soon as you get home. It doesn't matter if it's late but you need to call," she said.

There was an edge to her voice; it almost cracked as she spoke. There was noticeable apprehension and a touch of fear in the way she repeated, "Call me."

"Mom, you okay? I mean if you don't want me…."

"Just call me," she said again. "And be careful; don't go wandering around somewhere alone."

"Mom, we'll be okay. We're just going up to visit, to see what this is all about. I'm sure there's nothing more to it than an old county house that creaks in the night," I said.

There was a short silence again before she said, "All right, drive safe and CALL ME," mom said.

"I promise, mom. Love you, don't worry," I told her.

"Love you too, Paulie."

I hung up the phone staring at the wall wondering what she was worrying about. Mom was a very quiet woman, a very caring woman. She always worried about me, her youngest and I must add she never stopped spoiling me. As I said, she was certainly my best friend and as I became a young adult, I was able to talk to her about most things without leaving anything hanging in the air. This conversation disturbed me although I didn't understand why.

"You ready?" Debbie asked as she bit into her sandwich while hurrying to the kitchen door.

"My mom seemed a bit worried that we were going to the house," I said as I closed and locked the door behind me.

"Your mom always worries about you," Debbie replied.

Whenever my band played out of town, it was a ritual that I drive by my parents' house. My mom would always be sitting on the porch waiting to wave or sometimes throw an Italian hand gesture at me. We've been a lot closer since her first heart attack. Really, I think I wanted to be sure that *she* was okay not the other way around. As I pulled away, Debbie asked me what the box was in the back seat.

"I thought I could trade a box of potato chips for my life when we pull up to their house! Maybe he'll be less apt to shoot if I give him the ransom," I chuckled.

"I told you, the gun isn't loaded and I'm sure by now there aren't many people coming to the house," she said.

It was only about a 15-minute drive to Crosby's from our house. Crosby's Dairy has been in business since the late 1800's. It was, without a doubt, one of the greatest places to take the family for treats. As kids, we would ride our bikes down the back Hinsdale road from north Olean to get our favorite ice cream desserts. We always made one stop on the way. Just about waist high, a pipe, jutting out of the side of Boot Hill, offered the coldest, most refreshing spring water imaginable. We'd always carry our canteens to fill so we could quench our thirst on our 6-mile round trip bike ride. Years ago, Crosby's suffered a severe fire and, like most local dairies, fell by the wayside, and was sold. It's now a quick stop convenience store offering the typical staples as well as self-serve gasoline.

We arrived at Crosby's around 7:30. I pulled into a parking spot and Debbie went in to call Clara. While waiting, I noticed the traffic was heavier than most evenings on the Olean-Hinsdale road. Most of the traffic was heading back toward Olean. It was just a few minutes when Debbie returned to the car.

"Okay, Clara said to be careful 'cause there are still a lot of cars on the roads."

That explained the heavier traffic that evening. Debbie went on to tell me that Clara informed her that the roads are dirt and some areas are really washboard.

"There are a couple of ways to get to her house but she said this is the easiest from Crosby's. Turn on Flannigan Road and, right after you pass the fire hall, you turn left onto Congress road. Follow Congress to the 'Y' in the road and continue to the right onto Wagner—"

"Slow down! Let me get to the first road, will ya?" I asked.

We came to Congress and I followed it to the "Y" and veered right onto Wagner Hill Road. If you will, imagine a somewhat typical country road: houses, maybe an eighth of a mile apart, surrounded by large open fields. I couldn't believe the amount of traffic coming toward us. In a matter of a few brief minutes, no less than 12 vehicles passed us heading back toward Hinsdale. In the '70s, Wagner Hill was a winding, dirt road with numerous ruts creating a washboard effect. At least the traffic was moving at a reasonable rate of speed. I stayed right at 15 mph going up and around the tightest curves. As we approached the top of Wagner, the driver of a car approaching us was waving his hand. I slowed to a stop as he pulled along side of me.

"Hey, if you're going to the haunted house, turn around; the only thing you're gonna see is a nut with a gun at the end of the driveway!" The man said and continued on. A car horn honked and I looked in the rear view mirror to see a car behind me. The driver was waving his arm in a motion to "move it." I continued on and questioned Debbie on the rest of the directions.

"We should be close to their turn. Clara said Wagner would flatten out and their turn is to the right: McMahon Road. Look for a bus stop shack and a big tree and barn on the side of the road," she said.

There was a house just ahead on a hill and a car blocked the driveway. There were three cars in front of us, several parked on both sides of the road and several coming toward us from the other direction on Wagner Hill. There were at least a dozen people walking in both directions to and from the parked cars. The road looked more like that of a secondary parking area when all the parking lots were full at a Country Fair.

"Good God! All these people are ghost hunting?!" I exclaimed.

"There's the shack!" Debbie shouted.

I was so busy watching the people running back and forth on the road that I had missed it. I went up the road a bit to try and find a place to turn around. There were no other houses in the immediate area where I could use their driveway to turn around so I had to drive a ways before I was able to find a wide enough spot in the road to make the u-turn. I wasn't familiar with the area and it appeared most of the dwellings were more like cabins. Later, I learned that most were camps used by hunters that come up from the cities during the hunting seasons.

After finding a suitable spot to turn around, we headed back toward McMahon road. There were a couple of cars coming out of McMahon road so this time it was easier to spot. The second was a pickup with what appeared to be a bunch of teenagers in the bed of the truck screeching and hollering. "The ghosts are gonna get you, boo hooo hoooooo ha hahaha." We turned onto McMahon and continued for about two hundred yards when I came to a sharp turn to the left. A couple of people were walking toward us on both sides of the road and we could see three more walking through a field back in the direction of the barn.

"This is nuts!" I said. "I would never tolerate all these people trespassing on my property." Continuing on, the house didn't come into view until we were nearly at the end of the road. It didn't look like the typical haunted house you generally see in the movies. Just as I was about to take the last turn to the right that led to the back of the house, a man walked out from the side of a big pine tree in the front yard with a gun aimed directly at the hood of the car.

"Stop and get off this property. There's nothing here for you to see," the man yelled. The sight of that gun and the look on his face scared the hell out of me. I had to remind myself that he was carrying an unloaded weapon, but that didn't lessen the fear I was feeling at that moment.

"I thought he was going to be keeping an eye out for our car, Debbie!" I exclaimed.

Debbie leaned over from the passenger seat and yelled out my window to the man (Phil was it?) that we had been invited by Clara and that she worked with her at B.O.C.E.S. He somewhat lowered the aim of his equalizer and walked over to my door.

"Hi, I'm Paul and this is Debbie. She works with your wife," I told him.

"Clara said it was okay to stop by," Debbie said again.

He looked in the car and scanned the back seat. He seemed to be a bit calmer, turned around and yelled, "Phil!" He turned back to us and said, "Hi, I'm Gordon, Clara's brother. This is Phil."

Another man approached from the front of the house and took the gun from him. Clara's brother told me to pull to the back of the house and park. I pulled up another sixty feet or so and shut the engine off. Just then, a slender woman and a boy of about sixteen approached the car from the back of the house. "That's Clara!" Debbie said. She exited the car, walked over to Clara and gave her a hug. I felt safer now and I exited the car. "Clara, this is Paul—Paul, Clara," Debbie said, introducing us. Clara and I shook hands. Clara introduced the boy who had walked over to the car with her as her son, Mike.

"Nice to meet you both," I said as I shook Mike's hand.

"Looks like you have quite a lot of visitors tonight," I said.

"Yeah, well these goddamn visitors can get right the hell outta here too." Said a voice from behind me.

"Paul and Debbie, this is my husband, Phil," Clara said.

"Nice to meet you, sorry if we came at the wrong time," I said, shaking his hand.

"No, you're fine. Clara told me you might be stopping by, but I wasn't paying attention to who was driving what car. Can't believe this goddamn many people are so interested in our problems," Phil said.

"Come on you two, let's go into the house," Clara said.

Dusk was beginning to fall and it was a beautiful night. The temperature was still in the mid-seventies and the sky was clear. The house appeared to be an old farm house. The main structure was two stories but the end of the house was only one. To the north of the house, past the large back yard area was a good sized pond and I could see a boat on the bank. Further north was a large field and beyond that more open land. Directly behind and above their property you could see another home or camp if you will. Walking in the back door you entered a sort of mud room where visitors could shed their overcoats and dirty footwear, before entering into the kitchen.

"Come on in and meet Father Al and the rest of the family," Clara said. Debbie and I followed Clara through the kitchen and into the living room.

"Father Al, this is Paul and Debbie. Debbie works with me and Paul is her fiancé," Clara said.

Father Al, a short stocky man, puffing at a pipe, rose from the recliner he was seated in and shook both our hands. "I'm very pleased to meet you both," he said.

"Nice meeting you too, Father," I said.

Mike walked into the living room, excused himself past us, and entered a room off the living room. I could overhear him having a discussion with a female.

"Make yourselves comfortable on the couch, you two," Clara said, motioning for us to have a seat.

Father Al returned to the chair he'd been sitting in as Mike and a pretty young girl of about 15 walked from the room Mike had entered a few moments before.

"Hi," voiced the young lady as she sat on the edge of a chair.

Mike excused himself again as he continued walking to the kitchen.

"This is my daughter, Beth Ann. Honey, this is Debbie and her fiancé Paul," Clara said.

"Hi, Debbie, nice to meet you. Mom's talked about you. Hi, Paul, nice to meet you too," Beth Ann said.

Clara excused herself to go to the kitchen where she called out to her daughters, Mary and Laura. "Mom says you work at B.O.C.E.S with her, Debbie. Do you like working there?"

"Yeah, it's okay. I'm in the data processing room. It gets boring at times but I work with a lot of nice people, including your mom," Debbie replied.

"I don't know if I could sit all day and type. It seems like it would get tedious," Beth Ann said.

A loud thump resounded from above and everyone in the room jumped. I looked to Father Al for his reaction as two girls walked around the corner and into the living room, Clara following.

"Mary, Laura, this is Paul and Debbie," Clara said.

With a chuckle, Father Al said, "By the look on your face, Paul, that noise had you thinking it was something else, not the girls. Am I correct in my assumption?"

"I don't know what I was thinking, Father, but I guess I'm expecting to hear or see something," I responded.

Mary, the youngest daughter, said hello and Laura gave us a shy smile.

"Girls, you need to get to the dishes and then we can all have some dessert," Clara said. Beth Ann, getting up from her seat, offered to help and the three of them went to the kitchen. Clara walked in and sat in the chair where Beth Ann had been sitting. On either side of the chair Clara was seated was a birdcage, each housing one parakeet. Both were communicating with one another in aviary song. The wall opposite Debbie and me was decorated with several pictures of the family hanging between two windows facing the front yard. There was a door on the south side of the room that, at the time, I believed led to the front porch. I later learned it had been converted into a closet. There was one window on the north side of the room, which faced their pond as well as the rest of their property. There was an old upright piano between this window and what I later learned was Beth Ann's bedroom. As I was glancing around, Clara told Debbie and me that the picture of Mary that had the letter opener in it was on the wall opposite us. I got up to look at but Debbie remained in her seat.

"You woke up and it was just stuck in the picture?" I asked.

"No, actually, we were watching TV. I believe I was the one who looked up and noticed the letter opener balanced in Mary's picture. I had forgotten I even had the thing. When I resigned from my job in Buffalo, I brought the opener home and have no idea where I put it. This was the first time I'd seen it since." Clara explained.

A door closed loudly; we all became silent.

"Goddamn people, they sure have their nerve walking wherever the hell they want to," Phil was heard grumbling as he made his way through the kitchen, and to the doorway of the living room.

"You had to expect something like this was going to happen once the story was published, Phil," Clara replied.

I was shocked! I couldn't believe Phil had spoken that way in the presence of a priest. I wouldn't have dared to say hell in front of a priest unless I had been referring to hell. I looked at Father Al and he didn't seem remotely bothered by Phil's comment.

"Well, this better not go on very long. I can't be here day and night, ya know," Phil said.

"I know, Phil, I know. We'll call the State Police and see if they can put a road block at the end of the road tomorrow," Clara replied.

"Why don't you take Paul and Debbie on a tour of the property?" Clara asked.

"No, thanks," Debbie said. "I'll stay here and visit with you if you don't mind."

"Chicken," I said. "I'll come with ya, Phil."

Phil waved his arm for me to follow. Walking into the kitchen, I saw Beth Ann tending to something in the refrigerator. Mary and Laura were at the sink. We walked into Mike's room, which was toward the side of the house just off the kitchen. It wasn't a very big room, with shelves on the walls, his bed, a dresser and a guitar in the corner. I looked at the shelf before leaving the room. I assumed the chess set mentioned in the story had been on that shelf. I noticed there was a chess set sitting on top of his dresser now.

"I'll show you the upstairs now, Paul," Phil said as he walked back into the kitchen.

The stairs leading to the second floor were on the north side of the kitchen. There was a tiny bedroom on the right of the top landing. On the left was the large master bedroom. Another small bedroom lay off it.

"This is Clara's and my room. This one," Phil said pointing to a closed door, "Is Mary's room and the one off the landing is Laura's. Mary's room seems to be the worst in the house but there's got to be some goddamned reasonable explanation for what's happening. Some nights, we'll all be downstairs and it'll sound like someone's dragging the goddamn furniture around up here. Don't ask me, I think it's a bunch of crap," Phil said.

As we were descending the stairs, Phil pointed to the crawl space that was above the stairs. "Lots of noise in there some nights, probably one of the raccoons or some other animal trying to get in. Let's take a walk out by the pond," Phil said.

As we descended to the kitchen, I saw that Mary and Laura were finishing the dishes; Beth Ann was elsewhere. Phil exited the kitchen first, as I stopped for a second to look into the bathroom off the kitchen when Laura looked at me and said, "You know they're here too, don't you?"

I said nothing; I just looked at her, puzzled. The look on her face when she said it troubled me. She said it so seriously, so firmly. As I turned to go outside, Mary gave Laura a light swat on the arm. I don't believe Phil heard Laura and I didn't ask what she might have meant. Phil grabbed a flashlight from a shelf and we walked across the back yard to the pond. I hung on to Phil's shirt because the night was as dark as coal and I didn't know the lay of the land. It was a clear night, still quite warm and the crickets were singing their discordant song.

"Watch the run-off here, the ground is soft and muddy," Phil said.

There was a little stream of water trickling down from the front edge of the pond toward the field to the front of the house. As we approached the backside of the pond, Phil asked if I noticed the cold spots. I had, but thought it was normal to experience cold draughts of air in the country especially near water. I dismissed what he might have been suggesting.

"This is the side of the pond where the girls have seen the woman," he said.

"Is this the one you call the dizzy bitch?" I asked.

He turned around quite abruptly and shone the light directly in my face.

"Yeah, it is. I don't know who she is and don't really give a damn," he sounded perturbed.

Was he angered by my question? I didn't press to ask what upset him. Rather than walk around the pond completely, we turned around and headed back toward the house on the same side as we had walked out. Neither of us spoke until we reached the back of the house. As we neared the back door, instead of entering, Phil continued to walk around the side of the house toward the front. I followed.

"Let's see what Gordon's up to," he said.

As we arrived at the front yard, we noticed Gordon, talking to a man and woman who were in their vehicle at the end of the Dandys' drive. We continued to walk the length of the road to the first turn. I looked at my watch and saw that it was 9:15. There were still vehicles traveling Wagner Hill Road and there was another backing down the road ahead of us.

"Do you believe these goddamned people? I'll bet anything this shit will be going on for weeks," Phil said.

"Well, I hope not for yours and your family's sake," I said.

"I just hope Clara remembers to call the State Police tomorrow. Being Saturday, they might not have a car available to sit up here to keep these goddamned people off our road," he said.

We were at the turn in the road and Phil told me this had been the spot where Clara and a few others have smelled what they thought was the aroma of pipe tobacco.

Phil stood beside me silently for a couple of minutes and uttered, "Gotta be some goddamn, reasonable explanation for all this shit. Come on; let's go back to the house."

As we were walking back, the vehicle that had been at the end of the drive was heading toward us. We moved to the side and as the driver approached slowly, he expressed his apologies for coming up and said he hoped all would be back to normal soon.

"Thanks a lot," Phil said as he kept walking toward the house.

You know they're here too, don't you?

The words Laura had said to me as I was leaving the house had been going through my thoughts since Phil began the outside tour. Who are *they* she was referring to, the ghosts? I didn't know anything more than what I was told. I didn't feel anything except a bit uneasy while we were walking outside. I'm sure that was nothing but apprehension born of expecting to see or hear something startling. Cold spots? Nah. Those, I was sure, were nothing more than cold pockets of air caused by the air cooling quicker around the pond. I hadn't experienced any on our walk since leaving the back yard area. I didn't see or hear anything out of the ordinary....no odor of tobacco smoke, no specters roaming the hillsides, not a moan or groan from the darkness; nothing. Just the quiet sounds of a beautiful night in the country.

I had read the story one more time before leaving the Fountain and it stated that a psychic had been at the house that day and told them, according to what Mr. Schnettler reported, that he had felt that the spirits haunting them were that of a mother, father, a young son and a grandmother. Supposedly, he felt that they had been occupants of the property years past and they wanted the Dandys to leave. Now, I must say, I find that psychic's conclusion simply ridiculous. I'd read several ghost stories and have seen movies but I don't ever remember an entire family being the 'hauntees.' I didn't really know that much about the paranormal world but, if they were truly being visited by dearly departed souls, what are the chances it would be four members of the same family? Remote? I had the understanding that most "lost" spirits remained earthbound because they had unfinished business or that their deaths were so traumatic they didn't know they were dead. Reading that second explanation sounded just as absurd to me as the psychic's conclusion that several members of the same family were responsible for the haunting.

As we approached the side of the house, we saw no sign of Gordon. Obviously, he'd gone inside. Just as we turned the corner at the back of the house, Phil's flashlight went out and a very cold air mass engulfed us.

"You feel *that*, don't you?" Phil asked.

Yes, I felt it. Or, was it feeling me? It hit us so suddenly and sharply that it had taken my breath from me. The ambient temperature couldn't have been below 72 degrees and the air that had encompassed us felt like that of a deep freeze when you opened the door. It wasn't anything I had ever felt before on a warm evening—never. It made the hair on my arms and neck prickle and my senses go to red alert. We walked in the back door and as Phil was about to set the flashlight on the shelf, it turned on.

"Okay, can we get inside, please?" I said.

Phil chuckled, turned the light off and opened the door. I felt uneasy. No, I was scared. Even though I expected to see or hear something, I didn't really *expect* to see or hear *anything*.

Clara, Debbie, Father Al and Beth Ann were at the kitchen table, Mary and Laura were in the living room watching TV and Mike was in his room listening to music.

"Well?" Clara asked.

"It's quieting down outside. We could see one car by the tree while we were walking and a couple passed by on Wagner," Phil said.

"Yeah, and we just walked through a blast of Arctic air too," I said.

Phil gave a light chuckle, Clara and Father Al looked at one another.

"Cold spot?" Clara asked.

"Yeah, it was cold all right," I answered.

"Well, it was colder than any I've felt, I can tell you that," Phil said.

"Umbrella night?" Clara asked.

Beth Ann scooted her chair slightly closer to her mom after she said, "umbrella night."

"What does that mean, Clara, umbrella night?" I asked.

Phil grabbed a beer from the refrigerator and walked upstairs.

"Well, it's what I say when things begin to go wrong, when the energy of the house starts to build. Usually, it's more than just one thing that happens, not just a cold spot. Maybe it will be noises, or the burners on the stove turning on. Or it might be the water flowing from a faucet with no one turning it on and the basement door rattling," Clara said.

"It's getting late, Paul. We really should get going and let them get some sleep." Debbie interrupted.

"I'm sorry, Debbie. I didn't mean to upset you," Clara said.

Father Al reached to Debbie's hand and gave it a soft pat. It was obvious he was an extremely kind man. A very soft-spoken man yet you could sense he had an inner strength. I supposed being a priest, you had to be strong and have great compassion for all those that come to you seeking guidance, and help.

"It is getting late, Clara, and I had a nasty day at the Fountain," I said.

"Yes, Debbie was telling me at work and finished the story tonight while we ate some cake which, by the way, you and Phil missed out on," she said.

"I'll certainly take a rain check on that," I said.

"Our door is open whenever you want to visit," Clara replied. She continued, "All of my family lives in Buffalo and mum and dad don't get out visiting as often as I'd like. You're welcome any time."

"Oh nuts, I brought you guys something and forgot to bring it in," I said.

26

I stood and turned to the door and immediately hesitated in opening it.

"Let me walk out with you, Paul," Father Al offered. With Father's words, an almost instantaneous feeling of protection came over me. There are no words I could use to explain the relief I felt. For the lack of a better explanation, think of the worse toothache or pain you'd ever experienced and have it stop *immediately*. It was so complete, so genuine and so holy.

"Thank you, Father. Was my reluctance that obvious?" I asked.

Father Al stood, placed his hand on my shoulder as we walked out the door with Debbie, Beth Ann and Clara following. I walked to our car, opened the back door and lifted the box out.

"What's this?" Clara said.

"Not much, I grabbed all the potato chips and had planned to offer them to Phil as a peace offering so he wouldn't shoot me," I replied.

Everyone laughed and Clara gave me a smack on the head. "Well, now I'll have to give you ice cream *with* your cake when you return," Clara said.

I grinned. "Sounds good to me."

I shook Father Al's hand and thanked him and Clara again. Beth Ann was holding on to her mom's arm and looking toward the pond. Were we being watched? Was this going to be an "umbrella night" as Clara explained? Debbie and I got into the car and she locked her door.

"Tell Mike, Phil and the girls we said goodnight, Clara," I requested.

"I will, and thank you!"

"Drive carefully; it was very nice meeting both of you," Father Al said.

"Thanks, Father. It was nice meeting you too and thanks for the protection!" I exclaimed.

Father Al gave a subdued chuckle, and they all waved as I began backing the car around to leave.

All in all, with the exception of an Arctic blast to the face, it seemed to be a normal night of visiting friends. Sure, there was a bit of apprehension and nervousness because we didn't know what might happen but I guess that was to be expected. Even though the different things mentioned in the story kept going through my mind, I kept thinking that they're maybe imagining many of the things they talked about. Clara said she had a thought that maybe she had put the letter opener in the picture caused by stress or something. That didn't sound rational, stress or not. She certainly didn't appear to be the type of person who would do anything remotely like this under any circumstances. They were a normal family in every sense of the word. They had three dogs and two cats which just lay around the house. Two raccoons and a pet skunk which, by the way, I wanted to see but didn't get the pleasure. I'd never seen a skunk up close unless I was running away from it! Everything I expected to see or experience just didn't materialize other than a cold blast of air. However, it wasn't just cold—it was freezing! If I had paid close enough attention, I'm sure I would have noticed my own breath!

It was nearly 11:30 p.m. and there were no vehicles in the area. There are no streetlights on these country roads and the only light we could see was from a house on the other side of Wagner Hill Road. I had meant to ask why there were no other houses on their road. If their house were over 100 years old, one would think there might have been other houses on their road. I'll try to remember to ask the next time we visit.

You know they're here too, don't you?

What the hell? Why didn't I at least ask Clara or even Father Al why Laura would say that to me? Why in the world would a 13-year-old girl assume that a perfect stranger knew something about paranormal activity or ghosts? Did *she* know, really know? Alternatively, was it something she put on herself simply because of all the talk about the house the other members of the family had as part of their conversations every day? There were many questions to ask. We only visited for a few hours, yet I felt I *had* to have answers but why? Even if their house was truly haunted by spirits, why did **I** feel I needed answers? I didn't know these people. I've heard of other supposed haunted houses in the Olean area yet I didn't seek them out. I've never purposely gone looking for haunted houses. Sure, Debbie worked with Clara but I didn't know that, not before the story came out. Why did I ask Debbie to get permission for us to visit tonight? Puzzling.

"So, what did you think? Are they being visited by the ghosts of yesteryear?" I asked.

"I don't know what's happening. Honestly, I do not want to know. I like Clara and they all seem to be really nice people but it's not something I'd like to be around on a daily basis, I can tell you that much," Debbie replied.

"I'd like to live out in the country like they do. Look at this road, their house, the only house on it. No nosey neighbors sticking their nose…"

The car stalled; it stalled dead. No prior hesitation, it just quit, along with the headlights.—a complete shutdown, and directly under the big tree at the beginning of McMahon road.

"What the f….."

"Oh, this is not what I call funny. What is…? "Debbie interrupted.

"I don't know, Deb. It's never stalled in all the time we've had it," I said. *We've had car trouble, broken bones, and equipment failures*

Part of a quote by Clara from the story in the Olean Times Herald and I remembered the statement very clearly at that moment. The night was black, *pitch* black. Looking out the window, you couldn't see ten feet in any direction. We both rolled our windows up and I locked my door the same time Debbie was reaching in the back to lock the rear doors. "I don't like this one bit," I said as I turned the key in the ignition.

The battery didn't even click as a battery usually does even when totally drained.

"I saw something!" Debbie shrieked.

"Oh, you did not; don't you lose it. There's nothing there, hear me? It's probably just an animal. We're in the country," I said.

"Animals aren't ten feet in the air! Dammit, I saw something in the tree above us!"

I turned the key several more times. Nothing.

"It's probably just a loose wire in the ignition or something," I said.

"That's not going to make the headlights go out and certainly not the dash lights!"

She was right.

"There's something outside the car, I'm telling you, there's something outside!" Debbie said, becoming hysterical.

"Please, Debbie…. Goddamn it, there's nothing outside. It's your imagination. Just please shut up and help me figure out what the hell is wrong!" I said. I snapped. Imagination or not, I was scared out of my wits. Looking across Wagner Hill Road, I could see lights in the house no more than an eighth of a mile up their driveway. The thought of leaving the car and walking in pitch black was out of the question in my state of mind. There is no way Debbie would allow me to leave her alone and she sure as hell wouldn't have trekked the distance with me. There *was* something! I couldn't see it or hear it but I could *feel* it. How? My mind was playing against me and I tried my best to make it obey, yet there *was* something or someone outside the car. I told myself it was my imagination but the feeling was getting stronger. I dared not look up from the steering wheel because, if I saw what I *felt,* I would lose it. All the while, these thoughts whirled through my mind; I was twisting the key so hard in the ignition I expected it to break at any moment. All of the windows in the car were closed. The air was heavy, hard to breathe. Was this shock? Time wasn't moving, at least not from my perspective. So many thoughts were crossing my mind and I surely wasn't thinking rationally.

"Do something!" Debbie shouted. "Get us off this fucking road, NOW!"

I couldn't move. I refused to look out the window; there's nothing there. Our imaginations were running rampant and I, in some way, needed to get control of a situation I shouldn't have put us in.

"We're okay, Deb. I'm sure the engine's going to turn over in a minute and we'll be on our way home," I said calmly, yet my mind was screaming at her to not say another word.

"Oh, God, what was that? WHAT WAS THAT!?" She screamed so loud every nerve became frazzled and every hair on my body stood at attention.

A glimmer of light that seemed to come in from behind the car sparkled on the dash. I wondered how there could be any form of light where we were sitting in this black void. It came again, glinting against the metal pieces of the dash and this time I caught a glimpse of it in the rear view mirror. Suddenly it was brighter, sweeping across the tall grass and weeds on both sides of the road. It took a few seconds for my mind to accept what we were seeing. Then the realization snapped home—it was the headlights of a car coming down the road behind us. Relief was not in a hurry to accommodate my mind's needs. The fear I was realizing sitting at the end of this road, under this huge tree, so close to a supposed haunted house, was overwhelming. I can't even imagine how Debbie was coping, what sort of mental torment she was attempting to stave off. The car pulled right up to my bumper, the headlights; the overly welcomed light at the end of the tunnel warmed our sight, our hearts. Looking in the side view mirror I recognized the friendliest face I would ever want to see at this moment in time; Father Alphonsus Trabold. The calm didn't come instantaneously. The fright of these past few minutes (seemed like hours) held fast to each nerve ending. My senses wanted to let out a scream irrigated with tears to cleanse the anxiety from my system. Still, I knew everything was going to be fine. Debbie was already in full sob mode. I raised my arm to place it between her and the back of the seat and she pulled closer to her door; understood.

"Car trouble?" Father Al asked.

I opened my door and instinctively and without hesitation, wrapped my arms around a man for whom I knew my admiration would be stronger than for any other human being.

"Thank you, Father. I have no idea, it just quit. It's never acted up like this before," I said. I got back in the drivers seat and told Debbie everything was going to be okay. Father Al leaned in my window to ask if I was in park.

"Yes, it's in park. I turned the key so hard so many times I'm surprised it….."

The engine came to life on the first turn of the key and the rest of the electrical system followed. The dash, the headlights and radio all came on.

"You better have a mechanic take a look at it," Father Al said.

I looked out the window and up at Father Al's kind face.

"I believe *Someone* has sent me the best mechanic available," I said.

He bent down, looked across to Debbie and asked if she was okay.

"Yes, Father, I'll be even better when we get home." Debbie replied.

"Off we go then—I'll follow you home to be sure you get there safely," Father said.

"Thanks, Father. We live on south Sixth Street; I hope it's not out of your way."

"Not at all" he replied" I drive right down west State Street to get to Saint Bonaventure," he replied.

"Thanks." I said again.

I waited until Father Al got into his car before pulling onto Wagner Hill Road. Not only because he was *my* "shield" twice in one night, but I wanted to be sure he wasn't going to fall prey to unseen forces.

The ride down Wagner Hill was slow and cautious while the rest of the ride home was bleak and silent. I tried to talk to Debbie several times but she wasn't interested in interacting. I honestly didn't think she was interested in hearing me talk but she didn't have the energy to tell me to keep quiet. I felt horrible, not physically, not even mentally, just miserably and completely horrible. If all the things mentioned in the story were true, and they've experienced any of them more than once, how in God's name had they coped? It was 12:19 a.m. We were just about at the end of Congress road, ready to turn right, back to the world we knew was real. I looked over at Debbie. She was fast asleep. HOW? Exhaustion; shock perhaps. Father Al was about three car lengths back. What did he make of all of this? I didn't know at the time how he had gotten involved with the house. Was he called upon, did he volunteer to assist after reading the article or had he been a friend of the family? I was sure to have answers to this and many other questions soon enough. We were just passing Crosby's at 12:23 a.m. I wish they had been open; a chocolate milkshake would have sure hit the spot.

We pulled up to the house at 12:35 a.m. I tapped Debbie lightly on the shoulder and she woke with a start. She picked up her purse and exited the car without saying a word. I got out and walked back to Father Al's car. I assumed Debbie had forgotten Father followed us home because she hadn't noticed him until she reached the front door, at which time; she turned around and came back to the car. Father Al got out of his car when he saw Debbie returning.

"Thank you for saving us, Father. We'd probably still be sitting there if you hadn't pulled up," she said giving him a hug.

"Not at all, not at all. Thanking me is not necessary. I did nothing. I'm sure once you have the car checked out you'll find it was a short or something," he replied.

"Just the same, thank you again and it was very nice meeting you. I hope to see you again," Debbie said, rubbing his shoulder.

"You too, Debbie, sleep pleasantly," Father said.

"I'll be in shortly; I just want to talk to Father for a second, Deb," I said.

"Okay, I'm sure I'll be asleep before my head hits the pillow," she replied.

As she walked away, I turned to Father Al and told him what Laura had said to me. He didn't respond immediately but thought while chewing on his pipe.

"Paul, I believe Laura is gifted. I also believe a lot of the activity is centered on her. Rather than go into detail at this late hour, I'll just say that many times poltergeist activity revolves around children approaching puberty. In this case, there appears to be more than a poltergeist at hand. As for her statement to you, I don't believe I can offer a definitive answer. She might have made the same statement to someone else if they had walked into the kitchen," Father explained.

"It wasn't just *what* she said, Father, it was the look in her eyes and how she said it."

He thought again before speaking.

"When you arrived at the house, did you feel or sense anything at any time before you and Phil went outside?" He asked.

"I don't believe so, just maybe apprehension. I think part of the reason we went to the house was to see something, or even expected to see something," I said.

"Yes, yes, but did you feel anything while walking through the house with Phil or when you were in the living room with the rest of us?"

It was my turn to think. "When we came down from upstairs, and just before going outside, I did look into the bathroom. I think we've all had the feeling of being watched or stared at one time or another and that's the feeling I had. Maybe it was an overactive imagination, or just the fact that we were in a supposed haunted house but it just seemed I had a feeling or a thought, um..." I said pausing, thinking of the proper word.

"A premonition?" Father Al interrupted.

"I don't know," I said. "Just I felt that there was someone looking at me from the bathroom. I know that sounds strange 'cause I knew there was no one there."

"Was it the same time that Laura said what she said?" Father asked.

"Well, I looked into the bathroom and began to go out the back door and that's when Laura said it."

"Maybe she sensed the same as you and noticed you looking into the bathroom. It could have been the expression on your face. I don't know, Paul. What were your thoughts when you experienced the cold spot in the yard?"

"Well, initially, I just didn't understand. Later, I thought it wasn't natural for air to be that cold on such a warm night without there being a source for it." Hearing myself saying those words gave me a chill. What had been the source for air that was as cold as winter? It just wasn't the coldness of it; it was how it overcame me.

I continued, "For a few moments after, I felt like you would feel after a near accident, only there wasn't the adrenalin rush accompanying the feeling but more of a draining, exhausted feeling." I explained.

"Our minds are fragile; when fear is involved many emotions are distorted and can become warped. There are disturbances happening at the Dandy house, and I am not, at this time, in a position to define what the reasons or sources might be. I will support Clara, Phil and their family in every way I can whether it be spiritually or just as a supportive friend. I will do the same for you, Paul." Father said.

"Thank you, Father," I said. "I've taken enough of your time and I appreciate your helping us tonight. I just don't understand what happened to the car."

"You're welcome and I'm sure you'll find that it was just an electrical problem. Have a good rest tonight," Father replied.

I walked with him as he got into his car. He gave a wave and friendly smile as he drove off. I stood there for several minutes but instead of thinking of all that had happened tonight, my mind was a total blank. I sat on the steps and smoked a cigarette before going into the house. After about ten minutes, I went in, drank half a Pepsi and turned off the lights.

"Shit!" I whispered. "Call your mother!"

I really didn't want to call her this late but if I didn't she'd be mad for a week. I hesitated at the phone then dialed. I was about to hang up on the fourth ring when a sleepy voice said, "Hello?"

"Hi, mom. Sorry it's so late, we just got home."

"That's okay, I told you to call. Everything alright?"

"Yeah, everything's fine. We had a nice visit and we met a really nice Friar from Saint Bonaventure."

She paused for a few seconds before asking, "A Friar? What was a Friar doing there?"

"He's a friend of the family," I told her. "He was just visiting like we were, mom."

"That doesn't sound right. The house is supposedly haunted and they have a friend who is a Friar? Did he come up to bless the house?"

"That wasn't mentioned. He really didn't say much about the house. Actually, I spent most of the time with Phil, the father. We walked around outside and he told me about some of the stuff that's been happening."

"What stuff?" She asked.

I didn't feel this was the time or the right way to tell my mom anything about the house. I told her I would be over in the afternoon and we could talk then. She agreed; thank God. There really wasn't much to tell but I still didn't want her lying in bed thinking something worse. I rechecked the kitchen door and went into the bedroom. Debbie was fast asleep as was I a few minutes later.

CHAPTER II

Debbie woke me around 7:45 to remind me she was spending the day with her mom. I usually opened the Fountain of Youth at noon on Saturdays but today I would prepare for advertising the fixtures, equipment and other items. I ate a bowl of cereal before starting the day. I called Freddie J. with the vending company to tell him I was going out of business and to arrange for them to pick up the pool table and other games at the Fountain. I then drove to Tops Markets to get some boxes for packing, after which I went directly to the building. Pulling up to the Fountain of Youth I observed Hank K. standing in front of the Lincoln Diner. He walked across Third Street as I exited my car.

"Hey, what's the plan today?" He asked.

I told him I was going to get everything in order to get ready for the sale. "I have no idea what to ask for anything, Hank."

"Well," he said, "I talked to Mrs. M., a local antique dealer and she agreed to stop by and take a look at what there is."

"Oh, Pam's mom?" I asked.

"I don't know who's mom she is, all I know is she's an antique dealer and works out of her house," Hank said.

I believe I knew to whom he was referring. I went to school with her daughter and my band played at her daughter's 16th birthday party. In fact, I bought a couple of items from her to decorate our house.

"Well, she said she'd be home most of today. She'd be more than happy to come over, take a look, and give her appraisal. She said there might even be something she's looking for," Hank told me.

I grabbed a couple boxes from the trunk of the car as I was telling Hank to give her a call. "Tell her I'll be here for about an hour and a half."

"I'll give her a call now," he said as he walked back toward the diner.

Even with the electricity off, there was plenty of sunshine flooding through the front windows to help me get my work done. There wasn't really much to pack except my personal belongings. Since everything was to be sold, I figured I would set all of the glasses, bowls and silverware on the front bar. Even at my young age of 21, I could appreciate the age-old beauty of this grand building. The first business here was a general store. Not only could you purchase the everyday staples, you could also bust a gut loading hundred pound bags of grain and feed on your wagon for the sale price of just $1.40. I tried to imagine what the talk of the town was as patrons came in to buy a three-cent loaf of bread or a nickel five-pound bag of sugar. I'm sure there were many interesting stories told by Olean's founding fathers right where I was standing.

I went to the back room to see if I had missed anything the night before. There was a huge safe in the back room that had to weigh near a ton. The first thing Hank told me about the safe was not to lock it because no one had the combination. Okay, what the hell good was it? Obviously, I never placed the daily receipts in it. I unplugged all the video machines and neatly wrapped their cords around the back hooks. I went behind the bar and removed everything from the shelves. I totally forgot to clean out the containers that held all the toppings for sundaes. There were many: hot fudge, caramel, butterscotch and all the other favorites. There were more containers with chopped nuts, sprinkles, cherries and sliced almonds. I threw all the dry toppings into the trash and washed out those and the rest in the double sinks behind the bar. It was beginning to hit me; the Fountain of Youth was closed as of now. We had a lot of fun, those four months with the pool and chess tournaments and listening to the newest songs on the jukebox. I wasn't much older than the kids who came in and it was easy relating to them. Olean High was just two blocks from the Fountain and many kids came in after school to ruin their appetites. Not only did the kids come in to play pinball, video games and pool, but also there were twenty or so of my regulars that played checkers and chess every visit. After a month or so, the kids began a chess tournament. One boy just couldn't be beat. He'd have you in checkmate in ten moves or less. I can't remember his name to save my life but he was one of the best I've ever seen. My brother, Mark, would bring his wife Pat and their three kids: Tom, Jeff and Valerie in for an after dinner treat on occasion. I didn't have a thriving business but what I had was good and, like any new business venture, it would have taken time. I was going to miss it.

Hank and Mrs. M. came in about 10:15. We recognized one another immediately. "Hi, Paul. I didn't put two and two together when I saw the story about your purchasing the Fountain. I'm so sorry to hear about the fire. Hank told me they're going to have the building razed. That's just nonsense, to tear a building as beautiful as this down is an outrage."

"I agree, but that's the bank's decision. There isn't much for kids to do around Olean, but I guess they feel a parking lot is more important," I said.

"Well, let's see what you have. I'll give you my best estimates on value. I might even see something that strikes my fancy."

Mrs. M.'s first interest was the marble chairs and tables.

"Oh my, these are beautiful and in terrific condition." She said quite excitedly.

"Mr. and Mrs. Questa purchased these sets when they began the business over 50 years ago," I told her.

"There is another table that has a small crack in the top in the back room," Hank told her.

Mrs. M. continued looking at the rest of the items that were available. She pulled from her purse a small spiral notebook that had numerous names and numbers written on the cover in different colors of ink. She flipped through several pages before finding a blank one and began making notes of every item available for sale. Upon finishing her appraisal for each item, she sat at the end of the bar and explained her conclusion. All total, the items together were appraised at just under eight thousand dollars!

"Wow, do you really think I can get that much for everything?" I asked enthusiastically. The purchase of the business only cost me twenty five hundred dollars. If I could nearly triple my investment, it would be wonderful.

"Well, everything you have here is in terrific shape. The mirrors are beautiful and, being as large as they are as well as beveled, they should bring a premium. The back bar is your pricy item and should bring at least twenty-five hundred from the right buyer. It's all hand carved, Paul!" She exclaimed as she tapped me on the head.

She went on to tell me that each table and chair set was worth between three and four hundred dollars. The fans should bring a hundred and fifty each and the rest of the items appraised for anything from one to forty dollars.

"Now that's my appraisal on the antiques but not for the coolers or any of the marble. The bar is made of fine Italian marble and someone who is looking for such marble will probably make you a nice offer," she said.

Louie M., owner of the Downtown Deli walked in and greeted us all.

"Sorry to hear, Paul. I used to love coming here when I was a kid. I think the bank is making a big mistake. Olean has lost too many of its historical buildings," he said.

"I agree, Lou, but there's no changing progress as they call it. I even offered to help with the cost of the rewiring."

"Well, it's not just the rewiring the bank is concerned about, Paul. The building needs a new roof, most of the plumbing is original and part of the back foundation has a few cracks. Granted, all of these things can be corrected but it would cost a great deal, more than they're willing to pay," Hank said.

"Isn't that what it's all about with these beautiful old buildings, to keep them intact? Only memories remain of many of Olean's charming buildings. It's a shame another is only going to be remembered by a picture in a book of Olean's historical landmarks."

"Well, I came in because I'm interested in the bar for the Deli. I spoke to the Questas about my interest in the past but they wouldn't hear of it. It will just about fit perfectly and will certainly add to the charm of the business. I'll make you the same offer I did the Questas, Four thousand."

Silence gripped the room for a good ten seconds before I was able to speak. "DOLLARS!?" I blurted, as soon as I was

40

able to raise my lower jaw that dropped to the floor after Louie made the offer.

"Wait a minute, Paul. This is your first offer and you haven't even advertised yet, have you?" Mrs. M. said.

"Christ, I should have kept the business. I knew you were interested in the bar, Lou, but not *that* interested," Hank said.

"Come on, Mrs. M, There probably aren't going to be many people around the area that are going to be interested in it. And besides, Louie will keep part of the memory of the grand old place right here in town. Not to mention, how much time is the bank going to give me before I have to be out?"

I was happy with Louie's offer. Selling the bar alone will give me a $1,500.00 profit, and I liked the idea of someone in Olean purchasing and preserving it.

"Well, I did go to the Olean Times Herald and placed an ad today. Tell ya what, if you're willing to keep your offer 'til the end of the week, Louie, and no one else shows interest in the bar, it's yours," I said.

"That's fair enough, Paul. When does the ad run?"

"It'll be in Wednesday and will run through Sunday," I told him.

"Okay, if anyone does show any interest will you let me know?" Lou asked.

"Yup, I sure will," I said.

Louie told us he had to get back to the Deli, wished me luck and said goodbye. Mrs. M. wrote a copy of everything she had written in her notebook and handed it to me telling me to use it as a reference for selling the items.

"Thanks for coming and helping me, Mrs. M. I would have been lost if someone had asked me what I was asking for something.

"Let them make an offer and go from there. If it's close to my appraisal, you'll be okay. I don't know what to tell you about the coolers though. Perhaps Hank can help you there he's in the restaurant business."

"Yeah I can do that," Hank said. He seemed irritated or even angry.

"Well, I have another appointment in about an hour so I have time to get some lunch. What's the lunch special at the diner today, Hank?" Mrs. M. asked.

"Goulash."

"Would you care to join me, Paul?"

"Don't mind if I do, Mrs. M. I can't resist Hank's goulash!"

I folded the notes Mrs. M. gave me and slipped them in my shirt pocket. We all walked out, I locked the door and we headed for the diner across the street. I noticed my friend, George standing in the window of G&G Music throwing a kimey at me. Don't ask, you'll never understand.

As usual, lunch was good at the diner. The food was home cooked and the servings were usually generous but I had only about half as much on my plate as Mrs. M., making me wonder again about the anger? The diner was an original coach car from the Erie Railroad.

"Lou's offer really is respectable, Paul, but at least see if anyone else shows interest in the bar." Mrs. M. stated.

Hank said goodbye to Mrs. M. but turned around and snubbed me when I passed the register. I thanked Mrs. M. as she walked to her car that was parked on State Street. What was the matter with him? Was he mad because Louie made such a large offer for the bar? I didn't have any plans for the rest of the day. Debbie wouldn't be home for another three and half hours so I returned to the Fountain and decided to go to the basement and do something I had planned to do since I bought the business. Two metal sidewalk grates covered the basement window wells that were nearly full of decades of dirt and debris. I had planned to dig them out and finally had my chance to do so. I carried down a kerosene lantern I had brought to the building to use for light when we were going to bring up the soda tanks. There was an empty 55-gallon drum in the basement that I used to put the dirt from the wells in. The basement was dank and musty, and the floor was dirt. Only the slightest daylight was able to break through the darkness at the top of the basement windows.

Damn, there's more dirt in here than I thought, I muttered to myself.

I began digging, using a small, folding army shovel to dig into the years of compacted dirt. The dirt was very hard and dry at the bottom of the wells and crumbled easily. It was too difficult searching the dirt by pushing it around on the shovel. I realized I needed something to sift the dirt rather than search each shovelful with my hands. I went upstairs to look around the back room for something that might work. I grabbed an old screen, took it back down with me and placed it over the top of the drum. This was easier. I moved the dirt around on the screen and left a small opening at the edge of the drum to push what I had searched into it. I couldn't believe the number of coins I was finding! I'd been collecting coins for the past six or seven years and this was a joy. I found every denomination, and was trying to look at the dates of each coin as I wiped off the dirt. I was finding coins back to the mid 1800's! With my excitement rising, I decided to completely dig out the wells and examine the coins more closely later. About four inches from the bottom of the well, I found a two-ounce milk bottle. I don't recall the name of the dairy but it was a sample milk bottle. Imagine, many, many years ago, they gave out samples of milk! The window wells were nearly three feet deep and as I said, the dirt all but filled them. By the time I had finished removing all of the dirt, I had found over 120 coins including four Columbian Exposition Halves, five silver dollars and the most valuable, a 1922 penny. I can understand someone dropping a penny or maybe even a nickel in the 1800's, but to drop a half dollar or silver dollar and not request the owner to retrieve it for him or her was strange. Actually, most the coins, with the exception of many pennies that had corroded due to the many years of moisture, were semi-valuable because most were in excellent shape.

It took me over two hours and three short-lived conversations with pedestrians who, while passing by, looked into the noise filled voids beneath the grates to observe me digging in the dirt. I put all my newly found treasures into an empty can and went back upstairs, extinguished the lantern and washed up behind the bar. There were many businesses in Olean that had these same grates over their basement window

43

wells. I wondered how many others were as full as these were, and if they might contain items that are even more valuable.

You know they're here too, don't you?

It was as if I heard Laura say those words at that very moment. I wasn't thinking of the house, nor was I thinking of what she had said to me. My thoughts were consumed with the idea that I may have discovered a fortune in my now cleaned-out-probably-for-the-first-time-in-80-years window wells. *No, I don't know anything*, I said quietly to the cleaned condiment containers.

I stood there for a few of minutes thinking about what had transpired last night, grabbed the can containing the new additions to my coin collection and walked out the front door. A slight breeze swirled around me, drawing out the musty smell of my clothes, absorbed from the basement that I had occupied the past two hours. I sat down on the stoop and lit a cigarette. I looked at my car parked in front of the Fountain. It's never stalled before last night. Stalled? Hell, it died! No lights, no horn, no electrical anything, that is until Father Al walked up. It hadn't given us a problem since, not even a hint that it was going to hesitate on starting. Coincidence? Of course it was; I'll get it checked.

It was nearly four and I needed to get moving. My band was playing in Port Allegany, Pennsylvania tonight. Debbie would be getting home in about half an hour and I wanted to stop and see my mom before I went home. I drove down State Street to my parents' house. They lived at 109 north Eighth Street in their three-bedroom house. I liked the house but the back yard wasn't large enough to accommodate a picnic table, which also meant less lawn for me to mow when I was still living at home. That was something I didn't mind. Since my brother and I moved out, and after mom suffered her heart attack, my parents slept in separate rooms. My dad suffered extreme cramps and Charlie horses in his legs, especially at night, and he didn't want that to disturb my mom's rest. He also often dreamt of animals coming through the mattress, but we'll leave that story for another time! I turned on Eighth

Street and pulled in the neighbor's adjoining driveway to back up and park in front of the house. My dad, who worked for the city, was already home and there wasn't enough room for two cars in the driveway without partially blocking the neighbor's driveway. Dumb design. Both my parents were on the front porch, which told me they'd already eaten.

"Howdy," I said as I sat on the steps.

"Well, now what are you going to do?" My dad asked.

"I suppose I'll look for a job. I still have the band, dad, and we do good. I'll find something in the next week or so."

"Well, you'd better; you have a baby on the way," he reminded me.

"I know, dad. Debbie is working too, ya know."

"Yeah, but not for much longer. When's she due, March?" He asked.

"Will you two quit arguing?" my mom pleaded.

"I told you it wasn't a wise idea to buy that business. George goes into business and you think you have to do the same. Jesus, Mary and Joseph," dad said. Something he said often.

"Mrs. M. came in today and gave me an estimate on the fixtures. Also, Louie M. dropped by and made an offer on the back bar. He said it would be a nice addition to the Downtown Deli. He offered $4000, dad!"

"Believe it when you see it," dad said.

"Gee, I'm glad I stopped by," I said with a bit of cautious sarcasm. "Hey, mom, I cleaned out the window wells and found a lot of coins and a miniature milk bottle; two ounces!"

"That'll pay the bills," dad muttered.

"They're in the car, I'll get them, mom," I said with a sigh.

My father got up and went into the house as I walked back to the porch. I sat down next to my mom in the chair my dad had been sitting in. "Most are very old and in great shape."

"They're filthy!"

"I know, I only cleaned a few of them. As I was digging I was wiping them off to see what dates they were, but then I started finding so many I stopped cleaning them and just kept digging. I figured we could go through them together," I explained.

When I first started collecting coins, I met an elderly man, Walt B., who was the auctioneer for the Portville, NY coin club. He taught me a lot about collecting and what to look for. I would visit him and his wife at least once a week and we'd compare our new finds. He collected for decades and dedicated an entire room of his house to his hobby. When I was younger, we would walk to the bank and each of us would carry either a fifty-dollar bag of pennies or a hundred dollar bag of nickels back to his house so we could go through them. Phew, that was a job carrying them! Do you have any idea how much 5,000 pennies or 2,000 nickels weighs? My arm ached at the thought of carrying them! I started doing the same thing and brought them home so mom and I could go through them. We had an absolute blast. There were still a lot of wheat pennies, a few Indian heads, war nickels and lots of older coins as well as a few buffalo nickels still in circulation in the late 60's. Mom and I would dump the coins out onto newspapers that we would spread out on the table. We'd take out all the 'keepers' and would have to wrap the rest. The coins were loose as all came from the city's parking meters. The bank wouldn't accept loose coins from the public so we had to roll them. Mom really enjoyed going through them with me. She really didn't have much to do these days. The only thing she had to look forward to was going to bingo a couple of nights a week with either my aunts or my father.

"You go through them, mom. I have to get home, Debbie will be there in a few minutes and we're playing tonight," I said.

"No, I'll wait until you have time to go through them too," she said.

"Go ahead. You always seem to be the lucky one. You find better ones than I do when we go through a bag," I insisted.

"Nope, I'll wait," she said.

"All right," I said as I got up. "I'll call you later. I'll stop by tomorrow and we can check them out." I kissed her on the cheek and we both walked in the house, she was carrying the can. My dad was sitting in his recliner reading the paper.

"I'll see you later, dad, I'm gonna get home and start dinner," I said.

"Okay, be good" He ordered, barely looking up from his paper.

Mom walked me to the door and past her antique library case she had purchased from the Saint Bonaventure University library. The case was filled with every shape and size ceramic elephant, zebra, monkey and other exotic animals.

"Okay, I'll call you tomorrow and we'll get at those coins but you can go through them if you want. You don't have to wait for me," I told my mom.

"I'll wait, go home and get something to eat. Don't forget, I still want to hear about your visit last night," she said.

I put an arm around her neck and kissed her head. "I know, mom. Love you."

"Well, then quit making me worry," she said.

"Worry about what?" I asked...

"Anything—goodbye!" she said and gave me a gentle push out the door.

Walking to the car, I really understood just how fragile my mom was. She was tough in her own way but fragile because she worried about everything whether it was warranted or not and that weighed on her. She always tried to please everyone and never had anything negative to say. When I was younger, I didn't understand, but she was the perfect mom.

It only took me about two minutes to drive the short distance home. Debbie's mom was very punctual and I was sure she had already dropped her off. Debbie was sitting on the steps going through the mail.

"Hi, how was your day?" I asked.

"It was okay," she said, as I leaned down to give her a kiss.

"You hungry?" I asked.

"Starved!"

"Want me to cook something or do you just wanna get something quick?" I asked.

"I'd kinda like Arthur Treachers if that's okay?"

"Sure, that sounds good actually. Wanna go with me?" She was already on her way to the car before I finished asking. We drove to Arthur Treachers/Kentucky Fried Chicken, which was on the corner of Eighth and State Streets. As I drove past Eighth Street, I could see my mom was back on the porch reading the paper. My dad was probably fast asleep in his recliner, snoring away, his glasses still adorning his face. I drove around to the drive-thru and ordered. Debbie must have been starving because she said to order two extra pieces of fish; after all, she was eating for two.

"My brother called and said he wanted to come by tonight," Debbie said.

Debbie's brother Tim and she were very close and spent a lot of time together.

"Clara said she and Father Al talked after we left. Father Al seems to think you are a, what did she call it… a sensitive," Debbie said.

I looked at her puzzled. "A sensitive? What am I sensitive to?"

"I guess he thinks you can feel, or maybe know when something is, um, around. I don't know. Clara said those that experience vehicle problems usually have something about them that connects to the house in some way," she explained.

"What?!" I exclaimed. "Are you saying the spooks not only affect people's cars but that the people themselves can be affected?"

"Huh?" She asked with a confused look.

"How can *I* be connected, as you say, to the house? I'm sure there are others who may have 'felt' *something* while on the property or in the house, but their feelings and mine may have been nothing more than an overactive imagination," I said.

I pulled up to the window and paid for our food. I continued forward allowing the next car to pull to the window as Debbie checked the articles in the bags.

"I didn't say it. Father Al did. And what was it that Laura said to you that seemed to upset you?" She asked still digging in the bags.

48

You know they're here too, don't you?

I sat staring through the windshield hearing those words so clearly in my mind once again.

"Whast cee shay?" She attempted to ask again with a mouthful of fish.

The blast of a car horn shocked me out of my trance. I looked left before pulling out of the drive-thru and into the turn lane.

"She said I knew they were there too but what she said didn't upset me. It puzzled me," I said.

I drove down eighth and stopped in front of my parents' house.

"Hi, mom!" Debbie yelled to my mom past my head nearly shattering my right ear drum.

My mother waved back and asked how she was feeling.

"Fine, but I'm always hungry," Debbie said.

"Yeah, and if I don't get my hands on some of this food, I'm not going to get any. She decided on Arthur Treachers. Got me outta cooking," I said.

"Well, go home and eat and be careful tonight." Mom replied.

"Okay, I'm sure I'll see you again in about an hour when we drive by."

We all waved goodbye as I pulled away.

"What time is your brother coming over?" I asked.

"He said he'd be over around 6:00 or so."

"There's a help wanted sign at the sub shop. I'm gonna stop real quick and fill out an application. I'll be leaving about 6:15; I guess I have the time. We start at 9 tonight and we still have to load the equipment in the truck," I said.

"Yeah, go ahead, you can stop."

CHAPTER III

I stopped at the West Side Sub Shop to get the application, and yes, there was an East Side Sub Shop too, with the same proprietor. Tim C., an acquaintance of mine who worked there, was taking an order from a man at the counter when I walked in.

"Yeah, smother it in peppers... no, you know better than that, SMOTHER it with 'em," The man said as Tim was spooning on some of the hottest peppers this side of Mexico.

"Man, your mouth is gonna hate you when you bite into this, not to mention another part of your anatomy later!" Tim said in his typical comedic way.

Tim was a clown. I think he could find something funny about anything. He has a great sense of humor. Sometimes I'd crack up for no reason just listening to him talk. He missed his calling; he should have been a stand-up comic. He wrapped the customer's order and threw an olive at me.

"Hey, Tim," I said, returning the olive which hit him squarely on the forehead. "Got an application available?"

"I sure do, if I can find them. Oh, here they are," he said, pulling up a pad of applications from under the counter, along with a chunk of tomato that he obviously picked up from the floor. He threw the piece of tomato at me and it hit in the center of the glass in the front door.

"Missed," I said.

"There's a little mustard on some of the applications and most are oil soaked but none have pepper,." he said again in his comical way.

He tore one off and handed it to me and, indeed, it had a stain on it, several actually.

"Gimme another one, Tim. I don't want the owner to think I was eating while filling it out," I said.

"Shit, it doesn't matter to him. He'll think it fell off his own shirt. Every time he comes in here it looks like he'd been eating something. He's always got some sort of food dribbled all over his messy ass shirt. Damn slob!" Tim exclaimed.

If I were hired to work here and I was fortunate enough to work the same shift as Tim, I was going to like it no matter how boring or mundane the work might be. Everyone liked Tim except some of his former teachers. He, like me, was always getting into mischief in school....nothing terribly serious, just silly stuff.

"Sorry about the Fountain, man. Always some damn thing happening to make our lives miserable. You weren't even open that long were you?" Tim asked.

"Nope, bought it in April. I can't believe the bank won't repair what needs to be done to keep the building standing," I replied.

"What do you mean keep the building standing? I know you're closing, but don't tell me they're knocking the building down?!"

"Yeah, there are several things that need attention but the bank has decided to tear the building down instead of making the necessary repairs," I said.

"Aw, that's too bad. What are you going to do now?" He asked.

I looked at Tim and then at the application I held in my hand.

"Yeah—okay," he said.

"I still have my income from the band too so hopefully we'll be okay. But I'll tell ya something else; the antiques are worth quite a bit," I said.

"What antiques? Oh, the Questas'? What, you got 'em locked up in the basement or something? Gonna sell them to the highest bidder?" He said so straight up and as matter of factly as if he were talking about something serious.

"Yeah, I'm gonna hold a special, two for the price of one!"

"Remember the time I was combing my hair while playing pinball and she almost pulled the damned hairs outta my head when she grabbed the comb?" He asked. "Did ya ever think some day you'd own the same business and you could lock them in the basement for safe keeping?"

This guy was a crackup; no wonder everyone liked him.

51

Still laughing I said, "Anyhow, Louis M. came in and made an offer on the back bar to put in the Downtown Deli. Four grand, Tim! Shit, I only paid $2500 for the business and to be honest, I didn't know the fixtures went with it. My dad did and he said he would have really insisted that I NOT purchase the business if there hadn't been something of value in case I didn't make a go of it."

"Thank God for our fathers. Without 'em, we wouldn't be here," Tim said.

Tim always had a look on his face after one of his little quips. A look of either, "did ya get it," or "well, are ya dumb, I just made a funny."

I continued filling out the application while Tim was taking an order from a woman. I glanced up once to see. As she was fumbling in her purse, Tim was making gestures indicating how top heavy she was. It's not so much the way he would say or do things, it was more of the expression he would have on his face at the time. When he would laugh, it was as if it were a chore. Something could be funny as hell, side splittingly funny, and he would give out this two second shot of laughter and go right back to being straight faced. Watching him laugh was funnier than whatever he'd said to make you laugh.

"Thank you, ma'am, and come again … all over my—did ya get it filled out?" He asked.

It's the expression; the damned expression.

"Yeah, there are a couple of words where the ink smeared and didn't come out too clearly 'cause of the oil."

"That's okay, he can't read anyhow. So, what are you gonna do tonight?" He asked.

"Gotta play in Port Allegany," I said.

"Man, you must get a lot of groupies hanging around....all those girls wanting a little personal musical serenade," he said.

"Well, there was a time, but not now, I'm spoken for. I can't go down that road, Tim."

I noticed yesterday's paper lying on a chair behind the counter. The front page was face up. While staring at it, I started thinking about everything that happened and what we had talked about.

"Paul, earth to Paul."

You know they're here too, don't you?

"Paul!"

Thirty seconds must have passed before I heard Tim's voice. Prior to his snapping me out of it, all I could hear was Laura asking that disturbing question.

"Sorry, Tim, guess I was day dreaming," I said still staring at the paper.

Tim turned around to see what I was fixated on. He picked up the paper and laid it on the counter. "What, you didn't see this?" he asked.

"Yeah, I saw it, up close and personal too. Debbie and I went up for a visit last night like about 100 other people. The dad and I walked around the property as he explained some of the stuff that's been happening."

"You're shittin' me? Take me, take me, I wanna see a ghost! Take me with you, dammit!" He exclaimed.

"You're working! But I'll ask if it's okay if I bring you up sometime. Besides, we didn't see any ghosts," I said.

The expression was there. Here I was, standing in front of a person who was capable of the sharpest quips and one liners imaginable. Anything you say could be a set up for this character.

"What, you have to hold a séance, set up the Ouija board, spin a pendulum, draw a PENT O GRAM on the ground, what?"

"You know what I mean," I insisted.

"Yeah, I do, but I'm going with the flow right now," he said.

Tim was a joy to be around. He should hire himself out as a "cheerer upper" for anyone having a bad day. I thought very highly of him. (I can't believe for a moment he thinks I tampered with his brakes!)

"Be sure he gets the application and put in a good word for me, okay?" I asked.

"All right. Let me know when you're going to go up to the house again. I didn't read the whole story, is it really messed up?" Tim asked.

"I can't say right now."

A woman walked in with her young son screaming about not wanting a sub for dinner.

"Our car stalled when we were leaving and it kinda scared the heck outta both of us," I said.

"Oh my God, the car stalled, you're kidding me right? My car stalled once and I nearly dropped dead right over the steering wheel. I was never so scared in my life!" Tim exclaimed.

Some need a straight edge to draw a straight line. I, on the other hand, would prefer to use Tim's humor.

The woman was telling her son that a turkey sub was really, really good and all he could say was "No, no, I want to go to McDonalds!"

"Can I help you, ma'am?" Tim asked.

"Just give me a sec please, I'm sorry about this," The woman said.

Tim told her "no problem" as he walked with me toward the door making a choking motion after getting behind the woman.

"Who lives there, a family, an old couple? How many people? What's going on up there? Tell me, tell me!" Tim exclaimed.

"No, it's a family with four kids, three daughters and a son," I explained.

"Daughters? How old are these daughters?"

"Never mind! Well, Beth Ann is seventeen I think. Her sisters, Mary and Laura, are eleven and thirteen," I said.

"I'm ready to order, sir," The woman said while trying to corral her son.

"Is that respectively or don't you know? Be right there ma'am. Let me know when you go up again. I'm off tomorrow so if you go up, call me," Tim said.

"I will. I'll see ya later," I said.

I was halfway out the door when Tim leaned out and said quietly, "Hey, take this kid up there. Maybe the ghosts can scare him to be a good little brat! Hi, Deb, See ya later, Paul."

"Hi, Tim," Debbie said waving from the car.

I closed the door shaking my head....something I did often when Tim had the last word.

"Sorry I took so long. I filled out the ap and Tim said he'd put in a good word."

"That's all right." Debbie said. "I had another piece of fish while you were in there but I left you three pieces."

"That's enough; you know I don't like to eat a lot before a job," I said.

We pulled down our street and saw that her brother was already waiting on the steps.

"Hi, Timmy," Debbie said as she walked up the steps to the apartment door.

"Hello. Hi, Paul, where are you guys playing tonight?"

"Port Allegany, we're gonna be playing outside on the tennis courts. I'm glad it's a nice warm night," I said.

We all walked in and I took a quick shower. This is my seventh year playing professionally and I still experienced butterflies before a job. I didn't understand why because I really enjoyed playing. We were a three piece band, bass, guitar and drums, and had been three pieces for the past two years. George and I had been in several bands together, and at one time had a five piece band. We even attempted adding a couple of brass instruments, sax and trumpet, but it didn't work out the way we had hoped. I always thought the band we had in the years, 1971–74 was the tightest we'd ever had. Our bass player, Jamie, was terrific and had the showman qualities needed in a rock band. It was an extremely enjoyable time of my life.

I finished getting ready and expected George to be picking me up at any minute, even though it was a custom for him to be an average of ten minutes late. We always got started on time, but in many cases we were rushed. At times, I really believe he did it on purpose to see me sweat.

"George called, said he was on his way," Debbie said.

"I'm ready to rock and roll! I just don't know about playing outside. The fog comes in, the electronics get damp and zap, your hair is standing on end!" I said.

"Just be careful, that's all you can do." Debbie's brother said. Just then the horn of the milk truck squawked. You couldn't mistake it, it sounded like a duck with a cold.

"See ya later," I said as I kissed Debbie goodbye.

I walked out to the truck, opened the bi-fold door and stood in my appropriate place on the passenger side as I did on every trip to entertain the masses.

"The ritual drive past my parents,' if you would please," I told George.

We drove around the block, up Seventh, down State, and turned on Eighth Street. There was my mother, as usual, sitting on the porch and ready to hail an Italian salute to me as we drove by.

"Hi, Mrs. Kenyon." George shouted as we slowly passed by. I waved and mom gave her customary wave back, yelling to be careful. When we were in our teens, sometimes our parents would go to some of our gigs. More times than not, they were the ones hauling our equipment, at least until we had so much and became more than just a garage band. We were lucky when George and I were 16; our organist, Don B. was 21 and drove. He would borrow his father's pickup to haul the equipment. One year we played every weekend, just two weeks shy of an entire season at a bar called, The Telemark Inn in Ellicottville, New York. My parents celebrated their 25th wedding anniversary at the Telemark and I never felt so honored being able to play for them. We didn't finish out the season that year because a State Trooper asked to see our ID's and, when he noticed that three of us were only 16, he said our, "Crystal Grapin" days were over in any bar in New York State.' Little did he know, we changed the name of the band and played there again the following ski season. Oh, the name of our band was, "Crystal Grape," which was shortened from, "The Liquefied Crystal Grape Rebellion."

We bought the milk truck in 1972 when we re-formed the band. We purchased the 1953 Divco from Kent's dairy and painted it black by hand. Then we had a sign maker create two big signs, one for either side. The name of our band was Blackstone Jury but the signs didn't exactly read that way. When George and I arrived to pick the truck up at the sign painter's house, we looked at one another and said nothing. On either side of the truck were these, what appeared to be big, white clouds. And written in bold, black lettering on each "cloud," quite professionally I might add, was, "Black Stoned Jury!"

"Oh, my God!" I exclaimed. "Black *Stoned* Jury? What are people gonna say when they see us pulling up with this name, in a black milk truck?"

"I don't know." George said. "I have no idea."

I could only imagine what Tim C. would come up with when he saw the truck. We talked to the gentleman who did the work and he had no intention of redoing the signs or giving us a refund, not even a break on the price for the signs. Of course, looking back, if we had insisted and explained it wasn't what we ordered, I'm sure the courts would have been on our side. My goodness, we were naive, even at 21. Anyhow, the name stuck and everyone saw that we weren't stoned in any way when we were entertaining; or when we weren't entertaining for that matter.

"Is Jamie gonna meet us at your parents to help load or drive straight to Port Allegany?" I asked George.

"He's probably already there. He couldn't get out of it this time. He has to drive down State Street to get to Port A."

Jamie lived in Franklinville, NY and more often than not, our jobs were in the opposite direction. We really couldn't expect him to drive the 20 extra miles just to help us load the equipment into the milk truck. We practiced in George's parents' basement and Jamie had to drive to Olean for each session. I guess it was fair that we took care of the loading.

We arrived at George's parents' and indeed, Jamie was already there with much of the equipment already outside the ground level basement door. We loaded everything up rather quickly, each of us slinging our usual smart cracks towards the others. George's brother, Joe, also came down to help us load. And as usual, George said, "Get outta here, eggshell, we're already loaded," I know I was told why he always called his brother eggshell, but I don't remember. Call him that today and your head will look like a *cracked* eggshell! George and I jumped in the milk truck while Jamie drove his station wagon.

There really wasn't enough room for three to sit comfortably in the front of the milk truck. Actually, I don't think there was enough room for Jamie in the front of the truck when no one else was in it. Once when we played at the Cabaret in Olean, George and I were outside talking to Ralph P. Jamie had come out to tell us something, and Ralph said, "Get outta here you fuckin' earthquake."

George and I performed our usual a cappella fashion the entire drive to New York's neighboring state, making up songs about things we'd see during the trip. We arrived, set up, and played the three hour gig. The fog stayed away so no one ended up looking like they'd stuck their finger in a light socket. The tennis court dance turned out great and there was quite the crowd.....mostly high school age kids. What I thought was nice, there were a couple of adults to keep an eye on things. It was a benefit dance for a student who had taken ill near the end of the school year. There was always one person who stood out at every job we performed. This night it was Igor....at least that's what we called him. He led everyone in dancing their hearts out for the cause; it was a good time. Generally, we would stop on the way home to get something to eat but the vote was unanimous: we were all too tired. George and I drove directly back to Olean and Jamie to Franklinville. We decided to leave the equipment in the truck until our next practice which was scheduled for Tuesday.

George dropped me off shortly after 2:30 a.m. As I climbed into bed, Debbie reminded me that she and her mother were going to Buffalo to do some shopping today. They wouldn't be leaving much before 9 but she said she wanted to remind me because I'd probably still be sleeping when she left. Despite the usual ringing in my ears after playing, I was asleep very quickly.

CHAPTER IV

I woke at 12:40; Debbie was surely on her way to Buffalo with her mother. I was starved! I hadn't had anything to eat since Arthur Treachers the night before and, even then, I only ate two pieces of fish. I scrambled up a couple of eggs, made some toast and drank a Pepsi. I called my mother and told her I'd be over about 2 p.m. at which time I realized I'd forgotten to get the new edition of Krauss's coin prices. It didn't really matter since being able to spend some time with mom was all I looked forward to. I decided to walk over, it was only two blocks. I was standing at the corner of Eighth and State Streets when Tim C. yelled to me as he was driving by. He did a u-turn and pulled into the Wooden Nickel parking lot. I walked across the street to see what he wanted.

"Hey, I just tried to call you but you didn't answer," he said.

"I can't reach my phone from this corner, the cord's too short."

There! I got him for a change, yet he still had the expression on HIS face.

"Asshole... can you start work Tuesday, you'll work 5–10 with me."

"Sure, sounds good. Do I need to wear anything special?" I asked

"Well, Saran Wrap would be good if you want to keep your clothes from looking like Jim's. No! Just wear regular clothes, cufflinks are an option. You're gonna be working in a sub shop, you're going to be getting oil, mustard, mayonnaise, and pickle ju...."

"Okay, okay, I gotcha! I'll be there at five," I said.

"You need a ride somewhere?"

Oh boy, now's my chance to get him twice in one day. My parents' house was only two doors down Eighth Street. I got in the passenger side trying to keep the grin off my face; it was trying so hard to leak out.

"Go down Eighth Street," I told him.

"Okie-dokie"

No sooner did Tim C. turn the corner and drive 100 feet I yelled, "STOP!"

It obviously took him by surprise; I might have even frightened him. He hit the brakes so hard I was propelled into the dashboard! The look on his face was priceless.

Laughing very hard I said, "This is my parents' house."

"You asshole! You first class, unabridged ASSHOLE!"

"I'm sorry, but then again, I'm not. The look on your face when I yelled stop will be in my memory forever. I finally got the king of practical jokes," I said.

"Yeah, well, if you don't get outta this car in the next three seconds, this king is gonna shove his crown up your ass!"

"Okay" I said, still laughing. "I'll see you Tuesday."

That felt good! Putting one over on Tim C. usually has to be planned out very carefully. Now, there was retaliation to worry about!

Mom and I spent about 2 hours going over the coins while my dad was fiddling around in the basement. We found several semi-valuable coins in really nice condition. We both had a piece of apple pie she had baked that morning. I knew something was on her mind and finally she let it out.

"So, tell me more of what's been happening in Hinsdale."

"There's not much to tell, mom. They told us they've heard noises in the house and Beth Ann hears voices outside her bedroom window. Oh, and there are cold spots outside around the pond and the yard. I thought that was normal because it's always colder around water, isn't it?" I asked.

"It's not normal to hear voices outside your bedroom window unless there's someone there. It's also not normal to wake up and find burns on your body. Did anyone show you these burns?" She asked.

"No, I think that happened a while ago. They didn't even talk about that last night," I said.

"When you and Mark were kids, I told you that I was a white witch, mainly as a joke, but I *saw* things sometimes. I guess today they call it being psychic, not that I think I really am. You know your cousin, Caroline, is psychic; she was born with a caul. Do you remember the day you stayed home from school? I guess you were about seven. I was upstairs cleaning the windows and I suddenly became frightened. Do you remember?" She asked.

"Yeah, we've talked about it before. But what has that got to do with the house in Hinsdale?" I asked.

"I had a dream and, in the dream, I saw a green house. On the wall of the front porch hung a wreath of pink flowers. It looked awful; the two shades of colors didn't go together. The day I was cleaning the windows I saw a hearse drive down the street and stop at Mr. G's house. I knew right then what had happened, I remembered the rest of the dream when I saw the hearse and I REALLY knew what had happened. Mr. G. had died in his sleep and I had dreamt it the night before. And how many times have you had your 'goosies' and things happened shortly after? Those feelings you have that you call 'goosies' are more than feelings, I think they are psychic energy that you have," mom explained.

"But mom, what has that got to do with the house?" I asked again.

"I just worry that something might happen, that you might be able to see something you won't want to see. Something so frightening it will stay with you the rest of you life," she said.

She appeared to be really worried about this and I didn't understand why. I've never heard of anyone ever being injured by spirits if they even existed. I think if I did see a ghost it would be exciting as well as scary. I couldn't think of anything that might happen that would, as she said it, stay with me the rest of my life. I had to ease her worry.

"Mom, I don't think there's really anything to worry about. The family has been experiencing these things for some time and no one's really been hurt. Maybe they're making it up, I don't know. But I can promise you this, if I feel, really *feel* there's any danger in being there, I won't go again. I'm very interested and curious as to what's happening in their house and that's all. You need to stop worrying; nothing bad is going to happen. In the time we were visiting, no one was ever any further away than one room from someone else. Everything will be okay. By the way, I start work at the sub shop Tuesday. It's probably only part-time but it'll help. It will certainly make dad stop worrying so much. I don't know why he's always carrying on anyhow. I play one night and make almost half as much as he earns working all week," I said.

"He worries 'cause Debbie's carrying his grandchild," mom said.

"We'll be fine," I said.

"You oughta go down stairs and tell him. I'm sure it'll ease his mind."

I got up and walked to the basement door. "What're ya doing?" I asked my dad when I reached the bottom of the stairs.

"Fixing this damned pipe. I had to put a piece of PVC in 'cause the old pipe is rusted through and leaking like a sieve," he explained.

"Need any help?" I asked.

"Nope, just finishing up."

"I'll be working at the sub shop starting Tuesday. I don't know how many hours a week yet. Tim C. caught up with me on my way over here today and told me," I told him.

"Is he the thin kid that works there?" Dad asked.

"Yup, he's a joker if there ever was one."

"He's a good kid; I know his father," dad said.

"Yeah, he's pretty cool. All right, if you don't need me, I'm gonna get going. Debbie went to Buffalo with her mom to do some shopping so I'm gonna clean the apartment before she gets back," I said.

"All right, take it easy. Hear anything more on the fixtures?"

"No, there'll be an ad in the paper starting Wednesday. I'm sure some of the stuff will sell," I said crossing my fingers.

We both walked upstairs. Mom asked if I wanted to stay for dinner and I told her I was going home to clean the apartment.

"Okay, well be careful."

"Careful about what?" Dad asked.

"Nothing." Mom replied.

"Humph." He responded, dismissing his curiosity.

CHAPTER V

It was late afternoon when I started walking back home. I decided to call Tim when I arrived to see if he knew how many hours I'd be working. There were at least three or four other people working there, I would imagine no one was full time.

"Hello?" Tim answered.

"Do you know how many hours I'll be working, Tim?"

"Short memory, huh? Yeah, let's see, you're working 5–10. I believe that's five hours. An easy way to figure this out is to start at five and count up to ten. However many fingers you are holding up will be how many hours you'll be working but don't put a finger up for the first hour 'cause you'll be one over," he explained

"Per week, moron, and I'll put a finger up all right!"

"Oh, why didn't you say that? No, but I'm sure he'll have a schedule on the wall you can look at when you come in Tuesday."

"What are you doing later tonight?" I asked.

"Dunno, why?"

"Well, I'm gonna clean up around here then I thought, if Debbie doesn't mind, I was thinking of driving up to the house," I said.

"I'm in! Hey! Do you think Brian could go too? I told him you went and maybe the next time you go he could go too. He's really interested. What do ya think?"

"I don't know. Phil can be a real bear. He's so tired of everyone bothering him and his family. I haven't even asked if you could come up yet, let's not push it. I'll call Clara now and I'll call you back," I said.

"Yeah, you're right, screw him. HA! Okay, call me back and let me know."

"Bye," I called the Dandys and Mary answered. "Mom, it's Paul."

A few moments went by, "Hi, Paul, what's up?" Clara asked.

"Would you mind, um, is it okay if I….." I stuttered.

"I told you, you're welcome anytime. Just don't come knocking on the door at 3 a.m.!"

"No, of course not. A friend of mine, Tim C., would like to come up too. I'll be working with him at the sub shop. He's a really nice guy; he'll make you laugh," I told Clara.

"Oh Paul, I could use a good laugh about now. I'm sure it'll be all right. What time had you planned?" She asked.

"Well, I'm waiting for Debbie to get home. She went shopping with her mom and should be home any time."

"Yeah, Beth Ann and I just got home a while ago ourselves. We drove to Buffalo to get Laura and Mary. Will Debbie be coming too?" Clara asked.

"No, probably not. The last thing she said to me is that the next time she comes to visit, the sun will be shining when she gets there, AND it will be shining when she goes home!"

Chuckling, Clara said, "Smart girl there, Paul."

"All right, well, we'll see you after a bit. If it gets too late we won't bother you," I said.

"I don't know what too late is these days. It seems we're always up 'til 2 or 3 a.m., but I don't think I will be tonight, I'm bushed. Phil said the traffic was horrible today. I can't believe these people! They drive up the camp roads, we shoo them back down the road and they curse us. Sheesh!" Clara said.

"All right, see you later," I replied.

We hung up and I began cleaning the apartment. I didn't believe Debbie would mind if I went to visit, but I didn't want to leave everything for her to pick up. Besides, I had the day off and had plenty of time to tidy up. Our apartment has only one bedroom and we kept the place in order most of the time. Debbie arrived home about 9 p.m. and said she was exhausted. She had to work tomorrow and was going straight to bed. I told her I'd like to go up tonight and that Tim was going to go with me. She couldn't have cared less; she was in bed and sleeping before I had new batteries in the flashlight. I called Tim and told him I'd be over by 9:45 and, if he had a flashlight handy, he needed to bring it. He lived in east Olean, which was basically on the way to Hinsdale. When I turned on his street he was already walking to the curb in front of his house.

When he entered the car he asked, "So, since I'm going it must be okay. You obviously talked to, who?"

"I talked to Clara, the mom," I replied.

"Okay, and—is anything happening, are we going to see ghosts, did a headless horseman ride through their yard?" Tim asked. "You're nuts! There's something seriously wrong with you, did you know that? I called; I asked if it was okay to come up—if *you* could come up, that's it. I told her you'd make her laugh."

"How?" Tim asked.

"Oh, Christ, just be yourself and you'll have the spirits fleeing!" I exclaimed.

"Is this flashlight bright enough?" He asked as he flashed it directly into my eyes.

"Come on, man! I mean, I know we're right down the street from Olean General but are you trying to become a patient when I crash 'cause all I can see now is a white light?!" I yelled.

"Sorry, just wanted to be sure the flashlight was bright enough," Tim said softly.

"Flashlight my ass, beacon more like it!," I exclaimed.

"It's okay then, huh?" He asked.

During our drive to Hinsdale, we engaged in small talk about the sub shop, my band, things in general. I told him I didn't want to talk about the house because there really wasn't much to say, nothing to speculate on. It was Sunday evening and generally you wouldn't see three vehicles between Olean and Hinsdale. Yet by the time we reached Crosby's, eight or nine cars had passed us heading toward Olean. One can only guess where they were coming from. Tim was getting fidgety by the time we turned onto Congress Road. In one sense, I felt it was ridiculous driving up here at this time of night, yet on the other hand, it felt compelling to get there. I always thought of myself as being level-headed; now I began to doubt that. I did have an interest in the paranormal and things that go bump-in-the-night but I couldn't shake the feeling that somehow I was supposed to be there. Maybe it was because Debbie worked with Clara and that they were friends. Possibly I felt obligated to help some way. But what help could I possibly be? What was it I thought I could accomplish by being there?

As we reached the rise of Wagner Hill Road we could see a couple of cars parked just past the turn-off to McMahon Road. It was getting close to 10:30 p.m. and there were still people hanging around this quiet rural area in hopes of catching a glimpse of something. Well, what were Tim and I doing here? Weren't we hoping to see something? As I turned onto McMahon, two men were walking toward us on my side of the road.

"Are those guys ghosts?" Tim asked.

Of course I knew he was joking and his question didn't warrant an answer. I slowed as we got nearer to the men and one stuck his hand up as if he wanted me to stop.

"You probably shouldn't drive up this road," The man said, continuing to hold his hand up.

"Why's that?" I asked.

"Well, a friend of ours was up here a couple nights ago and he said some nut job was at the end of the driveway with a gun," he explained.

"He was probably protecting his property and family from all the *other* nut jobs trespassing on their property," I said.

The man looked at his friend who glanced him a "who-the-hell-are-these-guys" type look.

"So, what is it that you're doing up here at this late hour?" The other man asked.

"We're here to spell the nut job guy with the gun so he can get some rest," Tim said.

It was very difficult not to laugh at Tim's reply. Actually, I should have just let him do all the talking right from the get-go. I'm fairly certain he would have said something so straight-faced and so off-the-wall, these guys would have probably left their vehicle and run home, or worse, beat the hell out of us! The man who first talked to me seemed offended by the remark but I didn't give them a chance to say anything more. I continued driving up the road, made the left hand turn to the end of McMahon road and drove to the rear of the Dandy homestead. I hadn't noticed if the men had gotten into just one of the vehicles. There were two cars parked alongside the road and there could possibly be other people traipsing around the adjoining fields. The latter would make more sense, though, because the first man did say a friend of theirs was up here the other night. It wouldn't make sense for them to drive separate cars if they were both here for the same reason, whatever that may be.

"Great comeback, Tim. I hope they aren't gonna be assholes and come walking back up the road searching for trouble," I said.

"Well, if they do, they'll get some. I don't know what kind of trouble; we'll have to find the gun you were talking about. Wait a minute, GUN!? Who had a gun and why?" Tim asked.

"Gordon, Clara's brother, was at the end of the driveway the other night with an unloaded .22 rifle. There was so much traffic they didn't want people getting around this corner and trampling all over the place. Phil must have gone to work, his car's not here," I explained.

"Where does he work?" Tim asked.

I told him he worked in Buffalo but didn't know how he was able to manage it since he ended up chasing people away all day instead of getting the sleep he needed.

"Buffalo? Does he drive to work every day?!" Tim asked.

"Yeah, sure does. It's gotta be tougher than hell even without everything that's happening here," I said.

"Damn, that makes for a long ass day, God!"

I pulled the car as far forward as possible and angled it so we were facing the pond. There's a right-hand turn into their driveway when you get to the end of McMahon Road. If you pull all the way forward, you basically end up at the edge of the back yard. On the right side of the yard a field, to the left is the main part of the yard and further out, their pond. Past the pond is the majority of their eight acres of property extending to the tree line. At the back of the yard is a rise, at the top of which were the Dandys' closest neighbors. They must have had a spectacular view of the lower valley.

"We gonna go in and meet everyone?" Tim asked.

When we turned into the drive, neither the living room lights nor those in Phil and Clara's bedroom were on. There was a light on in Mike's room on the driveway side of the house. Being parked at the back of the house, we could see the windows of Mary's and Laura's bedrooms. We could barely make out a dim light in Laura's room and of course, there was no light glowing in Mary's disturbed room.

"It looks like Mike's the only one awake, Tim. I didn't see lights on in any other part of the house. I could tap on Mike's window and see if he's up. Usually, he and his mom are up late because there are so many cars traveling the camp roads but Clara said she probably wouldn't be up late when I talked to her. I know she and Beth Ann went to Buffalo to get the girls today. Maybe Clara went to bed early because there are no cars to worry about, plus she might be tired from driving to and from Buffalo. She hasn't been getting a lot of sleep these past few days. Besides, if someone were awake, they surely would have investigated us when we pulled in," I said.

"But they knew we were coming, right? Did you tell her what time we'd be up?" Tim asked.

"Not exactly. When I talked to her I told her I was waiting for Debbie to get home and then we'd be up," I said.

Tim was evidently upset that he wasn't going to get the chance to meet everyone. I had a sneaking suspicion he really wanted to meet Beth Ann because I had told him she was a very cute girl. I was surprised that no one heard us drive up. Perhaps everyone was so frazzled from the past few days *and* nights, they were getting the needed rest they deserved. I was contemplating tapping on Mike's window, but since he didn't come out when we drove right past his bedroom, I decided it best not to disturb him.

"Let's just sit here for a while and watch," I suggested.

"Watch what? You can't see 30 feet past the hood of the car!" Tim exclaimed.

"We do have flashlights and we can walk around back and to the front of the house."

"I'll be happy just sitting in the car for now, thank you," Tim stated.

CHAPTER VI

This was a rare occasion: Tim was silent for a change. Actually, we both were. We sat quietly for what seemed to be at least half an hour. Eventually, our eyes became accustomed to the darkness and we were able to see the far distance to the pond. You couldn't really see details other than the shape of the house, but we could discern the trees and the lay of the land. We were able to distinguish shadows against the house. Toward the side of the house, near the front yard, the huge pine tree stood guard on the left of the driveway, tall against the dark night sky. We could hear the sounds of the night being gently carried on the evening's light breeze. I caught a glimpse of movement against the back corner of the house, more a shadow than movement. I waited, focusing my eyes on the exact area and readying my flashlight which I held against the outside of my door.

"What are you looking at?" Tim asked.

"I don't really know if I'm looking at anything. I thought I saw something, like something dark against the house," I said.

Tim picked up his flashlight (beacon!) from the floorboard and rested it on the frame of his open window. He was leaning as far forward as he could; chin almost resting on the dash, squinting, as if to push the darkness out of the way.

Rustling.

I brought my light up and pushed the button, flooding the side of the house past Mike's bedroom window and further, toward the pine tree where the noise seemed to come from. There was nothing; nothing visible. It sounded like cloth of some sort, some kind of material flapping in the wind but there was no wind, only a slight cool breeze. I panned the whole area again, moving slowly from the edge of the road where it meets the driveway and toward the front yard near the pine tree. Tim was all but sitting on my lap gazing out my window following the beam of light.

"I heard it," he said

"Yeah, but it could be anything and nothing. It might have been an owl flying from the tree or a small animal running through the tall grass in the field," I said.

"Yeah," Tim breathed.

We hadn't been parked there for more than an hour, but our senses were becoming very acute by this time. At least I know mine were. I heard a slight noise again. I looked out the window and down at the ground. There was a small piece of paper no bigger than a quarter sheet of writing paper on the ground about three feet from the car. Every now and then, a light breeze snuck its way under the edge and I could hear it move against the dirt driveway. Perhaps that's what we heard when it was further down the drive? It wasn't quite the same sound but at a distance it may have sounded differently. About fifteen minutes later, a light shone in Mary's room. It was a very dim light, but easily visible from the darkened yard. The harder one focuses in the dark, the easier it is for the eyes to play tricks. We stared at the bedroom window and it seemed the light flickered. It became brighter and then slowly dimmed out as if gradually moving away from the window. My first thought was that Clara opened her bedroom door. There may have been a light on in her room, and as the door was closed, the light diminished.

"Which room is Mary's again?" Tim asked.

"That one, the one where we saw the light," I explained.

"But I thought you said she doesn't sleep in there since, well, whatever," Tim wondered.

"She doesn't, I don't think she does anyhow," I said.

I told Tim my theory of what we just seen. He thought it over a few moments and said, "Yeah, sure, that makes sense... I guess—yeah."

Both Tim and I smoked but neither of us had lit a cigarette since we pulled into the driveway. We were probably thinking the same thing—if we lit one, someone will be able to see where we were. Well, that didn't matter anymore since I had just doused the countryside with a three cell flashlight while Tim lit up the area with his miniature lighthouse. No sooner did I light one, Tim was tapping my arm to hand him my lighter.

"We should have brought some pop and chips or something with us," I said.

"Shit, if I'd known we were gonna be camping out tonight, I'd have brought some hotdogs and buuuunnnns!!" Tim whined.

My lit cigarette fell from my lips, down my shirt, and onto the seat when Tim said buns. You had to know him to really appreciate his humor. His reply, even though it was a bit sarcastic, sounded fine until he whined buns.

A female's voice.

The words were indistinct, but we both heard them. My first thought was it may be Clara in the kitchen, or in Mike's room or possibly in Laura's room. We probably heard her because the window was open and she was saying something about the car in the driveway. Maybe she didn't recognize that it was mine and she was voicing her concern. I half expected to see a light pointed directly at us, checking to see who we were, hearing someone telling us to get the "hell out of here," or seeing a State Police car come speeding up McMahon Road. Instead, we heard the voice again but this time it was very obvious that it came from Tim's side of the car.

"Holy shit, uncle!" Tim said as he rolled his window up faster than any power window I've ever seen.

Tim placed his light directly against the window and pointed it while I aimed mine over the roof of the car in the same direction. It's not normal to hear someone talking, someone who sounded like they were just a few feet from you and not see them. Unless, of course, there was some sort of obstacle separating you. The only obstacle between the source of the voice and us was Tim's rolled up window, which was now fogged up by his own breath.

"You know what? You have the house and the people in that house on your side of the car. I've got a fucking hill, some weeds and the goddamned invisible woman on my side!" Tim said, staring at me, his light shining on the floor of the car. I gave him a moment; I knew there was something else he wanted to say. He continued with, "Either we switch sides, or we're going back to Olean, we're gonna walk in the front door

71

of the sub shop, around the counter, and I'm gonna stick a spoonful of hot peppers up your ass!"

Under the circumstances, I was able to hold my laughter in. There was something quite remarkable happening at that moment and even though Tim was fairly comical in his last outburst, humor wasn't at the top of our emotions.

There was someone there, and I think it was the *someone* that Clara and her family members talked about. We were scared. Who wouldn't be? The rustling noise could have been dismissed, so could the light from Mary's room, even the shadow I though I saw by the back of the house. There could have been, as Phil so often offered, "a reasonable explanation" for these incidents, but the voice, on the other hand, could not be explained. Unless there was a radio lying alongside the car or the nearby hillside was wired for sound, there could be no mistake: this voice came from '*someone.*' For obvious reasons, I decided to roll my window up as well.

CHAPTER VII

We sat there expecting to hear a voice again at any moment. We couldn't see far from the car and we surely couldn't turn our lights on with the windows up because all we would see is reflections from inside the car. About 10 minutes after hearing the voice, a light came on in Mike's bedroom. I tapped Tim on the arm and nodded toward the side of the house. He glanced at the window for a second and returned to staring out his window.

"Mike's awake. I'm gonna tap on his window and ask him if everything is okay in the house," I said.

"No, noooo you're not! You're not going to get out and leave me here and I'm not getting out to go with you, so you think of another plan where we both can LIVE!" Tim replied.

It was safe to say we were both on edge at that moment but even with the fact that we were sitting outside a haunted house (yard?) in the middle of the night and hearing the voice of someone we couldn't see, Tim still had a way of making light of things. I don't think he was trying to achieve that but he did for me.

"Okay, I'm gonna back down the driveway and when I get to his window, I'll reach out and tap on it," I said.

"See, now you're thinking. Neither of us has to leave the fort, captain."

I made a six point turn to get as close to the house as possible. I had to be careful because there were a few planks of wood alongside the house near Mike's window. I edged up so close that I barely had to lean out of the car window. I tapped twice and waited about thirty seconds but Mike didn't pull the curtains back. I tapped again and the light in the bedroom went off. I looked to Tim for a second and back to the window just as a bright light hit me in the eyes. I was so startled that I jerked away from my window and hit Tim's jaw with the back of my head.

"Oh, SHIT, that hurt!" Tim yelled.

Mike turned the light up to his own face, I guess to let us know it was him. When he did, Tim gave out a shriek.

Thinking back, it was funny but I know it wasn't funny to him, not then anyhow. You know how we've all held a flashlight under our chin to create eerie shadows, especially during Halloween? I'm not entirely sure that was Mike's intention, I would doubt it, but it had that same effect. Mike opened his window to talk to us.

"How long you been out there?" Mike whispered.

"About an hour and a half, maybe a little less," I said.

"At the window?!"

"No, we were parked at the end of the driveway. I called and told your mom we were coming up but when I didn't see any lights on downstairs I thought it was best not to bother anyone," I said.

"Yeah, she told me to keep an eye out for you but I guess I crashed, sorry," Mike said.

"No problem, Mike. Oh, this is Tim—Tim, Mike." They greeted one another through the open window. "Hang on, let me get something on and I'll be out in a minute," Mike said.

"Watch out for the lady. You can't see her but she's there.....somewhere," Tim said, as he was scanning the back yard through the windshield.

"Huh?""Mike asked.

"I'll tell you when you come out," I said.

I started to pull back to the end of the driveway and Tim told me to pull straight in and not turn toward the pond.

"I don't want to be parked so close to the bottom of the hill again. Just pull it straight in," Tim said.

Mike walked out the back door a minute or so later carrying a flashlight. He panned the back yard and turned toward the pond, shining the light back and forth several times.

"What's he doing? Didn't he hear what I said?" Tim asked.

"I'm sure he's kinda used to what's been going on, he lives here, remember?"

"Yeah, but if I lived in a haunted house, I wouldn't be looking for the haunters," Tim said.

"Isn't that what we're doing, looking for the 'haunters?'"

"Yeah, but I go to the zoo to look at the animals too. But, if I lived there, I sure as hell wouldn't be making it a point to

74

go looking for the godddd dammmmned things if they weren't out in the open!" Tim exclaimed.

Mike walked over to the car and got in the back seat. We told him all that had happened since we arrived; what we'd seen and heard. He told us that about 9:30 he'd become sleepy and decided to lie down. His window had been open then to allow the night breeze to come in. He said he heard someone shouting and it sounded like they were down by the tree at the beginning of McMahon Road. "Probably some ghost hunters." He told us. He felt himself drifting off and was sure he'd heard a woman outside his room saying something. The voice was loud enough to stir him but not loud enough for him to make out what she had said.

"I looked out and shone the light into the driveway. I didn't see anyone and honestly, I didn't really care, I was beat and wanted to go to sleep. I tried to stay awake and watch for you to drive up but I got really super-tired. If the woman was with someone and they were just walking around trying to see a ghost, well, more power to them. The doors were locked and no one has caused any damage or anything. I think everyone is just curious. I closed the window and fell asleep really quick."

"Mike, was the woman's voice really soft? I mean, I know most women have soft voices, but was she more or less whispering?" I asked.

"That's what it sounded like to me but it also sounded like she was trying to get a point across about something," Tim added. "You know what I mean? I couldn't make out what was said, but it was said in a way like, shit, how do I explain this? Like, 'you need to pick up your clothes, NOW!' Not those words, but there was a demand, *inflection*, that's what I'm trying to say, dammit, inflection! Even when someone is whispering, when they get to the end of a sentence and they're kind of upset or are demanding something, they have that certain tone—that's what I mean."

"I don't know. It's possible; maybe. I was too tired to pay attention; I just knew it was a female. I thought it was mom at first but I was sure she was still upstairs. It sounded like she said something about help. Not so much, 'help me,' but more like 'you help.'" Mike replied.

I thought for a minute and mentioned the second car that was parked at the end of the road. It may have belonged to someone other than one of the two men we met when we arrived. If that were the case and one of the people who came in that car was a woman and she was the one we heard outside the car, there would be no possible way she or anyone she might have been talking to could go undetected by our lights, especially Tim's. There wasn't cover of any kind, no bushes, buildings, or ridges where someone could hide under or behind that our lights wouldn't catch. After much thought and discussion, the only tentative explanation we arrived at: We heard the voice of *someone*. Possibly it was the *someone* the family talks about who is responsible for making strange noises in the house, or turning the burners on, or rattling the basement door knob. The voice might have been that of *someone* whom members of the family and others have seen in and out of the house or who's been seen crossing the yard. Perhaps it was the *someone* who has strawberry blonde hair and wears the overpowering perfume that several have smelled. Unless we were mistaken, it wasn't someone we were going to get to know or to sit down with and discuss the world's problems. It wasn't someone we would be apt to invite to share Thanksgiving dinner with us. No, the *someone* we're most likely dealing with has problems all their own. One of those problems may be trying to solve, 'how to move on.'

"Do you really think we heard a ghost talking?" Tim asked. "If we did, was she talking directly to us, trying to tell us something? It sure as hell sounded pretty close to the car. I just wish I had heard what was actually said."

"Yeah, this is sort of like when people take pictures of U.F.Os. They take a picture but it's rarely clear enough to make out any detail. Or some people claim they've been abducted by aliens but there never seems to be concrete evidence they actually were," I said.

"I'm surprised mom hasn't gotten up to at least go to the bathroom. Lots of times when she does, she'll check on everyone to make sure we're okay," Mike said.

"Well, let's stick around another half hour or so and see if our visitor comes back. Ya know something we didn't mention? If the voice belonged to someone, you know, someone like us, living, we'd have heard them walking through the brush at the end of the yard or in the field behind us. There is just no possible way anyone could have been outside the car without our seeing or hearing them," I said.

"Yeah, we pretty much established that already," replied Tim.

My window was still rolled down since I'd begun talking to Mike. He had rolled his down when I said we'd stay another half hour. Tim's window, and I could totally understand why, was still up. Five minutes or so passed. None us had said anything. I'm sure Tim and Mike were deep in thought as I was myself. When I was walking the property with Phil Friday night, I had hung on to his shirt as we walked to and from the pond. I only let go when he whipped around to confront me when I had mentioned the 'dizzy bitch.' Was that whose voice we heard? Another possibility entered my already reeling thoughts: if it was a ghost we heard, why didn't it come right up to the car and let itself be known? What's with the voice but no visible presence? If there were an answer to this, I'm sure Father Al would know it. He could shed some light on this as well as other questions I had stockpiled in my memory. Has this house always been haunted or troubled as Father Al would call it? Did the previous residents have problems with the paranormal? Were they bothered with daily disturbances or did they have apparitions roaming the land? Seems that, if they had, there would have been some mention of it by either Bob S., the reporter who had interviewed Clara, or someone else who had knowledge of it.

I reaffirmed something I had planned. This little adventure this evening made me determined to visit the bookstore and look for something on the paranormal and anything I might find on hauntings. My friend, George Stephan, worked for a local company that made deliveries of products to the neighboring towns. One of the towns he delivered to was Lily Dale, NY. Lily Dale was a spiritual community of psychics, mediums and others involved in the paranormal world. I had ridden with him on occasion and I remember an event that was sort of shocking yet comical when we entered the narrow streets of Lily Dale. There was a young girl of about 20 chasing after a cat. The animal finally stopped and the girl was able to pick it up. The girl was in the road ahead of us, some 25 feet or so. George made a comment to me. Something like; "you'd better get that cat before someone runs it over." As we got closer, the girl, clutching the cat to her chest, glared at George as we drove past. There was no way she could have heard him, he was talking to me in the cab of the truck still 20 feet away. Yet, her look said that she was challenging him to "dare run over my cat!" We both felt that was very close to what her look meant and it was creepy. I can't believe all of these spiritualists are fakes. Some, if not all, must have a gift. Certainly, those who are gifted in the spiritual sense aren't going to allow fakes or frauds to be part of their community. I mention this because of what Father Al had said to Clara about me—that I could be a sensitive. Is Father himself gifted, and if so, is he able to deduce if someone else was? I had had feelings in the past; I always refereed to them as "goosies." I guess that was because I would sometimes know when something was going to happen. I think we've all got psychic abilities. Some people's are stronger at birth and others learn to tap into them over time. I was determined that I was going to learn whether or not I was one who had any gift at all.

Mike was shining his flashlight toward the pond, slowly panning left and right. There was a light cover of fog settling over the water, reflecting the light and creating shadows on the ground. On one pass, it appeared there was a separate column of fog within the shrouded cloud of mist on the left bank. It was obvious to Mike because he panned back left and fixed his light in the area.

"Strange, isn't it?" Mike asked.

"What?" Tim asked.

Mike kept the light trained on the edge of the bank. Tim, chin again nearly resting on the dash, was peering through the windshield. There was no real shape to the separate mass we were watching but it was definitely different from the rest of the fog, now quickly accumulating over the pond and spreading to the far side of the back yard.

"That's creepy," Tim whispered.

Was there such a thing as fog anomaly? Eventually, the column of fog blended with the rest of the cloud and was no longer discernable.

"What do you make of that?" I asked.

"No idea, but we'll add it to the rest of the stuff happening around here," Mike said.

I've seen pictures of apparitions in books and I really couldn't say if that's what we had seen. I can say, I don't ever remember seeing a separate "chunk" of fog in the vertical position. Sometimes when driving, you'll pass through pockets of fog and come to a clearing and then back into the mist. This fog appeared to have more mass to it than that of the surrounding cloud. I found myself thinking what I had heard Phil say on numerous occasions, "There's gotta be some reasonable explanation," I was hoping there was.

"Okay, I guess it's time to go," I said.

"No, not yet. Let's hang out for a while longer," Tim said.

"I know I'm ready for bed. You guys can hang out if you want, but I'm gonna go back inside," Mike said.

"It's nearly two thirty, Tim. Aren't you tired?" I asked.

"No, are you?"

"Not really but what do you want to do, just sit here?" I asked.

"Yeah, why not? Maybe the woman will come back and we'll hear her better."

"Okay, you guys," Mike said wearily as he opened the back door. "I'm heading in. Nice meeting you, Tim. I'm sure I'll see ya later," Mike said.

"Oh, yeah, I'll be back. This is kinda fun, creepy, but fun. Nice meeting you too, Mike," Tim replied.

"Night, Mike. Thanks for coming out, sorry if we woke you," I said.

"You didn't. I went to the bathroom and just got back to my room when you tapped on the window. Besides, we're usually up 'til 2 or 3 a.m. chasing people outta here. I was just really tired tonight. I guess it all just caught up to me. I don't think I'm gonna tell mom about the voice you heard. You can if you want, but she's been edgy the last couple of days and I don't want to add any more for her to worry about," Mike said.

"That's fine. We won't say anything unless something else happens that we feel she'd need to know. I do have some questions for Father Al next time I see him, though," I agreed.

"I'm sure he'll be up in the next day or two. I'll talk to you guys later." Mike said.

Mike walked across the yard and entered the house through the back door. The light in his bedroom didn't come on so I assumed he simply went directly back to bed. Do people get used to the idea that their home is haunted? That, at any given time, something not of this plane, dimension, world, wherever spirits are trapped, could suddenly appear before you and you just take it in stride? That doesn't sound appealing to me in any case, nor does it sound like something anyone would be able to accept easily. Tim gave a good analogy that night regarding ghosts (or do they prefer to be called spirits?) Simply put, he said that it might be fun to visit a haunted house but it might not be fun to live in one.

We did stay a short time longer but we didn't spot any more dark shadows, voices or strange fog anomalies. We left the back yard about 3:15 a.m. and drove slowly down McMahon Road to Wagner Hill Road. As we approached the "hanging tree," I did feel a twinge of apprehension, fearing the car would have another hiccup. I hoped and prayed not. Father Al was certainly fast asleep in his residence at the Friary of Saint Bonaventure University. What a unique and likable man he was. I looked forward to having many discussions with him regarding his involvement with the paranormal.

The car didn't even quiver when we drove past the tree but I can't say the same for myself. When I stopped at the corner of McMahon and Wagner Roads, I thought of the two cars that were parked there earlier. It was too bad we didn't see if the two men had gotten into both vehicles. Then again, maybe there were other people in the area and they left while we were parked at the house. I guess it didn't really matter because I resigned myself to believe that whoever we heard outside the car wasn't anyone from around here.

After we had turned and were a good half mile down Wagner Hill, I explained the entire story about the car stalling to Tim. He was convinced that Father Al had to have had something to do with the car starting again. "It was just too coincidental to be a coincidence," he said. I felt entirely the same but then a thought crossed my mind that I kept to myself: I was always under the assumption that priests were called upon to rid places and people of evil spirits or demonic possession. Were they also called upon to cleanse a location of lost souls or aimlessly wandering spirits? Couldn't any of us have the authority to tell the particular *someone* who was stuck between planes to go away and not return? A decent person who might want to hang around an accident scene would probably leave at the request of just about anyone if they were in the way. But a disturbed person might need more persuading, possibly from a policeman. Are members of the clergy the policemen of the spirit world? There was so much I needed to understand regarding the paranormal and, for some odd and unknown reason, I was determined I was going to learn.

I dropped Tim off some time before 4 a.m. He reminded me again to ask if Brian could come to the house. I told him I'd rather wait until he was introduced to the entire family before bringing anyone else up. The Dandys have had more than their share of strangers coming unannounced. I'm sure as soon as things settled down it would be fine for Brian to come up for a visit.

On the drive home I wondered if Debbie might be upset that I was out so late. As I stated before, she was used to my coming in late from our jobs but this might be different. I would know the state of her feelings soon enough.

CHAPTER VIII

When I arrived home this morning, Debbie barely stirred as I crawled into bed and I fell asleep very quickly. I woke just past 9:30, took a shower, shaved, got dressed and went into the kitchen. There was a short note leaning against the toaster. "Hope you and Tim had a good time last night. My brother ordered pizza last night. Couple of slices in the fridge for your lunch. See you after work. Love, Me."

For breakfast I had two slices of toast and an orange since I forgot to buy orange juice. My plans for the day were made: I had to pay the electric bill; I was going to stop at Zemer's garage to see if he could look at the car real quick, and I wanted to go to the bookstore and library. I washed up the few dishes that were in the sink and began heading out the door when the phone rang. It was Mrs. M. She said she had a man who was interested in purchasing some beveled glass mirrors.

"Well, it just so happens, I have a few of those!" I said.

"He's going to be stopping by my house around 11:00. Is there any chance we can meet you at the building and let him have a look-see?"

"Sure thing, Mrs. M. I'm going to pay the electric bill and run to the library. I'll meet you there right after," I told her.

We hung up, I grabbed the appraisals that Mrs. M. had written for me and I left to take care of chore number one. It was only 10:15 when I left the pay station so I had time to stop at the bookstore and look around. I didn't particularly know what I was looking for but I figured someone would be able to help me. Olean was a small city and most of the stores were downtown on North Union Street. I had plenty of time; it was only four blocks from the bookstore to the Fountain. The clerk who worked at the bookstore was quite helpful. Most of the books pointed out to me were fiction about exorcism, possession and haunted houses. She was able to find a couple that discussed these topics in scientific, spiritual and psychological terms. There was one that particularly caught my attention: *Beyond the Senses*, I shied away from the first bunch she showed me but purchased the latter. Of course, with the news recently in the paper, the clerk asked me if I was looking for this subject due to the story in the paper. I told her that, on the contrary, I was just looking for something different to read. She gave me a curious glance as I paid for my purchase and left the store. It was nearing 11, so I drove down State Street and parked in front of the once Fountain of Youth. I unlocked and opened the front door and the escaping air was very hot and dry. "Damn, close the building up for a couple days and it becomes a tomb," I said to the empty room. It suddenly dawned on me that some of the condiments, the hot fudge, cherries, and other assorted toppings were put in the refrigerator on Friday. I guess I wasn't thinking that if the electricity was off in the front, it was going to be off in the back room—dummy!

Mrs. M. and a gentleman from Rue, Pennsylvania walked in about 11:15. I told Mrs. M. about the old coins and the miniature milk bottle I had found when digging out the grates while her friend went to look at the mirrors.

"These are beautiful!" He exclaimed. "What is your asking price?"

I looked to Mrs. M. for an answer. "Do you have the notes I jotted down for you?" She asked

I pulled the itemized list she had given me the previous Friday from my shirt pocket. They weren't in order and the sheet with the mirror estimates was the first one.

"Yes sir, for the larger one, I'm asking $300.00 and $225.00 each for the other five," I explained.

He pulled out what appeared to be a small calculator and was punching numbers on the pads. He walked to the adjoining wall and ran his hand over the edge of each of the mirrors. Punching in more numbers, he looked at the ceiling, I assumed at the fans. He walked back to the bar where Mrs. M. and I were standing and offered: "I'll write you a check for $1400 if you throw in the ceiling fans." He knew I was green at this and I'm sure he and Mrs. M. talked on their way over. I trusted Mrs. M. completely and if she thought the offer was fair I would agree.

"Shall we say, $1700.00, Dale?" I looked at my sheets and the mirrors combined appraisal was $1425 and at least $100.00 for each fan.

"Okay, last offer, $1550, take it or leave it." Dale said with a smile. That offer was just over $500 shy of Mrs. M's total appraisal for the fans and mirrors. I felt it was a fair price but what did I know? Maybe the mirrors were worth a grand each. I didn't know, but as I said, I trusted her. Mrs. M. had a good reputation in Olean and I'm sure she was looking out for my best interest. She looked at me and said Dale's offer was acceptable. I agreed, and he wrote me a check on the spot and asked if it would be okay to pick the mirrors up later this afternoon, about 2:30 or so. I told him that would be fine and made plans to meet him here at the agreed time. Dale said he had another engagement and excused himself. He thanked Mrs. M. for helping out and thanked me for doing business. He walked out and crossed the street to a pickup which I could see had a dresser and other pieces of furniture in the bed.

I stumbled over my next sentence when I asked Mrs. M. if I owed her anything for her help. She explained she had known Dale for years and bumped into him at an antique auction yesterday afternoon and told him about the items.

"Dale is a mirror freak, Paul. He owns a huge old homestead which has been remodeled and there are several mirrors that adorn his walls throughout the house. He loves traveling to antique shows all over the eastern seaboard, especially Maine. I'm pretty sure the mirrors will end up on the walls of his home; at least a few of them," she told me. "He can be quite opinionated at times, and loves to argue with people who offer items for sale but I guess he's an okay guy," she added.

"I really appreciate your help. I would've been lost without your looking out for me. Honestly, between you and me, I don't trust Hank's judgment," I replied.

Chuckling, Mrs. M. said she also had other stops to make and told me to call any time I needed help.

"Tell Pam I said hi," I told her.

"I certainly will. See you later, Paul"

After she left, I looked across the street and noticed Charlie G. talking to George. I decided to walk over and visit with them for a while before going to the library. Charlie was a good ole guy and always entertained us with his good ole day stories. I stayed for about fifteen minutes until George had a customer go into G&G Music.

I didn't have much luck at the Olean Public Library. I did find one book with a few stories offering accounts of poltergeist activity and various haunted houses in the United States and England. It seems there are an abundance of haunted castles in England and South Wales. People are probably hearing the voices of people who got lost trying to find their way out of these expansive bastions. Some of these castles covered as much territory as a small hamlet! After checking out the book, I deposited the check in the bank and returned home to eat the leftover pizza for my lunch. I read a little from each of my new books and then returned to the Fountain to meet up with Dale. I'd have to take the car to Zemer's tomorrow; I wouldn't have enough time today. I arrived at the Fountain shortly after 2:00 and Dale and three helpers showed up about five minutes later.

"Hi again, Paul, we're ready to take these off your hands, or off the walls as it were," Dale said.

"You know where they are, can I be of any help?" I offered.

"No, I've got my brutes with me, we can handle it. Hey, I see that haunted house made the news again," he said.

"What do you mean?" I asked.

"There's another story in the Olean Times Herald. The reporter wrote about all the phone calls he's been receiving, and talking about other hogwash regarding psychics and stuff," Dale explained.

"Oh, that's interesting. I'll have to check it out when I get a chance," I said.

Scoffing he said, "It's a waste of paper and ink as far as I'm concerned. These people must think everyone is as stupid as they are to think they're going to get the rest of us to believe their house is haunted." He continued with, "Either they're morons, or they're trying to make a fast buck by getting someone to buy their story."

I moved aside as two of his helpers were carefully carrying the first mirror out to a truck and wrapped it with thick, heavy moving pads. I was glad they walked out when they did and interrupted what I was about to say. Actually, it didn't take long before I did respond.

"Do you know them, Dale?" I asked.

"Personally? No, but I know all about people like them; loonies."

"Well, I have to disagree with you. I know these people, and they are far from being loonies as can be. Why is it when someone has a problem and they don't understand they start labeling them? I think it's crude to say something like that about someone you don't know," I said.

"Well, I'm sorry if I've offended you but people who start telling tales about ghosts walking around their house need some serious help. Eh, that's just my opinion."

Dale turned to help his third helper remove another mirror while I went outside to cool off, both from the heat of the interior of the building and from the heat that was building in me from listening to this opinionated, as Mrs. M. told me, loudmouth. I was afraid if I said what was really on my mind, he might rescind his offer on the mirrors even though I had deposited his check. I was so pissed at this guy, who didn't know the just Dandys from the Queen of England, that I walked over to George's store to call the bank to see if the check had cleared. We both had accounts at the same bank, The Exchange National Bank, so if he had sufficient funds it should clear right away. Five minutes after I walked into G&G Music, I had my answer: the check had cleared and the money was in my account. Since we had also agreed that all sales were final, I wasn't concerned about what I might say when I returned. I thanked George and walked back across the street to the Fountain. I lit a cigarette and stayed outside while they were inside removing the mirrors from the walls. They were finished working on the last one and brought it out to the truck just as I threw my cigarette butt into the gutter.

"Well, that's all of 'em. It was a pleasure doing business with you. He offered his hand to me, but I just looked at him, refusing to shake it.

"Hey, I said I apologize if I hurt your feelings but get real. You don't believe these people do you?" He asked.

"Ya know, it's not a matter as to whether I believe them or not. I just wonder how you would feel if someone called someone you knew, someone you had respect for and thought was a decent person, loony or stupid," I said.

He rolled his eyes and laughed, then said, "Take a piece of advice, kid: You oughta stay away from these people 'cause you'll be called the same thing. Take my word for it."

"Well, that's your opinion and you're entitled to it. Now, here's a piece of advice for you: when you take your new mirrors and begin to shove them as far up your fat ass as you can, be sure to start at the beveled end first, you arrogant moron."

I cannot believe I said that, especially with two of his helpers standing at the back of the truck just a few feet away. I looked at them for a split second expecting one or both of them to walk in our direction but instead, one of them actually gave me the 'okay' sign with his thumb and index finger. The other turned away and walked to another vehicle parked in front of the truck; I believe he was actually laughing.

Dale turned around and walked to the vehicle the second man got into. I got the impression they didn't agree with his philosophy. That felt good. I'll have to try that again sometime! It was time to go home, I really felt good! I stopped at the store and grabbed a copy of the Olean Times Herald on the way home.

CHAPTER IX

I was fixing Swiss steak when Debbie arrived home. It was one of her favorites. When she walked in she told me Clara hadn't gone to work today, that she had called in sick.

"Yeah, she's probably sick of hearing bodiless female voices talking to her," I said.

"Huh?" Debbie asked with a perplexed look on her face.

I told her what Tim and I had heard the night before and what the three of us saw in the fog by the pond. She sat at the kitchen table and listened intently as I told her everything while preparing dinner. I asked if she were upset that I had been out so late or that I had forgotten to tell her about the car and she told me not in the least. She said if I were interested enough to go up, it didn't bother her as long as she knew everything was okay. I'd always been a night owl even while still in high school. There were many nights when my dad would yell down for me to; "get my ass to bed" well after midnight. Debbie picked up the book I had purchased at the bookstore.

"What's this? You're really getting into all this spooky stuff, aren't you?" She asked.

"I just figure, if I'm going to be around something I don't know much about, why not read up and become enlightened? Oh, before I forget, I deposited a check for a little over fifteen hundred dollars today," I said nonchalantly.

"WHAT!? From where, how, who...."

"That was the sale price for the mirrors, but I had to throw in the ceiling fans too."

"Holy crap! That's almost what you paid for the business. How much do you still owe on the loan?" She asked.

"About $1275 but there's more to go and I hope it all does. We don't have any place to store it. So, when do you want to visit the Dandys next?"

"All right, I want to be honest with you; I don't like going there. Don't get me wrong, I like everyone, and I really like Clara, but I'm not that interested in what's happening. Actually, it does scare me because I do believe in ghosts and I really don't want to be around such things. I don't mind going for a visit now and then but, like I said, it has to be a nice bright day when we get there and when we leave, the sun better still be pretty high in the sky," she explained.

"Oh, I understand, you're a chicken!" She reached over to where I was standing at the stove and swatted me. "But really, I do understand. I remember the look on your face when the car died. You were more than scared. There was something in your eyes, I don't know, like you really did see something by the …."

"I did. I'm telling you, I did see something and it looked like, well, like a person," she interrupted.

"You didn't tell me that then. What was it you think you saw?"

"I know it sounds, um… nutty, But it looked like a man; it looked like a man was standing on one of the branches," she explained.

I didn't know if Clara discussed the so called "hanging tree" with her or not and I don't honestly remember telling her the story of a man being hanged there. If she did see a man standing (hanging?) in the tree, why is it I didn't see him?

"Maybe the shape of the branches gave the impression of a person. It was pitch dark and we were both pretty strung out," I said.

"I really don't remember where I was looking when you said you saw something, but it seems if I had glanced up at the tree I would have seen it if it seemed to be that clear to you. I really don't know what to think," I responded.

What is it with this paranormal stuff, are there some hard fast spiritual rules whereas some people see things while others, can't? Something I read in the book comes to mind; it stated that if you don't believe you won't see. (What rule # is this?) I believe—in something. Another passage I read says that spirits are actually left-over energy and we just refer to them as ghosts. Now, that sounds contradictory in some way. If all of these ghost sightings, not just in Hinsdale mind you, are described as being an apparition of *someone*, how is it fair to call the *someone*, energy? Was it energy that Tim and I heard outside the car or was it the energy of the *someone* escaping from their plane, dimension or whatever you'd call it, to ours?

For instance, a battery produces energy. I can see the battery but I can't see the energy. I can, however, see the *results* of that energy. That's where the contradiction comes into play. If what we see or hear in the spirit world is the result of energy, isn't the apparition or anomaly we see actually the source (the battery) that lets the energy come forth? I'd just read a few pages of the book I purchased, skipping through here and there, and it seems there are more opinions regarding the paranormal than there are stars in the sky. That's why there are believers as well as skeptics. I think my belief during this introductory time to the Dandy house was that I had an open mind. I wouldn't have said I was a believer or a disbeliever but if it looked like a duck and sounded like a duck, I'd probably agree and say it was a duck.

Debbie appeared a bit upset and said she was going to change out of her work clothes. I finished preparing dinner and set the table. I had an urge to call Father Al at the Friary but decided not to disturb him; I'm sure he had a hectic schedule. After all, I was no more than an observer, the Dandys were the ones who needed the help. I had so many questions I needed answers to but I thought it best to wait until the next time we met. Mike said Father would probably be visiting soon and I'm sure my answers would come soon enough.

Debbie walked out of the bedroom and asked, "So, are you planning on going up tonight?"

I really wanted to. Remembering back to this day, the day after Tim C. and I heard the voice outside the car, I had the feeling that I *had* to go. After last night, I believe the curiosity aspect of this "troubled" house had been taken care of—I don't believe I was curious anymore. Moreover, I had a feeling of needing to be there but I didn't know why it would come across to me that way.

"I don't want you to be upset if I go up. There's something that is...."

"I'm not going to be upset. You're a night person, ever since I met you you've been a night owl. Even when you come to bed earlier than normal, you watch television 'til the wee hours. You seem to be preoccupied with the house, and lately, when we're talking, I feel your mind is elsewhere. If there's something you feel you need to clarify about all of this, then by all means, find the answers. I don't like the idea of your driving to Hinsdale late at night by yourself. I was more comfortable when I knew Tim went with you. If something happened to the car or to you or you were foolish enough to go wandering off, there'd be someone there to watch your back. If you feel you need to know, then find out, or it's going to drive you and probably me insane," Debbie said.

"Pass the potatoes, please. I can't explain what I felt— thank you—after the incident with the voice, and I've thought long and hard on this, I had a strange feeling that she, whoever she is, never left the proximity of the car. I know that sounds ridiculous but that's exactly what it felt like. You know, when someone sits down behind you at the movies, there's that feeling of your immediate space being encroached upon. Then you get involved in the movie and for some reason you wonder if they're still there. You don't have to turn around, you don't even have to listen for them rustling their candy wrapper because your senses will tell you. If they're there, you can feel them. Does that make sense to you; do you know what I mean?" I asked.

"Okay, I got one that will maybe make it easier for me to understand if this is what you're talking about. We used to do this when we were kids—you're in a room and you turn off all the lights, you make sure no light is coming in through the windows. Someone blindfolds you to be sure you can't see at all, then you stand at the opposite end of the room and slowly spin around, then someone will aim you toward the other side of the room. Now you slowly walk forward with your hands straight down at your sides, and you try to get as close to the wall without any part of your body touching it. Yes, I do know what you mean, you can FEEL the wall coming but you're not exactly sure just how close you are. It might feel like you're almost ready to kick your shoe into the baseboard but you might still be two feet away! Is that anything like what you mean?"

I'm sure there was a name for what she just described. It sounds very much like sonar but do we transmit some sort of wave that would bounce off the wall and return? Is that how we know it's coming?

"Well, both of our explanations have something in common, I guess. I'm sure if you really key up your senses, you could do that anywhere, not just in a room you're familiar with. How's dinner?" I asked.

"Very good, thank you and I'd like one more piece of steak, please, but make it a small one," she said.

"I think Tim is at the sub shop tonight. I'll call over and see if he wants to go up with me. If he doesn't or can't, I won't go alone," I said.

It was early evening, around 7:30, I called and Tim answered. He was very interested in going again, but he said he wouldn't be finished cleaning up until near 11. He told me he'd like to drive if that was okay and I agreed. He said he'd be by to pick me up as soon as he was finished. Debbie was relaxing, scanning the channels on TV. I told her I was going to clean up the kitchen and then join her.

"You guys going?" She asked.

"Yeah, Tim's gonna drive and he'll be by a little after 11:00."

"That's late," Debbie said.

"That's when the talking lady comes out!" I said.

"See if you can find out what she wants this time," she said sort of sarcastically.

I put the leftovers away, washed the dishes and cleaned up the kitchen, then joined Debbie on the couch. She was watching Dobie Gillis. Maynard must have been asked to do something because he exclaimed, "WORK!"

During the commercials, we talked about B.O.C.E.S., where Debbie was employed. She had been a student trainee and just recently was employed to work in data processing. She liked it okay, but being pregnant, it was tough on her back to sit long periods of time. After Dobie Gillis was over, she asked me to get her a small bowl of ice cream while she looked for a good movie to watch. When I returned to the living room, she'd announced she wanted to watch, "The Bride of Frankenstein."

"Oh, no! Do you know how many times I've watched this movie?" I asked.

"Yeah, I know, you and George watched it a million times and you both know every line of the movie. It's a classic, shut up, sit down, and gimme my ice cream!" She exclaimed.

"You're gonna get fat!" I said.

"Good, now sit down," Debbie replied.

We were only about 20 minutes into the movie when I realized she had fallen asleep leaning against my shoulder. She couldn't have been sleeping very long because she handed me her bowl to set on the end table just a couple minutes prior. She looked far too comfortable to disturb. I reached around her to retrieve the book from the arm of the couch. I resigned myself to the fact that she was going to sleep until I woke her so I repositioned a cushion between myself and the arm on my side of the couch. This was a good time for me to learn a little about paranormal activity. I was really surprised that Debbie slept so long. She only woke once just before 10:30 and asked the time. She stretched, got off the couch and said she was going to bed. I followed her to the bedroom and lay down with her until it was time for Tim to pick me up. She was a good kid and had it together for someone so young. We met little over a year ago and one thing led to another and we became pregnant. It was harder than hell telling our parents. Her parents were divorced and she lived with her mom and two brothers, Tim and Mike before we moved in together. There were tough times ahead. I admit, I hadn't really grown up and having a baby on the way scared the hell out of me. I was 21 and she was 19: a baby having a baby. She could have done a lot better than me and in years to come, she did. I was spoiled by my mother and I guess my father was a little too light on me at the same time. If I had to do it over again, I think there would have been some drastic changes and I would have never agreed to leave New York State, but don't so many of us say we'd change things? Hindsight? Yeah, that's the answer to an answer.

CHAPTER X

It was 11 p.m.. I rolled over and gave Debbie a long hug, a soft kiss and whispered, "I love you." She didn't stir. I went out to the car and grabbed the flashlight I used last night. Tonight, I was going to be prepared. I went back into the apartment and snagged a couple of Pepsi's from the fridge and put half a bag of fig newtons in a lunch bag. I made sure I had my keys, locked the door and went outside to wait on the steps for Tim. It was only a few minutes when he pulled up.

"Look here, Mr. Kenyon, we're going to eat in style," he said holding a bag up to his window that obviously had food in it.

Approaching the car I said, "Damn, and all I brought are some cans of Pepsi and fig newtons."

"Well, then, we have dinner *and* dessert, even though we'll both probably have the shits after dessert—get it," he said.

Led Zeppelin's, "Stairway to Heaven" was playing on the radio when I got in the car.

"You guys play this, don't you?" He asked.

"Yeah we do, what did you bring?" I asked.

He picked up the bag that was sitting on the seat and plopped it on my lap. "I know you like tuna, so I made you half a tuna, no peppers and heavy oil. I made a turkey for myself and ham for Mike," Tim explained.

"Damn, did you put the oil on the sub or just soak the bag in it!?" I asked.

"Oh, sorry, there's a ton of napkins in the bag," Tim said.

I reached in the bag for the napkins to soak up the oil that was literally dripping down my pants leg. "Oh my God, the napkins are more soaked than my pants!" I exclaimed.

"Wait 'til we get there. There are some paper towels in the trunk," Tim said.

Driving down Union Street, Tim turned onto Main street because he had to go home to get his flashlight. He put it back in the garage just in case his dad would need it for something. It would be at least midnight before we arrived at the house. I called earlier today to see how Clara was, but Mike told me she had gone to the store. He said he hadn't told her that Tim and I had come up the night before. He asked if we were coming up again tonight. I said it depended on what time Tim got off work and if Debbie would mind my leaving. He said he didn't get up until noon and would probably be up quite late. I told him I'd tap on his window again if we came up.

We pulled onto McMahon Road about 11:45. There were no cars parked alongside the road tonight, and we didn't see more than four cars traveling in either direction during the trip from Olean. When Tim turned into the driveway we noticed the lights were on in Mike's room but no others that we could see from the front of the house. Mike obviously heard us tonight; he pulled his curtain to look out. Then it dawned on me: I wasn't driving, it wasn't my car. He may think we're some pain in the ass snoops. I asked Tim to stop as he neared the side of the house and Mike's window. I walked over and tapped on the glass and Mike opened his window. "Good, I was afraid you wouldn't recognize us and come out blasting," I said.

"Naw, I couldn't see who you were but I assumed it was you guys. There haven't been too many driving this far up at this time of night. Hang on, I'll be right out," Mike said.

"Hey, Mike, hope you like ham, I brought you a sub," Tim whispered loudly.

"Ya might want to grab something to drink, I only brought two Pepsi's," I said.

Mike gave an 'okay' sign and left his window. Tim started to say something to Mike but he was away from the window too quick. I returned to the car and Tim pulled ahead to just about the same spot I parked last night.

"You think Mike's a camel, he doesn't get thirsty?" Tim said.

"I wasn't thinking, at least I brought one for you," I said.

"Yeah, well look in the back seat, I brought us all a drink, so there."

Sure enough, he had brought a six pack of Pepsi. Tim's a good guy, always thinking of his friends. I'm surprised he didn't ask if Brian could join us tonight. They'd been friends for some time.

Mike came out with a flashlight and a glass.

"Hop in," Tim said. "Um, why do you have an empty glass?" Tim asked Mike.

"I dunno…. Paul said to get something to drink but I guess I forgot to put something in the glass," Mike said. "I guess I better go back in and put something in it, huh?"

"No, I'm just bustin' your chops, I brought a six pack, there's plenty for everyone," Tim said.

"I can't drink, mom would kill me!" Mike exclaimed.

"A six pack of Pepsi, Mike," Tim clarified.

"Oh," Mike said as he got in the back seat.

"Before you start pulling crap out of that bag, give me your keys so I can get the paper towels," I said. "Be careful, Mike, there's enough oil on these subs to keep the engine in this car lubricated for the next two years!" I said.

"Go get the towels outta the trunk. The oil is from your sub, ya guinea," Tim said.

I snagged the keys from the ignition and walked around the side of the car and opened the trunk. I grabbed the paper towels, shut the trunk as quietly as I could and returned to the front seat. I'd been thinking on the way up that I was going to suggest that we take a walk tonight. What could happen? If we saw something that scared us we'd run like rabbits back to the car. We couldn't be any more scared than we were last night when the *quiet one* was talking. (To us?) Something I read while Debbie was resting comfortably on my shoulder has been going through my mind. Some paranormal studies show an increase in activity when there is interaction with those who are haunting an area. I decided to wait until we started eating before telling Tim and Mike of my idea. I thought that if maybe we talked, "coaxed" whoever it was who was here, they might be more cooperative in communicating. It was worth a try.

"Let me lay some towels on the seat so you can set the bag on them," I said.

Tim handed Mike his sub and set his on the dash. I was left to attempt to unwrap mine without making a total mess of the front seat. I picked up a Pepsi from the floorboard and handed it to Tim. While we ate, I explained what I wanted to attempt. I said I thought it was a good idea to try and

96

communicate with whoever was causing the disturbances, to see if there was a way for us to understand why they were here, maybe even to console them.

"Console them?" Tim asked.

"Maybe they're in turmoil; lost. I was reading a book tonight and it said sometimes spirits don't know they're dead. They haunt places they're familiar with trying to understand what's happened," I said.

"Maybe they're demonic. Three of us have been burned, and what about the letter opener that was in Mary's picture? Not to mention the chess set that fell on me that was under books that weren't disturbed," Mike explained.

"Could it be they're trying to get someone's attention, to communicate a wrongdoing?" Tim asked.

"You want to get my attention? Tap me on the shoulder and say hi, that's how you can get my attention," Mike said.

We finished our subs and I suggested we take a walk down to the first turn in the road. This was the first place the smell of pipe tobacco was noticed. And possibly, we might hear a chorus of Gregorian chant.

"Are there any bears around here?" Tim asked.

"I'm sure there are," Mike said. "We're in the country and there are a lot of mountains."

"Maybe it's not wise to walk around at night. That's when they forage isn't it?" Tim asked.

"I think bears eat mostly during the day, Tim. Is it really bears you're worried about?" I asked.

"All right, let's go but the first sign of something moving, I don't care if it's a rabbit, we're coming right back here to the safety of my car," Tim said.

Tim seemed to have been losing those expressions of his face when we were at the house. They usually accompanied his humorous side. Perhaps he didn't really find any of this humorous at all. We walked slowly, in tight quarters, toward the end of the driveway and around the turn. The first turn in McMahon Road was probably 200 yards or so but seemed a lot further at this time of night. Thoughts begin to accumulate when you're faced with the unknown. Will someone jump out to the edge of the road from the field or will a specter suddenly appear ahead, and begin walking (floating?) in our direction? The imagination is a powerful thing; no wonder young children have so much fun at playtime. As children, our mind's eye can create anything we desire and it all seems so real to us—our imaginary friends, the car we created from an old crate—the invisible tea poured by the hostess for her friends gathered at an afternoon party. Ah, yes, that wonderful make believe world of childhood. Now, here we are, three young adults walking the road that's on the property of a supposed haunted house. Were all of these incidents happening at the Hinsdale farmhouse the concocted story of an over active imagination of an entire family? Some have spoken very harshly about this family since the story surfaced while others have offered their help. In some cases, they've offered to rid the home of spirits, some using very fascinating methods. These people too have been scoffed at, called kooks, weirdoes and sickoes. Mass hysteria, this is another explanation circulating among the townsfolk. Opinions are like, well you know the rest of the saying, everyone has one. It wasn't Tim's and my imagination at play and it certainly wasn't mass hysteria last night that caused us to hear a woman's voice in close proximity of the car. Whatever the cause was, or the reason we heard her, didn't really matter. We heard it, and at the same time—ruling out the chance of someone's imagination going to work when someone else says, "did you hear that?"

We walked to the end of the road; no one said a word. Anyone from a distance would think we were a search party. The beams of our flashlights were scanning to and fro and crossing one another like searchlights sometimes do in the night sky at the grand opening of some new supermarket. It was a typical, uneventful walk on a warm summer's evening with only the sounds of night keeping the darkness from being too quiet. We turned around, walked back toward the house and without anyone saying a word, continued directly to the pond.

"Watch the run-off," Mike said. "It gets pretty muddy on this side of the yard."

"I remember, I was out here with your dad," I said.

"I wasn't, thanks, Mike," Tim said smacking me on the back.

"Nehh," I said to Tim giving him a push.

"Is there anyone here that would like to talk to us?" I asked to the darkness.

"What the hell are you doing!" Tim exclaimed.

"I told you what I read in the book. It said to try and communicate," I said.

"Well, let them start the conversation or at least wait 'til we're in the car before you start conjuring up bodiless voices!" Tim said.

"Why, you gonna be less scared in the car than out here?" Mike asked.

"Probably not less scared but I'll be able to step on the gas and get the hell outta here!" Tim exclaimed.

I was thinking I needed to come here during the day. The first time I walked to the pond it was already pitch dark. Our flashlights lit the way but I needed to see all of the property in one fell swoop. The pond wasn't all that big, but big enough where you could launch a rowboat. By the way, theirs was lying against the far shore. We stood at the end of the pond near the boat and scanned the field that led to the tree line. Tim's light was the best as its beam reached the entire length of the field. You could make out the individual trees almost to the end of the Dandys' property. It was then, while Tim was panning his light back and forth and Mike was shining his light at the boat, that I had a feeling, a sense, that it wasn't just the three of us standing on the bank of the pond. I shone my light behind us, back in the direction we came toward the house and back again. Mike, who was standing maybe three feet from me, asked if something was wrong.

"No, I just felt like, I don't know, like there was someone else here," I said.

Tim turned quickly and began shining his light up and down rapidly to cover the path we had taken to the spot where we stood. Of course, there was no one caught in the beam of his flashlight and I didn't expect there would be. Yet the feeling didn't dissipate.

"Here? You mean, right here with us?" Tim asked, eyes wide.

"I don't know, Tim, I don't like the feeling but I have it," I said.

If I were imagining it, all well and good. But, there hadn't been a feeling of apprehension while walking out here and I wasn't thinking or expecting to see anything. It came over me very suddenly as if someone else had walked up to join us. Rather than get the two of them worked up I said calmly, "I'm sure it's nothing, just my imagination. Let's go back to the car and get something to drink." I began walking in the direction we had come. Tim skirted around me, not very quickly, but quick enough to be sure he wasn't bringing up the rear.

"Hey, You almost pushed me in the pond, ya dork!" I exclaimed to Tim.

"Well, that'll teach you to ask if there's anyone out here that wants to talk to us," he said.

As we reached the corner of the pond at the run-off, the feeling remained. Actually it seemed stronger than it had at the onset. I believe I did attribute this to my imagination. Honestly, I was hoping it was. We reached the car and we all took our seats as before. Mike handed over two, now warm, Pepsi's from the back seat. I declined and said I was okay. "I thought you wanted something to drink?" Tim said.

"I changed my mind. Actually, I have to take a leak," I said opening my door. I walked to the back of the car and relieved myself into the tall grass at the edge of the field. In a way, it upset me that I would have that feeling. Now I'll be worrying I'll have these feelings all the time because I'll be expecting them. Is this what Father meant when he said I could be a sensitive? How did Debbie explain what she thought it meant, *I would know when something was going to happen?*

You know they're here too, don't you?

"Maybe I do," I said softly, still standing at the back of the car.

"What?" Mike asked.

"I have mud on my shoe," I said.

I returned to my seat in the car, leaned on the back of the front seat and asked Mike, "What do you think is happening here, Mike? Do you think your house is really haunted by ghosts?"

"I don't know. There are a lot of things happening that require an explanation. Dad says there has to be a reasonable explanation but I can't think of one. We've all talked as a family about everything that's been happening. I do know one thing for sure; *no one* in this family stuck a letter opener in Mary's picture," Mike said.

It seems the question was loaded because I think I had just gotten shot by Mike's anger.

"I hope you didn't think I was implying..."

"No" Mike cut in. "But when you asked, I thought of some of the shit the kids were saying at school. Even a couple of my friends made a crack or two. They don't know, they don't live here, and when I asked them to come up, they just laughed."

"Screw 'em," Tim said, biting into a fig newton.

"Mike N., a friend of mine, got into an argument with one of the kids who lives in the Ischua area. I thought they were gonna start throwing fists but luckily a teacher came around the corner and they backed off. Hand me a couple newtons, please," Mike said.

We sat there for a good long while, talking about school, music, and some of Mike's friends. He said one of his friends, Randy, was a medium. He claims that he can put himself into a trance voluntarily. Now that's something I really didn't hold a lot of stock in, at least not the ones who say that spirits use them to communicate. I remember watching a movie, I don't recall the name, where I woman held a séance and spirits who were being summoned spoke through her. That just sounds like it should be an act in a carnival side-show. Maybe it's possible but I don't think I'd want someone from the spirit world getting all cozy in my mind!

"It's almost 4. Call it a night?" Tim asked.

"Yeah, it's been a relatively quiet night. Not too many cars after 9 last night. Nothing seems to be out of the ordinary out here, thank God. You guys coming up tomorrow night?" Mike asked.

"Not sure, tomorrow's my first night at the sub shop working with him," I made a motion with my hand toward Tim. "I don't know if I could handle that many hours with him," I said.

"Screw you, dorkus," Tim replied.

Mike opened his door and asked us to give him the bag and other trash that was left over from our meals. "I'll throw it away. Funny, no one but me knows you guys came up last night and tonight. I'll leave it that way for now. Knowing mom, she'd start worrying about you being out here all night," Mike said.

"All right, Mike, thanks and get some sleep; I'll give you a call if we're coming up," I said.

"See ya," Mike said as he walked to the back door.

Tim backed his car down the drive, leaving the headlights off so they wouldn't shine on the front of the house as we left. As he backed into the cut out at the end of McMahon Road he stopped. He was looking in the direction of where we were parked.

"What?" I asked.

"I thought—no, it was probably Mike," Tim said.

"It was probably Mike.... what was probably Mike?" I asked.

"I thought I saw Mike walking back to the house," Tim answered.

"Mike DID walk back to the house. Do you think you saw someone?"

Tim, rolling his window up, drove back down the driveway. When he pulled into the area we'd just left, he cranked the wheels to get a better angle of the pond area and the back of the house and yard with his headlights.

"Are we looking for someone?" I asked.

"I just wanted to be sure. I really thought I saw Mike....or someone, walking back toward the house," Tim said. "Let's stay for just a few minutes, okay?"

"All right, just a few," I said.

In less than a minute, the outside back door began to open very slowly. There was no light in the kitchen window and that in itself made the small hairs on the back of my neck stand on end. My initial thought was that Tim had seen someone but was it someone lurking about until we left to vandalize the property? Just then, the interior of the car was filled with light. It startled Tim so badly that he slid all the way over to my side of the seat. The back door opened fully and we could see that it was Mike. He walked to the car and Tim rolled his window down.

"Chrissakes, Mike, did ya have to blast us with the light!?" Tim exclaimed.

Chuckling Mike said, "Sorry, I didn't aim it directly at you, it just happened."

"Did you come back out when we were leaving?" Tim asked."No, I threw the trash away, went to the bathroom and straight to my room. I didn't even turn any lights on, why?"

"Tim said he thought he saw you go back to the house again," I said.

"I couldn't have gone back, I didn't come back out. You think you saw someone, Tim?" Mike asked.

"I don't know. We sat out here all night in the dark. Maybe my eyes are playing tricks on me. I came back to double check, that's all," Tim explained.

"Well, I didn't come back out, if that's any consolation. But I will if you come back a third time," Mike said, laughing again.

"We're not coming back. We're leaving now," I said, directing the statement at Tim.

"See ya later, again," Mike said, as he walked back to the house.

"How is it we don't wake anyone up with all the talking we do outside?" I asked, as Tim began backing out again.

"I don't know. Whose bedroom is whose with all these windows?" Tim asked.

I explained to him what windows were whose rooms. We do talk quietly when we're in the backyard and it did make sense that no one heard us. Clara's room is at the front of the house, Beth Ann's is at the opposite end of the house from

Mike's, and Mary and Laura's rooms are at the back of the house. Mary doesn't sleep in her room but with her mom. I'm not sure about Laura. Laura would probably be the only one who could hear us if her window were open. Both Beth Ann would see us for certain if she looked out her window when we were walking by the pond with our lights on. Obviously, if they woke during the night when we were here, it couldn't have been the precise time when we were by the pond.

As we approached the end of McMahon Road and the tree, Tim slowed to a crawl. "Now what?" I asked.

"Nothing, I wanted to see if the car would stall," he said.

"Let me tell ya, it was scary as hell. The first time up here for either of us, talking about hauntings and hanging trees and people waking up with burns on their bodies and you name it. Then we get here and the car dies. It didn't stall, Tim. Everything quit. I planned to take it to Zemer's and have it checked out today but didn't get to it. I'll get there tomorrow or should I say today?" I said.

"Yeah, I guess you should take it in, just in case there is something ready to go. But, what if he doesn't find anything wrong, electrically I mean?" Tim said.

"Then I guess the car's okay. There's nothing to worry about," I said.

Before turning onto Wagner Hill Road he looked at me then said, "Look behind us. If they don't find anything wrong, then you might want to find an exorcist for the car."

"Moron."

"I'd rather *be more* on than off," Tim said.

The country is so quiet, especially in the wee hours of the morning. There weren't a lot of houses along Wagner Hill Road, and about half of those were hunting cabins. Hinsdale proper is very small, with one central school. There are few streets that turn off Main Street and those all dead end. Most of the roads in the area are dirt the majority of which take you into another nearby village or town. All of the villages surrounding Hinsdale, excluding Olean, are very small. Most have a population of 10,000 or less. There are really no retail shops to speak of and the only place to get anything to eat is Crosby's. I'm sure everyone in town knows one another by first name.

"Are we going up again tonight after work?" Tim asked.

"We'll see. I don't want Debbie getting mad about my going up so much," I said.

"Didn't you say she told you if you really think you need to find out what's going on to go with it?"

Tim had asked me on the way to the house what Debbie thought of my going to the house late at night. I told him of the conversation we had during dinner. Still, I had it in the back of my mind that she was going to be in a bad mood some day and do what so many people do, use it against me. I can hear it now, "Well, if you hadn't gone to the haunted house so often this wouldn't have happened."—So on, and so forth.

"Still, I'll wait and see how she is feeling. I don't want to commit unless I'm sure," I said.

"What time does she usually go to bed?" Tim asked.

"Normally, between 9:30 and 10, unless she falls asleep earlier on the couch," I said.

"Well, there ya go!" Tim exclaimed. "You'll be working until at least 10:30 and she'll already be fast asleep. She won't even know she missed you."

"Yeah, it doesn't work that way, Tim. Wait until you're living with someone, you'll see."

"You can let me know when you come to work. I'll see ya later this afternoon," Tim said.

"See ya, thanks for the ride, Tim," I said as I got out of the car.

I unlocked the door, went to the bathroom and then directly to bed. Debbie would be getting up in about 2 hours. I tried to be quiet as always, but she had woke when I dropped one of my shoes while taking it off.

"Anything interesting happen tonight?" She asked sleepily.

"No, not really. Tim brought subs up and all I brought were two Pepsi's and a few fig newtons. I didn't even bring a drink for Mike," I said.

"A FEW fig newtons? I went out to get some while watching TV and more than half the bag was gone!" Deb said.

"I didn't take that many. I did have a few for lunch yesterday, and I took what remained from one row," I said.

"Right," she said. "Half a bag. That's all right, you like them more than I do. What do you mean; you didn't bring a drink for Mike. Has he been coming out too?"

"Yeah, but don't say anything to Clara. She doesn't even know Tim and I have gone up the last couple of nights. Mike said she might worry that we're outside all night," I explained.

"You should tell her in case something happens. I don't think it's right for her not to know you guys are up there. Do you just stay outside the whole time, or do you go in the house?" Debbie asked.

"No, we stay in the car most of the time. Tonight, we walked down to the first turn in the road and back. It felt kinda weird, but surprisingly, it wasn't really scary," I said.

"Okay, I'm going back to sleep, rub my back," She asked wiggling.

"I'm taking the car to Zemer's today."

"About time, rub my back!" She demanded.

Debbie leaned over and gave me a kiss. She rolled over and moved closer so I would have good aim at her back. I know if I started rubbing her back, I was going to get sleepy fast. Oddly, I didn't feel all that tired. I thought about the feeling I had while we were walking by the pond. I tried to dismiss it when it first happened, but my mind or senses wouldn't let it go. Even when we walked back to the car, the feeling felt heightened. I didn't know what to make of it; a feeling is a feeling, how or why would it get stronger? I wondered if Tim had really thought he saw something when we were leaving. He wouldn't have made it up, but he didn't seem all that worried about it after we got back to our, now reserved, parking spot. It was strange also that there was no fog this evening. The weather conditions seemed the same as the night before. I'm not a meteorologist, so I guess I didn't need to concern myself with that. As I began to drift, a vision of the Dandys' backyard came to me. I was thinking that I needed to go there in the day time. I wanted to see what the house and yard look like, and the pond, and the field to the tree line, and the hanging tree and the inside of the house. I want to see all of these things when the sun is shining. I want to know what it feels like in the day time. To see if it had the same sort of morbid feeling as it does when we're sitting in the car in the pitch dark. Does the time of day make a difference in what paranormal activity exists? If for any reason it did, then I would have to retract the statement I made earlier about having an open mind. I would instantly become a non-believer, because, if a duck looks like a duck at night, it surely would look like a duck during the day.

CHAPTER XI

I woke up late! It was nearly 1 p.m.. "Holy, shit, I'm staying up too late," I said as I jumped out of bed. I showered in a matter of minutes, got dressed and ran out the door. I opened the car door, sat down and immediately realized: Sure enough, it's happened many times in the past and here I am again, outside ready to go somewhere and I locked the keys in the house. "Dammit!" I went around to the side of the house and prayed the whole way, "please let the window be unlocked, please let it be unlocked." It was. I pushed it up, pulled myself over the sash and rip—I caught my shirt on a loose nail and tore the front of my shirt. "Oh, this is going to be a great day!" I said as I fell to the floor of the bedroom, banging my head against the dresser. I closed the window, took off my shirt and threw it on the bed. I grabbed another shirt from the closet and started buttoning it as I rushed to the front door. I almost had the door closed when I caught myself again. "Dumb ass!" I said as I returned to the kitchen to grab the keys. As I passed the counter I grabbed a handful of fig newtons, stuck one in my mouth and stuffed a few in my shirt pocket. I hopped in the driver's seat and started her up. "Zemer isn't going to find anything wrong with this damned car," I said to the steering wheel. I hoped he did, I wanted him to find a wire, or a connection, something that would have caused the car to stall that night. I didn't want him telling me there was nothing wrong with it because that might mean something I entirely didn't want to think about. Zemer's garage was on the corner of First and Wayne Streets. It would take five minutes or less to get there. I arrived around 2 and I could only see one car that he may have been working on. I walked into the garage and waited a minute at the counter when Joe walked in.

"Hey, kiddo, what can I do for you?"

"Hi, Joe, I wanted to know if you could take a look at the electrical system, the ignition I guess," I said.

"Tell me, what's it doin'?" He asked.

"Well, the other night, we were riding along and all of a sudden it just died."

"Stalled out on ya, huh?" He asked.

I explained the whole scenario to Joe, with the exception of its starting when Father Al walked up to the side of the car. I told him I tried over and over again and nothing at all happened and then suddenly it started.

"That's kinda odd. Did you check anything out yourself, maybe the battery cables, or the distributor?" He asked.

"Me?! I wouldn't know the distributor from the wiper motor!" I exclaimed.

"Sounds like the car's got a mind of its own," he said laughing.

He had no idea what I was thinking at that moment. Either it has a mind of it's own or it's being manipulated by unseen forces. "Do you have time to look at it today?" I asked.

"Well, I have a brake job I'm doing now. I could get to it in about an hour, that sound okay?"

"Will I need to leave it here; I can if it's going to take time to check it," I said.

"I'll have to start with the ignition and if I don't find anything wrong there, I'll move on to the starter and distributor. You say it just died, no clicking when you turned the key, and it hasn't done it since?" Joe asked.

"Yup, that's it. It hasn't hesitated on starting since and it never did it before. It was just that one time," I said.

"Why don't you drop it off in the morning and leave it. That'll give me enough time to really go over it. I could get on it after the brake job but if I don't find anything I'm gonna ask you to bring it back anyways. It could be a short in a wire connected to the battery or somewhere else. I'd feel better if I had a little more time to look her over," he explained.

"Is this gonna cost a lot, Joe?" I asked.

Laughing, he said, "No, I won't dig too deep in your pocket. Your old man's a good friend; I'll take care of ya. I'll probably find it pretty quick and it won't cost much at all, Paul," he said.

"Thanks, Joe. I might leave it later tonight rather than bring it in the morning. If I do, where should I leave the keys?" I asked.

"Leave 'em under the passenger seat, but make sure you take anything of value out of it. But don't lock it; the keys aren't going to do me any good if they're in a locked car," he said.

I laughed quite hard when he said that. "Okay, I'll remember *not* to lock it," I said.

"What's so funny?" He asked.

"I was in such a hurry to get over here, that I locked the keys in the house. I had to crawl through the window to get them and almost forgot to pick them up before going out the door again!" I explained.

"You're a chip off the old block that's for sure. I'll see you tomorrow, kiddo," he said.

"Do me a favor though, call me if you find something major before you start any repairs? I know you'll be fair, but I want to have an idea of what it's going to cost," I said.

"I definitely will call with the verdict before going any further."

"Thanks, Joe."

I left Joe's and decided I was going to surprise Debbie and pick her up from work. I had over an hour before she got off so I drove to Carol's to grab a quick hamburger and afterwards, I made a withdrawal from the bank. If Debbie wanted fast food, I'd need to get some extra money. I arrived at B.O.C.E.S. at 3:40, Debbie got out at 4:00. I waited out back where the employees parked so I'd see her come out. "There isn't a thing wrong with this car," I thought. It really was something to do with everything going on up there, I knew it. I guess I just didn't understand much of this paranormal stuff when it comes down to it, at least not first hand. I found it hard to believe something supernatural could affect anything electrical. We learned about sun spots and how they're able to disrupt radio, television and telephone service, but I've never heard of an incident where something supernatural drained the energy from a car.

Debbie and her friend would have walked right by me if I hadn't said something. "Hey, lady, want a ride?" I shouted out the window.

Her smile would be great at the Dandy house late in the evening, it was so bright it would light up the entire field.

"I don't know, I was always told not to take rides from strange men," she said.

"I might be strange, but I'm a musician, you could be my personal groupie," I said.

"Does this include dinner?" She asked.

"I'll even throw in strawberry shortcake for dessert if you continue to smile like that."

She ran around the car so quick she almost lost her footing. "Hi, Paul. How's the ghost hunting going?" Debbie's friend Susie asked.

"Hi, Susie. Haven't seen any yet, but we're ready to catch 'em," I said.

With a snide chuckle she said, "Maybe they'll let Clara come back to work soon."

"Have a good night, Susie," I said.

She continued walking to her car and Debbie was telling me to hurry up because I had to be at work in an hour.

"Okay, okay. But we're stopping at Service Store first," I said.

"For what?" She asked.

"Stuff for Strawberry shortcake!"

"You don't have to, but, okay!"

I drove down Genesee Street to Main and turned into the Service Store's parking lot.

"Shit, what do you want for dinner? Is there anything I can get here?" I asked.

"Grab some hotdogs and buns and get a gallon of milk too," Debbie replied.

I started walking to the entrance when she yelled, "GET SOME OREO COOKIES TOO!"

What's she going to do, put the Oreos in her strawberry shortcake? Somehow, I wouldn't put it past her. I got everything that was on my mental list and headed for the checkout.

"Hi, Paul. Hey, I hear you've been going up to that haunted house that was in the paper last week."

It was John D. I went to school with him. He was a drummer in a rival band here in Olean a few years back.

"Who told you that?" I asked.

"Deb S., she heard it from someone else," John said.

Oh boy, that was all I needed. Deb was the daughter of the reporter who wrote the story. I hoped he didn't plan on writing another article and adding me and Tim to it as "The Dandys' Haunted House Ghost Chasers."

"Yeah, we went up because Debbie and the mom, Clara, work together at B.O.C.E.S. No big deal, really," I said.

"That'll be $5.43, please," The cashier said.

"See ya around, Paul," John said.

"Yeah, take it easy, John." I took my change from the twenty I handed the cashier and walked out to the car. It was already 4:20 and I wanted to get to work a little early. We were home by 4:30. We went in; I threw a couple of dogs in a pan of water and put it on the stove for Debbie while she went to the bedroom to change. There was no sense in driving to the sub shop; it was literally up the street.

"How'd you rip this shirt?" Debbie said, walking into the kitchen, holding my torn shirt.

"I locked myself out again," I said.

"So you got mad and ripped one of your favorite shirts?"

"No, you goof," I said laughing. "I snagged it on a nail when I crawled through the window."

"Did Zemer's look at the car?" She asked. "I took it over and Joe asked if I could drop it off in the morning. He wanted more time to look everything over," I replied.

"You gonna get enough sleep to take it over in the morning?"

"Why wouldn't I?" I asked puzzled.

"Well, if you go to the house tonight and stay as late as you have been, you won't get but a few hours sleep," Debbie said.

"I didn't say I was going up tonight," I said.

"You can, I don't mind at all, I told you that already."

"Are you *sure*?" I asked.

"Yes, I'm sure." She replied.

112

Was she TRYING to get rid of me? She must have thought this was going to be an every night episode, going to the house. It had been kind of interesting, hanging out with the guys. I admit I felt guilty. She's here alone, and I'm up there sitting in a car doing what? Waiting, guarding? Probably to anyone who would see us, looking foolish!

"Pam said she was going to drop by about 7:00. I told her you were starting a new job tonight and she asked if she could stop by. I don't see her as much as I'd like anymore," Debbie said.

"That'll be nice. You guys were pretty close when you were in school," I said.

"Hey, it's almost 4:45; you'd better get a move on," Debbie said, looking at the clock.

"I'm gonna walk over, I'll make it."

She gave me a hug and kiss and I left for my new job, making subs for women with kids that scream that they "don't want a sub," and grave diggers who should be envied by fire breathing dragons. I walked in the shop just before 5:00 and there was no sign of Tim. Jim, the owner, greeted me, shook my hand across the counter and asked me to, "Come on back." He proceeded to show me where everything was kept; the rolls, different cold cuts, all the different bins filled with peppers, lettuce, onions, etc.

"We don't have a time clock, just write your time in and out, and initial it. Tim will be the one to show you how we make the subs, and he'll teach you how to operate the register. One thing, don't give 'em too much. Just put enough lettuce on to cover the meats and four slices of tomato for a full sub, two for a half. If they want more, you have to charge them for it. There's a price list on the back wall that'll tell you those extra charges," Jim said.

While he was telling me all the dos and don'ts, I noticed something Tim told me the night I was filling out the application; he was a slob! There were all kinds of stains on his shirt and tie. You could also see that he was obviously a pro at spilling because there were at least half a dozen set-in stains from previous spills. I noticed there were aprons hanging on

113

the wall and, it was fair to say, he probably didn't slip one on when he was making subs.

"Oh, yeah, when cleaning up, don't run the water 'til it's super hot. My damned water bill is getting higher all the time. Also, when you mop the floors, use this to measure the soap." He handed me a cap and I would really be exaggerating if I said it was any bigger than a thimble. "Use one capful for four gallons of water. Oh, and when you're done mopping, rinse the mop out really good. It gets pretty oily and I have to keep buying new mop heads 'cause they don't last," he said.

"Hey, fellas," Tim said as he walked in. Jim, the owner, looked at his wrist watch.

"It's 5:04, Tim. Here's a new employee and he managed to get here ten minutes early. Take notice of that."

"Sorry, Jim, I couldn't find my left shoe," Tim said. Thank God Jim was standing between Tim and me and there was enough stuff behind the counter for me to look at, because I would have burst out laughing so loud from the look I *knew* was on Tim's face when he gave that absolutely ridiculous excuse for being four minutes late. The fact that he said it so straight-faced was really making it hard for me to keep in the humongous laugh that so wanted to come out.

"All righty, Paul, watch Tim as he prepares the subs so you get the hang of it. Tim, just do what you normally do and …..(Holy Mother of God, the suppressed laugh was about to erupt) ….everything will go smoothly. Good luck, Paul," Jim said.

"Thanks, Jim," I said, holding back a laugh that was so close to the surface.

I dared not look at Tim until Jim was out the door, in his car, and at least a mile away. I know exactly how this was going to go down. I'll look at him, he'll have one of his expressions on his face, then he'll have that famous two second burst of laughter come out and go right back to being straight-faced. Jim was gone; it was time to turn around.

"You son of a bitch!" I said and the laugh came. I couldn't stop, and at that moment, a woman walked in but she had no effect on me at all. I couldn't stop laughing and, frankly, I didn't want to; it felt too good. Tim went to the counter and took the lady's order and came back to prepare it. I was still in stitches and full blown tears were streaming down my face. When I was somewhat composed I figured I might as well make it worse and asked.

"So, where WAS your left shoe? Where did you find it?" I asked, knowing his answer was going to be dumb.

"Well, I fell asleep and when I woke, I saw what time it was and knew I had to hurry. I sat up on my bed, grabbed my shoes and didn't realize I had already put one on my right foot. I was holding my right shoe but I didn't see the left one on the floor. It took me about half a minute to figure it out. When I got off the bed and looked under it, my left shoe fell off my right foot 'cause it didn't fit right," Tim explained with one of his expressions.

I was speechless; there wasn't one word that would come to describe the explanation Tim had given. Even his expression had no effect on me; I was numb. If he had made that story up on the fly—God help us all.

I didn't bother watching Tim make the first sub on my first day. I wouldn't have been able to see anything anyhow. He took the woman's order to the counter; she paid for it and left.

"Come here and I'll show you how to use the register. And for Chrissakes, don't create a lot of over rings, Jim goes nuts. Just be careful and you won't have a problem," Tim said.

We went over the keys on the register which were all marked with different subs. All you had to do was push the appropriate button and the price was automatically entered. Tim explained that over rings were done when people were going too fast and they punched in prices for extras and hit the wrong key. He told me one time he charged someone $2,335 dollars for 5 subs and a couple of pops. Of course, it should have been $23.35. I don't know why that would be difficult when doing the books; just move the decimal point over. It shows what was rung up, you can pretty much figure out what it should have been. But that wasn't my worry, I didn't do the books and I was very careful not to hit the wrong keys. Tim asked me to come help make some tuna salad.

"Tell me, Tonto, are we're heading out tonight?" Tim asked. "If you want, sure," I replied.

"It's okay with the little missus?" He said, offering another expression.

"I think she assumed we'd be going again. One thing, can you drive? I want to run home and drive the car to Zemer's tonight," I asked.

"He's not open late," Tim said.

"I know, I was there today. He didn't feel he'd have enough time to look at it and suggested I drop it by in the morning. I thought if I left it tonight I wouldn't have to worry about getting a ride home," I said.

"Ohhhhhhhh, so you *assumed* we were going tonight, huh?" Tim asked.

"You did ask this morning when you dropped me off, so I figured you'd want to go. I just planned ahead, you know, in case," I said.

"Uh, huh."

"Oh, damn, I have to make a call. We were supposed to practice tonight. I better call Debbie and ask her to call Jamie before he leaves Franklinville; it's long distance," I said.

I called and asked her to call Jamie and then looked at the schedule to see when I was working again before calling George. I had totally forgotten we were practicing tonight. I didn't work again until Thursday; same hours. I called George and told him, he said he hoped Jamie hadn't left yet and that tomorrow was fine. We usually started around 6:15, hopefully he hadn't left. He usually showed up late so chances are he hadn't. Debbie called me a few minutes after I hung up with George. She said his wife caught Jamie just as he was walking to the van. That was a good thing.

"We set practice for tomorrow night," I told Tim.

"That means no spook chasing," he whined.

"Not necessarily, we get done around 8:30. We can't practice all night for crying out loud. There are neighbors and George's family to think about," I explained.

"Oh yeah, those things happen," Tim said, with yet another of his expressions. He was definitely one of a kind. By the end of the night I felt comfortable with everything I'd done.

I didn't make any mistakes on the register; hopefully. I made ten subs on my own, and no one came back in, wielding a machete, and I didn't give out any extras without charging. I knew most of the people who came in. Overall, Tim said we had a really good night for a Tuesday.

"Let's clean up these messes you made back here," Tim said.

"Me?! You were the one tossing olives around like marbles, look there's still six or seven under that chair."

"Come on, you put the containers away and I'll clean the counters. Make sure you put the meat on the BOTTOM shelf but leave out the turkey and tuna. If you want tuna again that is," Tim said.

"No, turkey is fine, *light* on the oil. And what difference does it make if the meat is on the top or the bottom shelf?" I asked.

"If Jim comes in and sees them on the top, you'll be in there too. I don't really know why and never asked him. When you're done, get the mop water ready and use that Dixie cup on that top shelf to measure the soap, not that ant's hat he showed you," Tim explained.

"Aye, aye, captain," I said saluting.

We worked well together and were finished cleaning at 10:25. Everything was in its place and we were ready to head off to the country.

"I marked on your sheet that you had half a turkey," Tim said.

"Okay, marshal, let's get outta Dodge. What else you got in that bag?" I asked.

"Three bags of chips and a six pack." He replied.

"You should have brought four bags, I feel company coming tonight," I said.

He gave me a look as we walked to his car. He put the goodies in the back seat and I reminded him to go to my house so I could get the car. I remembered my keys, so I just hopped in and drove to Zemer's. Tim was following as I parked my car at the end of the building and got back into Tim's. Another thing I forgot to do, I didn't call Mike to tell him we were coming up. I'd been getting awfully forgetful lately and I'd been catching myself thinking about the house a lot. Not just thinking but fretting over it and that didn't make any sense to me. We were pulling onto Wagner Hill Road earlier than ever; it was only 11:05. As we turned onto McMahon Road, Tim stopped and this time I didn't ask anything, I saw it too. Up the road, about twenty feet past the tree, what appeared to be a woman walked toward us and then turned left into the field. She was out of beam of the headlight by the time she turned.

"Keep going; pull up just past the tree," I said.

"And?" Tim asked.

"And? I'm getting out—I want to see this; I've *got* to see this! What pisses me off; I thought about bringing a camera tonight and forgot. Oh shit, I forgot my flashlight from my car," I moaned.

"You're batting a thousand, aren't you? Mine's in the back seat," Tim said.

I reached around and grabbed Tim's light. "Move up a little further," I said.

Tim pulled up another thirty feet or so and I got out. When I exited the car, my feet had a mind of their own; I couldn't move. I just stood there, and I didn't even turn the light on. I was standing at the front of Tim's car but couldn't go any further. That feeling was there but that could have been because, as I said, I was expecting it. Under the present circumstances, it may have been genuine because there was a *sighting* and it was genuine. We saw it and we saw it simultaneously. It was *great*! I realized I was shaking and it surely wasn't due to the temperature. I don't remember if it was from being excited or scared—probably both. I wanted to walk right into the brush and see if I could follow whoever we had seen but I just didn't have the nerve. The pit of my stomach felt heavy and I had a nauseated feeling. I walked back to my door and asked Tim to turn the lights off.

"NO, no fucking way am I turning the lights off, and I don't know what you're doing, standing outside the car!" Tim exclaimed, quietly.

I got back in the passenger seat and closed the door. "Tim, isn't this what we're here for, to experience what this is all about? Aren't you the least bit curious if that could have been a ghost!?" I asked nervously.

"Yeaaaah, but can't I experience it from *inside* the car right now?" Tim asked, whispering.

I understood his feelings and I had to side with him—what *was* I doing outside the car after seeing this..... *her*? I don't believe I felt a threat of any significance but I did have an enormous feeling of apprehension and dread, yet I wanted to see. Some people are scared out of their wits before going onto a roller coaster but they still climb into that seat. The attendant locks the bar in place for safety and off they go, screaming in delirious fright. What's the difference? The bit more that I read in the book yesterday is that spirits can't hurt you, you can only hurt yourself by not being careful. I didn't know from what depths inside of me I'm dredging up this courage to want to walk into the field. When I walked the property with Phil and there was really no reason for me to be fearful of anything, I was just the same. Why now, have I seemed to become acutely aware of the unknown?

"Tell you what, let's sit here with the lights ON and wait for a return visit," I suggested.

"I'll do that, but I do not want to get out of the car yet, not now," Tim said.

"Okay, deal, but is it all right if I stand outside so I can hear better?" I asked.

"Sure, but right by the door in case I turn chicken and start peeling out," Tim replied.

"Okay, but tell me beforehand so I can get in, you're not leaving *me* here and I feel a lot safer with you here," I said.

"Oh, lucky me, I am now your guardian and protector, shit!" Tim exclaimed.

"I wish I could see the house from here to see if Mike was up. Maybe we should drive up and see?" I asked.

"Good idea! Get in, there's strength in numbers," Tim exclaimed.

I got back in the car and we drove off. The entire time, I was looking back hoping to see something, but the night swallowed everything fifteen feet away. When we got to the driveway, Mike's light was indeed on.

"Yes! Don't pull in; I'll go to his window." I got out, walked to the side of the house, and tapped. Mike was at the window in record time. "I forgot to call, I'm sorry," I told Mike.

"That's okay, I figured if you were gonna come up you'd....."

"Come on, hurry!" I Interrupted. "We saw a woman as we turned onto the road!"

Mike didn't say another word and was out the back door and around the side of the house in seconds, carrying his flashlight.

"Where?" He asked.

"Just past the tree! She was walking, Mike, and she walked from the road, into the tall grass, then into the field!" I exclaimed excitedly as if I were a child of 6 who had just spotted Santa.

We both jumped in Tim's car, he backed out and we were on our way back to the hanging tree.

"Did you see her too, Tim?" Mike asked.

"Yeah, and dumb shit here wanted to get out and chase her through the woods. He did get out, but thank God he didn't go any further than the front of the car," Tim explained.

"Cool!" Mike replied.

"Lord, save me from these two," Tim sighed. Tim took the last turn before we reached the tree and slowed down to a snail's pace.

"Come on, let's get there," I said.

He drove a little faster, then suddenly said, "okay, you want to chase this ghost, well let's go!" He stepped on it and we were parked under the tree in the blink of an eye. I grabbed the flashlight and got out. Mike was right behind me and, amazing as it was, Tim was the first one out of the car!

"We stay together, no one runs off if they hear or see something," I said.

"Yeah, and we only have two flashlights 'cause Festus forgot his," Tim said.

"We don't need to go anywhere, let's just stand right here and shine around the entire area. Hey, let's check for footprints, there has to be some if someone walked here," Mike said.

Shining our lights on the road, we did see footprints, loads of them, left by an army of spook chasers. People have been trampling up and down this road the past several days. We weren't going to find anything this way. Besides, does a ghost leave footprints? Somehow I doubted it.

Mike began walking into the overgrowth towards the tree.

"Hey, no one leaves the others," Tim said.

"I'm not leaving, I just saw something on the ground over there; it was just an old shoe."

"If it's a left shoe, throw it to Tim. He has problems keeping track of his left one," I said.

"Come on, let's go back to the car. We're not going to find anything out here except maybe poison ivy," Tim said.

"You getting a little creeped out, Tim?" Mike asked.

"If anything I'm pissed off that we didn't see her again. And tell me something okay, if this woman we saw was a ghost, fine. When we die, do we suddenly become dumber than a stump?" Tim asked.

"What'dya mean?" I asked, and knew I probably shouldn't have.

"Take us for instance, we're alive, and I could see us taking a casual stroll down a country road at a reasonable time of night. But I don't think anyone in their right mind would be roaming around through fields and shrubs in the pitch dark," Tim explained.

"We are, Tim," Mike said.

I knew, and I'm sure Mike did as well, what Tim was trying to say. I was positive Mike has already learned how to push Tim's buttons.

"But we wouldn't be if we weren't chasing after some dumber than a stump ghost! For Chrissakes, I know if I were a leftover 'cause I couldn't find my way to heaven, or the other place, and if I had the power to make myself visible, I wouldn't be playing hide-n-seek with the living. I'd walk right up to someone and say, 'excuse me please, but I seem to have lost my way. Can you please direct me to the closest stairway to heaven, 'cause my fucking feet are killing me from walking through these goddamn fields!' I mean, COME ON!" Tim explained in great detail.

It was always a good time with Tim. Mike and I looked at one another and burst out in the heartiest laughter imaginable. He had a very serious way of being comical even when he wasn't intending on being comical; or serious for that matter. I couldn't see his face but it was there—the infamous Tim C. expression. Lon Chaney had nothing on him.

"Well, am I right?" Tim asked.

"You need to bring this up with the board of directors of the American Psychic Society. Maybe in their research they can make it a rule with the spirit world that if you're lost, they could offer a number you can call for directions to your destination," I said.

"It would be simple too," Mike added. "They'd only have to give directions for north and south."

Mike and I were already at the car, and Tim was bringing up the rear.

"So what now, stay here, go to the house, or take a drive?" Tim asked.

"Let's go park at the house and walk out to the tree line," Mike suggested.

"You mean way the hell out past the pond?" Tim asked.

"Yeah. Dad has been mentioning the tree line lately, like there's something there."

"Dad, as in, 'there's got to be some goddamned, reasonable explanation,' dad?" I asked.

Laughing, Mike said, "He said a couple of times when he was out near the pond he'd get these feelings."

"What the hell, does everyone but me get feelings? Another thing, don't you guys think we need to start considering the amount of wild animals out here? There are all kinds of 'em you know," Tim said.

"Here we go with the wild animals theory again. If it were tigers, or cheetahs or even water buffalo, I'd be worried, but I'm not worried about raccoons, skunks and foxes," I replied.

Tim pulled up to the front of the house and Mike asked him to back into the cutout instead of pulling into the back yard.

"Why, did we get into trouble?" Tim asked genuinely (doubtful) concerned.

"No, but if you park aimed toward the road, we can see part of the way to the turn if you keep your headlights on. Mom had been talking to some people today and they said they could smell the strong odor of tobacco smoke, like pipe tobacco, at the turn but there was no one smoking," Mike said.

"That's sounds good to me. We can park here and watch for someone to light up. Yeah, forget the tree line," Tim said.

"We can still go to the tree line in a while. We won't even have to walk around the back of the house, we can walk straight there from the front of the house," Mike.

"Anyone hungry?" Tim asked.

"I could eat," Mike said.

"I brought us all turkey and there's a bag of chips for each of us too. The pop is on the floor, Mike," Tim said.

Mike handed a couple of pops over the seat and Tim passed out the sandwiches. We ate while Mike told us his mom wants to throw a get together on Labor Day. It sounded like it could be fun, and best of all, it would be during the day! Finally, a chance to come up when everyone was awake. We'd get to meet the neighbors and possibly hear some of the stories they may have to share. Mike said Father Al would most likely stop by and that would be a really good opportunity to talk with him about these "feelings." We might, at last get information about the former tenants, regarding any experiences or disturbances they may have had. It's a shame Clara has been so stressed lately. I'm sure this has taken its toll on the entire family. I wanted to ask Mike if things have been somewhat normal in the house but after asking his opinion last night and getting a rather defensive response, I was fearful the conversation might get into something he may have taken wrong. Yet, he hadn't said anything, so I assumed that things were fairly quiet inside. But what's with all this activity outside? It appears there's more paranormal energy out than in.

Sometimes people are haunted, not just locations. Did I read that somewhere or did someone say it to me? I didn't remember but it was familiar. Something about people being a sort of antenna that attracts the energy of the spirit world. Once again, without a professional or an expert on the subject to offer an explanation, I honestly didn't know what to make of it except to keep an open mind. The statement Tim made, his somewhat comical opinion and confusion as to why ghosts wander aimlessly, made a great deal of sense. If *people* can be haunted and they're aware of it, does this mean that every Tom, Dick, and Casper searches them out? I've heard of ghosts being seen at the Battle of Gettysburg and in the book I was reading....actually—skimming through, it is written that there are numerous castles in England that are notorious for their plentiful spirits. Why are only some folks who pass on, for the lack of a better word, permitted to hang about or return to finish something they started? Rather than assault Father Al with all of the questions I had, I planned to begin to seek for answers to some of these questions by doing some research on the subject. I didn't know where to start or whom to talk to, but perhaps a good starting point would be getting information from the New York Psychical Research Center, or the organization Father Al belonged to, The American Psychic Society. If I wanted to fully understanding what was happening at the Dandy house, I needed to know answers to some "why" questions. I had the feeling there was an enormous amount of work ahead of me if I were to continue to be involved with the house.

"You still with us, Paul? Do you want to take a walk out to the tree line?" Mike asked.

"Sorry, guys, I guess I was lost in my thoughts. Yeah, I guess we can. Are you coming too, Tim?"

"Ha, you were lost all right; Tim was the one who suggested it," Mike said, laughing.

"Yeah, but we need to make some rules to follow if we're going to be walking so far from the safety of the car and house," I said.

"What do you suggest?" Tim asked.

I asked them to hang on a second while I thought about it, and asked them to think of anything they could offer assuring our safety from *ANYTHING*.

"What if someone gets hurt and can't walk? Is one of us going to stay with him, while the third goes for help?" I asked.

"Also, what if one of us gets so scared we pass out? Are we going to...."

Mike interrupted, "It's the same as getting hurt Tim. That's a good question, what *WOULD* we do? I don't think there's much that we could injure ourselves on. We've all walked around out there and it's just like here except there are a lot of woodchuck holes in the field."

"Well, there ya go. Someone twists their ankle and can't walk. Do we carry them or does one of us come to the house to get help?" Tim asked.

"Oh, shit, we're worrying too much. I'm sure we'll all be just fine if we're careful," I said.

"I'm sure too." Mike agreed. "But we still need a plan if something were to happen. I say one stays and one runs for help and signals with their light when they get to the house."

"And what if the one running for help doesn't make it or we can't see them signaling because we're out of sight of the house? Then what?" I said.

"First, we make sure we only explore an area that's in line of sight with the house and if the person doesn't make it, they'll come back as a spirit and hopefully won't be as dumb as a stump and tell us! Let's just go and I'm sure we'll make the right decision *if* something happens, agreed?" Tim asked.

After we quit laughing at Tim's comment, Mike and I agreed, then thanked Tim for seeing the lighter side of it. We were beginning to get on each other's nerves and we all felt we'd be fine as long as we used our heads and were careful. We walked as far as we could toward Wagner Hill Road through the field that fronted the Dandys' house, and then began walking toward the tree line at the far end of the property. The walk wasn't bad at all. There were a few mounds of dirt and the occasional woodchuck hole but, all in all, it was an easy trek.

"I wonder if anyone is buried out here," Tim said.

"Well, I don't know how many cabins, huts, tents or what ever they lived in used to be out here over 100 years ago but people did tend to bury their dead in the most convenient location. Your house is over 100 years old, isn't it Mike?" I said.

"Yeah, that's what mom and dad said. Mom said the last family owned it for over 100 years; the McMahon's."

"No kiddin.' So the road is named after the first people that lived here, huh?" Tim asked.

"I guess, I don't know if they were the first but I assume they were," Mike replied.

We were almost to the tree line when Tim stopped. He looked at me, then back to the house and again back to me.

"You okay?" I asked.

"Yeah, I just can't believe we walked out here. The house is quite a ways away. If something did happen, it would take a bit of time to get back," Tim replied.

"We did good," Mike said. "We walked all the way out here without an incident. Now I suggest we start back. We accomplished what we came to do and there's nothing out here. Let's just head back and we'll do this another time."

He didn't sound like himself. I mean, it was Mike all right, but the inflection in his voice was different somehow, his personality changed or something. I think Tim picked up on it too because he was already heading back toward the house and the whole time, he kept looking over his shoulder at Mike.

"You okay, Mike?" I asked.

"Sure, we heading back?" He asked.

This was a put on, I thought to myself. Mike is trying to freak us out or something by acting differently. "Sure, we heading back?" He had asked. He suggested it with that, "not quite Mike personality." I was beginning to think we were all a little nuts. Too many variables and different ones every time we went up. I'm glad I was practicing tomorrow; I needed a break from this place. Tim was a few feet ahead of us, and Mike and I walked side by side. Every once in a while, he would stop and look back, either toward the tree line, or to our right, toward Wagner Hill Road and the property boundary. I didn't ask him anything because I didn't want to hear something I might take as a put-on and say something I didn't mean. I honestly didn't think Mike would deliberately fool us or act differently without telling us he did it as a joke, but with everything that's happened the past few nights, I left it alone. Tim got back to the car first and leaned against the trunk. Mike and I brought up the rear and stood on either side of him.

"What was that all about?" Tim asked directing his question to Mike.

"What was what about?" Mike asked, seemingly puzzled.

"You were acting weird when you said we accomplished what we came to do," Tim said.

"What do you mean? I don't remember…"

"Never mind that shit!" I interrupted. "Look!" I was pointing in the direction where we had walked last night, at the last turn in McMahon road that leads to the house. There was a dim light close to the ground and it was slowly moving down McMahon toward Wagner Hill Road. It was a soft light, almost like a fire flickering in the distance, swaying back and forth. It lasted for a few brief seconds and was gone. We lost sight of it at the end of the field adjacent to McMahon road due to the lay of the land and its proximity to the ground. "What the hell?" Mike asked.

"Dunno. It's so far away and we really can't see clearly from here, but it didn't look natural whatever it was," I said.

Tim was the first to get in the car. Mike and I jumped in a split second later. We arrived at the spot we first noticed the light. When there was no sign of it, Tim continued driving in the direction it had traveled down McMahon Road. There was no sign of it anywhere, on the road, or in the field. We drove to the beginning of McMahon and stopped at the tree. All of us exited the car and looked back toward the turn in the road. From this position our view of the terrain was limited as the land behind us, up McMahon Road, was a gradual rise and there was a slight bend in the road before the turn. If the light was anywhere between us and where we had first seen it, it wouldn't be visible from our position unless it was directly on the road or near the edge at either side.

Tim looked at us and said, "You wanna know what that looked like to me? I swear that looked like someone taking a leisurely stroll with a lantern! Imagine it, someone walking, lantern in their hand and …."

"Give that man a kewpie doll!" I interrupted. "It did look like that, minus one thing, Tim."

"Uh huh." Tim agreed. "I didn't see anyone carrying it!"

127

"Well, if someone had come down the camp road with a lantern, battery operated or kerosene, there would be enough light to reflect on the person carrying it. We would have at least seen their legs," Mike said.

"Mike, have things been quiet in the house?" I asked. I decided it was time to ask. I wanted to ask last night but decided it was best not to. I didn't want Mike thinking I was making any type of accusations.

"Mom, dad, Beth Ann and I were discussing how quiet is *had* been the past few nights. There were a few noises coming from upstairs when dad was getting ready to leave for work tonight but other than that it has been, I guess you could say, normal. Why do you ask? I mean, I know you're concerned, but why do you want to know?" Mike asked.

"We've been up here the past three nights and nothing has been happening inside. Could it be they're keeping their interests on us?" I said.

"Man, that's nuts," Tim said.

"Why do you say that?" I asked.

"We aren't the targets here, if it's okay to put it that way, and no offense to you Mike. This has been going on with Mike's family for a while, right? We're just up here hanging around more or less, eatin' subs and drinking Pepsi, although, I'd like a beer right now. Why would they turn their interests on us?" Tim asked.

"Cause we're the ones who are active, something to watch, everyone in the house is sleeping. If I had a choice between looking at someone sleeping or watching three dumb shits roaming around, I would choose the dumb shits," Mike said.

Sometimes people are haunted, not just locations. If spirits are attracted to a particular location, or house, perhaps what attracts them are the occupants, or human activity in the area. If there is something that keeps them bound to a location, maybe their only method of communication is to get the awareness of the people who are connected with that location, thus, making the statement valid to some degree. Then, this brings us back to the question, 'did the former tenants experience these manifestations, and if not, *why* not?' I believe it's safe to say, answers to paranormal uncertainties are somewhat elusive and there are many variations of answers given.

"I really believe we're keeping all their attention on us. We're not going to fully understand anything until we get answers from Father Al or I find something to explain why it is we don't have actual communication with whatever or whoever is causing these disturbances," I said.

"Was Father Al up today, Mike?" Tim asked.

"No, but I know mom talked to him. She said she was going to contact him and tell him things were a lot quieter," Mike replied.

"It'll be my luck that he comes to visit tomorrow and I have band practice. I'm going to get up here during the day and walk the entire area. I'd at least like to see what the area looks like without tripping over something," I said.

We all got back in the car and Tim drove back to the house slowly. We were looking on both sides of the road expecting to see something but, of course, we didn't. It's like anything, if you're looking for it, you can't find it, but any other time it's right under your nose. I wanted to bring up how Mike was talking prior to coming back from the tree line but decided not to. I had hoped we were going to be honest with one another and not fabricate anything just to get the blood pumping. Something I needed to check was to see if there was any record of someone being hanged from the tree. On our first visit, I remember Clara talking to Debbie and Father Al about the scarcity of records for the area. I would expect there would be something about a hanging though. It obviously wouldn't have been a legal lynching according to the rumors. In the south it was a daily occurrence and it was always racially related. I wouldn't think it would be something that could be swept under the rug in this tiny community. Hinsdale hadn't grown much in the past 100 years.

We parked in our usual spot in the back and we were all ready to call it a night. We were certainly getting braver; we weren't as frightened to leave the safety of the car after just three nights of visiting. I'm sure if the time came that an entity is suddenly standing alongside of us, we would have been back to hanging onto one another's shirts when we were out of doors.

"Hey, when am I ever gonna meet Dolly?" I asked Mike.

"Oh, I'm sure sooner or later she'll be out or mom will be holding her in her lap some night when you come up," Mike said.

What's—- who's Dolly?" Tim asked.

"Mom's pet skunk," Mike explained.

"Skunk?!"

"Yeah, we have our own petting zoo. Two dogs, two raccoons, two parakeets, two cats and Dolly. We did have three dogs but one died," Mike said.

"Sounds like Noah's Ark revisited, minus one skunk," Tim said.

"That's it for me; I'm ready to go in," Mike said.

"Well, we realized one thing tonight," Tim said.

"What's that, Tim 0 Thy?" I asked.

"We've got ballllllllllllllllllllllllllllsssssssAH!"

"Yeah, you can say that. Would any of us have had the balls if we were alone out here?" Mike asked.

"Nope, not me, count me all the way out of that one, no sir," Tim said.

"I'd have to agree, Mike, I'm not ready for a one-on-one with anything just yet," I said

"It's unanimous then. I'll see you guys tomorrow if you make it up. Mom may be going to Buffalo, she mentioned it but she wasn't sure," Mike said.

Mike started walking to the house when Tim yelled to him.

"Take the rest of these Pepsi's with you and give 'em to the kids, Mike."

"Thanks, Tim. See you guys." Mike said walking to the house.

"Ya know, I think you've been lying to me, Paul," Tim said.

"About what?" I asked.

"I'm beginning to believe Mike is the only one who lives in this house. That maybe he's an orphan and this isn't even the haunted house that was in the paper. You're just using me to help you to help him feel better about living alone out here in the middle of nowhere. He doesn't even have any sisters or parents, does he? That's it, isn't it? You're really slick, you are," Tim rambled.

"Where in the hell do you come up with this shit? Why don't you write a book for the mentally insane and title it, 'If You Think You're Nuts, Come and Walk in My Shoes for a Week.' You can even add a sub title, 'If, And When I Find My Left One,'" I said.

"Let's get the hell outta here before someone in a white coat takes us both away," Tim said, offering his two seconds of laughter.

We left the house and returned to Olean. I'm sure there was some truth to what had been said about the spirits holding their interests on us, and that had been the reason the house had been quiet the past couple of nights. There was no clarification from Mike regarding the atmosphere of the house during the day. Were the past few days uneventful because the spirits were working the "graveyard" shift this week? Does one need sleep when they're deceased? There were more and more questions with each subsequent visit that needed answers. Perhaps I could find more crucial information at Saint Bonaventure's library. I wasn't sure if you had to be enrolled to utilize the facilities but I would certainly find that out and soon. Surely, Father Al could steer me in the right direction if it was research I needed help with. I would doubt there would be any pertinent information about the history of Hinsdale, New York other than general history, but it would be worth the effort to check. Perhaps there were death records on file and we could cross reference names with dates and maybe, just maybe, causes of death may be listed. I was already convinced that much of this would be like looking for the proverbial needle in a haystack. Nonetheless, I was going to be diligent in my quest to acquire answers that would offer us a little more insight and understanding to what these occurrences happening in this rural country home meant.

"Do you have to pick up your car today?" Tim asked.

"If they're done with it today. I'm sure they'll get right to it this morning. Joe said he'd call me and let me know what it will cost to fix it," I said.

"That's good. Lots of garages do the work, *then* hit you with the bill. There oughta be a law about something like that," Tim said.

"I don't work tonight, but the band has practice. Shit, my ad's gonna be in the paper today. I forgot about that. Hopefully, there will be calls on the stuff for sale and, if there are, I'll have to be present to show everything," I said.

"Did you put the address in as well as the phone number?" Tim asked.

"Actually, I did, but I put our number in as well as the Fountain's. I called the phone company to keep the phone on until the end of the week; the fire department didn't see a problem with it," I explained.

"You're all screwed up, you know that?! You put the address in, so people are gonna come anyhow, whether they call or not. Plus, you say you put your home number in as well as the Fountain's number, right?" Tim asked.

"Yeah, what's the big...?"

"Shush! Remember when you got smart with me and said you couldn't answer your phone from the corner when I saw you the other day? You're also not going to be able to answer *both* phones today, *and* you're going to have to be there *all* day 'cause you don't know when people are going to show up, smart ass! I'm going home to my nice soft bed and *you* are going to drink plenty of coffee and keep your dumb ass awake *all day*!" Tim exclaimed with glee, digging at my stupidity.

"Oh, my God! Ya know what, I have a list of what everything was appraised at and if you..." I began, but was interrupted when Tim said,

"HA! Don't even say it. You got into this mess, you work your way out."

"Come on, Tim. You could be at the Fountain and I could be home in case anyone calls there. If someone calls I can..."

"No, no, no. Yeah, I'll be at the Fountain in case someone calls and you'll be home sleeping *until* someone does call. Nope. I'll solve this dilemma for ya right now. You placed two phone numbers in the ad and, if they don't get an answer at one, they'll call the other. Would you like me to take you to the Fountain now so you can get a head start on all the people that will be KEEPING YOU AWAKE?" Tim said, with many expressions.

"You're an asshole; did I ever tell you that? Well, I can get a couple hours sleep anyhow." I looked at the clock in the dash, it was 5:00! "Oh, shit, I can't believe we stayed so late tonight. I'll call you later, but I *doubt* I'll be chasing anything tonight except sheep as I'm counting them," I said.

"All right, maybe we both need a break but let me know. I'll see ya later; I need to get my beauty rest while you go to work!" Tim said, laughing.

As I was getting out of Tim's car, I slapped him on the back of the head. "There I feel better now, you prick!" I said.

"I will too, as soon as I get seven or eight hours of sleeeeeeeeep!"

I flipped him the bird as he drove off. He was a good friend, it's too bad so many years have passed by and his delusions kept the friendship from rekindling. I went into the house and it was only 3 a.m. His clock in the car is screwed up, it said 5! It didn't feel like we were there that long. I felt much better; I could still get a decent amount of sleep. I hadn't planned on heading to the Fountain until 10 anyhow.

I threw my clothes on the floor and jumped into bed.

"Good morning, sweetheart," Debbie said with a passionate kiss.

Oh, no!

Now, it *was* a little past 5:00 when I looked at the clock again and, of course, she was fast asleep. I was hoping for sleep to come fast! It never fails, you know you have to be up in a few, short hours, and because of this, you can't go to sleep. At least with me that's always been the case. I should be *dog* tired! Eventually, sleep came and it felt good. The last thing I remember before falling asleep was, 'how would I get back at Tim for his wise cracks?'

CHAPTER XII

"Where's the car? Did something happen last night, what happened. Are you okay?!" Debbie woke me with a vigorous shake, asking me all sorts of questions.

"What, what are you... oh, shit, I didn't tell you. I dropped the car off at Zemer's last night after Tim came by. When I was there yesterday, he suggested that I bring it by this morning, I thought I could just drop if off and not have to take it in this morning," I said sleepily.

"Shit, I thought something happened, that you got into an accident or it was sitting up there by that damned tree. Why didn't you tell me?" Debbie asked, rather angry.

I looked at the clock; it was 7:20. "'Cause it was almost 11:30 when Tim got here, I wasn't going to wake you," I said.

"Did you already know you were going to drop it off last night? Did you tell Joe you would be bringing it by last night?" She asked.

"Yeah, I guess I should have told you but I forgot. I was excited about going to work at the sub shop and honestly, I totally forgot," I said."

"Christ, I thought something had happened. You scared the hell out of me!" She exclaimed.

"I'm sorry, but if something had happened last night, don't you think I would have woke you to tell you?" I asked.

She now had that look when I knew I should find a place to hide. "No, 'cause you probably would have forgotten. You know, you've been forgetting a lot of things lately. You lock the door and forget your keys, crawl though the window to get them and almost forget them *again.* There's been other stuff too; you need to get more sleep, that's what I think," she scolded.

"You're right and I'm sorry. Remember, I have practice tonight. I'm gonna pay the bills today," I said.

"Susie's outside, I gotta go. And *you* remember you have practice tonight, I won't forget. Love you," she said.

"Love you too. I'll be at the Fountain all day today. The ad's going in the paper," I said.

"Well, then get some sleep!" She demanded.

"Huh??"

"The paper doesn't come out 'til noon. You have time to sleep. Again, I love you, see you later," she said.

Oh, my God! I set the alarm for 11:50 and buried my head in the pillow. I was sleeping before I was done digging in.

When the alarm went off, I thought it was still the dream I was having. I was a contestant on a game show and when one of the other contestants pressed their buzzer, it stuck. So much for the world of dreams. I got up, skipped the shower and went to the kitchen. I figured I'd have some toast then thought, "I'll just get the lunch special at the Diner." I went back to the bedroom, got dressed and *checked for my keys,* found them in my pocket and left. The Fountain was just 3 blocks up the street so I could walk it in a few minutes. I stopped at the diner to get the special. Today it was, 'tuna noodle casserole,' another favorite of mine. Hank came out of the kitchen and told me the guy at the end of the counter was waiting for me to get to the Fountain; he wanted to look at the marble.

"I'll tell him I'm here. Would you make me up the lunch special, please? Throw in two slices of bread. Thanks!" I asked.

"It'll be ready by the time you're done telling him you're here," Hank replied.

I walked over to the gentleman and introduced myself. He said he had been looking for a few large pieces of marble for a home in Buffalo, New York.

"The entire bar is made of marble, the sides, the top as well as the front. I'm ready to go over if you're ready to take a look," I said.

Hank set my lunch by the register. We walked toward the exit and I reached in my pocket to pay for my lunch.

"It's on me, get outta here," Hank said.

"Thanks, Hank!" I said. He seemed to be little friendlier than he'd been when Mrs. M. came in.

When the 'marble man' and I got outside, I observed a man and woman standing on the sidewalk in front of the Fountain. Holding my lunch in one hand, I fumbled with the keys to unlock the door. "Sorry, folks, it's pretty warm in here and the electricity is off. Take a look around and if you see something you're interested in let me know," I said.

I set my lunch on the counter and went to the back room to open the window. Hopefully, we could get a cross breeze if I left the front door open. It was stifling hot, and the air was heavy with the smell of mildew from the basement door being left open. A pungent smell of smoke lingered as well.

"What happened here?" The woman asked.

"There was a fire next door and the wiring is frayed, that's why the electric is off," I explained.

"It smells awful in here!"

I thought, if she spun around a bit, the smell of her overly applied perfume would surely have masked the odor of manure!

"How much for these coke glasses and these sundae dishes, young man," she asked.

"Fifty cents each, ma'am." I replied.

She began counting them as the "marble man" was measuring the dimensions of each piece of marble. "Oh my, this is beautiful; exquisite," he said, while looking at a picture he held in his hand. I don't know exactly what he was doing, because he'd measure a piece, write it down on a pad of paper, then measure it again and write it down on *another* sheet in the same pad.

"Would you take $60.00 for all of them?" The woman asked.

Is there something wrong with her math? I thought. I remember counting them and there were exactly 30 coke glasses and 72 sundae dishes. Now, that's 102 pieces in all and at fifty cents each….. "Sure, ma'am, that's fine. I have some boxes in the back and there are some newspapers that we can wrap them in."

"Lovely, that will be just fine," she said.

Lovely….. I went to the back room and got the boxes and paper. I placed them on the bar next to the woman with the noxious perfume and began wrapping them.

"Here, son, let me do that. She's very fussy about wrapping glassware," the man said.

"Have you a phone I could use, please?" Asked the "marble man."

"Yes, sir, right over there in the corner," I said, pointing to the back of the room.

He walked over and dialed a number. It must have been long distance because he started shoving coins into the phone as if it were a slot machine. He was on quite some time, at least half a pocket of quarters worth.

Mabel (I overheard the man call her that) and her male companion thanked me and handed me $60. I asked if I could help carry the boxes out but she said "Arthur" would take care of it.

"There's a bit of a tip there for you, young man. It should have been $51 but I believe the glasses are worth more than your asking price," Arthur said.

"Well, thank you, Arthur," I said.

He looked at me as if I slapped him across the face. That *was* his name, wasn't it?

The "marble man" hung up from his call and walked over to the bar again, talking to himself. He measured the longest piece one more time and then gave the most puzzling look. He shook his head and said aloud, "It is exactly the same size as the first time I measured it!"

"Be very careful, Arthur," Mabel said, holding a hankie to her face.

All right, the Fountain is closed, we know that, but did Rod Serling take over and is now in the process of filming an episode of The Twilight Zone?

"Sir, if you would," the "marble man" said, handing me the end of his tape measure.

He walked the length of the bar and then came back half way, folding the tape. Maybe I'm still asleep, that's what this is, a dream.

"I am prepared to make you an offer but there is one piece I do not need," he said as he walked to the end closest to the door and smacked the end piece.

"I do not need this piece. But for the rest, I am willing to pay, $2000."

As they say in jolly old England, "I think I just shat myself!" "Would you give me a second so I can call my father with your offer?" I asked.

"Absolutely. I can write a check or, if you prefer, I will go to the bank and acquire a cashier's check," he said.

"Just a minute please," I said, as I *tried* to walk to the phone.

It wasn't my father I was calling, but Mrs. M. I dialed her number and begged the wall where the mirror had been hanging to "please be home." She answered on the second ring.

"Mrs. M.! There's a gentleman here who has offered $2000 for the marble. Is that good? Mrs. M.? Hello, Mrs. M.?"

Excitedly and in a whisper, she said, "Tie him to a chair. Don't let him get away!" Now she added quite astonished, "My God, yes, Paul! I expected maybe $500 max for the entire lot *if* you found the right buyer. Who is he?" She Asked.

"I don't know, he said he was looking for marble for a house in Buffalo," I said.

"Oh, you have done well, Paul, very well!"

"Okay, Mrs. M., thanks again and I'm treating you and your husband to the best dinner ever!" I exclaimed

"That's not necessary; I didn't help you with this sale," Mrs. M. explained.

"Thanks again, but you're stuck!" I said.

"Bye, Paul—congratulations!"

I hung up the phone and walked back to the bar.

"Is everything, all right? Your father thinks the price it too low?" The marble man asked.

"No, No, it's not that at all, I just…"

"All right," he interrupted, " I can go as high as $2500 but I can do no better."

"Your first offer was…" I began.

"Not another word, please. This is so hard to believe….this marble; superb! It is a perfect match; he will be astonished when I tell him! Now, I think my offer is more than fair. I would appreciate…"

"That's fine, sir. Your first offer of $2000 is fine," I said, interrupting him.

I could have never forgiven myself if I had let him write a check for $2500. What I was going to say is that I couldn't believe that he offered two grand in the first place. Maybe they try to get more out of you in the big city, but I wasn't out to swindle someone.

"Now to schedule the pick up. I can have a vehicle and men here at any time, convenient for you that is, any time tomorrow. What's good for you?" The marble man asked.

"Is 2 p.m. okay?" I asked.

"Perfect! I'll run to the bank and get you a cashier's check, that is, if you're going to be here. Mr. Dennison is going to be ecstatic!" He exclaimed with delight.

"Yup, all day," I said.

"I'll see you shortly," he said.

He tipped his hand to me and left. All I could say at that moment and, I know it might be offensive to some, but, "Holy shit!" I was very excited with the sale of the mirrors. That along with the profit from counter sales and the share of the vending machines, squared me up with the loan and put a few bucks in my pocket. Selling the glasses for 60 bucks was nice. But, two grand for the marble? Now, if Louie purchases the back bar, I'll have done well for being in business four months! I still had the tables and chairs and the safe. I put all of the items in the paper; hopefully someone will be interested in those items as well.

I forgot about my lunch! I went to the bar and ate like a starving lion. As I was throwing the container in the trash, the "marble man" walked in carrying an envelope.

"Hello again! I called my client while I was at the bank and he is pleased, insane with happiness with the purchase! He asked that I offer you his thanks for making his wish come true. He's been remodeling a beautiful home for his daughter who was recently married. We have searched everywhere for marble such as this. Actually, we've been looking for just over a year! Here let me show you." The marble man said as he retrieved a few photos from his briefcase.

The marble in the pictures was exactly the same as the marble on the bar!

"I told him we have a perfect match and he was speechless! He asked me to be positively certain it will match and I assured there was no question, it was identical. Oh, here is your payment and Mr. Dennison insisted I must do a bit better than your asking price," he said.

I opened the envelope and sat down, luckily on a bar stool which was directly in line with my backside, or I would have continued onto the floor. "FIVE THOUSAND DOLLARS a BIT better?! Are you sh—kidding me? I have to be honest with you. I had an antique dealer appraise everything in here and she said I was lucky to get $500, and that's only if the right buyer came in. This is too much, I can't take this much money," I said, still astonished.

"I'm sorry; I didn't get your name," he said.

"Paul, Paul Kenyon."

"Well, Paul Kenyon, Mr. Dennison trusts my judgment and, most importantly, you have here what he needs to accomplish something he has been attempting to finish for two years. Quite frankly, I honestly believe if it were he here instead of me and you held out for more, he probably would have doubled what you now hold in your hands," he said.

"And what is your name, please?" I asked, handing him my hand.

"Alan Chambers."

"Mr. Chambers…"

"Alan," he interrupted.

"Okay, Alan, you have no idea what this means. This was my business and I was only open for 4 months. It's now closed due to the fire that occurred next door and to the decision of the ignorant people who are on the other side of this building who refuse to keep this building alive. I have a baby on the way and this will certainly help us in many ways. You tell Mr. Dennison, thank you very, very much and I hope everything goes great for his daughter. He sounds like a kind man, and if you are a representative of his, chosen by him, then I know he is," I said.

"And thank you, as well, Paul, that was very nice of you to say. My wife of 30 years thinks I'm on the road too long looking for Mr. Dennison's newest treasures but he has been very kind to us too. I've been in his employ for twenty years and the Dennison's have been great to us." Looking at his watch he said, "Look at the time. I really better get a move on. It was nice meeting you. I will see you tomorrow at 2 p.m. sharp." Mr. Chambers said.

"It was very nice meeting you too, Alan. Please, thank Mr. Dennison for me. I will see you tomorrow," I said.

"Good enough, Paul. You have a pleasant day," he said.

I opened the door for Mr. Chambers and he walked across the street to his vehicle which appeared to be the newest model of the Lincoln Town Car. I walked across the street to G&G Music to tell George what happened. His brother-in-law, Gary, told me he had just gone home but would be back. I asked him to ask George to stop over when he got back. He assured me he would tell him. As I was waiting for the traffic to pass, I saw Hank standing outside smoking a cigarette. I yelled to him and pointed at the Fountain. He walked over and stood on the stoop waiting for me to cross.

"What's up?" He asked as I stepped up onto the sidewalk.

"The marble is sold. The man who was in the diner bought it," I said.

"No kidding, what'd he pay for it?" He asked.

"I'll give you three guesses and if you're right, I'll split it with you," I said.

Hank guessed from $200 to $650 and then said I was lying, that one of those prices had to be right. I pulled the envelope Alan had given me out of my pocket and handed it to him.

"You gotta be fucking kidding me, five thousand dollars?!" He exclaimed.

I told him how the entire transaction went, from the beginning, to when I called Mrs. M., to where he thought his offer was too low. What really astounded Hank was the fact Mr. Dennison was so pleased with the marble that he more than doubled his first offer.

"So how much do I get for a finder's fee?" Hank asked.

"Finder's fee for what?" I asked.

"Well, he did come to the diner to wait for you and I bought your lunch," Hank said.

141

"You didn't buy it; you said it was on you," I said.

"Same damned thing, I own the fuckin' diner! You oughta give me something for selling the business to you," he said, stepping closer.

I couldn't believe what he was suggesting. I wasn't about to stand here and listen to him talk this nonsense. I started to walk past him into the Fountain when he grabbed my arm. "Listen, I brought Louie over the other day and I told other people that you were selling everything. I think you owe me something," he said.

"Hank, if I sold you a car and you decided to part it out and you realized more money selling it part by part; wouldn't you think I would have the right to ask you for some of the money you profited?" I asked.

"No, if you sold it to me I should be able to do what I wanted with it." He replied.

"There ya go, I owe you nothing. I can't believe you, but then I should have listened to my father. He said you weren't to be trusted. Although I do think the sale of the business was on the up and up and you were straight with me. But this conversation shows a side of you I didn't know, nor do I want to," I said.

I turned to walk inside and he grabbed me again.

"This is bullshit! You've sold the fixtures for a lot more than I thought you could ever get and I think I should get a cut. I even got Mrs. M. to come in and look things over. Don't tell me it's not fair," he said, now raising his voice.

"You're insane and if I were going to give anyone anything for helping, it would be Mrs. M. She offered her expertise for free, as a friend, and even after I talked to her, she insisted I owed her nothing. You bought the business from the Questas. If you still owned it, were in my position, had to sell out and Mr. Questa came to you demanding exactly what you are....that they wanted a cut, what would you tell them?" I asked, now madder than he was.

"Those senile old farts? I'd tell them to fuck off, that's what," he shouted.

"Well, this non-senile *young* fart is gonna tell you the same, go fuck off!" I said, ripping my arm from his grip.

"This isn't over." He threatened.

"Don't fucking threaten me, Hank," I said, taking my own step forward. I always liked talking to Hank when I would go into the Fountain when he owned it, but at this moment I was madder than I'd been in my entire life. If he and I had exchanged many more words over this, there inevitably would have been a problem. What's the term used here, he was trying to *strong arm* me?

"What's the matter with you? You sold the business to me and now you're pissed 'cause I've made a few bucks that you would have made if you were still in ownership. Well, I'm sorry you feel the way that you do, but you're wrong, and I think when you cool down you'll realize that," I said.

"You're a smartass punk, that's what you are. I signed the loan over to you and there's still a balance owed. I better see that money, and today!" He snapped.

It was true, I bought the business from him. He was gracious enough to carry the two-year note. Rightfully, I had another 20 months to pay the balance of the note, although Debbie and I had already decided to pay it up in full with the money from the sale of the mirrors to get it out of the way. Even though this thug was standing here threatening me, I still planned to pay it off. But I wasn't going to hear any more of this nonsense about owing him any more than what the note was for.

"Hank, I'll run to the bank and get the balance owed on the note right now. But you need to get the idea out of your fucking head that you are owed anything else," I snapped.

"Bullshit, you're making a killing here. And if Louie pays you four grand for the back bar, that means you'll make almost $10,000 profit! Give me 10% and we'll call it square," he said, face getting red.

"Go to the diner, Hank, get your thoughts right," I said.

"Look you little shit; I would have made that money if I hadn't sold the place. You won't even notice 10%, right?" He insisted. I could feel my blood boiling! He was relentless and delusional as well. There was no reasoning with this man and I didn't want this conversation to continue. Maybe he needed the money? Why else would he sell the business? He always seemed to be a pretty nice guy, and if someone had told me they'd seen him acting this way I'd have told them they were crazy. I know what anyone would tell me—I owned the business and whatever profit I made was mine. I'll talk to my father when I get done here—if I ever do! At that moment, Louie M. pulled up to the curb. He waved from his car and Hank repeated again, "This isn't over," then began walking back to the diner.

Louie got out and walked to the sidewalk where I was standing. "Hey, Paul. How's the sale going?" He asked.

I shook his hand and said, "Good, Lou, the mirrors, fans and all the marble is sold and for a helluva price too," I said.

"Good for you. Any bites on the back bar?" He asked.

"Not a one. It's yours if you still want it," I said.

I wanted out of this business, out of this building and off this street. It was too close to a man I *thought* I knew. What I knew of and heard about Louie, was that he was a well liked and respected businessman in Olean. I didn't know if I should have confided in him regarding the conversation Hank and I had but I did all the same.

"What?! You're not joking? Paul, you're 100% correct. If I sold you the deli and you found a billion dollars in a box under the floor, yeah I'd be pissed that I hadn't found it, but I wouldn't come chasing you down for my *cut*. Sheesh, you're really not joking, you're serious?" Louie asked.

"I'm sorry to say, but yes, Lou. He really went off the deep end, grabbing my arm, calling me names and threatening me; telling me this wasn't over," I explained.

"I'll be damned. I don't know, I like Hank, don't get me wrong, but this is scary. I'd at least make a preliminary report to the police if I were you; to protect yourself, you know, in case this escalates. I don't know how he can even think that way; that's nuts," Louie suggested.

"I don't know if I want to take it that far. I'm sure he'll cool off after he's had a little time to think about what he said," I said.

Just then, my father was coming down State Street in his bright yellow, Buick Skylark convertible. He spotted Louie and me and pulled up behind Lou's car. I couldn't wait to show him the check Mr. Chambers gave me, but was a little reluctant to tell him about the altercation between Hank and me. He sat in the car, obviously waiting for me to come over so I threw a, "come here" wave to him. He got out and walked over to join Lou and me.

"Hey, Sonny, what's new with you?" Louie asked.

"Just getting off work. How are things at the deli?" Dad asked.

"Good, good. I think the place will look a lot better once I get Paul's back bar out of the building. Have you two met?" Lou asked my dad.

My dad burst into laughter and said, "Yeah, a long time ago, Lou; he's my son."

"Son of a bitch, I didn't know that. I knew you had a couple of sons and you shared the same last name, but I didn't know Paulie was yours," he said.

"So you're serious, he told me you wanted it for the deli. Well, in that case, what are you waiting for, Paul, sell it to him!" Dad said.

"It's yours, Lou, I already told ya. It's not necessary to wait for other offers. The sooner you can get it dismantled and outta here, the better. I just want to get away from this goddamned place as soon as possible," I said.

"You're serious? Great, I'm ready to purchase!" Lou said.

"Hey!" My dad said, "What's with the language?"

I explained to my father the argument that Hank and I had. I know it would have been better for me to handle it with dignity and try and reason with Hank, but I if I hadn't told dad and anything got out of hand, so to speak, he would have really been upset if I hadn't come to him. "Where is he, at the diner?" Dad asked.

"Dad, it's okay. I'll talk to him tomorrow or some other time. Let him collect his thoughts and I'm sure he'll realize he was angry because I've made so much on the fixtures," I said, laying my hand on my father's arm.

"So much? How much is so much?" Dad asked. I handed him the cashiers check and, while he stood there with his mouth open, I told him what the other items sold for.

"What did you offer him for the bar, Louie?" Dad asked.

"Four thou, Sonny," Louie said.

"Jesus, Mary and Joseph!" Dad said, still staring at the check.

"I told you everything was going to be okay," I told my dad.

"Yes, you did. I'll be back in a minute." Dad said. He began walking toward the diner.

"Dad?" He continued walking. "DAD!" I yelled this time.

"I hate to say it, Paul, but I'd like to hang around for the fireworks." Louie said.

"Oh, shit!" I exclaimed. "I gotta stop him if I can." I said as I began running toward the diner. I was already too late. When I entered the diner my dad and Hank were already in an argument. I tried to say something and my father said he'd handle it.

"No, you won't, I will!" I shouted sternly.

There was only one other person in the diner, seated at the far end of the counter, and he proceeded to walk toward us, place his money on the counter, and slowly and carefully scoot around us.

"This was my business transaction and I will handle it, dad, please," I said.

The anger in my dad's eyes subsided. There had been other things he'd protected my brother and me from in the past and I believe at that moment, he understood that I could take care of this myself ; I wasn't a kid anymore.

"Hank" I said, "You were wrong in what you said and did earlier. I want it over and done with. You sold me the business and I agreed to your asking price. We had a contract drawn up by your bank, and I am now offering to pay that note in full, something I don't have to do. I have another 20 months to pay it off. When the fixtures went up for sale, I was hoping to at least break even so I would have the money to pay off the note. Well, it just so happens...."

"You made a fortune and I think..." Hank began.

"Please" I interrupted, "I don't care what you *think*....you can think anything you want but you're not entitled to anything, period. Where do you get off threatening me, and telling me this isn't over? It IS over, and I don't want to hear

146

another word about it. If I have any more problems, I'll file a police report and have you arrested for harassment. Do you understand?" I said.

"I don't know where *you* get off coming in here and harassing *me* at my place of business. I came over to see how you…"

My dad attempted to reach over the counter and I grabbed his arm, something I would have never thought of doing. For a moment, he began to push me away and stopped. He backed up and said, "Let me say something." He turned back to Hank. "You scrawny son of a bitch. You threatened my son because you're jealous he made a few bucks you couldn't because you sold a going concern to him that wasn't going anywhere but into the crapper. Now, my son thinks I was upset with him for purchasing the soda bar, but I was really angry with myself for not looking into the reason you wanted to sell, 'a good thing,' as you put it, so quickly. I made a phone call to the president of the bank and he informed me that the bank had already motioned for the building to be razed in September. Paul is bullheaded, he really wanted to own his own business and, down deep, I thought he could have made a go of it. I only wished I had made that call sooner and I could have explained this to him. He's bright enough to know it would have been futile to go into business knowing it wasn't going to be open very long. And here you were, trying to pan off this, 'good thing,' to get out from under it before it all came tumbling down. Well, you did. You got out from under it and Paul made himself—*himself*, you little worm, a nice sum of money. Now, I'm going to walk out that door and, if you so much as open your yap, you, like that building a couple doors down, will come tumbling down," my dad said with a look I remembered all too many times.

If I had been an innocent bystander, like Lou, who I hadn't known was standing at the open door of the diner, watching and listening this whole time, I would have given my dad a standing ovation for that performance. My father and I walked out of the diner and there was nothing said from the opposite side of the counter. When we got outside, Louie patted my dad on the back and said something to the effect of

147

not letting him sell anything to me. Of course, he was joking, attempting to calm my dad down.

"I'm sorry." My dad said as we reached the Fountain. "I should have told you but the deal had already been made. Maybe there was something that could have been done in lieu of the bank already making their decision to pull the building down but I thought it best to forget it and hoped you would make enough to pay for the purchase," dad said.

"Shit, it's not your fault, dad, I wanted to be in business and maybe it was because George *was* in business for himself. I don't know. But, thanks for setting him straight. I imagine he would have bothered me until he guilted me into giving him some money," I said.

"Then I would have been pissed! So, mister tycoon, how much did you make?" Dad asked.

"Hey, I don't mean to break up this family thing but I have to get going. I'll get with you on the bar, Paul. I'll make the necessary arrangements and give you a call," Louie said.

"Thanks, Lou. Whenever you need to get it, let me know," I said.

"Thank YOU, see ya, Sonny," he said as he went to his car.

The Fountain door was still standing open, so my father and I went inside. "You liked having your own business, didn't you?" He asked.

"Yeah, I guess, but it was long hours and I wasn't making much. Maybe in the long run it might have been better," I said.

"Well, it all came out good for you and that's all that counts. Use the money you made here wisely! Put most of it away, you have a child coming!" He said.

My dad wasn't a softie by any means, he was all business. He didn't have much education and worked hard from the time he was an early teen. There were a lot of problems in the house growing up for my brother and me but especially for mom. Those have all disappeared and now, finally, he and my mom have a very decent, quiet life. I'm sure my brother, like me, wished it had come much sooner. My dad told me he'd better get home. He was sure supper was already on the table. I walked with him to the door but before he walked out, I turned him around to give him a hug.

"What's that for?" He asked.

"'Cause you believed in me and you took my ground again. Now, I'd like to go over and finish the argument the way *you* wanted to," I said.

"Although I'm sure you could take him, I don't recommend it! If he comes over here you call the police, pronto," dad said.

"Go, get home, eat and fall asleep in your chair; tell mom hi for me," I said. "Matter of fact, give her a hug for me too," I added.

He walked out and turned around just as he got to his car. "Hey, that haunted house you've been visiting is in the paper again today," he said.

How the hell did he know I'd been going up there?!' I thought as he got in his car.

I hung around the fountain another hour or so and only had one call. Someone inquired about the ceiling fans and I explained that they'd already been sold. The only things left were the coolers, safe and all the silverware. Freddy Joseph is sending someone over tomorrow between two and three to get the vending machines. I still had my 50% of whatever was in them as well! I wasn't going to tell Debbie how much I made today; I wanted to keep it a secret. I know I wanted to give at least $500 to my parents just because.

"Oh my, God! The car!" I said to the marble that was soon going to be on its way to Buffalo. I went to the phone and grabbed the phonebook to look up Zemer's garage. I was getting forgetful, maybe I should take back what I said about being, "non senile."

"Zemer's," someone answered.

"This is Paul Kenyon; can you tell me if my car is ready?"

"Hey, Joe, Kenyon's on the phone. Just a second, please."

About a minute passed. "Hey, kiddo. She's ready to pick up," Joe said.

"How much do I owe ya, Joe, and what did you find wrong with it?" I asked.

"Hang on a sec…. $23.50 and there's absolutely nothing electrical or mechanical wrong with it. You're gonna need brakes soon, though," he said.

"Nothing? You sure there isn't a short that could have caused…"

"Paul" He interrupted, "We checked everything, that's why the bill is so high. Between Steve and me, we must have spent two and a half hours going over her on and off. I even called the dealership and they suggested looking at everything I already had. It had their head mechanic baffled too," Joe explained.

There it was, nothing wrong with it, and Zemer was a very good mechanic. What are my options now? Find a genie and see what she sees in her crystal ball? Was I just someone else who fell to the powers of the supernatural?

"Thanks, Joe. If I'm not there to pick it up before you close, leave the keys in the same place and I'll be over tomorrow to take care of the bill," I said.

"You got it, kiddo. Have a good day," Joe replied.

It was only 4:20; I might be able to catch Tim before he leaves for work. I'm sure he's looking for an item of clothing that he undoubtedly lost.

"Come and get me and drop me off at Zemer's before you go to work," I said, as Tim answered the phone.

"Oh Hello, Tim, would you be so kind as to give me a lift to pick up my vehicle?" He said very sarcastically.

"Come on! You have time, you asshole," I said.

"What's the matter, tired, didn't get any sleep 'cause you were playing clerrrrrrk all day?"

"I got plenty of sleep, well; enough anyway. The paper doesn't come out until noon so I slept just fine. Tim? Hello? You there?" I said.

He hung up! The jerk hung up on me. But I knew what he was doing; he didn't fool me for a second. He was on his to the Fountain. I went outside and waited. He's no more than five minutes away and he'll rush because he has to be at work at 5:00. Just as I thought, he pulled up, and it was just under five minutes. I hopped in and he was pulling away before I closed the door.

"What's the hurry?" I asked.

"Some of us have to be at work, you know. How'd ya do?" Tim asked.

"Eh, okay, only had two people come in. A woman and man with extremely bad math and worse perfume paid 60 bucks for some glasses and a real nice guy looked at the marble," I explained.

"Wow, 60 dollars! Las Vegas?" He asked.

"What?!" I asked.

"Are you going to Las Vegas now that you've made your fortune?" Tim asked.

"Oh, I forgot to tell you the guy that looked at the marble, bought it."

"You mean the *real nice* guy, as you put it?" Tim asked.

"He was real nice, very gentlemanly. Yeah, he was the representative for someone in Buffalo. He'd been looking for marble for over a year, he told me," I said.

"And what did this real nice guy pay for the marble, may I ask?" Tim asked.

I loved stringing Tim on. I wanted to keep it going but we were almost at Zemer's.

"Well, his final offer was $25 (cough) but he doubled it when he presented the check to me," I said.

"*Presented* the check to you? For what, $50 dollars? That's double $25 anyhow," Tim said.

We were pulling into Zemer's when I hit him with it. "No, No, my good man. I said $2500 but I had a tickle in my throat, so sorry. And the check *was* presented to me, for $5000! I'll call you later tonight," I said as I got out, closed the door, and waved in a dismissive way.

Tim got partially out of his car and it began to roll forward, so he jumped back in banging his chin on the door frame. "THOUSAND?!" He yelled

"See you later tonight and be careful! Sometimes cars have a mind of their own," I said as I walked into the garage.

"Yours certainly does if what Joe told me was right." Steve, one of the mechanics said.

"It did the other night, that's for sure." I said.

151

"It's ready to go and we didn't find a thing wrong with it," Steve said.

"Nothing? You're absolutely sure there isn't anything wrong?" I asked.

"Cripes, it sounds like you wanted something to be wrong with it," Steve said.

Did he say a mouthful!

I paid the bill and drove home, making a stop on the way to purchase a stuffed animal and a copy of today's paper. It was a long day, and it was going to be a long night with practice and then, undoubtedly, a trip to the country. I got home about 5:25 and found Debbie asleep on the couch. Why wouldn't she be asleep, with all the extra curricular activity early this morning? I thought. I gently set the little bear I got at the store right in front of her on the edge of the couch, went to the kitchen and closed a cupboard door just hard enough, not to startle, but to wake her.

"What the…oh, what's this?" She asked holding the bear up.

"Oh, just something for this morning. Sorry, I'm late. I just picked up the car and I have practice very shortly. You want me to whip something up real…"

"Jamie called," She interrupted, "there is no practice. One of the lead people didn't come in, so he has to work at least until midnight," Debbie said.

"That's too bad. Well, we have a lot of time on our hands then. Want to go out to dinner?" I asked. "Come on, let's go to The Castle," I suggested.

She got up from the couch and walked into the kitchen.

"The Castle?! What are you up to, mister?" She asked.

"Nothing, I just had a real nice day, aside from a misunderstanding with someone, but I believe this moment is ours," I replied.

"Well, let me get into something more appropriate. You should do the same. I'll take you up on that offer," she said.

"I need to take a shower after hanging around the Fou…."Her kiss stopped me in mid sentence and her words stopped my heart. Moments after our shower, we had an instant replay of this morning and it was wonderful; powerful. I can remember that evening as if it were yesterday; dinner hadn't been bad either.

I told Debbie everything that happened that day over dinner and also explained my intentions about the Dandy house. She understood perfectly, while I, on the other hand, and to this day, didn't understand why it was that was so important to me to find the answers to their paranormal disturbances. I knew that night, that I was going to be spending an enormous amount of time researching the paranormal and trying to establish the reasons for the *activity* that was tormenting this family. As I said, I didn't know why then, and I still honestly cannot describe the importance of my involvement with the activity that continues sporadically to the day of this writing.

The pages you've read thus far offer a little insight to some of the experiences my friend, Tim C., and I went through. You've also learned bits and pieces of my life and my growing up in Olean, New York. I feel these things are relevant because so much that had happened with my life in 1973. That was the year I met the Dandys and the shocks I endured over the next year drastically changed how I dealt with and felt about many things. The events at the Dandy house, which I took part in between August, 1973 and December, 1974 I pen from a vivid memory and from discussions with a few of those who were involved. I am only saddened that I hadn't spent enough quality, undisturbed time with my dear friend, Father Alphonsus Trabold after returning to my home town of Olean, some twenty-five years to the month from the year I had met this kind, dear man.

CHAPTER XIII

There was another article in the Olean Times Herald today written by Bob S. He wrote in response to the numerous calls, letters and people who had stopped him on the streets or while he was doing his grocery shopping. He was inundated with questions by everyone who was interested in the hot topic of the "haunted house." He wrote: *If you want to get something started the best possible way is to write something about the spirit world.* There was a lot of talk going on around the entire area about Hinsdale, New York's haunted house. Even the Buffalo newspapers, 70 miles north of Olean, have jumped on the paranormal band wagon and one writer in particular, Bob C., who writes for the Buffalo Evening News, had followed the story closely. It seemed everyone was talking, some excitedly, about the tucked away country home, now riddled by spirits.....everyone except the Dandy family, that is. In today's paper, Mr. S. stated he had only one truly negative statement made by one of his callers. A woman called saying, *"The Olean Times Herald must have lost its mind for printing such a ridiculous story, especially displaying it on the front page."* She went on to tell of a series of problems her family had to deal with and that spirits had nothing to do with them. Probably not, unless her house was haunted. Another caller on the positive side called in to say, *"I'm glad to see the story. It shows that people are bringing into the open things that have been going on for years, which they wouldn't talk about in public."* One negative call out of the dozens that Bob received after his story hit the newsstands supports one thing—either there are an awful lot of believers out there or, at the very least, people have open minds.

I would have called Clara today to talk to her about Bob's story, but with everything else that had happened and then going out to dinner, coming home, and hitting my third home run for the day, there just didn't seem to be enough time. I called Tim and asked if he wanted me to pick him up or was he going to swing by when he got off. He chose the latter; I would be ready. Debbie was asleep before 10:00, I would have thought sooner and I decided to read a little about the paranormal world before Tim arrived. As I read, it was like a kindergartner being sent to college and told to write a thesis on the World Wars. Some of it was straightforward and easily understood, but when they starting tying in the psychological aspect with the "supposed" abilities of the psychic, it became muddled. Spiritualism and the paranormal were wide open fields with many forms of study and beliefs. The book I was reading obviously wasn't going to be the source of what I needed to know or understand. It threw in cases of possession centered in third world countries with the exorcists being voodoo doctors and medicine men. It mentioned other cases in mental institutions with no more intervention than tranquilizers and shock therapy. There were only two references to haunted houses and the author's summations were brief and vague. There was also one small section on "out of body experiences," a subject about which I knew nothing. Supposedly, people's spirits are able to leave their bodies and travel to other locations at the demands of their hosts. I had heard of this phenomenon but didn't have any understanding of it. What if your spirit got lost or couldn't reenter your body? I didn't want to know.

It was nearly the witching hour and Tim would be here soon. I checked on Debbie and saw that she was holding onto the bear I had gotten her earlier today. I gently kissed her cheek and walked outside, after being sure I had my keys, to wait for Tim. Was Laura correct? Did I know what she said I did? I guess I knew something, so did Mike, and certainly Tim. Was it something she picked up just looking at me or was it like Father Al mentioned: that maybe it was the expression I had after looking into the bathroom? Were there places one could go to test for psychic abilities? Surely there were, but were the results reliable? I'd asked myself so many questions lately, I'd have to get a notepad to write them down, so when it came time to get the answers, I'd know what to look for.

It had to be getting close to 11:30 and Tim hadn't come yet. I was thinking I should go back in the house in case he calls. I wouldn't want the phone to wake Debbie. I was about to go in when he pulled around the corner. He pulled in the driveway and I got in. "I didn't think you were coming," I said.

"My car wouldn't start. Darndest thing too, it just wouldn't start," Tim said.

"Yeah, okay. Were you so scared that you almost dropped dead over the steering wheel? Isn't that what you said to me when I told you my car stalled?" I asked.

"No, really. It wouldn't start; nothing. Oh, our subs are in the back seat," he said.

"Yeah, change the subject, okay. What did you make me?" I asked.

"A pepper sub, no meat, no lettuce, no tomato, nothing but peppers," Tim said.

"Ah, my favorite. Did you read the paper?"

"Yup, it seems there aren't too many people who don't believe what's going on up there, doesn't it?" Tim replied.

"What I was baffled by is the statement made by the trooper about Gordon, or Phil, whichever one was warding off people with the gun. Someone called the police and the trooper said he didn't blame them for flashing a gun." I said.

"Yeah, until someone gets shot. Then there'd be a whole new ball game to fry!"

"What?!" Tim's brain worked in a very mysterious way.

When we arrived at the intersection of McMahon and Wagner Hill Roads, we weren't exactly surprised to see people in the area, due to the recent story in the newspaper. There were three vehicles in all, a pickup truck and two cars. There were several spectators standing at the rear of the car closest to the McMahon turn off. Tim turned onto McMahon slowly and a couple of the people waved to us, so Tim pulled over and stopped. Two women from the group walked over to talk to us.

"Hi, do you live on this road?" One of the women asked.

"Not exactly. We're here to relieve the other two guys that are standing guard at the entrance to the house at the end of the road," Tim said.

"Earlier on this evening we thought the police were here, because it looked like there was an unmarked police car with its lights on, chasing another car down the road. We did see something really weird about an hour after that....not all of us, just we two and the other couple standing by the back of that car. The couple who came in the pickup weren't here then."

"What was that?" I asked.

"The four of us were walking back down this way from further up this road. (She was referring to Wagner Hill Road.) We got maybe 100 feet or so from where we are now and we saw a boy, maybe 18 or so, walk to the middle of the road and toward us. Then he just disappeared! Angie here had her flashlight on him too. My batteries are about dead and it's not bright enough to see ten feet in front of me but hers is real bright. There just wasn't any place for him to go. He didn't run or turn up that road, he was just suddenly gone," she said.

"It scared us to death and we all ran to my car. He didn't look weird or anything and he was wearing those, what do you call them, the pants that Captain Kangaroo wears?" Angie (I guess) said.

"Overalls. What did he look like?" I asked.

"Yeah, overalls—normal. I mean, as I said, he was about 18, maybe 20, and had blonde hair," the first girl said.

"Yeah, that's about all I saw. I didn't really see his face that well but he did have blonde hair and was wearing overalls," Angie confirmed.

"We'll keep an eye out for him. Some people have been walking to the house by going up the camp roads to get a look at the house. We just wished they wouldn't, 'cause they have a couple of guard dogs up there that are really mean," I said.

"Well, good luck keeping an eye on this guy, because if he appears as fast as he disappears, he's liable to be anywhere at anytime!" Angie said.

"Thanks for the information. As for the police, we don't know if they were here yet today or not. One of the guys we're relieving is a retired police officer," Tim said.

Listen to this clown tell his story. It looked like they were believing what he was saying too. I supposed under the circumstances, there wouldn't be any reason for them not to believe him. Surely, everyone must think someone is watching over the property to keep trespassers out.

The other couple walked over to listen in. "Is that house really haunted? My friend said she could have sworn she saw a woman walking across the road near that big tree, but then she just vanished!" One of the women from the pickup said.

"I believe it is," said her friend who walked over with her. "We had three different ghosts living in our house when we lived in Belmont and it was really spooky."

"We've been up here since all of this started and we can't say for sure. We haven't seen or heard anything out of the ordinary," I said, leaning toward Tim's window to talk to them.

I had to tell them something negative or they may have attempted to make their way to the house even if they knew we were on the roads patrolling. There were many ways to get there; on foot, through the adjoining fields, or over the camp roads.

"Yeah, it's been pretty darned quiet while we've been here. Well, we better get to the house, the guys who are there now stay at the property above and if we don't show on time they'll just go up and leave the property unguarded. You have a good night. Be careful because the State Police usually stop in at least once to check on everything," Tim said.

We pulled away and started driving up McMahon road.

"That was smart, saying the guys stay right up the road," I said.

"Sure, if they didn't see someone coming down the road soon, they'd know I was feeding them a line of BS," Tim said.

When we turned into the driveway, Mike was walking around to the side of the house. Tim pulled up to our 'spot' and shut the engine off as Mike jumped in the back seat.

"What's up?" Tim asked.

"Well, Father Al was here for a while tonight. He played police and scared some of the people out of here. He even has a light he puts on his car. Beth Ann told me earlier, probably around 8 or so, that she thinks there was a woman, or *someone*, on her bed. Mom was up just a little bit ago, she was checking on Mary. I almost think she knows something is up. I put the pop you gave me last night in the refrigerator and she asked where it came from. I lied to her, I hated to but I didn't know what to say," Mike said.

"You should have told her we've been coming up. You don't think she'd get pissed do you?" Tim asked.

"Probably not, but she might be pissed at me when she finds out and I *didn't* tell her. I'll have to let her know tomorrow, unless she is suspicious and finds out on her own tonight," Mike said.

"What's up with this person in Beth Ann's room?" I asked. "I'm not really sure. I guess I haven't been paying attention or everyone else isn't telling me everything because Mary has been having trouble in her room too. Something else, mom said she's not sleeping well and gets up a lot. I'm wondering how she didn't know we were outside, especially when we're out walking around." Mike said.

"There were six people at the end of the road when we pulled in tonight. There were five women and a man in three separate vehicles. Four of them saw a person who fit the description of your blonde friend. The one who you and the girls have seen roaming the property. They told us he vanished before their eyes. Has anyone been driving all the way up the road tonight?" I asked.

"Actually, there was a car that came up to the first turn and parked for a while. I came out because I could hear the car driving on the road. I stood at the end of the driveway with a flashlight so they'd see someone outside and not get any ideas about walking up the rest of the way. I've had my window open all night and heard you guys coming too. I thought you might have been the car that was out there earlier. They just left about 45 minutes ago. Well, I'm glad someone else saw the kid besides me and the girls, if it was him," Mike.

"Everyone is curious, they want to see something. I'm sure it's the same for other haunted places whether there are people living in them or not," Tim said.

"You're probably right, and no one's causing any trouble or anything but they're sure pissing my dad off! Shit, we oughta put a gate up at the end of the road and charge people a buck each. Just let them roam where they want to as long as they don't just walk in and plop down at the kitchen table, like that one joker did!" Mike said.

"What the hell! Are you sleeping?!" Tim asked me, shaking my arm.

"Sorry, I'm worn out. When I got home this morning, Debbie and I… well, we got busy and I didn't get to sleep until after 5:00, then she woke me again just after 7:00 to ask where the car was! I went to sleep after she left but only 'til 11:30 or so. Then, before we went to dinner tonight, after I was at the Fountain most of the day, we got busy again. I could have taken a nap until you came over but I was reading the books I bought instead, so leave me alone!" I snapped, kidding.

"Poor guy, he didn't get to go nite-nite, Mike," Tim said.

"Eat it," I replied.

"I don't think any of us have the past few nights," Mike said.

"Oh, I'm sure the one who needs the most beauty sleep does, huh?" I said to Tim.

"I need it more. I have to slave for you two so you have something to eat every night," Tim said.

"I'm sick of subs!" I said.

"Me too," Mike agreed.

"Shit, I think we're busted! Mike, I think your mom's in your room," I said, after seeing a woman look out Mike's window.

If it were one of the girls, it was probably Beth Ann because whoever it was that looked out was taller than Laura or Mary.

"Damn, I'll go check. I don't think she'll really be upset, though. Be right back," Mike said.

"What's Phil like?" Tim asked.

"I don't know how to explain him, Tim. He seems okay but he acts like he's pissed all the time. He has no respect for the clergy by the way he curses with Father Al in the room. I know he got mad as hell at me when I mentioned the dizzy bitch while we were walking by the pond," I said.

"Dizzy bitch? Who's that, a rock group?" Tim asked.

"Yeah, they're the back up band for Sly and the Family Groin. Christ, it's the woman that's been seen dancing around the pond. When I asked him if the dizzy bitch was the woman the girls had seen, he became quite irate. He whipped around and pointed the light in my face. I thought we was gonna knock me over the head with it! He's okay, I guess. He has to be under a lot of strain with all of this happening and having to make the return to Buffalo every day. You'd really like Father Al, he's—oh, here comes Mike," I said.

Mike got in the back seat and said, "it wasn't mom."

"That's good. Do you think I should move the car away from the house in case she gets up?" Tim asked.

"It wasn't Beth Ann either." Mike added.

"Who was it then, Laura?" I asked.

"I don't think it was either of them."

"How do you know? Did you actually ask them?" I asked.

"I was in the house less than a minute after you had seen her and when I checked Beth Ann and called her name she didn't move. If it had been her, she would have answered. When I went upstairs, I bumped my elbow on the wall pretty hard. If it had been mom that came down, she would have still been awake and would have heard me on the stairs. Both Mary and Laura were sound asleep." Mike explained.

"Well, maybe they were just lying still and looked like they were asleep. You can't really tell in the dark," Tim said.

"No, I suppose not. But I know for sure it wasn't mom or Beth Ann." Mike said.

"Then, what are you saying?" I asked.

"If it *had* been Mary or Laura, they would have woke mom up and told her there was a car parked by the house; Beth Ann may have done the same, I don't know. If it had been mom, she'd have been out here because she certainly would probably figure I was outside too because I wasn't in my room." Mike explained.

"Well, you're not *saying* anything but you just said I lot. You think, just like I do, and I'm sure Tim too, that's it's one of your *visitors*, don't you?" I asked.

Here we are again, playing hide-n-seek. Will the real ghost please stand up and make yourself known? Why must it always be a game of, "be seen and quickly disappear?" Even in the movies, ghosts don't seem to hang around very long. They come; they get seen by someone, then poof, we'll see you around some blind corner at the next haunting.

I'm beginning to see where, in some instances, people are less frightened and become more aggravated and angry. If there is something you need to tell us from the other side, by all means, spit it out! Stop this—"Here I am, now I'm gone"— materializing head game stuff. We discussed this for a while and didn't give either side, the living or the not-so-living, credit for whoever was at the window. Mike said he had an idea his mom might be a little suspicious. We thought, if she saw that Mike wasn't in the house, she'd have figured he may have been outside with whoever left the Pepsi. It was possible Mike was standing guard possibly with a friend and that would be okay. She knew he always kept an eye on things when she went to bed, just in case any curious stragglers showed up. If it had been Clara or one of the girls at the window, they'd most likely mention it in the morning and Mike would let us know. We had agreed that 2:30 was the deadline tonight. We all had chores to attend to in the morning and Tim had to work an earlier shift at the sub shop. I wanted to be at the Fountain so I could man the phone properly, unlike today when I had my little incident. I was looking forward to seeing Mr. Chambers again and getting one step closer to clearing out the building. Mike, Tim, and I decided to take a walk all the way down to the tree and see if the people we talked to were still hanging around. We felt quite confident that if we encountered something on foot, we could deal with it without going off the deep end. After all, we've experienced several manifestations of one kind or another, and nothing terrible had come of them. It was fairly bright out and we walked without the aid of our flashlights. We'd stop every so often to observe and listen, not because any of us were worried or fearful of what might be lurking in the darkness, but because we were looking and *hoping* to see or hear or maybe feel something in the darkness. *Believe and you will see.* It seemed not one of us had much of a choice but to do anything but believe at this point. We were at the tree within 10 minutes and it had been an uneventful walk the entire way. The pickup truck was gone but the two cars were still parked in their same locations. We didn't see anyone around them, or walking in the area.

"Where do you think they went?" Tim asked.

We walked up to the vehicles and noticed that the windows were down but there was no one in either of them.

We continued walking on Wagner Hill Road for about half a mile to the spot where I turned around the first time I came to visit after passing the turn-off to McMahon. "This is strange. Maybe they went the other way," Mike said.

We turned around and back-tracked watching the field on the left for lights where one could cross to get to the house. We reached the cars; there was still no one in the vicinity. We walked a short distance in the opposite direction but didn't bump into anyone although we were startled by a deer that ran across the road behind us.

"How come animals don't haunt houses?" Tim asked.

"Oh, boy," Mike said.

"Well, if what Paul said was true, that humans stick around or come back because they have unfinished business or died suddenly and didn't know they were dead, then that deer could have been a ghost too. If they suddenly get hit by a car and don't know they're dead, they're gonna still be romping through the woods, looking for their cousin, Bambi, right?" Tim asked.

"Where'd you find this guy, Paul?" Mike asked.

"I don't know, Mike. I do know that he should be hired by the government to trick the enemy with his dissertations," I replied.

"Come on, let's go back. I have a feeling those people may have crossed over to see if they could get a closer look at the house," I said.

"Ohhhhhhhh, don't say 'cross-over.' Now we'll have four more to deal with," Tim said.

"Cross over the field to the house!" I exclaimed.

"Oh," Tim moaned. I couldn't see him, but I knew Tim had one of those expressions on his face to go with that, 'Oh.' There was still no sign of the people when we got back to the parked cars. We began walking up McMahon Road, now with our lights on, searching the adjoining fields on either side of the road. We slowly walked the entire length of the road back to the house and there was no sign of anyone.

"Where the hell are they? I wondered.

"Maybe their cars wouldn't start and they hitched a ride with the other people," Mike said.

"Both cars?" I asked.

"That's a possibility. Remember yours died down there by the tree but would they leave their cars there with all the windows down? I didn't notice if the keys were in the ignition but you'd think they would have rolled the windows up," Tim said.

"The keys were in the ignition, in the Ford anyhow. I checked when I walked by," Mike said.

"Aren't we a bunch of Sherlock Holmes'?" Tim said.

It was a little after 2 a.m. and we decided now was a good time to call it a night. Tim realized we hadn't eaten the subs and they were most likely not going to be any good now. Mike told him to give them to him, and he'd throw them in the yard at the edge of the field for the wild animals that would undoubted sniff them out. Mike took them to the yard, and after unwrapping them, let them fall to the ground.

"That's a waste," I said.

"Yeah, and I put them all on your name at work," Tim said. He assured me he was kidding and said that he had split them up.

"Well, at least we don't have to worry about drinking warm pop," Tim said.

"Why?" Mike asked.

"'Cause I didn't bring any, I forgot to grab them off the counter."

We said our "see ya laters," and Mike went in the house. Tim and I got in the car and left, heading down the road slowly while I shone my light out the window scanning for the mysterious owners of the cars. When we pulled onto Wagner Hill we observed that both cars were gone.

"How do you like that shit? I bet they were up near the house and doubled back through the field when we were walking up, wanna bet?" Tim said.

"Probably were, or maybe they walked this way further than we did and got back after we walked up the road," I said.

"Anything's possible. They might have walked to the top of the camp road and come down when we were heading back. We probably wouldn't have seen them while we were still at the house if they didn't use a light going up," Tim replied.

"Yup, that's another scenario but I can't see women walking without using their flashlights," I said.

"Somehow, my dad knew I was coming up here at night. I don't know if he knew we were both coming up, but he mentioned it to me," I said.

"Oh, um, I think I may have mentioned it to him when he came in a couple nights ago," Tim said.

"And why would you do that, may I ask?"

"I didn't think it was a big deal. I thought he knew you were going up, my parents did." Tim said.

I told Tim he probably thinks we're both nuts for going up there. He's not a believer in such things and would say it's a big waste of time. That's why my mother covered for me the other day when he said, "worry about what" to her. I'd never hear the end of it. "What are you doing wasting your time up there?" is what he'd ask.

Neither Tim nor I asked for clarification from Mike when he said Beth told him there was someone on her bed, and that Mary was having problems. You would think, under the circumstances, everyone would know the facts of every disturbance within the house. I was hoping that sooner or later, once Tim had been introduced to everyone, that we'd have the chance to sit in the living room or kitchen and see if anything happens inside. The house is supposed to be haunted but we've been getting our fair share of disturbances outside these past few evenings. I'd really been waiting to spend some time with Father Al so we might have a good chat about all of this and he could explain some things to me. I can just see him driving around chasing people off the Dandys' property. He's such a quiet little guy but has such a sense of inner strength about him. Here's an amusing piece of trivia about him: He doesn't allow any of his students to sit in the front rows of his classes. Those seats are reserved for the spirits, were they to choose to sit in. I understand that's been a rule of his for many years and it's been so regular that no one even takes notice.

I was dropped off about 2:30 and was surely ready for some good sleep. Tim asked if we were going up tonight and I told him I'd let him know at work. That's when Tim informed me that I'd be working with Brian tonight; he was off.

165

"Well, that sucks," I said.

"Nah, you'll like working with Brian. Well, you can call me, or maybe I'll stop in to see how everything's going," Tim said.

"All right, talk to you later," I said as I got out of the car.

I went into the bedroom and was *ever so quiet* so I wouldn't disturb Debbie. I wanted to *sleep* tonight. Sleep was quick and I wasn't awakened when she went to work.

CHAPTER XIV

I woke before 10 a.m., got up, showered and went to make breakfast. I had a couple of eggs, scrambled, and two pieces of toast. I left for the Fountain to answer any inquiries from prospective buyers who may call in. When I arrived I was pleasantly surprised to see Mr. and Mrs. Questa and their daughter, who lived in the apartment above, coming out the entrance to the upstairs apartment.

"What a shame, Paul." Ms. Questa said. "This place has so many memories for me and especially for my parents."

"It is a shame and more so for your parents who were in business for so many years," I said.

Mr. and Mrs. Questa looked lost standing in front of the grand, old building. They had such long faces. I hoped they left before Mr. Chambers showed up with his crew to dismantle the entire soda bar. Ms. Questa told me they had come by to pick up a few things from upstairs and would return this weekend when Geise Transfer and Storage would come to move her belongings. I felt sorry for the Questas because this building was all they'd known for decades and now, due to the ignorance of those who didn't understand the preservation of an historical landmark, they would see nothing but an empty lot when they pass by.

"You have a good day, Paul. I hope everything goes well for you." Ms. Questa said.

"You too, Ms. Questa. If you need anything, don't hesitate to let me know," I said, giving my former music teacher a hug.

Neither of her parents, who were in their seventies, said a word while walking to their car. Some business decisions were dumb, this one was the topper.

A large moving van pulled up to the Fountain about ten minutes later followed by Mr. Chambers in his freshly waxed Lincoln. He pulled to the curb behind the van.

"Hello, Paul, and how is everything today?" Mr. Chambers asked.

"It's just fine, thank you," I said. "Let me unlock the door and your men can start gathering up Mr. Dennison's marble," I replied.

While unlocking the door, it dawned on me that if they needed electricity for any power tools they were in trouble. As Mr. Chambers followed me in, I mentioned this to him and he said, "Not to worry, we have a portable generator and enough cord to reach around the building and back. I was fully aware that the building's power was off and made the necessary arrangements to be certain these lads weren't going to be unscrewing or cutting anything by hand. This marble is more like gold to Mr. Dennison and he wanted to be absolutely sure no harm came to it," Mr. Chambers said.

"Wow, I don't mean to sound—not sure of the word here, but it sounds like Mr. Dennison is more like a Diplomat or something," I nervously chuckled.

"Ah, in his own right, he could very well be. He's actually from San Diego and is in Buffalo preparing the house for his daughter. His son-in-law is an executive with the Ford Motor Company and was transferred here just over two years ago. Actually, it was just one month after his daughter was wed when he was transferred. He has a lot of respect for David, his son-in-law, and the house, as I said, was a wedding gift. Even though David and Colleen, his daughter, sought it out and chose it as the one they wanted, he said it was his gift to them," Mr. Chambers explained.

"What does Mr. Dennison do, if I may ask," I asked.

"You may. He's an executive for Shell Oil. He has an exquisite home in San Diego and the entire entry and bath are made from some of the finest Italian marble. His daughter has always said, when she started a life of her own, she wanted to have a bath exactly like her parents' home has. Thus, here we are preparing to relieve this wonderful old building of some of its character. Here, I have a letter for you from Mr. Dennison. Read it at your leisure," Mr. Chambers said, handing me an envelope.

"Thank you, Mr. Chambers," I said.

"Alan, Paul, it's Alan to my friends."

Alan went out to check on the men who were preparing to start the removal of the marble. I decided it was probably better to choose a later time to read Mr. Dennison's letter and stuffed the envelope in my back pocket. I was going to miss being here but it was okay now. I was ready to let go. I went outside and informed Mr.—Alan, that I was going to go across the street for a few minutes to visit a friend. He told me if there were anything he needed he'd get my attention but he was sure he had everything under control; I was certain he did. I walked across to G&G Music, but again, George wasn't there. Gary said he was out helping his dad with something. I went back to the Fountain and could see the men were ready to start work on the dismantling. They had started the generator and were walking in with several tools. I went to the back room where I could hear the phone if it rang. While sitting at the little table, I could see where the weight of the safe had actually imbedded itself into the wood floor. "That's one heavy son-of-a-bitch," I said to the lamp on the desk. If someone buys that thing, I'd hope they had someone like Mr. Chambers to see that it was handled properly!

I sat in the backroom for at least twenty minutes when the phone rang. It was someone asking about the fans and the marble topped tables. I informed them the fans were already gone, but all the tables were still available. The caller asked if he could come by within the hour and take a look, I answered in the affirmative. I took a peek to see how the men were doing. They had already dismantled the top and were working on the front. There were two braces on both ends, securing them from any chance of their tipping over. Mr. Chambers was not in the building. I walked out the front door to see if he might have come out for some air. His car was still at the curb where he'd parked it but he was nowhere to be seen. Then it hit me, he was probably at the diner! I sure hoped nothing stupid was going to be said to Alan but then again if it were, he would outwit the nitwit. I lit a cigarette and, before I'd finished it, Alan walked out of the diner and began walking this way. Alan walked with confidence, erect and very quickly. He appeared to be a man in his late fifties to early sixties, yet his hair was only beginning to show his years. When he reached the steps of the

Fountain he had a smirk on his face and looked as he was about to say something amusing. He looked back in the direction of the diner, let out a long sigh and said, "Absolutely aboriginal."

"What's that, Alan?" I asked.

"That man, the one with the cigarette pack neatly tucked in the folds of his, ahem, rolled up t-shirt sleeve. He sold you this business?" Alan asked.

"Yes, he did, why?"

Again he looked in the same direction and began laughing; it was a Santa Claus laugh, deep and hearty.

"He, in great length and exhaustive detail as to the transaction, said I should have handed the check I gave you to him. He told me he sold you the business for a paltry sum of money but feels since you've done so well with the items you sold since taking over, he should be rewarded with a commission of sorts," Alan told me.

"I'm sorry, Alan, I was hoping you wouldn't go over there. We had quite a discussion and he had me almost believing that I *did* owe him something but my father set us both straight on that yesterday," I said.

"And indeed, your father was unequivocally correct. Strange creature, I must say. Let's see how the work is coming, shall we?"

I think I caught it, I believe Alan was originally from England or perhaps Ireland. I detected a slight accent while he was talking to me. I may have missed it yesterday due to the overwhelming amount the check was written for. We walked inside and saw that the men had all but the right side dismantled. One of the men walked over and handed me about thirty or forty coins of different denominations. He said he'd found most of them on the floor under the front edge of the marble. I looked at them quickly and saw that one was an 1858 nickel in almost perfect condition.

"Holy cow, they're all in nearly mint condition and mostly nickels and dimes," I exclaimed.

"Give us a look." Alan said and now I *knew* he *was* English. 'Give *us* a look?'

"Oh my, yes. This is a superb specimen, it will bring a premium price in this fine condition. There are others here which would be great additions for the serious collector," He said, handing me a dime.

"Mr. Chambers? Sir, we're ready to begin lifting the pieces out to the truck." One of the workers said.

"Splendid, and in remarkable time; excellent job, lads." Looking at his watch he said, "We'll arrive at Colleen's home about 6 p.m.."

The person who had called about the tables and chairs walked into the building with friends. I went to the door to meet them. They took a look at the table sets and didn't think twice, they wanted them all, including the one in the back room that was damaged. I was made a fair offer and I accepted. Odd, they paid in cash and said they would be back about 5:30 if that was okay and I agreed. I went back to watching the men at work.

The men had an electric cart of some sort with a hoist attached to one end that could swing in a complete circle. Attached to the hoist were four cables and, at the end of the cables, steel beams about one foot by four feet in length and at least four inches thick. Watching them maneuver the marble onto these beams was a sight to behold. The cart moved very slowly and nearly walked up and down the step going in and out of the building. They had all eight pieces of marble in the truck, secured and padded in less than an hour and a half. I told Alan he could have the piece he didn't need. I didn't know if anyone would be interested in it, and if he didn't take it, surely it would end up at the bottom of the rubble when the building was razed. He thanked me and asked the men to come back in and get it. Alan and I walked outside and thanked one another for the business and wished each other well. He asked me if I had read Mr. Dennison's letter. I told him I hadn't but would. He insisted I didn't lose it because Mr. Dennison said something important in it. I reached around and felt that it was still safe in my pocket.

"Are you English, Alan?" I asked.

"Yes, sir, I hail from England, Brighton actually. I've been in the States since 1935," he said.

"May I ask how old you are?"

With a chuckle he said, "I was born in 1901, so that makes me seventy-two, October this."

I couldn't believe it; at most I would have said he was sixty-two. "If I look as good as you do when I'm 40 I'll be happy! I have to say, it was a pleasure meeting you and I hope you have a safe trip back to Buffalo and San Diego," I said.

"The pleasure's been mine, young man. You take care of yourself as well and the little tyke on the way," Alan replied.

We shook hands and Alan walked to the back of the van. The men were gathering the rest of their equipment. One of them was even sweeping the floor where the bar had been. These guys were first class in everything they did. There wasn't much sense in sweeping but I thought I would insult him somehow if I told him it wasn't necessary. They were all extremely polite and personable. The man who had been sweeping handed me six more coins he'd found while cleaning up. I thanked him as he picked up the last two short iron rods and took them to the truck. Where the heck did all these guys sit, I wondered? There were six in all and surely only three could fit in the cab of the van. Alan had walked back to his Lincoln and three of the men walked around the corner and up Third Street. The van and Alan waited about three minutes before pulling away. A new customized van pulled out of Third Street and I could see the driver was one of the workers. He waited for the traffic on State Street to lighten, then pulled out of Third Street, the driver giving a "follow me" arm wave to the driver of the moving van, and turned right. The van, followed by Alan, pulled away to follow the smaller van that had pulled out from Third Street. The workers in the moving van waved, Alan gave a blast on his horn and offered a "thumbs up" sign to me. A few days later, I was wishing I had gotten his phone number or at least his address to thank him again. After I opened the envelope and for at least six months after, I attempted to contact a Mr. R. Dennison who was an executive for the Shell Oil Company with no success. The envelope contained a short note from Mr. Dennison which read:

Dear Paul,

You were instrumental in helping me accomplish something I began to think I started in vain. When Alan called and informed he had found an exact match to a hard to find marble pattern, I was beside myself. I had experts in the trade searching the entire country, as well as abroad, for a match to my marble. Initially, we had an ample amount for the job at hand, but several slabs were cracked beyond repair in an, on-the-site construction accident. My only daughter, Colleen, is the light of my life, and her happiness is most important to me. Alan expressed your being overwhelmed when he presented you with the check for payment due. On the contrary, I am the one who is overwhelmed that I am able to finish my daughter's home to her liking. You will find enclosed, a gesture of thank-you, and I trust when you opened it, you had a stool at the ready. Yes, Alan told me of your near accident when presenting you with payment!

Much luck and gratitude,

R. Dennison

I didn't have a stool ready and, thinking back, the shock after opening the letter was worse than anything I had experienced at the Dandy house. Mr. Dennison had enclosed an added amount to the already, what I thought to be, overpayment.

The couple who purchased the table sets had come back with two pickups and their two sons. I helped them load the tables and chairs in the beds of the trucks and thanked them again. The only thing left was the back bar. I hadn't heard from Louie yet. If I didn't hear from him by tomorrow, I'd give him a call. It was 4:50 p.m.. I had to go directly to the sub shop to get to work on time. I would call Debbie and tell her all that's happened once I got organized.

It wasn't nearly as enjoyable working with Brian as it was with Tim. Besides, time was dragging because it wasn't very busy. We only had seven or eight customers and most only wanted a half or one whole sub, including the pepper loving grave digger. I made his sub and really poured on the peppers. I was curious to see if the peppers we served were as hot as they used to be so I stuck just one seed on my tongue. Oh yeah, they were hot all right! Debbie called sometime around 8 p.m. and said Father Al had called me.

"Father Al?! What did he say?" I asked.

"Not much, just wanted to know if you were available. He said it wasn't…. I forgot the word he used—oh, pressing, and he would talk to you next time he saw you," Deb said.

"Did he sound upset or anything?"

"No, not at all. He asked how we were, that's all. I'm just about to go to bed, I'm really tired. Did they get everything done at the Fountain?" She asked.

"Yup, and the tables and chairs are gone too. I've got a pocket full of money, they paid in cash," I told her.

"That's nice, are you going up tonight?"

"I don't know, I haven't decided. I want to, and on the other hand, I don't. I have to play tomorrow and Saturday and I wanted both of us to go visit Sunday," I said.

"During the day, right?" She asked, but it sounded more like insisting.

"Of course! I'm not going to have you screaming at me again." I said.

"We'll see," she said yawning.

She told me if I came home to watch the floor by the refrigerator; it may still be wet because she defrosted the freezer. Whatever time I came home, she would see me then, she said. A customer came in, and Brian was taking a cigarette break out back. I filled her order then went out the back door to do the same. No sooner did I walk out the back door, Tim walked in the front door, came around the counter and started throwing little bits of tomato pieces at me.

"Hey, what the hell? Jim's gonna see these out here and blame us, not you," I said.

"No he won't. He'll probably pick them up and put them back in the container. Are we going up?" Tim asked.

"I don't know, I'm kinda tired tonight. I have to play tomorrow and Saturday so it's gonna be a busy weekend. I want to go up Sunday during the day and spend a few hours so I can actually *see* something," I said.

"Neither of us works Sunday, can I go too?" Tim asked.

"Of course. You can ride up with us. I figured we'd go up about 1:00 or so," I said.

"Okay, that sounds good. Yeah, let's take the night off, I've got some other junk I can do tonight. All right, I'm gonna get. Give me a call sometime Sunday late morning," Tim said.

"Will do," I said, as he walked back around the corner and out the front door.

We only had three more customers before closing. The last one ordered five whole subs and all were very much custom. Some without this and that, some with this, that and the other thing and one, I started to write down because it was so complex. But the customer gave me the list he had been dictating from. Double this, no that, just a little bit of the other, but only on one side and be sure to spread the what-do-you-call-it on the bottom of the roll only and wrap it real tight "to keep it fresh??" Was this going to be shipped some where I wondered?

I made a half turkey sub for Debbie's lunch and a half meatball for myself. Even though I was a little tired, I planned to read for a while when I got home. We started cleaning up so it didn't take long to finish. We were out before 10:30 and I went straight home.

I unlocked the door, went to the living room to grab my books and took off my shoes. I went to the kitchen to put Debbie's sub in the refrigerator and, of course, stepped in a small pool of water. "She told you," I said to the orange juice bottle which I nearly knocked on the floor while putting the sub away.

I walked into the bedroom, sub in one hand, books in the other. I turned around, set the books on the dresser and returned to the kitchen where I could take the paper off the sub without disturbing Debbie. When I walked over to the waste basket, I walked into the same pool of water with my *other* foot. I walked back to the bedroom, only to turn around to get a plate from the cupboard. "Okay, stand here and think, is there anything else?" I said to the entire kitchen. No answer, I guess I was good to go. In the bedroom, now safe from puddles, I undressed and quietly got into bed with my sub but my books were still on the dresser! I got up to get them and Debbie said, "I guess there *was* something else, huh?"

"Huh?" I questioned her back.

"You asked yourself if there was anything else when you were in the kitchen. I guess you didn't remember 'til you got into bed," she said. "After you stepped in the water with both feet, did you wipe it up?" She asked.

"No, sorry—I'll do it now," I said getting out of bed again.

"I'm teasing you, dummy. I'll take care of it in the morning. There's just gonna be more by then anyhow," she said.

"Thanks, hon. I thought I'd read a little before going to sleep," I said, grabbing the books from the dresser.

"It smells like you're going to eat too," she said.

"Do you want some?" I asked.

"Just gimme a bite, then I'll leave you to your reading," she said.

Debbie was honest, she sat up, took a bite, chewed, swallowed and lay back down. She gave me a kiss as I got into bed and rolled over. I knew what that meant, "rub my back." I performed my triple duties impressively. While rubbing her back, I would set my book on my chest, pick up my sub, take a bite, set in back on the plate and resume reading. All while my right hand never stopped moving in circular motions on the flimsy material of her nightie. I probably looked like a well oiled machine because all the movements I was carrying out were beginning to be in a timed sequence—it pays to be a drummer.

My first involuntary, random thought that came to me while reading was a voice in my head that seemed to say, *I need your help!* I set the book down on my chest and listened carefully. Was that voice actually in my *head* or did I *hear* it? It may very well have been my imagination but it sounded like the voice Tim and I had heard outside the car. Maybe it wasn't the exact voice but when Tim had explained that there was a particular inflection to it. I thought it over and what I had just heard, whether in my head or not, was very similar to what we had heard that night. I laid there for quite a spell, half of the

176

half of my sub still on the plate, while I listened. Was I expecting to hear it again, isn't that asking a bit much? I thought, *Well, come on, if you're trying to communicate, let's have it, talk to me.* I felt foolish. Now I'm attempting telepathy; or maybe she was. Nonsense! I was tired. We'd gone to the house several nights in a row and the first couple were kind of frightening. I read for a while longer until my eyelids became too heavy to hold open. I set the book on the floor and the plate on the nightstand, reached to the lamp and turned it off. I had reread the bit about out of body experiences and thought, *What the hell, I'll try it.* I imagined the Dandys' backyard and concentrated on how it looked, where the house and spring house were. I imagined being above it all, looking down and seeing everything there. I kept my eyes closed and, after several minutes, I could actually see it in my mind's eye but that was all. I wasn't suddenly swept off on a paranormal carpet to the location, hovering above, observing everything below. I knew I was still in my bed. I could smell the sub about a foot from my nose. I could hear Debbie breathing and I heard the refrigerator kick on. It was probably spitting on the floor again so I'd have something to walk in when I got up in the morning and forgot that there was still some residual water dripping from the defrost cycle. *So much for leaving my body,* I thought. I rolled over and put my arm around Debbie. She moved back, closer to me. That's when I thought, why would I *want* to leave my body?

When I woke, I looked toward the kitchen and, sure enough, it was still the kitchen. I hadn't gone anywhere and, if I had, I'd gotten back okay. My sub was gone though. Perhaps someone else who had an out of body experience came in and took it. I'm sure Debbie disposed of it this morning. If people's spirits can truly leave their bodies and go elsewhere, can they bring something back with them? I know where I would go, and what I'd bring back if it were possible. I'd float over to Crosby's when I had a craving, whether they were open or closed, and get a chocolate milkshake. That brings up another question, are you able to go through solid objects? I'd have to find out for sure because, if you can't, I'd have to go when Crosby's was open. I'd have to wait until someone opened the door so I could drift in. That was enough silly thinking, it was time to get up. I figured there wasn't any sense in going to the Fountain today to wait for calls. Everything was sold except the safe and I honestly didn't think anyone would want that old iron box. I decided instead of waiting for Louie to call, I'd call him and see what his plans were. I called the deli and someone asked me to hang on. When he came to the phone he told me he could get in sometime tomorrow and see what would be involved in getting it out of the building. I suggested I give him a key to the front door and he could come and go as he pleased. Before I dropped a key off at the deli, I went to the bank to ask how much time I had to get the rest of the items out of the building. I waited for about fifteen minutes before the president came out to talk with me. He said there was no real rush but the sooner I was completely out, the sooner they could seal the building. I told him I would get back to him later this afternoon. When exiting the bank, I looked at the once Fountain of Youth. I actually became a little misty. I proceeded to go to the deli from the bank and gave Louie the key.

"Hey, kid. Everything okay?" Lou asked as I walked into the Downtown Deli.

"Everything is swell, Lou. I'm completely done with the Fountain and everyone that's involved with it," I said.

"That's good to hear. That was some show the old man put on; admirable too. I really expected him to do more than talk, if you know what I mean," Louie said.

"Yeah, me too, but I'm glad it ended the way it did. It would have just made things worse if it had gone any further. Well, here's the key. The president of the bank just said the quicker I was out, the quicker they could close up the building," I said.

"I'm sure we can get things taken care of in the next few days; probably by the middle of next week, I would imagine," Louie said.

"Hey, Paul." Joe N. said as he walked into the deli. "I got some new drums. I traded a guitar for them. They're in real good shape too."

"That's good, Joe. Now you can start playing drums too," I said.

He said, "Yeah," as he walked away.

"Okay, Lou, if you need anything, help in getting the bar out or something, give me a call," I said.

"Thanks, Paulie, I sure will."

I left the deli and went directly to Carol's for something to eat then, while eating on the run, I went to G&G Music to get some new drum sticks for the weekend. I was tougher than heck on sticks, even tougher on my hands, so I bought new sticks if we were playing both weekend nights. When I pulled up, George was in the window staring at me as I got out.

"I need sticks and a bottle of Pepto Bismol for tonight," I said.

"I have the Pepto Bismol but I don't have the sticks. You'll have to call Charlie for them, ah-ha-ha," George replied.

He was blocking my view but, when he moved, I saw the most spectacular drum set I'd ever seen. They were called Zickoes. They were clear and made of a resin compound. The size of the each drum was bigger than the standard sizes of other drum manufacturers and, after sampling their sound, that too was bigger. Within two weeks of seeing them, I had a set of my own and they were fantastic to play. The first major national group to ever use them was Iron Butterfly. You can hear the sound of this fantastic kit on their hit song, "Inna-Gadda-Da-Vida." Of course, George had been kidding about the sticks and I bought three pair of, "Rock Knockers."

We talked for a while, then I went home to have lunch and read some more. I lay on the couch to read after lunch and fell asleep. I didn't wake up until I felt Debbie shaking my arm.

"How long have you been sleeping?" She asked.

"Oh shit, I came home about 12:30 and had a sandwich. I laid on the couch to read for a while and that's the last thing I remember. What time is it?" I asked.

"Almost 5:00. I figured you needed the sleep so I didn't wake you. You don't have to load the truck, do you?" Debbie asked.

"No, we never unloaded after Saturday. Since we didn't practice this week, all we're going to have to do is get in and go," I answered.

"How much time do you have?" She asked.

"George said he'd pick me up about 6:00," I said.

"Oh, you have almost an hour," she said, pulling me up from the couch and toward the bedroom.

At least we didn't have to worry about getting pregnant, did we?

George was on time, it was 5:55 when I heard the sick duck summoning me to come out. Debbie told me she was going to her mom's tonight and she and her brother may go to a movie. I told her to have a good time and to be careful. We kissed. I ran outside and jumped in the milk truck. We did the usual drive-by past my parents' house where we exchanged our usual waves and we were off to the job. Tonight we were playing in Wellsville and it should go well. We were well liked in Wellsville and it was only a forty-five minute drive. Jamie will drive directly to the location.

Jamie worked for his father's company, Star-Dell Corporation in Franklinville, New York. Star-Dell was a vegetable packing plant and, from their hand packing assembly line, emerged packages of the usual vegetables: carrots, beets, radishes, lettuce and the like. Some vegetables were grown locally, others were shipped in by train. When we had visited Jamie, I walked through the plant a couple of times and observed how the production line worked. It was interesting to say the least. Most of the workers were women.

One side-note of interest: Jamie's father had converted an old railroad oil car into a bomb shelter. It had been buried on their property and was stocked with packaged foods (NOT all vegetables!) and bottled water in case of war or a tornado. Of course, both were extremely rare in this neck of the woods. The first time I went in I wanted to be eight years old again! It would have been a fabulous place to play war or have sleep overs! Ah well, those fun days are over.

The job went very well and, as usual, my ears were ringing in harmony. We stopped at a little all night diner on the way home. I generally ate breakfast food after playing and Jamie and George ordered their meals. George always ordered a chocolate milkshake with a Coke chaser. He first started doing that when we would stop at Langworthy's diner in Killbuck, New York. Langworthy's was probably our favorite place to eat after playing, and 'they were all sit-downs'. Again, don't ask, you won't understand.

I was dropped off and George took the milk truck back to park at his parents' house. It was just past 2 in the morning and I was ready for bed. I took a quick shower and walked into the bedroom. The TV was on, but Debbie was asleep. She had become accustomed to my turning it on after playing because I'd rather hear a late night movie than the ringing in my ears as I was trying to go to sleep. It was an annoying sound, that high pitched ringing that often changes tone. The bad news is, you'll get that after playing loud music for years but the real bad news is, it doesn't go away even after the playing has. I got into bed and was sleeping in no time.

The next morning, Debbie was up before me. I woke about 12:00 and was thirsty as the dickens. I went out to the kitchen and grabbed a Pepsi. Debbie was on the couch looking through an advertisement. I had a weird problem, I couldn't take more than two swallows of any kind of carbonated pop other than Mountain Dew without hiccupping. I didn't get the hiccups mind you, I'd only hiccup once and every so often, twice. The last time I actually had the annoying hiccups I was probably about ten and that was the LAST time. Strange.

"How was the job?" She asked.

"Good. Did you and your brother go to the movies?" I asked.

"Nah, we stayed at mom's and watched TV. Wanna go look around the stores today and see what kind of baby stuff they have?" Debbie asked.

"We can do that. Have you eaten lunch yet?" I asked.

"No, I was waiting for you, to see what you wanted," she said.

"We could go to Gomez's and get something," I said.

"No, that's way out toward Portville and there aren't any stores out that way that I want to go to," Debbie said.

She decided on Montgomery Ward's, yet we ended up going to almost every store that would have baby items. We didn't buy anything, we were just browsing. In four hours, we probably walked five miles, "browsing." We got back home about 5:00; I had about one hour before leaving again to play.

Tonight we were playing at a teen center owned by a renowned, "retired" belly dance, Tullah H. There was some enjoyment, because we were entertained during our breaks by this "retired" belly dancer, who, in my opinion, should have retired *many years* prior. She was doing the community of Salamanca, New York a service though by offering the kids a place to get together and enjoy music and whatever else was in those rooms upstairs that I had been told to stay away from by an older guy with no neck. Perhaps there were other "retired" entertainers who resided in those rooms that didn't want to be disturbed; obviously. Who was I to ask?

I got ready for that night's job about 5:30. Thinking back, we used to wear all the "in" clothing when playing. We used to wear Nehru shirts a lot and one time I was out shopping and found a really psychedelic one. The colors were bright enough to blind one if looked at it in bright sunlight! One odd thing that I didn't understand then : When I put it on, the buttons were on the wrong side. I figured it was because it was made in a different country until a friend of mine had said it had "darts." I wondered what she had been talking about and then she and her friend explained it to me. When I looked in the mirror, I did notice it had some "extra room" in the chest area. What did I know, I thought it was made in foreign country and it was "roomy." I never wore that damned thing again!

George and I pulled away in the Black STONED Jury's milk truck heading first for Eighth Street, then on to Cuba Lake to play at the Pavilion, which at some future time, due to all the kids dancing, would vibrate itself apart and fall into the lake. The entire building swayed to and fro and up and down, almost as if it had been resting on the waters of Cuba Lake like all the boats around it at each cottage's dock. I don't think many years passed before the building was, in fact, condemned and none too soon!

In the middle of playing, "Radar Love" something came over me. I don't know what but it was on the frightening side. I thought I heard or imagined the same voice I had when I was reading at home the other night. It was the same words, *I need your help!* I lost the beat when it happened and George looked over at me as if to say, "Something there?" I tried to dismiss it but the feeling lingered. I didn't hear it again, I was still hearing it and that made no sense to me whatsoever. During the rest of the evening the house was on my mind. I was glad I was going there tomorrow. I needed to go.

The night passed quickly. We finished the job, packed up and drove straight back to Olean, a twenty five-minute drive. George dropped me off and asked if Tuesday would be okay for practice. I told him I'd have to look at the new schedule and I would call him and let him know. I went into the house, took a shower and went to bed with the craving for the Dandy house in the afternoon. When I looked at the clock it was just a little before 1:30 a.m. I walked around to Debbie's side of the bed to see what time the alarm had been set for: 9 a.m. I got back into bed thinking, "That's perfect, we'll be at the house by 10:00." I closed my eyes, but sleep didn't come because I kept trying to remember what Mike had told Tim and me about the voice he had heard when his window was open. I was sure he said it sounded at one point like she had said, "I need you to help." That was very close to, *I need your help* and there was an inflection to it as Tim put it. What I heard, or imagined if you prefer, wasn't a plea for help, it was a *demand* for help.

Neither Tim nor I heard what was said that night. Though I can't say that what I heard is what we heard, something tells me they're somehow connected. Hopefully, Father Al will be there, and even though I might come across as arrogant, I'm going to ask him as many questions as I can remember. Sometime after 2:45 I fell asleep.

CHAPTER XV

Debbie woke me at 9:20 a.m. and asked if I wanted something to eat. I told her a bowl of cereal would be fine. She could choose.

"Do you mind if Tim rides up with us?" I asked from the bedroom while getting dressed.

"Nope, he called last night right after you left and we talked for a few minutes. You guys are really into this haunted thing, aren't you?" Debbie replied.

"Yes, and you asked that the other day" I said rather firmly. "There's something going on up there and I need to know what it is? Are you ready to go?"

"You haven't even eaten yet and your cereal is getting soggy," Debbie said.

I went out to the kitchen, sat at the table and ate my cereal in record time. I put my bowl in the sink, rinsed it out and called Tim. He answered the phone and I told him to be ready in twenty minutes and we'd be over to pick him up. I hung up and called the Dandys. Mike answered. "Hey, man. You guys coming up today? Mom said Debbie had mentioned you were," Mike asked.

"Yeah, we're going to pick up Tim and we'll be up in about an hour or less. Is there anything anyone needs?" I asked.

"Not that I know of. Let me ask mom." Mike said.

I heard him set the phone down and call to his mom. He picked it up and said, "If you wouldn't mind, would you stop and pick up a gallon of milk?" Mike asked.

"Sure will, Mike. We'll see you shortly," I replied.

I felt agitated, rushed to get something done and it was bothering me. I was running around the apartment like a chicken with its head cut off. I checked twice to be sure I had my keys, made sure I had enough money and asked Debbie at least three times if she was ready to go.

"What's the matter with you today?" Debbie asked.

"I don't know. I feel strange like there's something I have to do but I don't know what the hell it is! Clara asked if we could stop and get a gallon of milk. I can run into Service Store before we pick up Tim. Is there anything you want that I can grab when we get there?" I asked.

"I can't think of anything right off-hand but, if I do, I'll let you know." Debbie replied.

I felt pressed for time and had no idea why. It wasn't even 10 a.m. and it seemed like I'd been up all day. We walked out, I locked the door and we left to get the milk and pick Tim up. Service Store was fairly busy on Sunday mornings and this was no different than any other Sunday. I got the milk and decided to get two gallons instead of one. There were five in the house and they must go through milk like it's going out of style. Plus. I didn't know if anyone else was coming up today. I also grabbed two six packs, one of Mountain Dew, the other Pepsi. I knew Gordon had been up during the day and Clara had mentioned that her mother and father sometimes came to visit, just not as often as she would like. I was in line at the store and the woman in front of me had an overloaded cart and, to make matters worse, she had a handful of coupons at the ready to present to the cashier! For some odd reason, I didn't seem to have patience to wait for her to get through the line and I asked, "Hi, do you mind if I jump ahead of you, I've just got this milk and pop, and I've got a sick brother at home?" I asked. She appeared reluctant at first, but then sighed and said, "Oh, I guess so."

Wow, it was going to take me all of forty-five seconds to give my money to the cashier, take my change and be out of the woman's way. I'm glad it wasn't Christmas, I would have said, 'Humbug' to her! I almost ran to the car and hopped in. Debbie looked at me as if I had just robbed a bank and jumped into the get away car.

"Are you okay?" She asked.

"Yeah, I think so. I'll be better when I get ho… I mean to the house."

I drove out of the parking lot and down Second Avenue to pick up Tim. He wasn't outside, so I honked the horn. I don't think a full minute passed and I honked again. "Give him a minute to get out here, hon" Debbie said. "Calm down. There's something bothering you and if you don't want to tell me, it's okay. But, if there is anything I can do, please let me."

What the hell *was* wrong with me? I had a feeling of dread but about what? Going to the Dandys today shouldn't be any different than any other night we'd gone up. In a way, it felt similar to hurrying to get to the airport because you were running late for your flight. I took a couple of deep breaths and the feeling of urgency seemed to lessen. Tim came out a minute later and got in the back seat.

"Hi, Tim," Debbie said.

"Hi, Deb! Oh driver, could you possibly put the top down? It's going to be a beautiful day," he said to his supposed chauffeur who didn't own a convertible.

Tim's quip of the morning helped snapped me out of whatever the hell funk I was in. The tightness began to relax, I only wish I knew what caused me to feel that way. I turned on to Center Street from Second Avenue and then onto Main to head towards Hinsdale. Debbie reached over to touch my leg in a reassuring gesture. I looked at her, smiled and told her I was okay. There were still several cars driving the back country roads and I was sure some of their occupants were looking for the now famous house. We turned onto Congress Road and there was a car on the side of the road with about five or six teenagers standing alongside of it. One appeared to be looking at a piece of paper; a hand drawn map to the haunted house. Why did I think that? We continued on and saw yet a couple of more cars with teenagers in them. It's been over a week and they're still coming, looking for the house that was in the paper.

"Are these people all going to the Dandy house?" Debbie asked.

"Probably, the little bastards," Tim said with a guttural voice.

"We don't have movie star houses for people to pass by and gaga over, so the next best thing is a haunted house, I guess," I said.

When we came over the rise and around the bend of Wagner Hill Road there were at least six or seven cars parked along both sides. At the very least, it was dangerous. Where the hell were the State Police to clear this mob up? We turned onto McMahon and a car that was parked closest to the turn, pulled

186

down to follow us. I stopped quite abruptly, waited for the car to get close to mine before I got out; Tim got out too. I walked back to the driver's side of the car and asked the driver, a boy of about 18, who had a passenger of about the same age, what they wanted.

"Are you looking for the haunted house, 'cause we are too?" He asked.

"Do you see that dead end sign behind you?" I asked.

The kid turned around and looked through the rear window and said, "Yeah, what about it?"

"That means this road doesn't go very far, and where it does go is where we're going but you're not. I suggest you back up or turn around but whatever you do, don't fucking follow me up this road! There've been enough people coming up here harassing our friends and you're not going to be another one added to that list!" I snapped. Actually, I did snap and I had no idea why. It wasn't normal for me to be rude to a total stranger like this.

"We just..."

"I won't repeat what I just said. There are no trespassing signs posted all over. This is private property so unless you want the State Police climbing up your ass, you'll turn around and go back to where you were parked. Better yet, go to Crystal Beach or something and find a real thrill, 'cause there sure as fuck aren't any up here," I snapped again.

Tim began walking up to the passenger door of the kid's car as he started backing up. We both stood there until they were all the way back onto Wagner Hill Road when the kid almost backed into the ditch at the side of the road. We got back into my car and continued on up McMahon Road.

"That was so fuc..—cool! Sorry, Deb," Tim said.

"What'd you do?" Debbie asked.

"He scared the crap out of those kids. You didn't hear him? That was cooler than heck!" Tim exclaimed.

Normally, I would have handled that differently. I would have asked them nicely to back up, or told them they were on the wrong road. I don't know why I was so gruff. Tim might have thought it was "cool" but it was very much unlike me.

When we got to the turn to the Dandys' driveway, we noticed that Phil's car was blocking the road.

"Oh oh, barricade time," Tim said. "I hope no one comes out with a gun!" He added.

I didn't want to honk the horn as I assumed Phil worked last night and was probably sleeping. I got out and walked around to the back of the house and opened the outside back door. I was about to tap lightly on the kitchen door when Laura opened it.

"Hi," she said, looking at me with that sheepish grin I had become fond of.

She turned around apparently to announce our arrival when Clara walked up behind her and greeted me.

"Where's Debbie and this Tim character you told me about?" Clara asked.

"They're in the car. I came back to let someone know we were here. I was afraid of waking Phil. I'll go get them," I said.

"Just come on in when you get back here," Clara said.

I walked around the side of the house to see Tim and Debbie already out of the car. Tim was holding the two gallons of milk and Debbie was carrying the pop. I told them to come on back while I was looking at the spot where we heard the voice a few nights ago.

"What a difference during the day," Tim said.

"It looks like a regular, everyday house in the light of day," Debbie said.

I waited for them and we all walked in together. I took the pop from Debbie and Tim quietly asked if he looked okay. I told him I've never known him to look okay, then he proceeded to kick me on the back of my foot.

We all gathered in the living room where the introductions took place. After I finished introducing Tim to Clara and the girls and it was Mike's turn to say his "nice to meet you." Shaking hands, they simply said hi to one another.

Clara asked, "You two know each other. You're the mysterious Pepsi man, huh?"

The expression Tim had on his face was one I had never seen before, I imagined it might have been embarrassment.

"I had my suspicions but I didn't have enough evidence to start pointing fingers. So, Paul, how long have the two of you been coming up at night?" Clara asked.

"Our first night was last Sunday, right, Mike?" I asked.

"Yeah, that was the night you guys told me you heard the woman's voice," Mike responded.

"You've been coming up since LAST Sunday?!" Clara asked

"Yeah, Clara. And I've got to talk to you about that, Mike," I said.

"Yeah, Clara! That's it?"

I wasn't sure what she meant by that statement. Was I supposed to add something, an explanation or something? She stood there standing, staring at me as if she were waiting for me to elaborate or something.

"Yeah, Clara..... ma'am?" I said, questionably.

She burst into laughter and it was nice to hear after Mike telling us how stressed she'd been lately and not sleeping well. Hopefully, with Tim here, if he opens up because he really is shy around new people, he'll have her laughing most of the day. We'll all be laughing for that matter.

"You called me last Sunday and told me you and Pepsi Man here were coming up but I thought you hadn't made it. Every time I talked to Mike about you or Debbie he seemed to skirt around the topic and all the while you've been coming up here guarding the house; how sweet!" Clara exclaimed.

"Well, we haven't come up since Wednesday night. I couldn't Friday or last night because I had to play and Thursday we decided we needed a break," I said.

"No wonder the house was quieter than normal. You were keeping them busy outside!" Clara exclaimed.

"Now, didn't we talk about this very thing? Even Mike said if he were a ghost he'd rather watch three dumb sh… people than someone that was sleeping," I said.

"We live with the kids' father, we've all heard the 'sh' word before," Clara responded.

"Paul, Tim, let's go out for a walk and leave the ladies to talk about us while we're gone," Mike said.

189

"Yeah, get out of here. Go see what the place looks like when you can actually admire it," Clara said.

"You okay, Deb?" I asked.

"I'm fine, it's daytime, get outta here!" She replied.

Mary, Clara and Beth Ann laughed when Debbie made that comment. Laura sat on the edge of the couch looking at me. I was gonna have a chat with that young lady before we left today, you could bank on it! The three of us trudged through the field and to the tree line where we had gone on a previous night's quest. We still hadn't mentioned how Mike had acted that night but it had been on my mind. This might be the perfect time to bring it up. We walked a good portion of the length of the property, engaging in small talk and just looking around. I asked Mike if he remembered everything that we did that night.

"Yeah, we came out here and waited for a few minutes and went back to the house, why?" Mike asked.

"'Cause you were acting weird as shit mostly after we got out here and most of the walk back. You said something about coming all the way out here, that we had accomplished what we set out to do, or something strange like that," Tim said.

"Yeah, Mike, you said there was nothing out here and we could do it again some other time. Do you remember saying that?" I asked.

"No, I remember us talking about it being a ways out and I remember walking back. Did I really say all that?" Mike asked.

"We aren't making it up and even if you don't remember it, we wouldn't say you said it if you hadn't," Tim said.

"I don't remember saying anything like that, actually, I wouldn't imagine why I *would* say something like that. How long was I acting that way?" Mike asked.

"As I said, right after getting out here. We started heading back and a couple of times you stopped and looked back at the tree line or toward Wagner Hill. It was as if you were looking or watching for someone or something. It was really weird, Mike. We got about halfway back and you seemed okay. You were perfectly fine when we all got back in the car. Do you remember Tim asking you what that was all about?" I asked.

"Yeah, actually, I do. But you interrupted us and I didn't think to ask again what you meant. That's really weird, guys, I don't remember any of it, yet I think I remember the entire walk back, but I don't remember looking back at the tree line or stopping at all," Mike said, his brows drawn in perplexity.

Could it be more dangerous than anyone suspects being in the vicinity of this house? It's not likely that a spirit can make someone's personality change is it? That's demonic possession from what I understand and from the little I had read. That's not happening here, there was no way. We dropped the subject of that night and continued walking around the area. Maybe we would find a clue or something about the people who lived here or in the area. It was more like we were on a treasure hunt than anything. We were probably in the field for about an hour or so before we began walking back to the house.

"Did you mention to your mom about the woman that was looking out your window the other night?" I asked Mike.

"No, but I think now that we're all together, we should. We should tell her everything we've seen or heard as well as everything the two of you have. I really believe that if we keep a record of what's happening day by day, we'll have a better chance of understanding what the hell is happening and maybe why," Mike said.

"I agree with that," Tim said. "It's like putting little pieces of a puzzle together, the more we get connected, the better we'll see the overall picture." Tim added.

"Jesus Christ, what are we becoming, the new Psychic Volunteers Group Board of Directors?" I asked laughing.

"Hey, that's catchy, we ought to take it on the road," Tim said.

I picked up a small dirt clot and threw it at Tim. Instead, it hit Mike in the arm.

"Hey, what did I do?" Mike exclaimed.

We got back to the house and, just like the night Phil and I were out on the tour, we walked past the back door and headed for McMahon Road. We walked as far as the turn and could see there were still cars at the end of the road. We talked and wondered why they hadn't moved further up the road. It had to be the kid we told to get lost who was probably telling everyone else it would be best not to drive up. He wouldn't be telling a lie if he had.

I wanted Mike to show Tim and me where the sounds of the Gregorian chants were coming from, but we decided to go back to the house and get something to drink. The afternoon was becoming quite warm. We got back to the house and went into the kitchen where Mike got Tim and himself a Pepsi. I decided on a Mountain Dew; no hiccups in that bottle. We went into Mike's room and found a place to sit; I on the floor, Tim on the bed. We talked about everything that had happened since it first started. Mike wasn't really sure about everything. He knows the haunting started a couple of months ago but he thought it would be better for his mom to explain most of it.

"Who's the boy that everyone talks about, the same one the girls on the road the other night talked about?" I asked.

"I'm not exactly sure but supposedly a kid got killed in a buzz saw accident. It's the same description that fit the boy I saw a while back. I first spotted him when he was walking through the front yard, then he walked toward the pond and just disappeared, as if he fell into a hole or something," Mike explained.

"Did you go out and try to talk to him when you first saw him?" Tim asked.

"Nope, I just watched him, so did Mary and Laura," Mike said.

Tim was looking at Mike's chess set which was now sitting on his dresser. "Is that it?" Tim asked

Mike lifted himself from his bed to see what Tim had been referring to, "Yeah, that's the famous chess set and there's the Battleship game that landed on my chest," he said pointing to the corner of the room.

"Where was it when it fell on you, Mike?" I asked.

"On the shelf above the bed," Mike explained.

Looking at the shelf, no one could have doubted that the chess set and game box could have fallen very easily. It wouldn't require help from an unseen hand which was what everyone believed. My thoughts were on the call received by Bob S. from the woman correlating everyday mishaps with spirits; accidents will occur without the help of the supernatural. There were other fracases taking place some of which we've all been subject to but this I was I prepared to dismiss.

"Maybe they were a little off kilter and just simply slid off the shelf, Mike," I said.

Mike looked at the shelf, then back to me and said, "Yeah, that was a possibility, only, there was a ton of magazines on *top* of the Battleship game and the chess set was on top of that. The chess set fell first, and a little bit later, the Battleship box landed on me. How in the world could they have fallen and the magazines stayed on the shelf?" Mike asked.

Well, so much for my cross examination. Investigative works requires one to have the complete information before assuming or coming to a conclusion. I stood corrected with Mike's explanation. That may be why so many have been unjustly convicted: the defense involved in a case doesn't dig deep enough and misses a smidgen of crucial information needed to solve the mystery. The more that was explained about this house's perils, the more I was convinced we were truly experiencing a genuine, honest-to-goodness, haunted house. Although, hearing the woman's voice outside the car had me fairly convinced already.

"I have to apologize, Mike. My thoughts convinced me this was a slight accident any of us could have," I said.

"No need to apologize, Paul. I was under it all, it convinced me we had problems that weren't easily explained. There were so many other things happening that couldn't be explained before this happened. Of course, my dad thinks everything that's happened has an explanation. He doesn't necessarily have an explanation most of the time but that's either his defense against it all or he's just in denial to it all," Mike said.

We all had our opinions of what was happening, but Tim and I only heard what was going inside the house. I found it very difficult to believe what we had seen or heard and now, being offered even more concrete evidence of activity happening inside the house, it was nearly impossible not to believe. It was happening, we were experiencing it and that can't be denied no matter what anyone says. We experienced things that had no reasonable explanations.

CHAPTER XVI

"Let's add everything up since we've been coming here," Tim suggested. "The first night, you think you saw a shadow by the back of the house and then we both saw a light in Mary's room even though Mary doesn't sleep in it. Okay, both could have been easily dismissed as we discussed. Then there was the fluttering paper deal but the first sound we heard didn't quite sound like the sound the paper made against the driveway. I think that may have been *our* denial in that case. Now, we come to the mysterious voice in the hillside. We thought of every possibility to explain this away and there just isn't any logical explanation for someone to be heard but not be visible."

"The house is haunted, Tim," I said quite casually. "Not just the house but the whole damned area. But why hasn't it come to anyone's attention until now? Mike, the other night, when we heard the female's voice, you said you heard a woman too and it sounded like she was saying something like, "you need to help" or "help" something, I don't remember. Now, think really hard. Could she have said something like, "I need you to help me?"

"Like I said, I was really tired and I wasn't paying that close attention, but I've been thinking about what Tim said, that there was a demand in her voice. She did kinda sound mad and the more I thought about it, I think it sounded more like her voice wasn't so much by the window. It seemed as if it were coming from the end of my bed. But again, I was almost sleeping when I heard her. Why?" Mike asked.

I didn't want either of them to think I was making something up or losing my sense of reality; or worse, letting my imagination run wild. There was no reasonable explanation for me, someone who has no experience with the paranormal in any way, to hear a voice so clearly that sounded like it came from someone sitting next to them. I could almost understand it happening once, especially reading about such topics when it happened. But two times, and the exact voice and statement when that was the *last* thing on my mind, was to say at the least, bothersome.

"I've heard, at least I think I've heard, a woman's voice say, *I need you to help me!* twice. Once, while reading at home and last night while playing. Both times it was identical, same inflection—same voice—and the same words. It was just like listening to a line from a song. And to be totally and truthfully honest, I don't want to be someone who *hears* things unless someone else is hearing them too; get my drift?" I asked.

"All right, what are you boys up to?" Clara said peering into Mike's room.

"Nothing, mom. We're just talking about the house," Mike said.

"Clara, can I go up to Mary's room?" I asked but didn't know why.

She looked at me curiously and with a chuckle said, "Sure, if you want, but be quiet, Phil's still sleeping"

I walked out of Mike's room to the stairway and stopped. I looked up and I believe Clara and both of my ghost chasing buddies were standing at Mike's door staring at me, waiting for me to either go up or turn around with a change of heart. I started walking up the stairs, looking back to see that I had been correct. Tim had a quizzical expression on his face.

When I got to the top of the stairs, I turned around to look at the small door which led to the tiny crawlspace. *"We hear a lot of noises in there,"* I recalled Phil telling me when we were walking through the house. I moved forward a step and looked into Laura's room; the door had been open. *You know they're here too, don't you?* It was a typical teenage girl's room, with the usual teenage girl's environment. Another two steps and I was standing in front of Mary's room facing the door, which was closed. It was a bright sunshiny day. Outside the birds were chirping; so were the birds downstairs in the living room. I heard a noise come from Laura's room and out of the corner of my eye saw something dark move at the base of the door. Dare I look? It was Jinx, the family's black cat! I let out a sigh of relief. I wasn't truly prepared to see something even though I had come up for that reason. I placed my hand on the knob on Mary's door, slowly turning it and opening it even slower. It

195

was warm standing in the upstairs hall, but the air hitting my hand as it sought entry when swinging the door open was cold. There were no draughts present and the room was sun-lit and should have been as warm as the rest of the upstairs. The air was that of a closed up room, shades drawn, preventing the sun from splashing warmth into it. It was unnatural, unnerving, yet utterly fascinating to feel this peculiar phenomenon. As I was standing there, attempting to *feel* something, contemplating what could cause such a difference in temperature change, Jinx began rubbing back and forth against my leg. I bent down to give her a reciprocating rub when she stopped, arched her back, and let out a hiss rivaled only by that of a steam engine. It appeared she had her eyes fixed on something in the center of Mary's room, and after one more hiss, she turned and descended the stairs. I reached for the doorknob to pull the door closed and stopped. I wasn't going to be intimidated. I remember asking very quietly, "What do you want?" When I felt an ever so gently movement of the door's weight swing toward me—I let go of the knob and backed away. My thoughts were running wild. Did I just experience some sort of contact, understanding or communication, or was there suddenly a shift in the foundation of the house causing the door to move unassisted?

"Are you going to stay up there all day?" Tim whispered from the bottom of the stairs.

I walked to where I could see him and said, "Yeah, I'm coming."

I walked back to Mary's door but the door was closed tight against the jamb. Had I closed it when I heard Tim call up? I didn't remember closing it; I had planned to return to the room. I opened the door again and waited to see if it would close. It was probably a full minute and it didn't move in the least. Looking at the window, I could see that it was tightly shut, eliminating a draught causing it to close. I returned downstairs feeling somewhat exhilarated as well as disappointed. I wanted more; I wanted to understand. Everyone was now in the living room and they all looked cheerful except Clara. She was looking to me for something. Was she trying to determine from my expression or body language what had happened? What did happen? I opened the door, the air was colder than the rest of the house, a cat hissed and the door seemed to close on its own. None of this proved beyond a reasonable doubt that it was paranormal activity.

"Father Al isn't coming up today," Mike said.

"Dammit!" The word came out before I had a chance think about my response. "Sorry," I said.

Chuckling, Clara said, "We've heard worse. You'll get a chance to talk with him eventually. You ought to see if there's a time when you could go to the Friary and the two of you could sit and have a good chat."

That was an idea, but I'd been a little apprehensive about talking to him without someone, Clara preferably, being present. Then again, I shouldn't have been concerned whether or not someone was with me for support. I needed answers for what *I* was feeling. With what had transpired while standing at Mary's door that day, the only thing that may not have been experienced by someone else was the door moving on its own. Both Clara and Mike had mentioned that Jinx or their other cat, Fluffy, had been seen hissing at something that wasn't apparent to them. Everyone had talked about the coldness of the room, so that experience wasn't exclusive to me. But I felt the exertion on the door when it moved while my hand rested on the knob. Something other than just the jamb being out of square caused that door to move! And it wasn't just that, I had stood there for a minute prior to that without touching the door and it hadn't moved in the slightest. There was pressure against my wrist, slight as it was but I do believe there was a source of energy that had helped that door close—that I was sure of.

I has assumed everyone in the household had talked about these disturbances in great length, but I thought it was best to leave this alone with Mary sitting in the living room with us. There was no need for further discussion regarding the room she once called her own. I was so keyed up at that moment I was about to just blurt out, "Laura, why did you ask me, I knew they were here?" Luckily, I tamped down the temptation. This had all been very disturbing, yet my interest couldn't have been more intense. I knew in time that, without a doubt, I was going to understand a great deal regarding the world of the paranormal.

"Paul, tell us, what's it like working with Tim?" Clara asked.

"It's about the same as doing anything with Tim. You never know when he's going to sneak up on your sanity! I don't think he's got a serious bone in his body," I said.

"Come on, now, I've had some very serious moments," Tim said defending himself.

"Clara, if you were on a sinking ship with him and you were a thousand miles from shore, he would come up with something to say so that the last thing you would remember before gasping for that last desperate breath, would be the sound of your own laughter," I said.

"Tim, if you're that humorous, your presence would certainly take some of the gloom from this troubled old house," Clara said.

Every so often, I would catch Tim glancing at Beth Ann and she, in turn, would show the slightest hint of a smile that she was obviously trying to conceal. I knew Beth Ann had been going with her friend Jeff for a while so I didn't know what to think of it, nor was it my *place* to think anything of it. I just found it humorous. We visited until about 3:30 and decided it was time to head home. It was an enjoyable time, I only wish Father Al had been able to join us. I had made the announcement that we were going to leave. Clara, Debbie and Beth Ann were talking and laughing about something. This gave Tim, Mike and me a chance to talk about our next outing in the back yard. We went into the kitchen and discussed it. We all decided we'd come up tonight. Mike said he'd check with his friend Randy to see if he wanted to come up too. Everyone walked into the kitchen and Debbie, Tim and I thanked Clara for her hospitality. I was slowly getting to know this woman and, the more I was around her, the greater my feelings of respect for her grew. Not just because she appeared to endure the pressures of all that was happening so well, but I could see how close she was to her family and the relationship she had with Beth Ann, from what I had observed, was rock steady. They were best friends.

"Thank you for coming up. It was great seeing you again and, Tim, it was nice to finally meet you. The three of you seemed to have helped calm down the jumpiness of the house. You're welcome anytime to visit," Clara said.

"Thanks, Clara. It was nice seeing who lives here finally, I thought Mike lived alone and we just came up to keep him company. If you find any more Pepsi in the refrigerator you'll know I was here," Tim replied.

"Laura, why did you ask me what you did the first time we came to visit?" I said.

There, I said it. I finally asked, although I had hoped for a better opportunity than now, I didn't want to ask when everybody was standing around waiting for a reply. I could see that Clara was very interested in what it was she had asked and I felt I had put Laura on the spot and possibly had embarrassed her. But the reaction to my question with everyone waiting for an answer was just the opposite when she replied, "Because I knew you knew. I could feel that you could feel them and that you felt the same way I did."

"And what was it she asked?" Clara asked.

"When I was getting ready to follow Phil out the back door, I looked at Laura and she casually said, 'You know they're here too, don't you?'"

"Do you?" Clara asked, now putting me on the spot.

How was I to answer this? Did I know, really know, and, if so, what is the explanation I would have when I had to answer the next question that she would ask, which should be, "*How?*" I thought for a few seconds and responded with how I perceived it all.

"Yeah, I think I do. Although, I'm not sure what might be apprehension or what may be a genuine paranormal sensation or if I even know the difference," I said.

The only way, for me that is, to distinguish between the two was the circumstances that surrounded the unsettling feeling. If my senses had been piqued by something that might have had unnatural causes, then of course, my psyche was going to be wide open for assault. For instance, the first time walking the property, talking about the incidents that had taken place, surely I, or anyone who had an open mind, would *think* every little sound, the slightest movement glimpsed from the corner of the eye could be unnatural, given the surroundings and frame of mind. On the flip side, if an unsettling feeling strikes you unexpectedly, such as a voice suddenly heard with no apparent source or an immediate change in the ambiance of a room, chances are you may be experiencing a psychic impression. There's no question—it's an argumentative topic. The non-believers share the line, "I'll believe it when I see it, and that's a justified statement. With those who believe, I have concluded that some believe much too easily and much too much. I have met several people over the years who believe they have had a paranormal experience every time they visit a place that's supposedly haunted. I don't know how the subject came up but I remember talking to someone years ago who told me some stories about hauntings. Nearly every place this person lived was haunted and, if a place hadn't been he had many friends, not one friend but many, who had haunted houses. Plus, the ghosts were very accommodating to him every place he lived. There was always some form of communication with them and they would even leave notes in the dust on, his furniture. Obviously not a very good housekeeper, this "keeper of spirits." Another acquaintance I have told me of a spirit that resides in his friend's house. He told me if you put a bottle of milk on the kitchen table, the spirit will knock it off. He went on to explain that this would happen if you placed the bottle on the table ten times in a row, it would be knocked off each and every time! He invited me to witness this astonishing paranormal activity. I had gone on *three* separate occasions and on all three visits I was disappointed. Still, I'm sure it's safe to say, we all have known someone who has had supposed spirit problems at one time or another.

It was too bad Tim didn't get to meet the infamous Phil but certainly his chance would come. It was a good idea that Phil parks his car across their driveway keeping the really brazen ones from driving right up to their back door which did happen one time. I believe that was the individual who boldly walked in the back door, sat down at the kitchen table while they were having dinner and announced, "I want to see a ghost!" There's always one in the crowd.

When we were about to drive by the tree that afternoon, I glanced at Debbie. She looked back at me with a challenge, "I don't even care. It's daylight. If it stalls, I'll walk right back up this road to the house and sit down," she said.

I could look it up, but why bother? I believe there's a little bit of "I'm afraid of the dark" in all of us or, more likely, afraid of what might be camouflaged in that darkness. Apparently, the unseen forces which shut down the car's system as we neared the hanging tree were absent that evening or they're not interested today. We passed without a slightest hesitating twinge of the car's electrical system. There were a few vehicles traveling the quiet country roads as we were heading back into Hinsdale proper and we assumed some were people who lived in the surrounding area. Others were probably those still hoping for their chance to seek proof of life after death. Just as anything else new to the masses, people come by the scores and eventually the numbers diminish. Luckily, for the Dandy family, the interest in spectral sightings had lost some of its luster.

We stopped at Crosby's on the way in to Olean because I wanted one of their famous shakes; Debbie chose a hot fudge sundae and Tim a cone. As always on Sunday, Crosby's was busy with families coming to enjoy their favorite frozen treats on their post afternoon drives or returning from visits of family and friends; or possibly haunted houses! Both Tim and I were scheduled to work at 5:00 today. I dropped him off and Debbie and I stopped at Service Store on Front Street to pick up some essentials. We arrived home about an hour before I had to be at work. I cooked up some burgers and we talked about what Clara, the girls, and Debbie discussed while the three of us were roaming the country side.

"Honestly, I don't feel comfortable in the house. Almost everything we talked about was what had been going on there these past few months," Debbie said.

"Well, they're experiencing it all the time and probably have nothing else to talk about. Maybe they needed an outside ear to listen for a change," I said.

"Clara says there's always someone calling or stopping by who's offering help. I wouldn't have minded talking about work or our baby who's coming. Anything but the noises or disturbances in the middle of the night, or the voices that are heard outside Beth Ann's bedroom window. That's okay for you, I understand, but I'm really not interested. Even in the day time I have an uneasy feeling in the house. I did accept Clara's invitation to come up Labor Day but I think that's probably gonna be about the last time I go up for a while," Debbie said.

"I understand and I'm sorry that you feel uncomfortable, honey. I wish the circumstances were different, you really seem to like Clara and the girls," I replied.

"Oh, I do, I love Clara. She's very nice and I like talking to her; the girls are adorable. I'd just rather not be up there. Why are you looking at me like that?" She asked.

"Maybe I shouldn't go up so often. If you'd rather I didn't ..."

"No." She interrupted, "I wasn't saying it to make you think I didn't want you to go. I really don't mind. I know you have a lot of interest in it. I have to say I don't understand why, but it's fine. I'm interested too but not enough to go up as often as you. I'd like to find out why everything is happening too, but I think I'd rather find out from you than see it first hand."

"Even so, any time you don't want me to go just tell me. There's going to be plenty of times I can go," I said.

Little did I know then, for the first several months I was there as much, if not more, than I was at home. And in time, she became interested enough to make the occasional visit. I understood why she wouldn't want to discuss the house exclusively. She shows a slight interest when I would tell her what happened, but I think she asks out of respect, to be polite. When I tell her about the house, she listens, but not attentively. I'd be the same if someone were telling me about their going bass fishing every weekend. I'd listen, but really wouldn't give two beans.

I got ready for work after eating, then went to Richardson's to get bread when Debbie informed me we had forgotten to buy a loaf. It was already 4:45 but the store was only seven blocks down State Street. I asked Debbie to come too so she could drop me off at work and keep the car at home. I made it to work a couple of minutes before 5:00. Tim was already behind the counter mixing up a container of tuna. I joined him on the employee side of the counter, put on an apron, and checked the fridge to see if we had enough vegetables.

"Hey, there's half a container of tuna still in here," I told Tim, holding the container for him to see.

"You want fresh for tonight, don't you?" Tim asked.

"What's the difference? This was made this morning according to the tag," I replied.

"True, but Jim made it. He's so stingy, you're not even going to know there's mayonnaise in it," Tim scoffed.

"So then, take some of this tuna, put it in a separate container and add a little mayonnaise. Problem solved," I said, offering Tim one of my own expressions.

"You think you're so smuckin' fart, don't ya?" Tim said, tossing a tomato chunk at me.

Looking at the schedule I said, "Oh shit, he's got me scheduled for Tuesday *and* Saturday. Tuesday we practice and Saturday I have to play. I filled in the days I can't work in the box on the application. Fridays and Saturdays were the only two days I said I absolutely couldn't."

"I told you, he can't read. I'm off Tuesday and scheduled for Wednesday, I'll switch with ya. You work Wednesday and I'll come in Tuesday. Check with Jim about Saturday, I'm already scheduled. Maybe Mary can fill in for you even though she only likes working the East Side," Tim said.

"Thanks, Tim, I appreciate it," I said.

It had been busy that night. The walk-in patrons continued unremittingly all night, right up to closing time and we had six phone-in orders. Two were large, one was nine whole subs and another was five whole and three halves. There were only six rolls left on the rack when I locked the front door. We had nearly all of the cleaning up left because we didn't have time to get much done between customers. Not only did we have the regular chores but I made a hell of a mess when I dropped an entire bottle of oil on the floor and we tracked it all over before I had a chance to mop the majority of it up. Tim was thinking

203

ahead, he turned the water temperature up on the hot water tank. Jim kept it real low to conserve but you need plenty of hot water if you want to mop up an oily flub.

"You real hungry?" Tim asked.

"Not really. I agree, the heck with the subs. Grab some pop and chips. But throw that tuna you made into the other container and turn the water tank back to the setting it was on or Jim will have a fit," I replied.

"I already made a fresh container of tuna and yours was gone before 8 o'clock," he said, while readjusting the thermostat on the water tank.

"Off we'll be then, skipper," I said.

"All right, Gilligan."

We locked up and headed for the hills. It looked a bit like rain which would surely add to the gloominess of sitting in the dark. We pulled into the driveway at the stroke of midnight. There were no lights visibly glowing in the house. Even Mike's room was dark. He had told us he didn't sleep well last night and woke early from a noise that didn't repeat itself when he checked to investigate the source. He thought it was someone knocking on the back door but there was no one there when he went out to check. That happened about 6:45 a.m. After going back to bed he said he would drift in and out but didn't sleep soundly. He finally gave up trying and got out of bed a little after 8.

"Looks like everyone's sleeping," Tim said.

"Yup. What do you think happened with Mike in the field, really?" I asked.

"At first, I thought he was screwing with us, but after talking to him I don't know. He really acted like he had no memory of talking or acting weird," Tim replied.

"When we were walking back to the house, I kept looking at him and he really did seem different somehow. You know when someone is determined or maybe pissed, they have that look? He had an expression like that and the first time he stopped and looked back at the tree line, he said something but I didn't catch it 'cause he stopped and I kept walking," I replied.

"Well, the first time you start acting weird, I'll leave your ass here!" Tim said.

"I'd say the same for you but you have so many personalities I'd never know, would I?" I said.

We both had a pop and bag of chips and decided to walk around the house and down toward the first turn. I'd left my flashlight in Tim's car so I wouldn't take the chance of being absent-minded again and leave it at home. There was a cool breeze tonight and the possibility of rain was still in the air. We walked around the house and stopped at the front for a few minutes scanning the edge of the field we had walked this afternoon.

"Why'd you wonder if anyone was buried around the field?" I asked.

"I don't know. Like you said, people buried their dead in the most convenient places. I'm sure this has always been a field and there's a lot of empty land all around this place. I'll bet ya within half a mile of where we're standing there's an unmarked grave," Tim replied.

"That could be, and who knows how many settlers were killed by Indians in this area and vice versa. Most of this country belonged to the Indians before it was stolen from them. The entire field might be a mass graveyard. Come on, let's go to the "smoking corner," I said.

We walked down to the first turn in the road. At night, you're not able to see much of anything without the aid of a light. There were no lights whatsoever anywhere on the road all the way to the house. Talking about graves earlier really gave one something to think about. Not that I'm suggesting the haunting of the Dandy house had anything to do with graves in the area, but there probably were random burial plots around the country side. Something else Debbie brought up during their conversations about two sisters who were into the occult many, many years ago: the Fox sisters. Supposedly, they traveled the area conjuring up spirits. They were best known for the "knockings" that were heard when they would hold séances. Eventually, when searching about information on the sisters, I found that they had admitted they created the

205

knockings by cracking their toe knuckles. Interesting, I thought.

"Feel brave enough to walk to the tree?" Tim asked.

"Sure, after you," I said. "Did someone offer you brave pills lately?" I asked.

"The road is wide enough, we'll walk together," Tim replied.

"Ah, not as brave as I thought." I said.

We walked to the tree and continued onto Wagner Hill Road to the spot most people parked their vehicles. It was very quiet tonight with the only sounds being the breeze stealing its way through the tall grass and the staccato sound of the crickets. Occasionally, we would hear a dog barking in the distance. Sound traveled a long way in the country but, when down at the Dandy house, you only had one side that was open to flat ground that led one's sight to any distance. We stayed around the corner of McMahon and Wagner for probably ten to fifteen minutes, then began the walk back to the house. We barely jumped when a rabbit scurried in front of us across McMahon road.

"Hey, we're getting better, huh?" Tim said.

We were almost to the driveway when we heard a car coming down Wagner Hill. It appeared to slow and eventually stopped. We stood waiting to see if we would spot the lights coming up the road, but instead, it began moving again and we could see it continuing on down Wagner Road. Probably someone stopping to take a nature break, I thought. We turned into the driveway and our flashlights went out—*both* of them! Of course, as was the custom, we began banging them against our hands to no avail. I listened, looked and *felt*. There was nothing. No voices, no movement, no *feeling*. We continued walking toward the car and I stopped and said, "Look, shit I think it's Phil," It appeared Phil was standing near the spring house, looking up at the girls' windows.

"I thought he was at work, there's no car here," Tim whispered.

"Yeah and I don't know why Phil would be standing out here. Whoever it is, it looks like Phil's stance and body type," I whispered back.

When we got around the side of the house and next to Tim's car, Phil, or whoever was gone. Obviously, he walked around the other side of the house and toward the front. I wasn't sure if we should go after him or not but he knew we were here, Tim's car was parked in the drive and Clara told us she was going to tell him we'd been coming up every night to keep people away.

"Come on. Let's go around front and see if he walked out there," I said to Tim.

We walked back to the front, around the other side and into the back yard. No Phil.

"What the hell?" I questioned.

Could he have walked out to the pond and, if so, why? Possibly, while we were walking to the front of the house, he simply went in the back door. I could understand the car not being there, he may have had a mechanical problem, but what would he be doing standing in the back yard looking at the house, not to mention, the only logical way to get to the house was up McMahon Road. He sure as hell wasn't going to walk through the fields! I was fairly sure now that it wasn't Phil, but who else would it be? The next question was, why did both of our flashlights go out at the same time and just before seeing (Phil)? Now, again with the thought it might have been a trespasser, we decided to go back to the car, cautiously.

"Keep your eyes open!" Tim whispered.

"No shit!" I replied.

We got into the car and kept our eyes on the back yard, the back door and the rear of the house. It didn't make sense. If it was Phil and he did have car trouble I'm sure he would have turned a light on either in the kitchen or upstairs. There was no doubt in my mind, he would have made it a point to wake Clara and tell her he had trouble, to *complain* to her that he had car trouble. From what I've seen and what Clara had said about him, he would have made a production of it. We waited for about twenty minutes and saw nothing. Another ten minutes went by. Tim and I probably sounded like teenage girls when both of our flashlights, sitting on the seat between us, suddenly came on.

"What—the—shit?" I exclaimed, as I tossed the flashlight to the floorboard. Tim repeated my sentiments and added a few choice expletives of his own. I expected Tim to say something more. He was probably waiting for me to say something but neither of us said a word for several minutes. There was a powerful energy around us, there was no question, but what? I had wondered, if Tim had tried to start his car when the flashlights were sitting on the seat, dark and useless, would the car's electrical system be just as dead? Would everything have been affected, including electrical items in the house, or was it just our flashlights? Answers to these and many other questions will be given on next weeks show, folks!

"Isn't this fun?" Tim asked. "Go knock on Mike's window and ask him, no *tell* him to see if his father is home."

"I'm not gonna wake him up! I'll call tomorrow and ask if he came home early." I said.

And if Phil hadn't come home early, then we either had an unwelcome guest on the property, or we had just met the newest member of the house's entities. I don't remember anyone mentioning an adult male as *someone* who'd been seen other than the boy Mike and the girls had spotted walking through their yard and did the disappearing act by the pond. The person we saw fit the description of Phil to a 'T' and not that of a blonde haired teen. We sat in silence for another twenty minutes when I had to get out for relief.

"No sense, in going one at a time, I need to go too," Tim said.

Without either of us suggesting, we both shone out lights over the entire back yard, hillside and side yard before exiting the car. Seeing nothing, not that that made a difference, we got out. I heard a 'thump' and Tim nearly yelling said, "Oh, son-of-a-bitch!"

My waterworks stopped in mid-steam as I nervously asked, "WHAT?!"

"I dropped the goddamn flashlight in my pee!" Tim quietly exclaimed.

Everyone in the house should have woke up from my laughing so loud. "In your *pee*, you afraid of offending the ghosts by saying piss?" I said, laughing uncontrollably now.

"Shut up, you asshole!" He exclaimed. "Now what am I going to do?"

"Don't bring it in the car, that's what you're gonna do. Take it to the pond and wash it off," I suggested.

"Yeah, let me run right over there, and while I'm at it, I'll ask the dizzy bitch to dry it with her flowing '90's dress for me too!" Tim snapped.

We certainly had our share of emotions while visiting the house every night. One minute I'm seeing someone disappear into thin air and the next I'm laughing so hard it causes my side to hurt so bad it felt like appendicitis.

"I'll go with you. Come on," I said. "I'll get some paper towels from the trunk."

I returned to the driver's door, reached in and took the keys from the ignition, opened the trunk and retrieved the towels. We walked toward the pond but when we got to the opposite side of the house I shone the light in that direction.

"What?!" Tim asked.

"Nothing, just looking," I said.

"Why the hell can't we just go in the kitchen and wash the light off?" Tim said.

"You nuts, that's their home! They hear enough doors opening and closing when there's no one there to help them— I'm not about to enter their kitchen unannounced," I said.

"Well, it would be easier and a hell of a lot closer," he insisted.

We got to the pond and Tim bent down to rinse his flashlight off. I was very apprehensive that my light would go out again and that was a thought I didn't need rolling around in my head.

"Hurry up, I said rinse it, not give it a bath!" I scolded.

"Shaddup and gimme the towels," Tim said.

I handed Tim the towels and he wiped the flashlight off. We began walking back toward the car when we heard what sounded like someone walking through the tall grass along the shore of the pond behind us. I quickly turned and scanned my light across the length of the pond pathway—there was nothing. When I turned back, Tim was already at the car and getting in but he entered the passenger side. As I started to laugh the sound came again. So did the *feeling*. I had turned to stone, I didn't turn around and I didn't run to the car, I stood frozen in place and suddenly I was blinded by Tim who was shining his light directly into my face. I prayed he wasn't, at any moment going to yell, "RUN" when the light trained on me found its beam reflecting off something I dared not imagine. Every hair on my body was a-prickle, every sense heightened to their limits. My mind told my feet to "do their stuff," but they were set in fast drying cement. Every imaginable scene from every ghost story I'd ever viewed replayed through my mind. It felt like I was drifting, being carried on the cool breeze that was at my back. Was it the breeze, or was it the tip of the Arctic freeze that slapped my face the night Phil took me on my first journey into this haunted land? As I stood there, the air began to get much cooler; cold, and the *feeling* began to intensify with lightning speed. I was expecting to hear a voice once again.

You know they're here too, don't you?

Oh baby, do I, and *right* here, right *now*. I wasn't alone, I knew that. There was a presence with me but the insurmountable feeling of fear was subsiding and a feeling of profound sadness overcame me. Was it sadness for myself because I was standing here like a rooted tree, because I wanted so badly to run my ass off to the safety of the car, or was I receiving a psychic connection from the presence that was nearby? I believed the latter because it was extremely strong. So was the initial feeling and the only feeling of my own I was aware of was my own dark fear. The air was cold—very cold—too damned cold for such a balmy evening.

"What the hell are you doing?" Tim yelled.

Tim's voice was like a sledge hammer, releasing my entire being from the cement it had been encased in. I remember saying aloud, "I'm here to help if you need it." As I began walking back to the car, I stopped when I was below Mary's window and shone my light at it. I saw nothing but curtains on the other side of the glass. Curtains that covered our world from the pain, sorrow, and possibly an ominous evil, destined to force a family from their home. I walked to the car and told Tim through the driver's side window that I stopped to listen, listen for any sound that may have been near the pond.

"You all right? What the hell were you doing standing out there?" He asked.

I didn't want Tim freaking on me so I didn't tell him the feelings I had experienced. There was no proof it was anything but my own fear and imagination working overtime.

"Nothing, I was just trying to imagine why anyone, you know, anyone who wasn't with us anymore, why they would be here. I mean, not just inside like you'd think when a house is supposedly haunted but why out here, by the tree and other places people have seen apparitions?" I said.

I explained to Tim how I felt and he was beginning to think I was acting the way Mike had in the field. I assured him that wasn't the case, that I had just felt strange. I didn't explain everything to him as it happened because, I know, it sounded absolutely insane but it felt very real; very believable. I chose my words carefully and explained to him something he would believe without looking at me like I should seriously consider checking myself in. When you talk to someone who is baring his soul to you, you listen with compassion and caring. In those brief moments that I stood near the pond, that was the sensation I had, as if someone were telling me something heart wrenching. There was no voice to listen to, no one telling me the horrible dilemma with which they were faced. It was a total feeling of sadness, the same emotional upset we have all felt at times with only a thought to bring it on. My newest question was: Are any of the family members or anyone else coming to this house having, even remotely, similar feelings? Did this mean I was a sensitive as Father Al had suggested and was it controllable, was there a way to, "dial in" to a particular frequency? When the time finally came and I had the chance to talk with Father Al for any length of time, I had forgotten some of the questions I wanted to ask because more important ones had come to mind.

Over the next few months, Tim and I, and sometimes I alone, continued to visit the house frequently. We didn't experience a "disturbance" with each subsequent visit but we were able to deal with it when we did. Therefore, I won't bore you with the visits when we were merely aimlessly walking the property or sitting in the car eating subs, which after a while became quite an expense! I had determined that from the weekend soon to come until the Dandys moved out, to spend as much time as possible to make an effort to understand why all of these disturbances were taking place and why I had been besieged with compelling feelings to do so.

We're now getting to the gist of the story which will lead you through some very disturbing times, from several isolated incidents within the house to Mike's horrible car accident. And thence to the visit the following spring from a world-renowned psychic attempting to aid Father Al in ridding the house of what Clara called, *The Umbrella Nights.*

CHAPTER XVII

It was a week before Labor Day, 1973. Debbie had already confirmed with Clara that we would surely be coming for a picnic on the holiday. Louie M. called to tell me he had a crew ready to get the back bar out of the Fountain on Tuesday. He was sure they'd be able to finish the work that day. I asked him to call me when they were finished so I could pick up the key and return it to the bank. I had spent numerous hours researching information on the paranormal at both Olean Public Library and Saint Bonaventure's Friedsman Memorial Library. I thought I would have better luck at Olean's library than I had the first time but there was only a smattering of information on the paranormal. Friedsman Memorial was another story. I found so much, it would have taken me years to digest the information. Naturally, one book is much like another, defining the different aspects of the paranormal. But that was okay, because I was finally understanding some of what I yearned to know. Saint Bonaventure is a Catholic University and I expected to find quite a lot on the subject and indeed, I had. I received several odd looks when I went to the information desk to be pointed in the right direction. I filled about 50 pages with information I had taken from some of the books I chose to flip through and wrote down the names of others I wanted to get the next time I visited. During one of my fact gathering visits, I called the Friary before leaving hoping that by some off-chance Father Al might be available. I was told he was in class. I'd already assumed that he would be since it was late in the morning. I left my name and home number and asked that they give him a message to call me at his earliest convenience. I had high hopes that he might call before I went to work.

Last night's episode near the pond really had me wired. I wanted to talk with Father Al so badly to see what he would make of it

I left Friedsman Library with my miles of written data, went home and called Clara. I wanted to be absolutely sure there would be no problem with my spending time at the house.

I didn't know then how much but it turned out to truly be a case of home away from home. When I called, Mike answered. Come to think of it, nearly every time I called he seemed to be the one to answer.

I talked with Clara for about ten minutes. She said she half expected me to seek permission to come to the house often. After all, Tim and I had been going up regularly for a some time. "What would be any different?" She asked during our conversation.

"Would it be possible to come in on occasion?" I asked.

"I'm sure it wouldn't be a problem. What are you going to do, just sit there?" She asked with a chuckle.

"Probably so," I felt stupid asking, "Can I come in and hang around?" I asked.

"Oh, what the hell, you'd be one more protecting the family from the every day drudgery of the ghosts. What does Debbie think of your coming up so often?" Clara asked.

"She says she understands why I do. She doesn't like talking about the house. I really believe it frightens her more than she lets on," I said.

"Yeah, I could tell. She seemed uneasy when Beth Ann was talking about the voices she hears outside her window. Okay, Paul, I need to get some stuff done around here. I'll talk to you later or see you sooner!" She said, again with her chuckle.

"Hang on, Clara, just a sec... did Phil come home early last night?" I asked.

"No, he came home his usual time, why?" She asked, a little uneasy.

"Tim and I went for a walk last night and, when we got to the driveway, We could have *sworn* Phil was out back looking up at the house. We walked back further but whoever was standing there disappeared. We walked around to the front of the house and didn't see anyone. I thought it was Phil and he went in the back door while we walking toward the front," I said.

This disturbed Clara as much as it did Tim and me. It's possible that it *had* been someone trespassing but where did they go? It was bothersome to Clara because this meant, as I stated earlier, that this a different entity from the others that had been seen.

We hung up and I went to the kitchen table to start reading. I had about three hours before Debbie arrived home from work. I spent the rest of the afternoon reading prior to preparing dinner. I was startled when the phone rang. I had hoped it was Father Al but it was Clara. She related a strange incident that had happened earlier today. Every alarm clock in the house had gone off at the same time. I asked if they were set for the time they had gone off and she informed me that not one of them was set except hers which was the usual 7 a.m.

"Is there any significance to the time they went off?" I asked.

"None that I'm aware of. What's more puzzling is Mary's alarm went off too and her clock hasn't worked for some time," Clara replied.

She said they'd gone off at 1 p.m.. I jotted this down in a notebook. A commonplace procedure for me since the night Tim and I heard the woman's voice. In the beginning, I had just written down what had happened but, after the incident with the voice, I started writing down dates and times as well. Maybe there would be a pattern with the incidents which occurred at the house that would help with the investigation. Whether a pattern was developing or not, I thought it was a good idea to keep track. She also told me there was another incident of cold air last night. It blew the back door open. Is cold air bad and warm air good, I wondered? I explained what had happened the night before when Tim and I went to the pond. I believe if Tim hadn't said something, I wouldn't have moved and I would have completely felt the evil side of this phenomena that I wholly believed was present. In the material I had been reading, case studies determined that oftentimes there was a malevolent presence at work where many different manifestations were recorded. The incident I experienced near the pond made me feel fear, not frightened by the thought of a spirit being present, but a deep, gut wrenching feeling of fear that changed to sadness. I believe this was the result of two separate psychic energies or entities. If only the sophisticated

215

instruments of today were available during the investigation of the Dandy house.

Tim had called during our dinner and said he might not be available tonight. He said he started feeling poorly when he arrived at work but he would let me know if he began feeling better. I read for quite a spell while Debbie watched TV. It was 10:15 p.m.. We both woke with a start when the phone rang. It was Tim. He said he would be over at the usual time but I told him I would walk up to the shop. It was very hot in the apartment, as if the heat had been turned on. I saw that the living room window was open and the curtains were billowing from the breeze coming in so why the intense heat? Debbie walked into the kitchen and asked if I had planned on baking something. I didn't know if I had told her I was going to and forgot, or if she was suggesting I was baking now. Obviously, I was looking at her quizzically because she said very sternly, "You left the oven on and the door open!"

I hadn't touched the oven. I had no reason to. I had gone out to get our dinner.

"Not me," I told her.

"Well then who, the boogeyman?" she said, trying to be funny.

Oh, the thoughts that were conjured up when she said *that*! No, I didn't believe there were spirits turning on the oven so wipe that thought from your mind. But I was miffed, I had no idea how the oven happened to be on. She blamed it on my current forgetfulness and said she was going to get ready for bed. I used the bathroom while she changed. I went in to say goodnight when I finished. "Be careful tonight, I had a bad dream," she said.

"Dreams don't mean anything. They're just left over thoughts or something," I said.

"Oh, well, I had a leftover thought of you having an accident?" She said.

"Maybe you want me to!" I said waiting to get a smack; I did.

We said goodnight and I walked into the living room.

"Make sure you have your keys. I noticed them on the oven you forgot to turn off." She yelled from the bedroom.

"I didn't turn it ON!" I yelled in return. *I didn't.*

Walking to the sub shop, I thought very hard about it. "I—Did—Not turn it on," I said quietly to the cracks in the sidewalk. I was relieved that she wanted pizza tonight. I didn't want to cook. I had no reason to turn the oven on, period! My pizza had just come out when I got to Warner's and I NEVER reheat pizza *She* must have! It didn't matter. The oven was off and I was at the sub shop.

"Sub tonight?" Tim asked.

"Nope, not hungry, maybe some pretzels though," I said, as I pulled a pack from the rack.

"Grab me a bag of green onion and whatever for Mike," Tim said.

"One g'onion and one regular coming up," I said.

Tim had finished his chores and we walked out less than a minute after I walked in.

As we were driving to the house, Tim asked what I really felt last night. I had to tell him; if he thought I was a nutcase that was fine. We had to be honest with one another, it wouldn't be right any other way, and we were spending a lot of time together at the house.

"I understand the sad feeling you had. I can relate to that. I think anyone could. But, how did you *get* the feeling, especially the way you explained the fear? Were you afraid and then suddenly sad, or... what the hell am I trying to ask here....did....."

"I don't know, Tim," I interrupted. "No, I wasn't feeling sad at all, I felt the sadness from; whoever—*them*—the ones at the house or at least one of them anyhow. No, I felt the sadness from one and fear from another, I assume. It was kinda like listening to a country station, then flipping to a rock station."

"The Dandys? How could you feel how they're feeling?" Tim asked.

"Not the Dandys! Come on, you know what I mean," I said.

I needed Father Al to explain this stuff to me, it was frustrating. I wanted to know how I was able to pick up emotions from *them.* I can't pick up on Tim's feeling or Debbie's. If I was going to pick up anyone's, it should have been Debbie's. Sure, you can always tell when someone is upset but they're tangible feelings. You can see their expressions, their body language. That's a sense, not a *feeling*. How can one be a sensitive, if that's what we're talking about here, with the spirit world, but not with that of the living? The material I had been reading didn't explain any of this. Surely, I wasn't reading the proper material that would enlighten me with what I'm experiencing.

We pulled into the driveway, as we had so many other nights.

"I'm gonna put a time clock at the end of the driveway so we can keep track of our hours," I said.

"What, and charge them?" Tim asked.

"Yes, Tim, so we can charge them. It was a joke." I said, punching his arm.

"Ouch, I know. So, did you ask anyone what time did Phil get home last night?" Tim asked.

"You mean this morning? It's getting foggy," I said.

"Oh, so you're telling me it wasn't him last night?" Tim asked.

"Nope, probably the guy from the corner with the pipe," I said.

"I wonder who it really was. It could have been someone from one of the other camps who heard about the house and came down to snoop," Tim said.

"Oh yeah, I'm sure. Just wandering around, takin' in the sights. With no flashlight! I'm sure he had great eyesight and didn't need a light like the rest of us," I said.

"Look—son of a bitch!" I said.

There was already a layer of fog low to the ground when we pulled in but it was building rapidly over the pond. There was something more interesting tonight: the column of fog we had seen had brought a "fog friend." There were two columns and they were drifting in our direction.

"Headlights!" I quietly exclaimed.

Tim was so excited in getting them turned on, he hit the horn and we both nearly flipped over the seat. The sound of the horn didn't phase the columns in the least but the car was at an angle so the headlights weren't directly on them. Our flashlights were bright enough but the headlights would have filled the area much better.

"I wanna walk over there, Tim," I said.

"Go ahead, be my guest," he replied.

One column had moved to the opposite end and up toward the ridge facing the camp above the Dandys' home. Something extremely interesting: the column wasn't shrouded by the fog cloud. It was alone! The back door opened and Mike appeared.

"Shine your light to the pond, Mike!" Tim yelled.

He really didn't need to. Tim and I had both our lights trained on the column that was about half way the distance of the pond from the closest end to us.

"Holy shit!" He said as he walked side-step toward the car, keeping his eyes directed toward the pond.

"Ya wanna, Mike?" I said after I had gotten out of the car.

"Sure, Tim? Come on," Mike said.

"Ohhhhhhhh, shit, alright," Tim said as he slowly got out. "No running, and we stay *close* to each other, remember our rules" I said.

As we approached the pond, the column was still drifting toward the spot the other had gone, which wasn't visible from our vantage point. We were still forty or fifty feet from it as it continued to move upward toward the ridge. There was no way for us to walk in that direction. There was too much brush to make our way through. It would have been tough in the daylight, I wouldn't have dared to try it at night. This was a remarkable sight; there is no possible way that we were observing natural atmospheric conditions. There was no changing my mind as to what we had witnessed, unless one day I happened to be watching the weather forecast and the weatherman gives a report such as: *"Tonight the low will be hovering around 55 with a few lingering showers. Patchy fog will develop, so let's be careful on that morning commute, especially around those random columns of fog that so often materialize for no apparent reason."* To this day, those visions seen that night aren't the least bit "foggy" in my memory.

We didn't move from the shore of the pond for ten to fifteen minutes, standing quietly scanning the hillside hoping for another glimpse. Mike suggested we go around the side of

219

the house to the front. We quietly walked past Beth Ann's window and walked to the front yard .

"What are we doing out here?" Tim asked.

"I'm curious. Beth Ann has been hearing voices outside her window and I thought maybe what we just saw might be the source," Mike said.

"Ah, you mean our 'fogmen'"? I said jokingly.

"Or fogwomen. Beth Ann usually hears a woman's voice," Mike said.

I was planning to tell Clara that it was possible that some nights Beth Ann was hearing our voices outside but when Mike told us she usually heard a woman's voice, it ruled out our nightly conversations. I believe I did tell her at one point but it still didn't make Beth Ann feel any better. While we were standing just around the corner from Beth Ann's room in the front yard, a soft glow of light appeared on the same side of the house. It had been the light in Clara's bedroom illuminating to the side yard from the front. I had hoped we didn't disturb her. We were the last ones who needed to deprive her of her sleep. We left the front and walked around the driveway side of the house, back by the car. The kitchen light was on and Mike went in to see if everything was all right.

"Grab my Mountain Dew, would ya, Tim?" I asked as he opened the door to get himself a Pepsi.

Mike returned outside and told us that the burners on the stove were on full blast. He also said his mom wanted him to come back inside.

"She's stressed. I know she tries to joke about some of the things going on but I know it's tearing her up inside. Dad hates leaving us at night in case something really bad were to happen, and I know mom doesn't want to see him go. I'm going in. Be careful out here. If you need anything, rap on my window," Mike said.

"Okay, Mike, thanks. Tell your mom we're sorry about all of this and if she's angry in any way that you've been coming out, tell her it was my idea," I said.

"I don't think she mad at all, just tired of everything. Actually, I believe she's happy you guys come up. For a few days it was quieter in the house and we all figured it was because you were outside. Also, if the crowds came out like they had been, they'd see you and think twice about sticking around. I'll see ya," he said as he went inside.

"The burners were on full blast?!" Tim exclaimed. "That could be dangerous as hell! Assholes!"

When Tim said, "assholes," he turned from facing me and directed it toward the pond. It was obvious who he had directed the comment to. That was dangerous, very dangerous to have the burners on. What if someone absent-mindedly set something on one of the burners and that were to happen? We all know what the outcome would be, and the only way out from upstairs is through a window. This was unquestionably the evil side of their troubles in the house. That's not the way a non-malevolent energy would try and attract someone's attention. Let's not forget the incident with the chess set and Battle Ship game in Mike's room, or the three burns members of the family found on their bodies, or the letter opener in Mary's picture. I began to fear there was something worse that would happen and soon. Tim and I decided it was time to have a seat so we returned to the car. It was still foggy but it wasn't as dense in the yard as by the pond. I was panning the pond area and caught something that appeared to glint in the light. I panned back in the direction where I had seen it and it was there again. It wasn't something that was glinting, like a piece of shiny metal. There were two eyes looking directly into the light.

"Cat?" Pondered Tim.

"Probably, or some other small animal," I said.

The eyes didn't move. We were sure it was an animal but they didn't have the glow that most animals' eyes have. All the same, we dismissed it as simply a night forager looking for a meal.

There was an interesting side to all of this, almost enjoyable. We were getting a first hand experience with what apparently was a genuine haunting but we were visitors who could come and go as we pleased. The Dandys were in this for the duration or until they couldn't take it anymore. When Clara described how they had fallen in love with the house with its quiet country setting, and how they had made the necessary repairs to create the home-sweet-home they'd always wanted, it tugged at my heart to see what had happened to her and her family. To many not familiar with the Dandys, it was easy to tease and make jokes, or to ridicule and call them names. They weren't guilty of anything, they didn't ask to be thrown into a paranormal frenzy, to have their stress levels go off the charts. It wasn't clear as to why these manifestations began when they did or why the Dandy family was the first to experience them. Were they? One conversation that came up sometime near the end of 1973 troubles me and I had never made it a point to clarify it with Father Al before his passing. I am certain that Father Al had mentioned that he had been contacted by another priest from the Buffalo, New York area after the story was published in the Buffalo papers. The priest informed Father Al that he had been summoned to the exact same property to deal with identical problems many years prior. There was a letter written to the Olean Times Herald September 6, 1973, by one of the former McMahon family members in protest to these allegations which were taking place at their beloved homestead. When I read the letter I was angered and had attempted to contact this person with no success. I found out years later than Father Al had corresponded with this member of the McMahon family, as well as her sister. I offer you the second of two letters written to and published by The Olean Times Herald September 6, 1973. This letter was signed by Mrs. Elizabeth McMahon Rowley of Olean, NY.

I quote:

"Your various articles in the Times have been talked over from mill to meeting, even to the point of disgust, with erratic statements being printed without proof to substantiate them. My dear mother, deceased not quite a year, owned the large farm until about four years ago, rounding out over a century in the McMahon family. The talk of 'ghosts' has done irreparable harm to many little children who now refuse to go to bed alone at night. I believe my beloved former home in the Haskell Flats has been desecrated. Please print my outraged sentiments to your 'haunted house' stories.

Meanwhile, the present owners continue claiming the presence of unearthly spirits while awaiting a financial offer which will help them sell the place."

If those who had said all the horrible things about the family had talked with them, observed how their youngest daughter reacted to the slightest noise and went running to her mother for protection, were to experience what we had in such a short period of time, they would probably say, "shame on us." And if they didn't possess such emotions as guilt, compassion or caring, then I will say it for them, "Shame on you." As time went on, it was apparent how this was affecting every member of the family. They had no intention of selling their home. They put everything into that house and I don't mean just financially. They put their blood, sweat and love into it. They searched for a very long time before finding what they thought was their dream home. As for finances, there was a great deal of that went into the house as well. The McMahons' beloved home may have been loved by them but it certainly wasn't apparent when it was purchased. It took a lot of TLC and it had been given that and more when the Dandys moved in. I felt it so unfair for this family to be judged as harshly as they had—they were the victims, not the criminals. It was a shame more of those who ridiculed the family hadn't gotten to know them. I guarantee you if they had, they would have changed their attitudes.

There hadn't been any more activity prior to our leaving that night. Some nights I would feel totally drained after leaving the property. I'd been sleeping better than I had when I was still tending to the Fountain and didn't understand why I felt like I had run a marathon. Not only that, but I sometimes felt a strange sensation when leaving, as though I shouldn't, or even more strongly, that I mustn't leave. I didn't know what the hell that feeling was or why it came so often. Actually, I looked forward to getting home and going to bed so it wasn't a conscious thought by any means. It was an emotion that made me feel very restless, unsettled. When Mike told us the burners of the stove had been on, I thought about the oven at home. I didn't mention it to anyone and didn't for some weeks until something else happened. I found it very hard to correlate the oven with the happenings at the Dandy house, but stranger things have happened involving the paranormal.

When Tim dropped me off he reminded me that we switched shifts. Not that I forgot but it was good he told me just the same. When I got inside, I walked over to the oven and tried to remember if I *had* turned it on. I didn't; I-did-not-turn-it-on; period. I used the restroom, threw off my clothes and fell into bed. I glanced at the clock. It was 4:25. That was the last thing I remember. I didn't wake until 2:00 that afternoon when I heard the phone ringing. It was Father Al.

CHAPTER XVIII

"Hello, Father, thanks for returning my call," I said.

"Hello, Paul. Firstly, how is the car? Did the mechanics find your troubles?" Father asked.

"No, Father, I believe you did that night. They went completely over everything and couldn't find a thing wrong with it. They even consulted with the dealer hoping they had an idea. They were baffled, Father," I said.

"I see, I see. Well, Clara informs me that you and a friend have had quite a time outside the house: voices, apparitions and shapes in the fog. Explain some of this to me if you will," Father said.

I told him everything and he listened intently with an occasional, "uh huh, uh huh" response as I spoke. I explained to him all of the different feelings I'd been having, how one minute I would have one sensation and moments later it would change. He asked me what I thought they meant to me but I found it difficult to describe it. Part of the response he offered me was surprising and somewhat startling.

"Paul, some people produce psychic energy and it's very likely you are one of these gifted people. It's not something to be frightened of I assure you, but it's very difficult for some to deal with in the logical sense. I will explain it to you the same as I have with others who have realized they were gifted. It could be a shock, so I trust you will have the faith to understand that it's okay, okay?" Father asked.

I was very apprehensive in what he had to say next, and frankly, I nearly asked him *not* to explain it to me. "All right, Father, I guess I'm ready. I guess if I really want to understand, I'd like to hear it from you," I said.

He had a great laugh and offered it to me before saying, "Some spirits will use those who emit or produce psychic energy to manifest themselves, not necessarily directly to the person all the time, but that energy can be powerful enough for manifestation to occur within an area. I believe that Laura is very gifted and poltergeist activity is generally centered around a child of puberty age, more often with a girl than a boy. There

225

are different forms or levels or psychic energy, and, I believe, since it appears that when you are at the house there is more activity, that you are also producing these energies," he said, pausing. He went on after a few seconds, "Oddly enough, this is why known psychics are sometimes brought in to assist the police in murder cases. It's not just the fact they are known for being psychic but they are utilized for their psychic energy hopefully to allow them to pick up the residual energy of the murdered person to gather clues. Fascinating, isn't it?" Father said.

"Father, are you saying I'm psychic?" I asked.

"To a degree, Paul, we all are. Yes, yes, and I believe there is so much we as teachers, doctors, and investigators of the paranormal can learn from these untapped powers. The mind is very powerful and I am certain that our soul, our 'psyche' has much more potential than our minds," he said.

"So, it's okay for me to have these feelings, they're not going to drive me insane or anything?" I asked.

That quiet little laugh, "No, no, oh my no, not at all. It can be frightening but I don't think I have to tell you this," he said.

"But why haven't I picked up energy other places? Surely the Dandy house isn't the only place where spirits are," I said.

"There was already an abundance of paranormal activity at the Dandy house before you arrived. You thrust yourself into the middle of everything and in doing so, and being fearful, you opened the door, if you will, of your own energies—allowing, sharing these energies with those already present and active at the house. There are no perfect answers, Paul, one can only summarize given the information and facts along with knowledge learned from other paranormal cases. Another thing I'd like to add—the more you're subjected to psychic energy, the stronger these feelings you are experiencing are going to become and you will begin to pick up energies of others as well. At times, you'll get little nuances from people around you, and during someone's emotional upset, it will be very strong. You had mentioned growing up that you experienced, as you call them, "duckies," that forewarned you of things, am I correct?" He asked.

Laughing, I said, "Goosies, Father, I call them goosies."

"Oh my, well, either way, they're a sort of fowl, yes." He said, offering his own laughter. "Well, these, "goosies" are most likely energies you're picking up from individuals or the surroundings," he explained.

He asked me if I was understanding what he was telling me before continuing and I told him that I was.

"My best advice to you is to always use caution, be mentally strong and always keep your faith above all. *Listen* to the feelings you receive, mentally tune your mind to them and in time, you will find that it's very possible, even likely, if you possess and release strong energies, that you may fully understand what these feelings represent. When a feeling comes to you, when you are confronted with it suddenly, it is a sharing of energy from both you and another. And as I said, this isn't only with those who become earthbound, this energy can be shared by the living as well. If you are prepared mentally, attempt not to consciously assume what is being sent psychically, but rather listen, not with your ears, but rather with your mind. Your psyche is fragile when truly dealing with these energies and it can be very demanding, both physically and mentally, draining you. I hope this gives you some insight to the sensitivities of the human spirit and trust I've not frightened you too badly," he said.

Father's chuckle at the end of his lecture on the abridged version of psychic phenomena kept my mind from being overcome with what he had explained to me. I didn't know if I felt better understanding what these feelings may have meant as explained by Father Al, or if I'd have been better off having the sensations and wondering why I had them. Either way, I was given something to think about. One concern I had—was I going to create more havoc by going to the house?

Debbie called shortly after Father and I ended our conversation. She asked whether I minded if she went to dinner with her brother. Of course I didn't and reminded her I had practice tonight. I told her about my conversation with Father Al and she was shocked by his opinion. She asked if I was going to the house tonight but she already knew the answer. I told her I would see her in the morning and that Clara said if there were ever a problem not to hesitate to call when I was at

227

the house. I read a little more then rooted around the kitchen to find something for dinner. I decided on a couple of slices of cold pizza, and no, I wasn't going to reheat it, I never did.

"I don't know how you happened to be on yesterday but I didn't touch you," I said to the oven as if I were scolding it.

I read even more while eating, and left the house around 6:15. I wanted to see how Tim was doing at the shop before going to practice which started at 7:00. It had been slow Tim said. That allowed him to get all of the prep work for the next day finished within the first hour of work. I explained what Father Al had discussed with me. Tim wasn't nearly as shocked as Debbie but he said from now on, if something happens that's really frightening, he's going to blame me.

"You remember that when the time comes and I have to save your butt. I'll be back after practice. I'll take a half of a meatball tonight, I didn't have much for dinner," I said.

"Parmesan?" Tim asked.

"Dumb question," I said as I was walking out.

We accomplished what we had set out for at practice that night although my mind had been elsewhere during most of the session. I had a feeling of apprehension, I didn't know if it were due to my conversation with Father Al that afternoon but I'm sure it was most likely part of the reason. We finished at 9:00 and I decided to go back to the sub shop early to help Tim clean up. I walked in about 9:15 but Tim wasn't inside. I thought I'd seen him standing outside when I was driving down the street. I walked around the counter to see if he was outside having a smoke break and, just as I rounded the corner, he walked in with his head covered in an aluminum, cone-shaped hat. He was nonchalant, went about picking up the counter and saying nothing. He was baiting me and I absolutely refused to say anything about his cone head and I knew my ignoring him was eating at his very core. I asked him if it had been busy. He told me it was fairly steady for a while then slowed down and he had the time to get everything done with only the mopping and cleaning of the counters left. I couldn't let him down, he looked as if he worked diligently on his new head attire.

"That's not going to help, everyone knows you have a pointed head," I said.

"It'll be your head now, bucko. If you're sending out energy and the spooks use it to make themselves visible, then I'll wear this so I won't get any residual effect from it, just like superman uses lead," he said.

"The lead shields superman from kryptonite doesn't it?" I asked.

"Well, if it's lead that works on kryptonite then maybe aluminum will guard against psychic energy," Tim said.

Two women who were chattering about Bingo walked in. Tim, with no hesitation walked to the counter and asked what he could get for them. They both gave him their order, never taking their eyes off his noggin. He walked to the back counter to prepare their subs as one women whispered to her friend. He wrapped their subs, took them to the front and the women paid. They turned to leave when one of them looked back and asked, "Sir, why do you have aluminum on your head?"

Tim explained that he was involved in a scientific study involving evil spirits to find out whether or not they can be effectively warded off with aluminum shielding. I believe one of the women said something about marijuana when they walked out the door.

"I'll mop the floor and, if you want, I'll clean off the counters so you can take the necessary nap you obviously need," I said.

"You mop, I'll get the counters," Tim said.

One never knew what might be rattling around in the head of Tim C. He might have been a nut but he was as sincere a friend as anyone could be graced with. I really don't know what he meant by, "tampering with his brakes."

Tim threw our subs in a bag with some chips as I grabbed three Dew's, three Pepsi's from the cooler, and my Polaroid from under the counter. We double checked everything and walked out. Tim left his space-capsule shaped tin hat in the window nook.

"You weren't wearing that thing all night were you?" I asked as we walked to the car.

"No, you said you'd be done around 9:00 so I kept an eye out for you. When I saw you coming, I came back inside and put my hat on," Tim said.

"I figured as much," I muttered.

We drove to the house but I asked Tim to continue on Wagner instead of turning onto McMahon. "Where we going?" Tim asked.

"I want to go to the end of their property near the tree line across from Wagner. I believe there's some connection to the way Mike was acting the other night and that area. I don't really know what, Tim, but there is something out there. It's kinda ridiculous trying to find anything at night but I just want check the property along the area," I said.

"Okay, are gonna walk the field?" Tim asked

"No, I just want to go out and stand there a minute or two," I said.

When we were across from the end of the Dandys' property we stopped and I got out while Tim stayed in the car.

"I shoulda brought my hat, you know," he said.

I walked to the edge of the road, looked across the field and in the direction of the house. I knew there was something about this area. I could feel it the night we all walked out here and I felt it again when we came up in the afternoon. But what was it? What was I feeling? For some strange reason, I believed the person I mistook for Phil and this area have something in common but I just couldn't figure it out. I had been outside walking up and down Wagner Road for probably five minutes when Tim asked me to return to the car.

I felt silly in the sense that I had no idea what I had been trying to accomplish walking the edge of the road and feeling for something that I didn't know I was feeling for. But I was certain that there was something important involving the tree line area of their property. I got back in the car and we drove to the house. There were no lights on in the house but there was a glow coming from the kitchen window. The burners? We both got out and walked to the back door. Indeed, the burners of the stove were on and must have been on for some time because they were bright. The door was locked so I went around to Mike's window and tapped quite hard. Mike was at the window moments later and I informed him of the burners. He left the window and we returned to the back door. By the time we arrived, he'd already opened it.

"I don't believe this shit! Last night and again all day today mom said, and now tonight too," Mike said.

"Unplug that damned stove before you guys go to bed." Tim said.

Clara called down to Mike to ask if everything was okay. He told her Tim and I had asked for a flashlight. Of course this wasn't the truth but we had taken care of the issue and there was no need to worry his mom any further. Apparently she went back to bed because she didn't come down and we were relieved she hadn't. The stove incident was certainly getting out of hand and it wasn't something to take lightly. Spirits, ghosts or whatever, this had to stop before a tragic accident were to occur. Obviously, Clara had taken extreme precautions making sure there was nothing flammable within the proximity of the stovetop since this had been happening all too often recently. Mike thanked us and we went back outside. Since I only had two slices of pizza for dinner, I decided to eat my sub now and instead of sitting in the car, I ate at the picnic table. Tim retrieved his dinner and joined me.

"Originally, there was a barn where the pond is now," I said to Tim.

"How long as the pond been there?" Tim asked.

"I don't know. I guess the McMahon farm was really big at one time. Again, I forgot to ask Clara about the absence of other houses on this road. There's some kind of foundation on the other side of the road across from the tree. At least I think it's a foundation," I said.

"When we finish eating, we can drive down and take a look," Tim suggested.

"Sure," I said, feeling just a bit uncertain suddenly.

I went back to the car to get my drink. When I returned, Tim was shining his light toward the pond. Our night prowling eyes were back but now that we were out of the car and had a better view straight to the pond. We realized there was no cover, no tall grass for the animal to hide in.

"Okay, I see eyes, but where is the varmint itself?" Tim asked.

The feeling was not unlike the one I had the night I had become a statue on my way back from the pond. It was difficult to remove the fear of uncertainty from what I was sure was the psychic energy I was feeling. Receiving an explanation regarding all of this from Father Al was wonderful but dealing with it was another matter all together. There seems to be an absence of logic surrounding the paranormal, because if this were a sort of manifestation we were observing, where is the rest of the materialization? Are we only permitted to see parts of an entity? Senseless. For obvious reasons, we returned to the car.

"Come on, what the hell?" Tim whined. "This isn't making any sense, it's stupid."

"I agree, and I just thought of something," I said getting out of the car.

"What are you doing?" Tim asked while I was walking toward the back door of the house.

"There's a lantern inside the back door. I'm going to get it and place it on the ground where those damned eyes are. Maybe we'll get a better look at it and see what kind of animal it is," I said.

I took the lantern off the hook it had been hanging on and walked toward the pond and the eyes. They did exactly what I expected them to do, disappear. "Little shit," I muttered. I lit the lantern and placed it on the ground approximately where we saw the eyes. I walked back to the car and no sooner did I sit down, the eyes were back.

"You gotta be goddamn kidding me, take a picture!" Tim said impatiently.

"Come on, let's walk out there again," I suggested.

Surprisingly, and without hesitation, Tim walked with me. I took a picture before we got all the way out, but the only thing that showed up in the photo was the lantern. It was too bright. We were maybe fifteen to twenty feet from our little friend when he disappeared again. But the eyes didn't *move away*, they just did what so many manifestations do, they were simply gone, as if the animal closed its eyes.

"You son-of-a-bitch!" Tim exclaimed angrily.

"We're not alone, Tim. Now, don't go running off. Just stay here....please. It's not a negative feeling, but I believe we've been joined by someone," I said.

I feel helpless trying to explain this to you because this was very unique to me. One day, I'm closing my business because of an unfortunate fire and soon after I become a paranormal investigator. It felt as absurd to me then as it may sound to you now but it was happening. As time went on, my predictions became ever so much more accurate. Not only when Tim and I were "on patrol" but in many instances when the house was full of people. I'd announce a warning, a premonition, or something to be wary of and my caution would be warranted. I took another picture toward the far end of the pond and when it developed, we got a picture of just that, the far end of the pond.

"Nice picture. So, who's with us, the fogmen?" Tim whispered.

I laughed at the thought that he could make the situation light hearted.

"There isn't any fog. But I think there's more than one *person* very close. Let's just walk back to the car *slowly* and see what's next," I said.

"What do you mean, what's next?" He said as we began walking, almost tip toeing.

"I don't know what I'm feeling. It feels okay but then again, it feels bad. I wish there were a code that came with these feelings so I'd know what was what or who was who," I explained.

I wasn't always perceptive in distinguishing good from evil but I was becoming very accurate predicting something at hand psychically. It was extremely disturbing because, although I had become very interested and the excitement of this newfound "gift" was mentally stimulating to say the least, it tormented my thoughts. The emotion was like that of a crack in a dam holding back a swollen reservoir. The turbulent waters became so strong against the dam's face until it eventually crumbled, spilling the water with such force that it devastated everything in its path. I feared that my own reason would crumble from this rush of psychic energy. I had asked Father Al if I would go insane, although I don't believe I actually meant insane but, nonetheless, the feelings were so powerful I was concerned what long term effects they might have. If it were to get to the point of being too difficult to cope, I would have just stopped going to the house but with the help of Father Al and a tremendous amount of studying, I was able to control the amount of energy I could withstand. To this day, over 35 years later, I still don't know how.

When we got back to the car we looked back to the pond. The lantern was still burning but there were no bodiless eyes looking in our direction. I had to believe it was an animal, they were so near the ground and really, what other explanation could there have been? Not *everything* had to be related to the paranormal at a haunted house. The feeling remained even after we sat in the car. I tried to *listen* to the feeling, as Father Al explained, but it wasn't speaking. I had absolutely no idea what I was listening *for.* We sat expecting to see the return of our nocturnal visitor but it didn't come back. I walked back to the pond and picked up the lantern. There was a great deal of energy in this area but I, being a "novice" sensitive wasn't able to tell the virtuous from the malevolent. What seemed quite thought-provoking about this whole, give energy-take energy deal, was the idea that the longer you're subjected to it as Father Al stated, the more it appears you really become a sort of paranormal catalyst. I half wanted to simply stand at the far end of the pond, to offer my energy to see what results would come of it but this was a case where the half that didn't wish to be the guinea pig declined the idea. I walked back to the car and placed the lantern on the ground allowing it to cool before returning it to the entrance of the house.

"Ready to drive down and see if what we were talking about is a foundation?" Tim asked.

"Yup, go ahead," I said.

"You all right?" Tim asked.

"I guess so. I just wish I was better at figuring out what it is I'm supposed to be receiving. It's there, it's strong, very strong at times but I can't understand how to interpret. It's so damned frustrating! It's like listening to a conversation of a distant radio station with a weak signal. You hear bits of the conversation as the signal fades in and out as you attempt to put together a coherent message," I explained.

"Your antenna needs work. Maybe you oughta wear my 'hat,' It might work as an antenna for you and a shield for me!" Tim said, with one second of laughter.

"You're an idiot, an aluminum hat creating, missing shoe, class A, idiot!" I said.

"But I can be the life of the party. You said that yourself," Tim said with a smirk.

"I take it back. Forget the fuckin' frogs in science class. You should be the one dissected and studied. I'm sure you wouldn't jump out of water that gradually got hotter either," I said.

Checking the side of the road across from the hanging tree, it appeared that there were the remains of a small foundation. It wasn't as expansive at that of a house but all the same, something once stood at the corner of McMahon and Wagner Roads. While walking the area, we heard singing and it excited us both as it may have been the Gregorian that have been heard several times. The voices didn't linger on the breeze more than a few seconds so neither of us could really be sure. I don't believe it was. I somewhat recognized the melody and it didn't sound like what had been described to me by Clara and someone else from the vicinity. We hung around the hanging tree (no pun intended!) for about fifteen minutes then returned to the house. While the two of us paced back and forth hoping to catch another rendition, I told Tim it was probably a good idea to check with Hinsdale's historian. As mentioned before, records were so incomplete and scarce for small town America, that it could be assumed I wouldn't be overjoyed with what I would learn of the area. The county seat, Little Valley, New York, would surely be my best bet to search for information on land deeds. They also had miles of maps of the area from as far back as the late 1700's. Hopefully, they would have better compiled records for the little township of Hinsdale.

It had been quiet; no sounds, no apparitions, nothing to stir the psychic nerve, so we drove back to the house. Laura's bedroom light was on when we pulled into the driveway. Was something the matter? Surely if there had been, Clara would have summoned us inside unless a disturbance occurred shortly after we drove down the road. Tim suggested I check with

Mike but his light was off and Laura may have just gotten up to use the bathroom. I listened, but there was nothing. Maybe energy had to be present for me to feel anything. Perhaps I couldn't just perk my "psychic" ears and hear something. I agreed on the latter. A few minutes passed and the light in Laura's room went out. I got out of the car, picked up the lantern and returned it to its hook in the back entry. When I returned to the car, I told Tim it was time to go. He thought I was upset the way I stated it and, in a way, I may have been. Nothing else was going to occur that night, at least not outside, and I was sure of that. This will sound off the wall, but when I walked across the yard to return the lantern, I had the strangest sensation that *they* were regrouping; gathering together to combine their energies and wait to confront the Dandy house in force. I did not want that to happen but many times that was exactly what *did* happen. There were small thunderstorms that would come through and pass in minutes. Then there were massive storms that stalled overhead with their torrential rains and thunderous skies filled with the most spectacular displays of high powered energy. Those nights had happened at the Dandy house in the past and, with the way the energy had been sporadic this past week, and what I felt that night, I believed there was going to be a series of high energy nights to come; very soon. Clara was aware of it as well. I was just a guy who was interested in psychic phenomena and now I found myself in the middle of what was going to truly be "Hell on Earth."

CHAPTER XIX

I woke the next morning about 11:30, sat up in bed and was soaked. I knew we were supposed to have an unseasonably warm day today but it was hotter than hell in the apartment. I walked to the window and before I got to it I could see that it was open. The breeze coming in was certainly cooler than the air in the apartment but it wasn't what was making the apartment so torrid. I left the bedroom to use the bathroom when I noticed the oven door open. Yes, it was on, and the first thing I thought was Debbie was playing a prank on me. After going to the bathroom, I called B.O.C.E.S. and waited for her to come to the phone. She swore she didn't do it, that it would be silly to waste the gas for such a stupid joke. I told her I'd see her this afternoon and hung up. I was angry. I didn't and wouldn't believe it had a damned thing to do with the Dandy house nor was I ever convinced it had. I thought there had to be a reasonable explanation—oh gee, now I sounded like Phil but there had to be; there *must* be. I called Saint Bonaventure and left word for Father Al to please call me ASAP. I couldn't believe how pissed I was. If there was any remote chance this was somehow connected with the Dandys it was going to stop and stop NOW! This was my house and there was no goddamn way anyone or *anyone* was going to intrude. I sat down at the kitchen table and with no help from the heat of the kitchen, felt my blood boiling. Father Al was the expert and I couldn't even accept his word in the beginning when he said, "you can bring *them* home with you." I got up from the table and took a long, cool shower; it didn't help. I didn't even get dressed before returning to the kitchen. I poured a bowl of cereal, added milk and began eating; standing in the middle of the room. When I finished, I put the bowl and spoon in the sink, turned around and literally without thinking said, "Get the fuck out of this house NOW! Return to where you came from and don't ever come back, You Son-Of-A-Bitch!"

I was zapped, I felt as if I'd been electrocuted. I was so distraught when I made that statement so suddenly, even surprising myself that it had come out, that it drained me.

Won't drive me insane, eh? At that moment, I decided I wasn't going to the Dandys, at least not for the next couple of nights. It truly hadn't disturbed me to experience what I had while at their house but I was thrown a curve ball when I realized you could be followed. What was this going to be now, tag-a-long time every visit I made to the house?

"Hey, I visited you several times, now it's your turn to visit?" Bullshit! Maybe whatever or whoever was causing the disturbances at the Dandys felt they were supposed to be there, I don't know. But they are *not* welcome in my little piece of the world. They're not welcome at the Dandys either but it was apparent there is a connection as to why they *were* there and, hopefully we'll convince them that it's time to move on from there as well.

I called Clara to tell her what had happened but there was no answer. As soon as I hung up the phone it rang. It was Louie M. telling me the bar was now at the Downtown Deli.

"Hey, I have a bank draft here for you any time you want to pick it up," he said.

"Okay, Lou. I'll stop in sometime this afternoon, thanks," I said.

He hesitated before asking, "You okay, Paulie?"

"Sure, just under the weather a little I guess," I said.

I told him I'd see him a little after 1:00 and we hung up. The apartment began to cool off and I decided to get dressed. I really wanted to go to Lily Dale and search out someone that might be able to tell me something about all of this. I had heard stories about a few of the psychics there who some were extremely gifted. There were several so-called psychics in Olean too: tea leaf readers, palm readers. You know, the ones little old ladies go to seeking information about their recently departed husbands and the like. You go to their houses, give them fifteen or twenty bucks and they offer you general information that pertains to just about anyone who walks through their door. Some of the time they can even give specific detailed information regarding your family life. Yeah, after you'd been there several times and they go to their files to refresh their psychic abilities before you arrive or after they've heard or read about your recently deceased relative who wants you to know that all's okay on the other side. Did the word 'bunko' as in the phrase, 'bunko squad' come into use after the authorities starting busting all these fakes and frauds within the psychic circles? Since the definition of bunko is, *a trick or scheme that deceives people into parting with money,* I'm sure it did. I don't believe the bunko squad has ever been called in to check a resident of Lily Dale.

The following few days were uneventful at least in the appearance of disembodied eyes, late night walks, flashlights that go out at a moment's notice and drifting 'fogmen/women.'

But, overdue visits with my parents, Debbie's mom and other things that had been neglected had been taken care of. I was kept abreast with the house because Clara called to tell me Father Al had been up early one evening to say Mass at the house. He always seemed to be there when I wasn't. Clara also told me of other apparitions and disturbances experienced by others who were in close proximity to the house. I felt a feeling of depression when not visiting those few days and I think it may have possibly been attributed to an underlying emotion of guilt I felt as well. I asked Debbie if, by chance, she might want to visit the Sunday before Labor Day but she told me she was going to be spending time with her brother and besides, we were going to be there the next day for a picnic. I had played both weekend nights prior to Labor Day so I was able to keep my mind occupied at least part of the time. Tim was antsy about not going up, but he understood why with all that had been going on the prior week. One thing I was extremely thankful for, it hadn't been any warmer in the apartment than it should have been that time of year.

Tim and I talked about going up Labor Day eve and decided against it because we were going up Monday early. Tim had a prior engagement with his parents and wouldn't be able to make it but said he might drive up late afternoon or early evening if we were still going to be there. Of course, it depended on getting someone to trade shifts with him. He said he would call ahead to check.

Debbie and I went to bed early to get a good night's sleep and I needed it. She had talked quite a bit about being apprehensive but had already accepted Clara's invitation.

Besides, there were going to be many people there and maybe that will keep the activity down to a minimum—one could hope. We woke early, took showers and prepared to head to Hinsdale. I was glad we didn't live in the big city and would have to deal with all the Labor Day idiots on the roads and those who didn't understand that drinking and driving wasn't a good mix. I didn't know what time we would be eating so I suggested we grab something just to keep the hunger pangs at bay. We both had a bowl of cereal and left the house about 1 p.m.. I stopped at Service Store and grabbed a couple of big bags of chips, some pop and a bottle of aspirin. I had one hell of a headache beginning to pound. Still, I felt today was going to be good, that we were going to have a nice time visiting. When I spoke to Clara, we both had agreed there was going to be no chit-chat about this past week. Today was to be a day of rest and enjoyment. The traffic was moderate going up the Hinsdale highway but that only meant there were more than five cars within eyesight. There were more vehicles on Congress road but I'm sure that was due to so many camps and cabins in the area. Surely many from Buffalo were coming down to get away from the rat race but they'd all be leaving tonight to return to the hustle and bustle of city life.

We arrived at the house about 2 p.m. but there weren't as many cars as I expected parked in the Dandys' driveway. Mary and Laura were outside tossing a ball around and Lassie, one of their dogs, was trying to intercept each throw. Clara came out, obviously hearing us pull up and said we'd be eating in about an hour. Surprisingly, we were the only ones there beside the family. Clara's parents and brother left early to beat the traffic, Father Al hadn't been able to get away, and Mike was at a friend's party. I was disappointed, I was really looking forward to a sit-down chat session and having a few laughs. I believe I got my wires crossed when I spoke with Clara and misunderstood what time we were to eat, and what time her family would be leaving. Just the same, we were going to have a picnic and possibly Tim may join us later. I took the chips and pop into the house and Debbie went in to see if there was anything she could do to help in the preparation. Just moments after entering the kitchen the feelings began. I didn't want this to happen today, I just wanted to visit with friends and leave all this paranormal crap out in the fields, at the pond, and in the branches of the hanging tree. I wasn't sure if apprehension were partially to blame or if it was totally the house. I decided to wait a bit and feel it out. This was a day of togetherness and watching the girls and dogs play in the yard. And it was also important for me because I wanted to ask Clara to bring Dolly out from her favorite hiding spot so I could hold her without the risk of having to take a tomato sauce bath.

I looked at Clara and she was already looking at me. Somehow she knew I had already started to pick up the activity and it was strong. It seemed the kitchen was filled with it. I walked into the living room and acted as if I were playing with the birds in their cages but they too knew. They were silent in the middle of the afternoon and Beth Ann's room was sending me vibrations across the living room. It was not going to be a quiet afternoon. I wanted to pull Clara aside and try to explain what I was feeling but I didn't want to alarm Debbie and, frankly, I wanted it to STOP! I returned to the kitchen and grabbed a pop from the refrigerator. I stood at the end of the kitchen table watching Clara and Debbie get the fixings ready to take out to the picnic table. My back was to the stairs and I might as well have been leaning against an electric fence because every square inch of skin on my neck and arms was being stimulated by an energy source that I knew was coming from Mary's room. Clara's *umbrella* had totally covered the entire house as the three of us stood in the kitchen: Debbie and Clara, just about to take the food outside, and me, knowing this was going to be an afternoon not forgotten soon.

It was warm in the kitchen but not warm enough for my shirt to be wringing wet with perspiration. I could see that Clara wanted to say something but instead, she announced that it was time to get the food outside. The three of us walked out the back door, each carrying something tasty to place on the picnic table. Laura was attempting to remove the ball from Lassie's mouth. Mary was already seated and Phil was walking toward the yard from the pond. I didn't see Beth Ann and that disturbed me. We all sat down to eat when we heard a vehicle pulling in on the side of the house. Jeff, Beth Ann's boyfriend, had arrived and Beth Ann walked to the back yard with him. She obviously was waiting for his arrival out front and I was relieved to see her. I was sitting facing the pond with Debbie seated on my right, Mary at my left. Clara, Phil and Laura were on the opposite side and Jeff and Beth Ann attempted to squeeze on the corner next to Laura. Jeff decided to stand and allow Beth Ann to take the inch or so he would have gotten if he had sat down. With each glance toward the pond I became more restless, more sure of what was happening. I didn't know my comment several nights ago would have been happening that day but it was soon to be realized. All the energy of the Dandy house was fully charged and preparing to let loose. I stood up for a second pretending that I had a pain in my leg but it was actually a headache. The pain in my head was throbbing, pulsating and it was all stemming from the end of their property; the tree line. I was sure that the pond area and the tree line were the two most affected areas of the property besides the house itself. I needed to see, *listen* at that moment what it was *they* were trying to tell all of us.

Calmly but sternly I said, "I need to walk to the tree line now, I'd like someone to come with me but if I have to go alone I will. There are answers there that will help us understand what it is they want."

Debbie grabbed my shirt and Clara was all but ready to tie me down. Phil was upset enough for a split second that he said something I didn't ever think I'd hear him say in front of his daughters. He very angrily said, "The fuck you are! You're not going anywhere near that goddamn tree line, with or without anyone."

Clara immediately got up and told us all to go into the house. My head was on fire with sounds, electricity; something. I didn't actually hear anything but it was so full that my head felt heavy, my brain had somehow solidified. I wouldn't have even called it a headache, it didn't really hurt. It was more like if you looked into a blinding light and you were actually able to feel the bright beam. All of us took something from the table and carried it inside. I wouldn't allow myself to look any place but the pond the entire walk to the back door. I knew they were here and they wanted something: answers, revenge, peace, to be free; all of the above. There was no comparison between any night since Tim and I started coming up with today. The word "war" kept creeping into my head and I didn't have a clue as to why that word would be the word of the day, but it wouldn't leave my thoughts. It didn't dawn on me until I was taking Debbie home. We all went into the living room and took a seat, I chose the floor. The birds were quiet, they were lifeless sitting on their perches, as if watching an invisible cat, waiting for it to climb up, open their doors with its claws, and rip them to shreds. We tried to converse but the air was heavy with energy, yet we talked uneasily. I don't believe we were in the living room more than ten minutes before "Bigfoot" starting stomping around upstairs. I almost laughed when Debbie said someone was being awful noisy. Clara said, "Look around, we're all here."

I ran upstairs and, very reluctantly, opened Mary's door. I could hear Clara and Phil yelling for me to stop but there was no stopping this time. The cold was that of the blast I received my very first night there. But the fear and hatred I felt was overwhelming and it scared the hell out of me. I wanted to run down the stairs so goddamn fast and out the back door without a moment's thought. I was standing at the door to the room of a beautiful little girl who no longer had a room. That saddened me but it angered me a whole lot more. I stared into the room, looking at the lamp that had been broken numerous times, or had it been numerous lamps that had been broken? I thought of Father Al and did as he warned and kept my faith strong. The longer I stood there, and I had only been there for maybe a minute, the more frightened I became. There was nothing but evil in this room and I felt it wanted to take from me what I was feeling myself, energy. I knew I had to confront whatever it was that was holding this room hostage even if it was just with words. I had nothing else I could have confronted it with. I gave it my best shot.

"Whoever, whatever you are, you are not welcome here. You are not wanted here. Get out, get out of this house and take your evil with you. You are nothing, and you have no control over anything or anyone in this house. I am more powerful than you and I demand you leave. You may have been strong once but you're dead and are nothing. Go back to hell you son-of-a-bitch!"

I don't remember exactly what I said but that's pretty damned close. I was pissed and I felt strong; until I turned my back after closing the door. Phil was standing at the bottom of the stairs and I could see the fear on his face looking at me. Dear God, the energy, if that's what it was, consumed me. I felt like I would never make it back to the safety in numbers of Debbie and the Dandys. At the risk of being accused of over-dramatization, I felt like I was walking in slow motion. I had no energy; I was drained. As I reached the middle of the stairs, I heard the most awful racket in the crawl space directly above me. Phil heard it too because he took two steps up to look above. I didn't feel like the victim of an earthquake, I felt *like* the earthquake. Almost as if something was tearing me apart from within. By the time I reached the bottom of the stairs and Phil, I'm sure it was no more than 10 seconds, I was mentally exhausted. I will be dramatic now, I felt as if I had fought the enemies of both World Wars single handedly! I couldn't wait to see the faces of those in the living room only six feet from the bottom of the stairs. Phil walked with me to the living room. People say before or during an accident that they see their lives flash before their eyes; something flashed before my eyes but it wasn't my life, it was someone else's. I just didn't know whose.

I made it to the living room in one physical piece. Mentally? My mental faculties were all over the damned house, from top to bottom, in and out. I only thought of one thing after entering the living room. "Where's my Mountain Dew?" I asked.

Debbie handed it to me and whispered as she leaned to hand it to me, "I'd like to leave soon."

"You okay?" Clara asked. Although I believe she truly knew the answer.

"I think he just went toe to toe with something in Mary's room," Phil said.

"I told that bastard in Mary's room to get out! How long was I upstairs?" I asked.

Clara said, "About two or three minutes."

And at the same time, Jeff said, "Three minutes tops."

"Jesus, coming down, I felt like I'd been up there most of the summer! I'm sorry, Mary."

"What happened, you look awful, and what have I said about going anywhere alone?" Clara asked.

"Just a lot of something upstairs. I'm sorry, Mary," I said.

"You said that twice, Paul, for what?" Mary asked.

"Because you can't sleep in your room," I said.

I almost felt like crying, but I'm sure that was due to the conflict I had just encountered and the look Mary had on her face. It probably doesn't seem like much but I believe this was the first house the kids all had a room of their own and they were all such great kids. I'd like to look up the people that caused them so much grief in school and give them a piece of my mind! We stayed until the sun was getting too low in the sky for Debbie's liking and prepared to leave. Clara and Debbie gave one another a hug as did the girls and Debbie. As I reached the kitchen, Mary came out and gave me a hug and thanked me. She was so innocent and vulnerable to all of this. So was Laura but she knew and felt what was happening and I in turn, could now sense, really sense that from her. Phil said to be careful driving home because the traffic would be getting heavier. Yeah, we'll see six cars within eyesight! He was still stuck in big-city-mode. We said goodbye to Beth Ann and Jeff as Clara walked Debbie and me out to the car. As Debbie was going around to the passenger side I turned to Clara and said, "It's not going to stop, Clara. There is an awful lot of energy here today and it's not going to give up."

"I know, I know, I feel it too and it really scares me. What's up with the tree line, anyhow?" Clara asked.

"I feel there are answers there. I don't know what but something's out there just as there are answers around the pond area. I may be back, with or without Tim, after I get Debbie home. It's going to get bad," I warned.

Driving down McMahon we were silent. Everybody has that sixth sense, everybody has psychic energy to a degree and Debbie was feeling something. Probably fear, an enormous amount, and that was to be expected today but I knew it was going to be a whole lot worse. Driving past the hanging tree I all but dared something to happen but we were allowed to pass without incident. I asked Debbie if it would be okay to go back up and she replied, "You know, you're nuts, but I admire your courage or stupidity, whichever it is. I don't feel anything the way you do but I feel tension I guess and that's enough. If you are really feeling this energy, why do you continue to fool with it?"

"I don't know," I said with no emotion. I didn't know and really never did. To this day I still don't.

We got home and went inside. I was going to call Tim and decided against it. I wasn't sure if I wanted to go another round and I truly knew there was going to be more than one round left. I was sure I had overcome the energy in Mary's room until, as I said, I closed the door and walked away. *They* brought out their big guns when I turned to walk away. The sensations and psychic energy I felt walking down the stairs was ten times what I felt in the room and that was frighteningly intense. It was a taunt I was receiving, a knock down, drag out taunt then *they* let me free. Why, because they weren't finished with my smart-ass arrogance? I hoped not. I had hoped that was all they had and, if so, that could be beaten in time. The Dandys needed someone a little more experienced than a paranormal rookie to accomplish the task at hand. I wasn't a psychic, I was the biggest nobody in a psychic world of nobodies. Hell, I would have never believed I had a bona-fide psychic bone in my body even if every test that could be administered proved without a reasonable doubt that I had. Does Father Al get these overpowering feelings when he's performing an exorcism or confronting an evil spirit? I sure as hell hoped so, because if he didn't, then I should have gotten the hell out of there when the getting was good. I tried my best to put the feelings I had out of my mind and went into the kitchen to see what Debbie was up to.

"I didn't eat much, did you?" She asked.

"No, but I'm not hungry. Do you want something? I'll make it." I said.

"How 'bout a peanut butter and jelly sandwich?" She asked.

"Grape jam or strawberry?" I asked.

"Grape, NO, strawberry!" She replied.

I made her sandwich and placed it on a paper towel. We were talking about Beth Ann's boyfriend, Jeff when the phone rang. Debbie answered, it was Father Al. "Hi Father, how are you?" Debbie asked. "Hon, it's Father, he wants to talk to you."

After our usual greeting, Father began: "I understand you and Debbie just got back from the house. Clara said things were becoming quite active while you were visiting," Father said.

"Yeah, it was, Father. I had a bit of an incident in Mary's room that I'd like to....."

Father interrupted, "Paul, all hell's broken loose. Clara said there are apparitions everywhere, inside and out. If you're available, would you care to accompany me back to the house?"

"Father wants to know, he'd like me to go..." I began asking Debbie.

"Go, do what you can, you'll be okay, Father will be with you," she said.

"Yes, Father, do you want me to meet you there?" I asked.

"No, I'll pick you up, if that's all right. You live on South Sixth Street, correct?" Father asked.

"Yes, Father, I'll be waiting outside." I said.

"All right, okay. I'll see you shortly then, Paul."

Both Clara and Father Al were right, I was beginning to predict more accurately as time went on. It could have been a hunch or a wild guess when we were at the house earlier but I knew it was only the beginning of a traumatic night. I expected everything to cease immediately when Father Al arrived at the house. We would soon find out if that would be the case. He was at our house within fifteen minutes and we were on our way for his first bout of the evening and my second. I only hoped I had enough stamina to make it though another round and that it wouldn't involve Mary's resident.

Father Al looked tired and worried but more than that, he looked apprehensive and anxious. I could feel his inner strength, his unfaltering faith. We didn't speak until we got to the end of Union Street when he simply asked, "Is there anything that you believe you can feel from here?"

I didn't know how to answer that. I surely felt apprehensive as well as a little frightened. I didn't like the way he had said, "All hell has broken loose" during our phone conversation. I imagined Clara's call to him and how she may have described what was happening at the house. I didn't know what to expect. Our conversation seemed to start on the light side, as short as it was, but he became very restless when he explained what Clara had said. "Apparitions everywhere." I may be brazen in saying, big deal because if that's all that we were going to be confronted with, it would be no more that what had happened over the prior couple of months. Although this did confirm what I had felt several nights ago: a building of energy. I prayed that what I had felt after leaving Mary's room wouldn't be the catalyst, the prime mover in what we were heading to.

"I don't know, Father. I haven't told you yet what I felt in Mary's room. It was so foreboding and powerful. I can't tell if I'm just apprehensive thinking about how strong and overpowering it was or if I can still feel it even this far from the house. Honestly, if I had to take my best guess, I'd say a little of both," I said.

"Explain to me, with your best description, what you felt both physically and mentally when you entered Mary's room," Father Al asked.

"I'll try, Father, but let me start from when we arrived. When we walked...."

"I'm sorry to interrupt, but tell me your frame of mind before you left your house and on your drive to visit the Dandys."

It suddenly occurred to me: he was testing me. He wanted to evaluate the level of my psychic gift. I had to be sure it wasn't apprehension that replaced logical thinking. I couldn't allow my fear to cloud my judgment. I felt confident that I could separate the logical from the far-fetched and the imagined from the tangible. I began: "I had a good sleep last night. I didn't dwell on the events that occurred over the past week and I was looking forward to having a good visit with the family. I felt good this morning and was excited thinking that we were going to have a nice picnic with good friends. I knew Debbie didn't like going to the house and I may have felt a little uneasy thinking how she would cope but I personally had no fear. I was maybe a little apprehension thinking about the visit. I did have a headache start after we left our house but I sometimes get them after playing. It had already begun to subside by the time we reached Wagner Hill Road. Seeing other people at some of the camps made it all the more possible that this was going to be a good day; a day of friends and family," I explained.

"You had good thoughts on your way up, good, good. When did you begin to have feelings?" Father asked.

"God, I mean…. well, as soon as I walked in the kitchen door," I said.

"No uneasiness feeling when you turned onto McMahon Road or after arriving?"

"No, not at all. We walked in and it hit me," I said.

"And absolutely *no one* said a word to you suggesting something had happened prior to you walking into the house?" He asked.

"Not a word, everyone seemed happy. The girls were playing catch and everyone else seemed just fine. Clara and I exchanged glances when I entered the kitchen and I think we both knew something wasn't right. I wasn't thinking negative, I surely wasn't afraid of anything. Actually, I had lost most of the fear even during our night time visits. I was prepared to have an enjoyable time but the energy I felt after entering the house was more than anything I'd ever felt in or out of the house, ever. Not that it was that powerful but it was a complete sensation. I wanted to know where it was coming from. I walked into the living room and the birds were as still as knick-knacks. The feeling was still with me but not as strong as in the kitchen. It was when I was standing at the bottom of the stairs that I knew, I *knew*, Father, that it was going to be a bad day," I said.

"I see, yes. Did you attempt to dismiss it, to just think positive thoughts?" Father asked.

249

"It would have been trying to disregard that you had an abscessed tooth! And it didn't get better after going outside. In a way, it got worse. There is something about the tree line too, Father. Something extremely powerful, something that could take your will from you. Why do I feel this? Why can't this just leave these people alone and let them live peacefully? Why can't it leave *me* alone?" I asked.

I was coming very close to breaking down and the promise I made to my mother had been broken, that I wouldn't go to the house if I felt any sort of threat. All of my emotions were in turmoil. Yet I didn't feel I had a choice, I must go and not let myself be beaten by this psychic bully. Father asked if I wanted to turn around. No, there *was* no turning back, not now. I had no desire to give up and would continue to fight whatever it was. I composed my thoughts and explained my feeling about the tree line and the experience in Mary's room.

"During your initial, let's call it, confrontation, after opening the door to Mary's room, did you visually see or audibly hear anything?" Father asked.

"Hear? No, but I can say that there was no threat of ice melting in that room. And even though I thought I was dealing with a most ominous energy, I found myself checking just how cold it was by lightly blowing air out. I was amazed; I could see my breath. Oh, I also remember a sudden odd feeling come over me as I was going down the stairs. The extreme power that I felt in Mary's room hadn't dissipated. Actually it became much stronger as I was walking down but there was another feeling of; I don't know, I think desperation is the best way to describe it. A better description I could give possibly would be as if you were left alone and you knew there was little hope of being found. Does that make any sense and. if it does, please tell me how the hell I can feel this so strongly. Sorry, Father."

He gave a subdued chuckle when I said hell before he responded.

"I believe you're very sensitive to psychic energy and I am sure you offer the same. If most of what you are experiencing is as strong as you say, and apprehension and imagination has little to do with it, then you are extremely sensitive. Regardless of the amount of psychic energy felt, it

250

carries with it a degree of fear. Also, apprehension is always going to be something you can never shut out totally once you've been exposed to any level of energy. If you truly felt the energy to be that overwhelming upon entering the kitchen and believe the source was in Mary's room, you are indeed extremely sensitive," Father explained.

We were already at the 'T' in the road of Wagner Hill. There was only about a mile left to go. Father Al had one more thing to say.

"I want you to attempt to calm yourself, clear your mind as best you can of what happened today. Try to think good thoughts. Don't think or expect the worst and don't display anger. Exude control, compassion and above all, really try as hard as you can muster not to show fear. Evil, if this is what we're dealing with, thrives, feeds on fear; it gives it a power source; don't fuel it," Father said.

I don't believe Father Al looked away from the road as he was driving until he said those last three words; and then he looked directly at me. I tried as best as I could to control all of my emotions, especially fear, but it was difficult. We had no idea what was going on at the house, now it was only two tenths of a mile down McMahon road. As we turned the corner into the drive, we could see that all of the lights in the house were on. Father Al pulled all the way to the back and turned toward the pond. As he was hurriedly getting out, I told him I'd be there in a second, I had to pull together. As I got out of Father Al's car, I saw Phil and Clara coming across the back yard heading for the side of the house. I didn't know what to do or where to go. Father Al had gone inside, Jeff's motorcycle was still here so I assumed he was either inside or in the front where I couldn't see. I thought for a moment, walked in the back door and walked around the kitchen table as to not have to walk past so closely to the stairs. No one was downstairs and I had no plans of ascending the stairs, not yet, not alone. I went out the back door and headed for the front of the house when Tim pulled up—my partner in this supernatural investigation; I was very glad he made it. I walked over to his car and he told me that Debbie explained what had happened, that Father and I had gone up to help. He had to work tonight but closed up half an hour early and didn't really care after talking to Debbie. Tim reached in the back to grab our flashlights and we both headed for the front yard. Beth Ann and Jeff were on the porch and Clara was talking with Father Al; I didn't see Phil outside. Tim and I walked around the house in opposite directions to look for him. Before I had gotten all the way around, I heard Tim yell. I ran as fast as I could around the house and when I reached the back yard, he yelled to me from the pond. He said that someone had pushed him in!

"You okay? I asked. "Yeah, my pants are wetter than hell, but I'm okay," Tim said.

"You were pushed in, and by who?!" I exclaimed.

"I don't fucking know, the fogmen, the dizzy bitch, or some dumb as a stump, son-of-a-bitch!" Tim yelled, shining his light to and fro across the pathway of the pond..

"Ya sure you just didn't slip?" I asked.

"Yeah I'm sure, I felt someone or something push me!" He exclaimed.

We walked toward the back yard. Neither Clara nor Phil knew we were here yet. We walked back toward the front when Jeff told us he thought he saw Phil walking down the road, supposedly looking for a trespasser. Trespasser? We decided to walk at least to the first turn to see if he had gone that way, calling his name. There was no sign of Phil and he surely wouldn't have gone walking through the fields or up the rise so we headed back to the house. On our way, we heard a scream and began running, I tripped over Tim's foot as we were running and did a head plant in the road.

"Son-of-a-bitch, that hurt!" I yelled, as Tim helped me up, laughing as I had during his round at the spelling bee.

We reached the yard and Beth Ann told us that Mary had seen a woman in her window. I asked Tim to go with me to Mary's room. He was reluctant at first but I explained he didn't have to come up. I asked him to stand at the bottom of the stairs in case I needed help. He agreed. We entered the back door and with some hesitation, I darted up the stairs, two at a time. I nearly fainted!

Phil was just coming out of his room. "Every fucking light was on up here and we hadn't been upstairs most of the night!" He exclaimed.

"I came up to check Mary's room," I said.

"Forget it, just go downstairs where everyone else is," Phil said.

He looked awful. If it were possible for people to age ten years overnight, he had accomplished just that. He went to each room and turned the lights off as I went back downstairs. Tim and I went outside just as Mike and a friend pulled into the driveway.

"What the hell is going on? I called and was told to get home, that the house had gone insane!" Mike said.

"I'm not sure exactly, Mike. I just came back with Father Al," I replied.

Mike and his friend went to look for his mother while Tim and I went toward the edge of the pond to see if we could locate Phil. Everyone was yelling they were seeing apparitions everywhere and I had wondered, as dark as it was, if possibly we were occasionally seeing one another as we were all running around the property. At one point, Mike and his friend jumped in the car and drove down the road. I couldn't believe they were leaving during all the havoc but Beth Ann and Jeff said they went down the road in search of what Phil thought was a trespasser. I could only imagine he thought there was a trespasser because I don't feel he has fully accepted his home was haunted. I didn't know what it was going to take for him to finally give in to the idea that there was nothing reasonable about any of this.

Clara finally realized that Tim and I were here and the only words she said as we rounded the front of the house was, "Thank, God!" as she continued to walk toward the car with Laura and Mary, who had been hanging onto to her tightly. The three of them got into the car and drove up the road. Maybe Phil had asked them to leave. There was so much confusion, no one really knew what anyone else was doing. We caught up with Father Al, and barely slowing our pace, I introduced him to Tim. They said hello to one another as we went in opposite directions. Clara and the girls returned a few minutes later and it appeared Clara was carrying a light as bright as the one Tim blinded me with; twice. Tim and I rounded the house once again and he said he thinks he saw someone in the house. I didn't doubt it, as we were all in and out trying to keep track of who was where. A few moments later, Beth Ann said there was a girl in her room and Clara went in to investigate. As the evening progressed and things began to calm down, Beth Ann, Clara, and the girls went into the house. Mike said his dad wasn't going to work and Father Al was going to stay until morning.

While we were talking with Mike, he introduced his friend to Tim and me. We finally had the pleasure of meeting, Randy C.

"Mike's talked about you, Randy. It's nice to finally meet you," I said.

"Thanks, you too. It looks like it's been busy up here tonight," Randy said.

"Yeah, Debbie, my fiancée, and I were up earlier and the house was bad then. At least Mary's room was. We left and Father Al called and told me Clara said the house was jumping. I came back up with him," I said.

"You gonna be okay, Mike? I have to get back to the house. We left everyone there." Randy said.

"Sure, I need to stay home anyhow, Randy, but thanks for bringing me up," I said.

"No problem, I'm sure I'll see you guys again. We'll have to talk. Mike says you can feel things before they happen?" Randy asked.

"Yeah, I guess I have a gift but I'll gladly give it away for the asking," I said.

Randy laughed and he and Mike walked back to the front of the driveway. Tim and I went in the house and saw that everyone was in the kitchen and living room. I told Clara that Tim and I would be outside if anyone needed anything. She explained to us what Mike had already told us about Father Al staying until morning and that Phil wasn't going in tonight.

"I understand you went swimming tonight, Tim," Clara said.

"Yeah, but I was persuaded to take a dip, it wasn't voluntary," Tim said.

They both laughed and that was good. Even the slightest humor helped to clear the negative energy which, from what I felt, was still moderate. As Tim and I were walking out of the living room, Father Al tapped me on the shoulder from where he was standing at the doorway between the living room and kitchen. I said to him, "There's still energy in the house, but I really wish I didn't know that," I also told him that Tim could give me a lift home. He offered a tiny, hard to muster, smile as we walked out. Perhaps it would be quiet now that he was here.

I asked Tim if he wanted to stay as long as we normally did and he said that was fine. We walked around the house several times checking the property line and the area around the pond. As we passed by Beth Ann's room the third or fourth time I could sense there was still something that didn't want to go. I meant what I had said to Father Al whole-heartedly, I really didn't want to know this. It was tough enough dealing with the living and the day-to-day tasks of life without having to worry about the afterlife.

It was fairly warm outside and Tim decided it would be better to sit at the picnic table to allow his pants to dry. He started to sit and, before his butt hit the seat, he stood up and came around to my side. He wasn't comfortable sitting with his back to the pond.

"You said a few nights ago that something was building. How do you know that?" He asked.

"I don't know, Tim. How do you know when a bug is crawling on your skin?"

"I feel it and I smack the little bastard," he said.

That was actually a rhetorical question but, after hearing his answer, it was basically what my answer should have been: I feel it. I guess there just isn't any other way to explain it. I stated before that at times I would get "goosies" and that is very much what I had been receiving at the Dandy house. I can't remember when the word goosies first came in to play. I'm certain it's been a word that was first used to describe these feeling when I was a young child. I wouldn't choose to call a feeling a goosie at the Hinsdale farmhouse. It was far too mild a word for those feelings.

We'd been sitting in the car for nearly two hours and it was nearly 2:30 in the morning. We both felt it was safe to go. Besides, Father and Phil were in the house. They could certainly handle anything that might happen. The incidents that happened last night should, without a doubt, place the Dandy house into the Registry of Haunted Houses if there is such a publication. If there isn't, there ought to be. Their house could be the first entry. Tim dropped me off at home and, rather than going inside, I sat on the steps and smoked a cigarette while I thought. I couldn't believe the forces they were dealing with. What's more, I found it difficult to think I wanted to deal with it again. I hadn't had time to clear anything from my mind before being thrown right back into it. I was thankful I didn't feel what I did that afternoon on the second visit. If I had, I may have never gone to visit again. Visit, who the hell was I kidding? Surely not myself. I had become fond of everyone. Well, Phil was just too miserable. I'm sure the house had something to do with it, but I have a feeling he wasn't much different before moving into their country home.

Even though Mary's room had the greatest paranormal activity by far, I believed it was the heart of the house. Still, she was the one I worried least about. I believed Laura, who appeared least affected by the trauma the house dished out, was at the greatest risk. I knew she was aware of everything happening within their home but she was keen to it in a different sense, as I was. She dealt with it differently and, if I may be so bold, I don't think Clara knew in the beginning how difficult it was for her, nobody could have. The house had distressed everyone inversely. Clara learned just how badly the house had affected Laura long before I or Father Al and it was devastating. Thinking about all this, I will say something so very important: Don't lose contact with those who have touched your life because it may be too late when you finally attempt to.

There was an interesting article in the Olean Times Herald on September 6, 1973. It was especially interesting to Tim and me. After reading it, we were both left speechless. It's difficult to say if the incident that took place was a direct link to the Dandy house but many believed it was. After reading the story and going over the previous weeks incidents at the house, it was a challenge to believe it was coincidental. Rather than summarize the incident in my own words, I have included the story as it was written. The first part of the article wrote of offers to the Dandys for purchase of their property, most being ridiculously low offers. The next piece read as follows:

Although concerned with the so-called hauntings, some residents of the area read something into a report last Thursday of an accident along nearby Emerson road. Alfred J, Cowell of Emerson Road called State Police about 2 a.m. to inform them his car, heading home, had struck a young man. However, he said, the victim could not be located when he stopped his auto to investigate. Troopers and about 25 members of the Hinsdale Volunteer Fire Department responded and conducted an intense search of the area. Troopers continued the hunt during Friday daylight hours, but no one was located.

Some residents immediately started 'ghost' stories, but State Police say they feel there actually was a "white male in his late teens or early twenties struck." However, they feel he may have had an illegal reason for being in the area and rushed away when he was not injured by the car.

According to the article, Mr. Cowell called the State Police about 2 a.m. to report the incident. Much earlier that same night, Tim and I spoke to six people who were parked at the bottom of McMahon Road. Four of them reported seeing a boy of about 18–20 walk toward them and vanish. A boy of approximately the same age and description was seen my Mike, Laura and Mary weeks earlier walking their property and disappearing as well. Emerson Drive is about half a mile from where the four ladies saw the boy disappear before them. It took some time to contact Mr. Cowell but when I finally did contact him, he informed me that when he struck the boy he had been traveling about 25–30 miles per hour. The State Police's report says the boy left the scene when he wasn't injured because he had been in the area illegally. Coincidental? You decide.

Over the next couple of weeks, Tim and I would continue to go to the house but not every night. My band played every Friday and Saturday night through most of September so those nights were out. Clara and I kept in close contact especially when we weren't able to make it up to the house. I had asked Debbie if she wanted to visit but she many times had something to do with her family or was reluctant to go. I had read libraries of books on paranormal activity and psychic phenomena and still found myself wanting. I was able to get together with Father Al at the rectory one Saturday afternoon and it was a most enjoyable time. We were even able to divert our conversation away from the paranormal quite easily. We shared family stories and he had told me how it had come about that he joined the Franciscans. We walked the campus of Saint Bonaventure and then had lunch at a nearby restaurant. He was truly a kind and caring man and he had a great sense of humor. He held his Franciscan values dear.

I called Clara to tell her I had a great afternoon with the funny little guy from Bona's. Laughing she said, "Isn't he remarkable? When you can just sit and have a conversation with him about something that isn't haunted, he can be just that, a funny little guy! You never did get a chance to see him in action when he was playing the policeman up here. He had people peeling off down the road in fear of getting arrested! He is a joy!" Clara said.

"Tim and I are coming up tonight. The other night we met a guy named Keith. What a nut! I don't know if you've met him or not, but he has a camp not far from the house. He's going to be around for a while so I'm sure you'll meet him. Of course, we told him all about the house and he's ready to help with the fight, even though he doesn't believe in such things," I said.

"Another sentinel in the night! The more the merrier, I say. You can all stay outside and keep the ghosts busy so we can sleep peacefully," Clara said.

"It's almost time to go to work so I'll talk to later or see you soon, whichever comes first, I guess," I said.

CHAPTER XX

Today is Sunday, September 9, 1973.

Usually the sub shop isn't real busy on Sundays so I took a couple of books to read between customers. I was working solo tonight, Tim was off doing who knew what but would be in about closing time. I'd thought about making him a sub and loading it with peppers but I'd probably end up in the pond as he did on Labor Day. There wasn't a lot of business tonight and, if memory serves me, it was near 9 p.m. when I began to feel a "goosie" coming on. Writing that word seem ridiculous but since that's what I've been getting and what I've called them since I was a kid, I may as well use it. I would say 80% of the time, I didn't know what they meant but when I was at the Dandy house and had one, well, it was obvious what it was about. Since being involved with the Dandys, I've only had two when I was away from the house that actually pertained to the house. Both were the voice. I sat at the counter, head in my hands as if I were reading, hoping something would be clear but nothing came. I tried to envision the house, the yard, the pond, the interior, but the feeling stayed the same. I called Clara on a hunch but there was nothing new to report. She had told me about Beth Ann's room. Beth Ann and her grandmother had smelled the perfume again but telling me that didn't make a connection come through. There was something, not necessarily involving the house at all, but the feeling stayed longer than usual. I began doing my chores prior to closing when Tim walked in. He began helping by getting the mop water ready and wiping off the front counter. I turned to him and asked, "You okay?"

"Yeah, why?" He asked.

"I dunno, just thought I'd ask. Look at the pictures under the counter. They're next to the camera. I was messing around and took a couple of pictures from the TV. I was gonna mess around with Mike and tell him we got a ghost," I said.

"That wouldn't be very nice," Tim scolded.

"I know, I was gonna kid around, he wouldn't believe me anyhow. Look at the lines through them. Electronic

259

interference they call that. You can hardly make out what they are," I said.

"I guess, is this a woman smiling or a water buffalo taking a drink?" Tim asked.

"If you ever go in to be analyzed, I'd like to go with you. What makes you think? Do you want a sub or not?" I asked.

"No sub, but I'll grab some chips. You eating tonight?"

"Nope, I had half a sub while I was reading, but you can grab me a bag of g'onion," I said.

"You think Beth Ann likes me?" Tim asked.

I looked at him as seriously as I could knowing what I was going to say, "Tim, nobody likes you and, of all people, why Beth Ann?"

"Come on, dammit, I'm being serious. 'Cause we've— you know, kinda looked at each other," Tim said.

"Oh, well then hell yes, especially if you've *looked at each other*. Did you forget about Jeff, Tim?" I asked.

"Forget I asked," he said, seemingly upset.

"Sorry. I was messing with you. I'm sure she likes you, you're easy to get along with. If you mean, *like*, like, I don't know. Want me to ask her?" I asked.

"No! Never mind, it was wishful thinking, I guess," Tim said.

Beth Ann was a very pretty girl and had a charming personality. At times, she acted much older than her age of sixteen but that would be expected being the oldest of three daughters. Her conversational skills were never awkward whether talking to young children or adults. She was very intelligent and articulate. She was mature for her age but as fragile as an eggshell dealing with the problems of the house. Still, she stood strong and dealt with the troubles as logically as possible.

"Everything's done, ready?" Tim asked.

"Let's go," I said, checking the back door.

Just as I stuck the key in the front door, I remembered my camera. I went back in to grab it from under the counter.

On our drive up, we talked about everything but the house, a habit we'd developed. It was similar to going to work. You don't normally talk about your job on the way in to work.

People were still chattering about the haunted house around town but fewer were driving up to see it. It was rare that anyone could be seen parked along the roadside late at night and Clara says the traffic during the day was nil. It wasn't new news but that didn't take away the fact that the Dandys were still extremely uncomfortable in their own home. The energy was getting worse; more powerful. There had been several psychics who had visited the house since the onset of these troubled times. There were many conclusions to the impressions received by them but there was a consensus by nearly all of them: **The Dandys weren't welcome in their own home and needed to be put out**.

I had contacted a gentleman in Hinsdale this week who supposedly had information on the local history and possibly the house as well. I was excited to hear that someone might have news that would shed some light on all of this. To my dismay, everything he told me I already knew. Actually, the only thing he did tell me was the name of the family that owned the land and that they had farmed hay. I didn't know about the hay bit but the name of the family had already been published. Then he really made my day and said they lived on McMahon Road. No help here but I thanked him for his information.

When we arrived, we parked at the beginning of the driveway rather than pull to the back, just for a change of pace. The only light we noticed inside was from Clara and Phil's bedroom. Any time we saw a light burning at this time of the evening we thought there might be something wrong. Clara's mom and dad had come up for the weekend but had apparently left.

"Do you think the kid who was hit by the car is the same one those people saw and the same one Mike and the girls saw?" Tim asked.

"It's really strange the four of them saw a kid that fit the description of the one who was hit on the same night," I said.

"Yeah, it's even a lot stranger that in all three cases he disappears without a trace too," Tim replied.

We didn't feel like sitting and got out of the car. Tim opened the back door to get the flashlights and said, "Shit, I left them home."

"You left what home?" I asked.

"The flashlights. I took them out when I cleaned the car and forgot to put them back."

"We don't need them. I don't plan on walking too much tonight. Let's go sit out back, though," I suggested.

We started walking down the drive when Tim turned to go back to the car."

"Grab my chips," I whispered loudly.

"That's what I'm getting. Pop too?" Tim asked.

"No, I'll wash the chips down with pond water," I said.

I sat at the picnic table and Tim set out midnight snacks on the table.

"Where's my pop?" I asked.

"What? You said you were gonna drink pond water!" Tim exclaimed.

I used a couple of choice words as I got up to get my pop from the car. When I returned to the back yard, Tim was gone from the picnic table. I saw him standing nearer the pond and that surprised the hell out of me. He didn't normally venture toward the pond unaccompanied.

"Come here," he whispered, not fully turning around.

I walked to his side and saw shadows moving about the water. As my eyes grew more accustomed to the dark, it appeared there was someone in the boat. The boat was moving away from us, toward the far end of the pond. We must have thought the same thing, because both of us turned and headed for Mike's bedroom window. We needed light!

I tapped on Mike's window and waited a few seconds. When my screech came, it should have woke the entire valley. The curtains moved, a girl's face appeared at the window, then backed away, causing me to yell out a good one. I backed up about three or four feet and Tim went dashing for his car. A second later, Mike's light came on and he opened his window.

"Hey," he said.

"Hey my ass, we just saw a girl in your room!" I said.

"Yeah, that was Beth Ann. She can't sleep in her room tonight. She's on the couch." Mike replied.

There ya go, Phil, "one goddamn reasonable explanation" finally scored! I assumed, not expecting to see a female at Mike's window. That's why neither Tim nor I recognized Beth Ann.

"What's going on?" Mike asked.

"We need a flashlight, we forgot ours," I explained.

"Okay, I'll meet you at the back door," Mike replied.

I waved for Tim to follow me and he got out of the car. When he caught up to me I said, "For someone interested in a particular young lady, it's terrible that you didn't even recognize her."

"Huh?" He asked, with one of his dopey expressions this time.

"That was Beth Ann at Mike's window," I said.

"Shit, I didn't see anybody. Your scream scared the hell outta me!" Tim said.

Mike handed us two flashlights at the back door.

We took them and walked toward the pond. I turned one on and it went out. Shaking it didn't bring the light back to life.

"Here we go again," Tim said.

He turned his on and it stayed lit. When we reached the near side of the pond we saw the boat on the far shore empty. At this time of night, a logical assumption.. Not only was it at the far shore, it was halfway up onto the bank. The bank is so inclined that it would take someone to actually pull it up or it would need one hell of a wind at its stern!

"Come on out here where we can see you, dammit!" Tim said.

Laughing, I said, "Well, you sure have become brave lately."

"I told you, I'm tired of their games, 'Now you see me, now you don't,' shit," Tim said.

We walked back to the table and had a seat. I looked at Tim. It was always easy to tell when he was deep in thought. There was something brewing in his head but that was usual. You just never knew what he was going to say. It was only another five minutes or so before he tossed out a question I had no answer to.

"Okay, millions of people have died, we know that. Oh, and that made me think of something even better to add to this: okay, millions of people, even Neanderthal men. So, why are only a certain few coming back to haunt places as 'fogmen' or half seen people or eyes or whatever they come back as? Also, how come everyone doesn't see them? Why doesn't every…"

Before I went insane, I interrupted with, "You need to stop thinking and rest your mind. We've talked about this before and I don't know any more than you do. There isn't enough room for the living! What the hell would it be like if everyone that died was still wandering around?" I asked.

"You're reading about all this crap, you should know more than I do. What do the books say?" Tim asked.

"That you should never go on an investigation with someone named Tim. I'm reading about paranormal activity and haven't read anything regarding who was allowed to come back. Most of it is too complex and, to say the least, confusing," I said.

He'd made a valid point. Spirits, souls, what have you, stay because of unfinished business or because their deaths were so traumatic. Tim and I have discussed this two or three times and he still made a very valid point. What I had read didn't offer answers to these questions.

"Why do we have such dumb conversations?" I asked with a sigh.

"Why is Beth Ann in Mike's room?" Tim asked.

"Mike said she couldn't sleep in her room but he didn't say why. I'd like to stay in her room one night," I said.

"HEY!"

"You idiot! I'd like to stay in her room because it's becoming more active! They're smelling perfume more often and Clara's mom has been having trouble when she sleeps in there too. But they say it doesn't feel malicious in any way," I snapped.

"Sorry, I didn't…. I'm sorry," Tim replied.

"Christ! Let's take a walk down to the turn now that we have flashlights." I tried the one that had gone out and it worked this time. Odd though, why didn't the other one go out too? We talked about how many different entities had been seen but it wasn't possible to say how many times the same one was observed. If I had to choose a favorite on the basis of being the most interesting, it would be the "walking lantern." Of course my least favorite would be whatever was in Mary's room. Seeing what appeared to be a someone carrying a lantern minus the "someone" was really cool. There was no threat or malevolent presence and the illusion was very interesting. There is no description for the thing in Mary's room other than pure, unadulterated evil. If what I felt on Labor Day was the residual energy of a human being, I couldn't imagine what kind of person they were when alive; possibly the cruelest, most malicious, and immoral creature there ever was.

After arriving at the turn on McMahon, we continued on, and walked up the rise in the direction where the Gregorian chant was heard. There was supposed to be a clearing, a perfect circle somewhere in the woods further up but it was certainly too late to think about checking that out at that hour of the night. Someone had mentioned that Druids once traveled and settled in this area. This was one topic I had read up on because I remembered reading about Druids a couple of years ago and I was sure they were located in Britain. A druid was a priest of an ancient culture of worship. I wondered, why of all places on earth would they choose Hinsdale, New York? After reading further, I learned that they converted to Christianity. I don't remember who brought the topic up but they said that druids worshiped trees and that sounded strange. Actually, druids worshipped the earth, the forces of nature and, seeing trees are part of the overall picture, I can see where they might get that idea. There was so much to think about regarding all of this and there were so many opinions as to what was happening and why. We needed an expert, someone from the psychic circles who knew their stuff and could really sink their psychic teeth into the heart of the problem the Dandys faced. We surely weren't going to find a listing in the yellow pages for what was required.

"We'll have to check out the clearing some day. I think Mike said he's been there, we can ask him to show us the way," Tim said.

"Yeah, I'd like to take a look at it—in the daylight! You ready to head back?" I asked.

"Walk to the tree and then head back?" Tim asked.

"I suppose, then we can call it a night."

As we were walking to the tree, Tim picked up a rock and threw it into the field alongside the road. I guess he expected to startle me but I didn't oblige him. Waiting for a reaction, he walked a few more feet and tossed another one.

"Did you hear that?" He asked.

"Yup, probably the 'black man' following us without his lantern. You might have caught me off guard if you'd thrown a bigger one the first time," I said.

"Asshole, I was trying to get ya, it's been too quiet tonight."

"Well, go into the house, up the stairs and knock on Mary's bedroom door. Your chances are good that you'll have a little excitement. Come on, let's head back," I said.

We walked back to the house and I put the flashlights inside the back door. Tim was already in the car when he said from his window, "Listen, did you hear that?"

I listened but heard nothing but the crickets and frogs. I was sure he was playing another game, something he's never done in the past, but what the hell, it was quiet and he was trying to enjoy himself.

"I don't hear it now," he said.

I walked to the car and as I opened the door, I heard a faint, almost crying like sound. Tim didn't say anything this time and I waited to see if it would come again.

"You ready?" Tim asked.

Very faintly, it was the same sound. It wasn't possible to tell where it was coming from and it was barely audible but it did sound very much like a child crying. I looked to the upstairs windows but didn't see any movement and the sound had stopped. Tim opened his door and came halfway out of the car as we both listened for about a minute. It came a third time and it was a bit louder. I shut my door and walked away from the car, toward the house; Tim followed. If you're familiar with the open country, you know a sound can be carried for some distance. It's sometimes difficult telling where it's coming from. I opened the back door and grabbed the flashlights. Tim and I walked to the edge of the pond where we listened to the sound as it wavered on the night air. We still couldn't tell where it was coming from but it was undoubtedly the voice of a child crying; more whimpering than crying.

"Are we walking?" Tim asked.

"No, the crying has got to be far off. I wouldn't know where to walk and I don't want to walk past the pond area; not just the two of us," I said.

"Ya know what, to me it sounds like the crying is muffled, like someone has their face covered," Tim said.

I took a picture aimed at the pond but there was nothing visible after it developed. He was perfectly correct, listening closely, the crying didn't sound that far off. It sounded as if a child's face were being covered or someone was holding their hand over its face. We walked past the run-off of the pond. Just as we were approaching the far side, the crying was louder just for an instant, then stopped. We stood there for at least ten minutes, shining our lights over the entire area. We didn't really expect to find the source of the crying and we didn't hear it again.

"It was loudest right around here," Tim said.

"Ya know, I can tolerate and try to accept all of the shit that's been happening, but this is a little difficult to deal with. I'm pretty sure there isn't some kid lost out here somewhere but hearing one cry and not being able to help really bothers me, Tim," I said angrily.

"I agree with you there, buddy. But, I have an honest feeling we wouldn't be able to help this one anyhow, you know?" Tim said.

There was no feeling but I expected one; I wanted one. Why wasn't the feeling there to go with the crying? There was obviously something paranormal happening yet there wasn't the slightest twitch of a hair. We slowly walked toward the back yard in hopes of hearing the crying again. It didn't come. Neither of us were ready to walk to the house and put the flashlight back; not yet. We stood at the end of the pond nearest the house for at least fifteen minutes.

"Rotten bastard! You dirty, rotten bastard," I said in the direction of the far end of the pond.

"It was a subdued cry, Paul. I really believe that," Tim said.

"Kids cry for a lot of things, Tim. When they get hurt, when they can't have what they want, or maybe when they're sad 'cause mom is leaving the house and the kid wants to go with her, and when they're frightened. I'm very familiar with being frightened when I was a kid and that's what I heard, a frightened child. The cry that turns into a whimper after you've cried yourself out. Son-of-a-bitch," I said.

"Come on, let's put the lights back and get going. Even if we could do something, we couldn't, you know?" Tim said.

Tim took my light from me and set both of them inside the back door. We walked back to the car and Tim patted me on the back and asked if I was okay. I didn't respond, and no, I wasn't all right. I knew that cry, when you're so sad and you just want everything to be alright. I think the kid we heard was very frightened and knew everything *wasn't* going to be all right. I felt my anger, my hatred for whatever caused that child to whimper. That made me begin to wonder—if spirits linger, do they linger in the state they were when they passed on? If you die sad or happy, are you that way always when you're trapped in a timeless, psychic, unbounded space? I hoped not.

"Hold on! Look!!" Tim yelled.

Backing out, when Tim yelled he was pointing at the spring house. There was a man running from the back side and headed for the pond. Neither of us hesitated getting out. We both ran to the back door and retrieved the flashlights. When we got to the end of the pond, we shone our lights into the field and spotted him no further than twenty feet in. This was a trespasser and we were determined to catch up with him and ask him what the hell he was doing here. Perhaps he had something to do with the child crying. As I jumped into the field from the edge of the pond, the camera bounced up and smacked me square on the nose. It hurt like hell and made my eyes begin to water. Tim was just a few feet in front of me and

268

he was yelling all kinds of things—I was amazed and amused as well. Here we were, chasing someone through a field at 3 a.m. like a couple of guard dogs. We were obviously in better shape than the fugitive because we were gaining ground. Just as we reached the tree line, the guy stopped and put his back against a tree.

Tim asked, breathing hard, "What the shit are you doing here?"

The man said nothing, he just stood there looking at us. As Tim asked again, I lifted my camera while jostling the flashlight in my other hand and took a picture. Even today the picture I took is very clear in my mind, the look on his face when the bulb flashed will stay with me forever. Tim lunged clumsily for the man. That surprised the hell out of me. The man was gone before Tim was on him. We both shined our lights on the tree he'd been leaning against. It was no more than six feet from us. In under five seconds Tim went running past me so fast a vision of Superman came to mind. I turned back to the tree and when I realized I was standing there alone, I turned and ran like the wind. Tim and I were in a foot race back to the house.

I ran track at Olean Junior High and had some great times; even broke a record. That night Tim was so far ahead of me, I felt as if I had been standing still! No time for psychic feelings and, if they were there, the pure fear I was feeling would have quashed them.

"Where the fuck did he go?!" Tim yelled.

"Go straight and up to the front of the house, forget the pond!" I yelled, camera banging against my chest.

I've never seen anyone maneuver a turn the way Tim had that night. He was headed straight for the far end of the pond and did a ninety degree turn without losing any speed! It looked as if he had been yanked by an invisible rope in the direction of his turn. Absolutely amazing! We got to the front of the house, completely out of breath and I pulled the picture from the camera while Tim shined his light on it. It was a good picture, very clear. It was definitely the person we chased into the field. We looked at it very carefully, then to one another,

269

back to the picture and directly at the car. Another foot race had begun!

"This is NOT a person!" Tim said, jumping into the driver's seat.

"Actually, I disagree with you. This is a person that's NOT!" I said, literally sliding over the hood of the car, dropping the flashlight in the process, as I opened the passenger door.

We assumed we caught either a trespasser or someone from a neighboring camp dead to rights on the Dandys' property. We were undeniably wrong. When we reached the tree line and I aimed the camera at the man, he was looking at us. Upon examining the picture, it appeared he was looking past us; he hadn't been looking into the lens of the camera, that was obvious. His expression held more than fear. he appeared terrified. But his focus was not on Tim and me. He stood with his back to the tree, arms raised, with one side of his face appearing to have been beaten. It looked bloody. His mouth was open wide and one could only imagine what sound might emerge, piercing the cold darkness of the tree line. I'd read about the human aura and, completely surrounding this terrified man, was an opaque, blue band of light. I truly believed we had chased a man who was running, not from us, but from a malevolent evil from his past. And I further believed that past was with us and was in waiting in Mary Dandy's room.

Tim and I stared at the picture until the lenses of our eyes burned it in our memory banks. Several hours prior, I had told Tim I was going to pull a prank on Mike and now we possibly had in our possession indisputable proof of life after death.

"Well, do we give the picture to Clara?" I asked.

"No, I think you really ought to give her the one of the water buffalo having a drink!"

"For your information, it wasn't a woman or a water buffalo, it was Archie Bunker, smart ass!" I exclaimed.

"You know, Mike probably would have acted as if he accepted it as a joke if you gave him one of your Archie Bunker pictures, but I think it would have really pissed him off. I don't really know, this picture might push him over the edge, not to mention what Clara would think of it. Ask Father Al, see what he thinks or let him see it first. My mom is like your mom, she thinks we're nuts coming up here. I wanna show this to her," Tim said.

"Go ahead, I sure won't show my mom and, next time I talk to Father Al, I'll ask him," I said.

We didn't talk after pulling out of the driveway. The radio had been on but Tim turned it off before we reached the first turn on McMahon Road. We were both buried in our thoughts. We'd dealt with being scared out of our wits, being uncertain of what was around the next corner, and now, this was something that upset our emotional state in an altogether different way. It hit me suddenly, thinking about the night walking back from the pond when I had felt two very strong sensations. It made perfect sense now. The feeling of sadness replaced the extreme fear that had come before it. That night, had it been the child's distress I had felt, and was that sorrow a direct result of the prior feeling of terror or was the terror I felt the psychic energy released from our friend in the field? Dealing with the paranormal has its complications.

CHAPTER XXI

Tim and I had taken a couple nights off from going to the house. We were both emotionally distressed after Sunday's incidents with the voice of the crying child and the disturbing chase with the night specter. He and I worked together Monday night and I had practice Tuesday. We needed a couple days rest to recharge. I had talked to Mike and we had a little get together planned with him and two of his friends, Randy C. and Mike N. He said he had spoken to Keith M., the guy I met a week prior and he said he may stop by as well. Neither Tim nor I worked Wednesday night so we got together to go to the house early. We arrived around 9:15 p.m. and Phil was coming down the road. We stopped alongside one another on McMahon and chatted for a couple minutes.

"Hey,: Tim said as Phil pulled alongside.

"You two oughta move in, for Chrissakes, you're here more than I am," Phil said.

Neither us knew how to respond and I simply asked, "Everything all right tonight?"

"Nothing's been right in that house for goddamn months. Mary was going on about the smell of perfume in the car and Beth Ann said there's been a smell in her room on and off for a week. I'm sick of the whole goddamn mess and finding a job around here ain't easy, at least not a job that pays worth a shit," Phil grumbled.

"Did you try Clarke Brothers, Phil? You're a crane operator and there are cranes in different departments of the plant. I have a friend in the grinding …"

"I gotta go, I'm late now," Phil said

Phil pulled away before I finished my sentence. I wouldn't want to drive the distance he did every night, and I'm sure the house is giving him a lot of stress, but he didn't have to be rude when I was trying to be helpful. Over time, I learned that had been his nature often, even when it appeared he was in a fairly decent mood. Tim pulled to the back of the house where Mike and his friend were obviously waiting for our arrival. All three of them had come; Keith, Mike, and Randy. Tim pulled up, parked and we got out. Introductions were made all around; the six of us decided what we were going to do. We had brought the picture with us and couldn't wait to see someone else's reaction.

"Well, I told Mike I'm not too sure I believe all of this is true," Keith said.

"Tim and I used to come up every night, Keith, and even after the stuff that's happened, I find it hard to believe too. I think if you hang around long enough you might change your mind," I said.

Tim walked back to the car, retrieved the picture and handed it to Mike. Mike turned his flashlight on it; he didn't need to say a word, his expression said it all. Randy snatched it from him while Keith looked over his shoulder.

"Who the hell is that?" Mike asked.

"Don't know, who does he look like to you?" I asked.

"He looks like somebody that's had the crap beat out of him! Who is he and where did you take this picture? Keith asked.

Tim and I explained the entire evening to them: the child crying, and our race to the tree line and back. Randy and Mike listened intently while Keith, on the other hand, interrupted several times voicing his opinions and disbelief. We couldn't blame him, it would have been difficult for anyone to believe such claims. We all sat at the picnic table and filled Keith, Mike N., and Randy in on what had been going on over the past few weeks. Randy had explained his skill, if skill is the proper word, of being able to put himself into a voluntarily trance. I thought this odd at his age but what about Laura? She was certainly tuned into the energies of the house and she was much younger than Randy who was 17. Perhaps there was no set age when someone becomes psychic. It appeared that Keith was a strong skeptic. None of us attempted to convince him that what we were saying was true and that he was wrong in not believing. He was an "I'll believe it when I see it" skeptic. When the time came, if in fact it did, he would be able to reassess his beliefs. Until then, we respected his opinion. Tim took the picture back to the car and we all walked down the road toward the hanging tree. I told Keith and Randy what had happened to my car the first night I had visited the house. Keith, of course, said there was something the mechanics overlooked, that there was probably a loose connection in the ignition, that somehow when I twisted the key, pulled it tight again.

"All right, Phil," I said.

"Phil?" Keith asked.

"Just kidding, I don't think Phil really believed anything until Labor Day weekend. He always said there was a reasonable explanation for everything," I said.

"What would make the burners on the stove come on by themselves?" Mike asked Keith.

"Someone in the house turned them on. Come on, you guys; as a joke." Keith replied.

"I don't think someone would jokingly risk setting the house on fire, Keith," Tim replied.

"This is serious, Keith. There's just too much that can't be reasonably explained no matter how hard someone tries. You don't suddenly hear a woman's voice or a kid crying in the middle of the night without something being out of whack," Mike said.

"Well, I would still have to see or hear something to make me believe it was ghosts that's causing all these problems," Keith replied.

We walked up the road, waited and talked a few minutes. Then we returned to the house. We saw that Clara was in the kitchen and Mike asked that we all go inside. After entering, Mike introduced Keith to his mom and Beth Ann. Now I saw what Tim had meant when he said he and Beth Ann "looked at each other." I think there was a little chemistry in the works there.

"So what do you think about the stories the boys have told you, Keith?" Clara asked.

Randy and Tim, said in unison, "He has to see it to believe it."

Everyone laughed and Clara suggested we go into the living room. Mary and Laura were watching TV, and two of their dogs were on the living room floor. Jinx was curled up on Phil's chair. We continued talking about the onset of the incidents and what had happened since. Thank God Keith hadn't mentioned the picture Tim and I took. I wanted to talk with Father Al before telling Clara. The living room wasn't very big and most of us found a seat on the floor as we talked. Beth Ann went to the kitchen and she gave Tim a cute little smile on the way out. I had to chuckle, Tim had actually blushed. Randy and Mike were talking about the party last week when there was a muffled thump from above. Beth Ann was back in the living room without hesitation and we all looked to Clara.

"Maybe it's going to be noisy tonight," she said.

Keith looked at me and then to Mike. "What does that mean?" He asked.

"There's no one upstairs," Mike replied.

"I'm going upstairs," I said, standing up.

"No you are not! Didn't you have enough excitement Labor Day? Besides, you may just make matters worse," Clara said.

"It's not Mary's room, Clara. There isn't anything negative," I replied.

"Paul, everything is negative about all of this. Just let it be and it will settle down," Clara said.

We continued talking and tried to get off the house as the main topic. Beth Ann hadn't finished what she was doing in the kitchen and was reluctant to go back in. Tim volunteered to go with her and Clara and I exchanged smiles; it was a good feeling. Tim really was a good person. I didn't know anything about Beth Ann's boyfriend, Jeff, but Clara had said they hadn't been getting along. I'm sure Clara would let nature take its course without any interference. Another noise came and this time it sounded more like something had been dragged across the room above us: Clara and Phil's room. Tim flew up the stairs and Clara yelled for him to stop but it sounded like he had made the landing before she got the words out. I left the living room to follow Tim. Beth Ann was standing at the bottom of the stairs and I asked her to go back into the living room with her mother. Before I got to the top of the stairs, I could feel the cold. Tim was standing in the hall just before

Mary's door looking at me. "It's fucking freezing up here!" He whispered.

"Tim, come back to the stairs with me, now," I said.

I was totally wrong, it was Mary's room and it was, as Clara says, 'jumping.' There was another muffled sound behind and above me; the crawl space. I motioned for Tim to follow me. We descended the stairs and returned to the living room. I believe I said something like, "Mary's room is cooking," something to that effect and Clara's expression was full of anger. I hoped I hadn't inadvertently caused that anger.

"I think I was wrong, Clara. I'm sorry," I said.

"There's no need to apologize but you need to listen to me; you both do. The energy has been getting stronger lately. I think if we acknowledge it, it draws even more energy from us. Remember what Father Al told you," Clara said.

"Tell me what's going on." Keith said.

"Walk upstairs and you'll see. It's probably 30 degrees colder up..."

"What did I just say, boys?!" Clara said, interrupting Tim. "No more going upstairs! Leave well enough alone."

Mike suggested we go back outside. Clara was indeed angry but I wasn't entirely sure if she was angry with us or if it was a combination of things.

"Oh sure, things begin to jump and you all want to go outside. Mike, you can stay in with us. Boys, maybe you should go now. I'm sorry but there's been enough excitement for one night," Clara said.

Mike sat on the couch next to Laura and Mary, also angry, as the rest of us walked into the kitchen; Clara followed. I turned around to apologize.

"I told you, there's no need to apologize, just do as I ask. I'd been feeling uneasy all night but what's new, eh? I just wished this would all stop and let us alone," Clara said.

Tim rubbed Clara's arm as he walked around her to return to the living room. He was only gone for a minute or two and returned to the kitchen.

"I'm sorry, Tim," Clara said.

"There's no need to apologize," Tim said with an expression that made Clara burst into laughter.

"If you need us, you know where we'll be," I said as we walked out the back door.

I had the same feeling I felt the first night when I passed by the bathroom. I glanced in and, as I looked back at Clara before closing the back door, her look told me she had felt it too. It may have been the beginning of another "umbrella night."

As we all walked to the picnic table, Keith asked, "What did you mean, Tim, that the air was colder upstairs than down and really, how much colder?"

"Well, run down to your favorite grocery store and walk into their freezer. That'll give you an idea of the difference. This is my first time feeling what everyone's been talking about. I couldn't believe the change and it wasn't that cold when I got to the top of the stairs. It came suddenly as if someone *did* open a freezer door," Tim said.

"Come on! It couldn't have been *that* much different. Maybe they had the air conditioner set really low." Keith said.

"Keith, I wish Clara had allowed you to walk up. It's gotta be one of the strangest phenomena. Oh and, um—they don't have an air conditioner," I said.

We talked for about an hour when Keith said it was time he got going. He told us if his car was at his trailer to stop in any time as he planned on staying in the area for a while. Randy and Mike N. decided shortly after to head back to Hinsdale and suggested we all get together again soon. Both Tim and I agreed and walked them to their car. Mike yelled at us from his bedroom window as we passed by.

"Sorry, guys, mom's pretty upset right now. There's been a lot of activity in the house the past few days and she's concerned that it's going to get the way it was Labor Day night," Mike said.

"We understand, Mike. It can't be too easy never knowing when things are going to 'charge up.' If she's still up, remind her to call to us if she needs anything. We'll probably be here at least a couple of hours," Tim said.

Mike said goodnight to us and we continued to Randy's car. I didn't know how to read Randy. There was something in his eyes I couldn't quite make out. Perhaps he did have a gift but I never felt any 'vibes' from him. As Father Al told me, you can't always get signs from others. Sometimes you're not able to feel some peoples' energy at all. It was hit and miss I supposed. Randy and Mike N. pulled out as Tim and I went back to his car. The lights were off in the living room now and we assumed everyone had called it a night. I often wondered how easy or difficult it was to go to sleep in a room by yourself once an incident occurred. There had been times when Mike or Beth Ann refused to sleep in their rooms and other times they hadn't had a problem at all. I guessed, until you experienced it yourself, it would be futile to try to understand. In the beginning, Tim and I all but crawled into each others pockets some nights, and now we have no problem walking the property, even separately. We didn't even have the nerve to walk from the car to Mike's window, some thirty feet, the night we heard the woman's voice. Although, I did feel fairly confident that Tim would not walk to the tree line alone at night; I was sure I wouldn't have either. I wasn't totally sure if I would have even in broad daylight but the chances were I would. On Labor Day, I had a tremendous urge to walk to the tree line and I was determined I was going whether someone went with me or not. After Clara all told us to go into the house, I was later very relieved that she had.

There didn't seem to be any activity outside tonight. Looking back over all the nights we had gone to the house, I realized that I had begun to experience a sort of static in the air before something occurred. I suppose it was a building of the psychic energy in the area. But I had been dead wrong tonight when we were in the living room. I did have that feeling, a heaviness in the air, that something might happen but it didn't feel negative, as I told Clara. What I couldn't understand when I followed Tim up the stairs: what kept the energy that was so powerful from leaving the room? This was one of those questions that had several answers in the books I had been reading, but there was one common theme to all of the answers; the energy was bound to a specific location. Then again, the energy may have just wanted to tell us to "get out." I didn't and don't like the premise to that answer. Are there truly boundaries that cannot for any reason be breached? Here we have a very powerful, malevolent energy that you could imagine would disregard any limits of space by which it was bound. Yet there was another, the boy who has been seen by many, who roams the countryside at will, going any place he desires. I have a problem agreeing that there are boundaries when dealing with the paranormal. It wasn't rational to me but, then again, rational means normal and we're talking, *paranormal*.

"I'm afraid to say it's quiet tonight and it's time to go, 'cause the last time we said that, we ran through the field like soldiers," Tim said.

"We won't say anything, we'll just leave. How's that?" I suggested.

Tim didn't say a word, he got up and started walking to the car. Nothing happened. I don't think it mattered whether we said anything or not. The night we cornered our late night friend against the tree was no more than a coincidence. There were so many mysteries surrounding the Dandys' haunting. We all had speculated on which entity was who and how they might have been connected to one another, if indeed they were. Clara told us how many different apparitions were seen Labor Day evening and Tim and I talked about which ones we might have seen or heard. I was most curious about my least favorite, whatever had taken up residence in Mary's room. Clara and I talked about the extreme cold and where it had been experienced: Mary's room, my first introduction to it when I was walking with Phil, another evening when the back door blew open and a tremendous, cold wind blew in and the night I had felt the cold creeping up on me when I was glued to the ground. Were all of these caused by one entity and, if it was the energy from Mary's room, we might just rule out the boundary idea. There were two or three apparitions of women who'd been seen. One with black hair, another, whom Clara had seen, with strawberry blonde hair and the one referred to by Phil as, "the dizzy bitch." I don't believe a hair color had been mentioned by the girls when they describe the woman by the pond but she may have had black hair possibly ruling out a third woman. There was the young boy and now, the man Tim and I had chased. Clara and I have spoken several times during the writing of this story and she mentioned a minister who came for a visit in hopes that he may be of some help. Neither of us can remember his name but we remember him laughing as he entered the house saying he had never encountered so many spirits in one place. Clara had called it a "Spiritual Convention." There was a great deal of area involved when you take into account where the apparitions had been seen in reference to where the house stood at the end of McMahon Road. The hanging tree at the beginning of McMahon is about $3/10^{th}$ of a mile from the house. The tree line at the end of the property is almost the same distance. The hillside where the Georgian chant was heard is at least a quarter mile from the house. The young boy with blonde hair seemed to have been seen the most and in many locations. Someone fitting his description and his ability to disappear before your eyes had been seen on the property, along several spots of McMahon Road and Emerson Drive, where he had possibly been hit by a car. With all the was going on outside, it was apparent to all that whatever held Mary's room hostage was priority.

CHAPTER XXII

Wednesday, September the 12th was the last night Tim and I had been to the house. I had been asked to stay at home on Thursday. Friday and Saturday I had played. Tim had something to do Sunday so I decided to go it alone that evening. I called Clara and told her I was coming up alone unless I could talk Debbie into coming. She suggested I come up before nightfall. I arrived around 7:30 and it really felt strange, almost unsettling that Tim wasn't with me. For the first time in quite a while, the feeling of apprehension fell over me. It was okay driving up and visiting but I hadn't looked forward to being alone outside.

I knocked at the back door and I was greeted by Mike.

"Come on in," he said.

"So, you couldn't convince Debbie to come, huh?" Clara asked.

"Nope, I didn't think she would want to come this late. If it weren't for Father Al pulling up behind us that first night, I don't think she would ever have come again," I said.

"Father told me a little of the story. Exactly what did happen? Come into the living room and tell me," Clara said.

"Hi, Paul!" Mary and Laura said as we entered the living room.

"Hello, girls," I said, returning their greeting.

It was quite warm in the house; stifling. None of the windows were open as there usually were.

"Have a seat, Paul. Would you like some Pepsi or Koolaid? It's either strawberry or cherry. I don't know which," Clara said.

"It's strawberry, mom, I'll get it!" Mary said.

"Thank you, Mary." Clara said.

She returned with a large glass, full to the brim. I took a couple of sips and set it on the floor alongside the couch.

"Where's Debbie, Paul?" Mike asked.

"She stayed home, Mike. She doesn't feel comfortable sometimes," I replied.

Beth Ann excused herself and went to her bedroom. Clara sat down between Mike and me.

"Phil still here?" I asked.

"Yup, I'll be getting him up in about half an hour." Clara said. She continued. "Tell me, what happened that night when you left?"

"Well, I don't know. I was driving down the road and just as we got to the barn..."

"You mean the tree?" Mike interrupted.

"Michael!" Clara said with a mom's frustrated chuckle.

"No, he's right," I continued. "We were basically parked right under the tree. The barn is a few feet further I guess."

"They're about even." Mike said.

"Go ahead, Paul," Clara said looking at Mike.

"The car stalled. It just simply quit; everything. The engine died, the lights went out and that was it. I put it in park and turned the key but it was totally dead. The battery didn't even click like a battery does even when it's dead. The dash lights would have shone a little even if the battery had died but there was nothing," I explained.

"Did you see or hear anything?" Clara asked.

"I couldn't see sh..., anything it was so dark. As for hearing, I couldn't have heard a jet if it was ten feet above us with Debbie screaming at me," I said.

"How long were the two of you sitting there?" Mike asked.

"Oh, maybe five minutes, maybe a couple more. Yeah, I'd say five minutes at least," I said.

"And when Father Al pulled up behind you, your car started?" Clara asked.

"No, I was still turning the key when he pulled up. I got out of the car when I realized it was him. Actually, I gave him a bear hug! I don't think it started until... it started just as he got to my window. I remember I was telling him I was turning the key so hard I expected it to break, then the engine started," I said.

"But you don't remember seeing or hearing anything?" She asked again.

"No, I didn't. Debbie said she saw something. She said it looked like a man standing on one of the branches," I said.

"Above the car?" Mike asked.

"I'm not sure where, Mike. I just remember her saying that," I replied.

"Supposedly, someone or more than one were hanged from that tree," Mike said.

"Yeah, that's what I heard; the hanging tree," I said.

"Supposedly, a man got a woman pregnant out of wedlock and he was hanged on that tree. She was stoned to death. That's the legend anyhow," Mike said.

I sat there for a few moments thinking of what they'd just said. Even if this were a fact, what has that got to do with a car stalling?

"Okay, so a guy is hanged and, if you drive by the place he was hanged, your car's gonna crap out on you?" I asked.

"Father Al said it has to do with energies. A vortex if you will. If…"

I interrupted, "A vortex? This is WAY beyond me, Clara. What the hell is a vortex?"

"Well, it's, let's say, it's the main source of energy. It's … dammit, I've got to get Phil up! Excuse me a minute," Clara said, jumping up from her seat.

"Mike, can you come in here a sec?" Beth Ann asked from the other room.

Mike excused himself and went into her room.

When I had first entered the house, the parakeets in the living room were chirping non-stop; they were quiet now. Phil came down stairs, said hi, and went back into the kitchen where he began talking to the girls. I can't imagine having to get up nearly three hours before going to work because the drive takes two thirds that time to get there. It stretches an eight hour shift into a twelve hour work day with the drive to and from work. Clara came down stairs, offered a smile, said she'd be back in a minute and joined Phil in the kitchen. Mike and Beth Ann walked through the living room and into the kitchen. Beth Ann was already dressed for bed in her pajamas and a blue bathrobe. She got an apple and walked to the telephone in the kitchen. "Anti social," Mike said.

"I'm calling Jeff. I'll be off soon," Beth Ann said.

"Young love," Mike said.

"We've all experienced that," I said.

"I hate leaving you tonight." Phil said to Clara, standing at the living room door. "With all these nuts roaming around outside, especially the goddamned kids looking for a thrill. I just hate leaving you."

"We'll be fine, Phil. Mike and Paul are here if anyone comes around and I'm sure the State Police would be here in a hurry if we called. They probably have us on a hot list!" Clara replied.

"I'll call you when I get to work or sooner if I stop along the way," Phil said.

"That's fine. Don't worry, we'll be fine," Clara said.

Phil came into the living room, carrying a beer and his lunchbox. He grabbed a light wind breaker that was hanging across the back of his chair. I don't quite understand the beer knowing he's driving to Buffalo but Clara didn't seem to take notice.

"Have a good night we'll see you in the morning," Clara said, as Phil walked out through the kitchen and out the back door. Moments later, we could hear the engine start. Mike's bedroom window must have been open because the sound of the car was much louder as it pulled away along the side of the house. That must be why Clara and Beth Ann came outside moments after I arrived.

"Give me just a couple more minutes and I'll be back. I want to get the girls some blankets and their sleeping bags. They're going to camp out on the living room floor tonight," Clara said.

"No problem, Clara," I said. She and the girls went upstairs together, most likely to get the blankets when there was a muffled thud. It sounded like it came from somewhere in kitchen. It was apparent only Mike and I heard the noise.

"Did the girls hear that, you think?" Mike asked.

"I don't know, what do you think it was?" I asked.

"Not sure but, if the girls heard it, they'd have been screaming," Mike said.

Thud

Mike and I looked to the wall and then to each other.

"Maybe it's gonna be an umbrella night," I said.

"Shit, there are more sounds around here, man. Let me go up and tell mom. She'll probably…" Mike broke off when he heard his mom coming down the stairs. When she walked into the living room, she stopped and looked at us both quizzically.

"Something's wrong?" Clara asked.

"We heard a noise. It sounded like it was coming from the front of the house, maybe on the far end of the porch," Mike said.

"I suppose it could be one of the raccoons on the porch. Or it could be some nosey people looking around outside or something," Mike said.

"Sure, Tim isn't here with me and suddenly people come all the way to the house!" I exclaimed.

"Well, if you have the nerve, why don't you and Paul grab a couple flashli…."

Thud Thump, only this time, it sounded as it the noise were coming from above.

"Mom!" cried Mary, Laura right behind, glued to her sister.

"It's all right, girls," Clara assured them. Beth Ann had also come out apparently when she heard Mary call to their mom.

"Mom, what's wrong?" Beth Ann asked in a pleading voice.

"Everything is fine. Just everyone have a seat and we're going to check it out. It's probably one of the raccoons or maybe Dolly thumping around," she assured them. "Mike, please grab the flashlights and we'll check out the front porch."

"Mom, the second noise didn't come…"

"Get the lights, Mike," Clara interrupted.

Mike opened the back door to the slop room to get the flashlights. He held one and handed the other to his mom.

"Here, Clara, let me have that. I'll see if Dolly's on the front porch. I've been waiting to see her," I said.

"Are you sure?" Clara asked.

"Yup, not a problem," I said.

Mike and I walked out the back door and checked the front porch. The beams of both of our flashlights were trained on the entire front porch. Nothing.

"Should we walk around the house and see if someone might have run when they heard us coming?" I asked.

"I know dad would and he'd be mad if I didn't," Mike replied.

"Okay, I'm with ya, Mike."

We walked across the front yard to the side of the house which faced the pond. We scanned the entire side yard as well as the pond but saw nothing. We walked around the house and to the back door returning to the kitchen.

"Nothing outside mom. It's getting a little windy, maybe something was blowing against the house," Mike said.

Thud—Thump—Thump

Again, at the front of the house. It almost sounded like something being thrown at the house. Mike was quick to act and ran toward the front windows. Clara yelled at him to stop but he was determined. I followed and we both looked out the living room windows.

"You bastards! Get the hell out of here!!" Mike was yelling at someone. "I've got a gun and I'll use it!"

We could see two dancing lights crossing the field at the front of their property. It clearly looked like two people running with flashlights, and we were sure of it when the beam of one of their lights flashed onto the person running with them.

"Who are you yelling at?" She asked.

"Idiots, mom!" He replied. "There were two people, well, at least two, running across the field."

"I'll call the State Police and let them know we've had people trespassing. Maybe if anyone who's still around sees a police car, they'll leave and not come back," Clara said.

I asked Clara if I could call Debbie. I wanted to at least tell her I hadn't been 'scared to death' as she put it, when I was leaving. It was nearly 10 p.m. and I didn't want her worrying. When I called, she told me her brother was still there and they were watching a movie. He might crash on the couch as long as he had the car home in time for her mom to go to work. She asked if everything was all right without adding any scenarios involving ghosts to the conversation. I informed her of everything that had happened and all was fine. I told her not to worry and I'd be home soon. The only thing she mentioned in our short conversation was the tree. She asked me if I was worried about driving by it; I told her no. That wasn't entirely true.

When I hung up the phone Clara told me I was perfectly welcome to spend the night if Debbie didn't mind. She informed me the couch was quite comfy and the girls didn't sleep-walk. She said it would make them all feel a little more secure with someone else in the house since Tim and I weren't going to be outside.

"Would you like me to call Debbie?" Clara asked me.

"Honestly, I am a little apprehensive about leaving without someone with me. I know that sounds kinda child...."

"Not at all," Clara interrupted. "I'll call Debbie back and ask her if it's okay."

"Let me know what she says and *how* she says it. I don't want her to be mad at me," I said.

Chuckling Clara said, "Okay, I'm sure she'll understand."

Clara called Debbie and she said she understood perfectly, about Phil being gone and about my being a chicken! Truth be told, I think I was more chicken to stay overnight than to sit outside or chase after specters. Six of one, half a dozen of the other. At that time it all seemed so foolish and immature. Today, looking back, it was justifiable in labeling myself a member of the poultry family.

We sat around the living room. Both Laura and Mary were fast asleep in their sleeping bags. Peering from the top of Mary's bag was a small stuffed bear named Bunny held tightly against her cheek. There was no sign of a friend of Laura's as she had her back to the center of the living room. She had burrowed deep within the confining comfort of her sleeping bag. Mike was relaxed in Phil's recliner, I sat on one end of the couch and Beth Ann was leaning against her mom on the opposite end. The only light shining in the living room was a solemn lamp which was placed on an end table at the side of Phil's recliner. A night light, casting shadows through the doorway of Beth Ann's room, was glowing from an unseen corner.

Beth Ann was nearly asleep on Clara's shoulder. I'm sure the reason I was here was clear to Clara and perhaps to some, if not all, of her family members: the connection I've made with the house. I honestly didn't know why I continued coming to the visit. Sure, I was curious—but why? As I stated long before, in the beginning it had crossed my mind that this had all been a big fraud. But could one believe that six family members could all be talked into being conspirators in such an unbelievable story, and for what purpose? I could almost have believed that the younger children might have been frightened into believing something the adults concocted but I couldn't believe that Mike and Beth Ann would have been involved. The looks on all of their faces whenever something out of the ordinary would occur was that of genuine concern or perhaps fear. Never did you see one member of the family glance to another with a "I bet this is scaring them" look. I believe if this had been a hoax perpetrated by the entire family they would certainly have slipped up at one time or another and it would have been detected early on. Now, after all the incidents Tim and I had experienced, it was undeniable, this house is truly haunted. I was in it for the duration now and I believe Tim was as well; although there may have been an underlying reason for him to be here.

"Clara, if the girls wake up and see me here, are they going to be okay? They aren't gonna freak out or something seeing me on the couch are they?" I asked.

With her famous chuckle, she responded, "No, I'm sure they'll recognize you. I leave the lamp on low for them, so they won't wake up in an entirely dark room," Clara said.

Clara shifted a bit and woke Beth Ann. She walked with her to her room off the living room—Beth Ann managed a "goodnight" before retiring. Remembering back, all of the children always looked a bit frazzled as if they hadn't had enough rest. Stress can take a toll on anyone, regardless of age.

Clara said goodnight to Beth Ann and told me she was going to get a pillow and blanket from upstairs. What was I doing? I had no idea what might happen with the threats I'd made to the energy in Mary's room and here I was, sleeping on their couch just a few months after becoming involved. I had the feeling if Phil came home early and saw me here, he'd lose his temper which always seemed to be just below the surface. Clara returned with the pillow and blanket just as Mike came in to say goodnight.

"Now, you know where the bathroom is, and if you need anything to drink there's plenty of stuff in the refrigerator," Clara said.

"I'm fine, thanks—actually, I'll use the bathroom now. Mike, kinda hang around the kitchen 'til I get out?"

Chuckling, Mike said, "Sure, Paul, I know the feeling."

Walking into the kitchen I said, "I've seen enough outside to last a lifetime, I wonder what I'll see inside?" I entered the bathroom and semi-closed the door.

It only took a second for me to realize how pitiful I sounded after asking that question. The words came out as if I were a little kid asking my mommy if the doctor was going to give me a shot. They must have sounded that way to Clara too because she gave me that, "aw, don't worry" look moms give their kids just before you *do* get the shot!

"Let me put it this way," Clara said as I returned to the living room. "If anything does happen, you'll be one of the first ones to know. But I'm sure everything's going to be fine, Paul."

It was very easy for Clara to say what was on her mind, feelings not spared. Not that she was in any way cruel, on the contrary, she was honest and to the point. She wouldn't leave anything to chance, she told it like it was and that's something I admire about her to this day.

"Goodnight," she said, as she bent to cover the girls.

"Goodnight, Clara," She walked to the table and clicked the lamp switch to the lowest setting. It was dim enough to sleep and bright enough to allow the light to spill into the darkness of the kitchen. It was also bright enough on the window facing the back of the house, *and the pond*, to reflect the contents of the room in the windowpane. If *someone* were looking in I wouldn't see them, but then, would I want to? I don't think so. Clara and Phil's room was directly above the living room and I could hear Clara's footsteps. But we also had heard these same sounds when no one was upstairs. I know if I had heard these footsteps above shortly after moving into a house, and knew there wasn't anyone upstairs, I'd have been out the door and passing Crosby's in record time. I wouldn't even stop for a chocolate shake!

The humming of the refrigerator and the even breathing of the girls were the only sounds piercing the silence of the old farmhouse. I suppose people become accustomed to the quiet of the country. Yet, lying there on the couch, it seemed I was straining very hard to hear the silence. The apprehension was there. The thought of something making a point to end the silence, to let it be known it was present, was gnawing at my nerves. Once, I consciously caught myself glancing from the two front windows to the kitchen and back rapidly, several times in succession. *That's it,* I thought, *build something up that isn't there and you'll believe it's there whether it is or not. Psych yourself out enough and you're certainly going to see or hear something.* That's a true statement, it is. The harder you consciously try to hear or see something the more likely you will.

I lay there finally closing my eyes, waiting for sleep to come. It had been at least half an hour since I heard any noise upstairs and I felt myself getting drowsy. My last thought before I was sitting up straight was the noises we heard earlier. We were all very relieved to learn the noise was caused by those still with us. At least that's what we assumed.

Thump

The sound was nowhere and everywhere. It was one muffled sound, not loud but very audible. I stared at the front windows, I looked to the kitchen for the source and listened for movement upstairs or from Beth Ann's room. Was everyone sleeping? Were they in their safe place, deep from the sights and sounds of the House near Hinsdale? I listened—I wanted to cross the room and turn off the light but I was afraid if I did, and the girls woke, they'd be terrified if the noise came again. I told myself to go to Mike's room and wake him. Certainly, he wouldn't be angry if I told him I heard the sound we had heard earlier. He was in charge and he would want to be sure his mother and sisters were safe from intruders, outside or in. I admit it, I churned so much up in my imagination I became part of the fabric of the couch and wasn't able to get up. If someone were outside looking in, they surely could see me and I'm sure by the look on my face, knew they had succeeded in scaring the crap out of me.

Thud

Below! That sound absolutely came from beneath me. The basement. Sure, the house is old, there were certainly spots around the foundation where an animal might crawl under to seek refuge. That was it, we're in the country, there were probably twenty little creatures within a stone's throw of the house at this time of night. Absolutely, a little animal out scavenging for food, looking for a new home! Sure, that was it, absolutely nothing to worry about, just some hungry animal......

Thump

What the hell, was everyone so accustomed to random noises that nothing woke them?! The girls were in closer proximity to that last thump. They're lying on the floor. Why was it neither of them heard it? Honestly, I had been glad they hadn't heard it. Normally, Mary sleeps with her mom and Laura sleeps in her own room. Clara said they felt safer knowing I was in the house. I was grateful that neither of them had been awake to see my expression which surely would have conveyed my emotional state. Yeah, I was frightened, not only due to the random noises, but the feeling that had gradually been getting stronger. It wasn't ominous but it began to build. I was also sure it wasn't Mary's room "cooking" when Tim ran upstairs to investigate and I'd been wrong. I hated the thought, but I needed another set of eyes and ears to share this with. I uncovered myself to leave the comfort of the couch to get Mike, when I caught a slight movement from the window facing the back of the house. A small pine tree obstructed part of the view from the side yard. The light of the lamp on the window glass made me believe it may have been the reflection of the blanket as I pulled if off. No, it couldn't have been the blanket, the couch was at the edge of the room and I would have had to toss the blanket to the center of the room to see its reflection. But with the light on in the room, I could barely see the pine boughs near the glass. What I thought I saw covered more area of the window than the tree did.

Thud—Thump—Thump

I looked at the girls; they were still sleeping.

"Paul, is that you?" Beth Ann asked.

I didn't want to alarm her, yet if something were to happen, I didn't want her to be unprepared. I thought for a moment and said, "Yeah. Sorry, Beth Ann, I dropped one of my shoes when I was taking them off."

"You dropped it three times........? Oh no!" Beth Ann exclaimed, fear in her voice.

She *had* heard it.

"Beth Ann, I think you should wake the girls and have them go upstairs," I said.

"Yeah, I think our friend is back," she said from her room.

Beth Ann came out of her bedroom a few moments later and on her trail was a strong scent of very potent perfume; flowery smelling. She said she wanted to get her mom and have her come down before waking the girls. *"Good idea!"* I thought. She went up to get Clara and the two of them returned quickly.

"What's wrong?" Clara asked sleepily.

"The same noise we heard earlier, Clara, but I don't think it was com...."

"I smell her," Clara interrupted. "Whoever she is, Paul, she doesn't represent anything that gives the sense of evil."

"Something does and it's still present," I said.

"Come on, Beth Ann, help me get the girls upstairs," Clara said.

Mary and Laura were reluctant to get up and, after Laura was completely awake, she looked at me, looked around the room and stopped to gaze at the window. I looked over and saw nothing, thankfully. I looked back to Laura as she stood up and she gave me a smile. "It's okay, he's leaving," she said.

Jesus, Mary, and Joseph were the first words that came into my head. I had to silently chuckle thinking I sounded, mentally anyhow, like my father. Mom and big sister accompanied Mary and Laura up the stairs. A few minutes passed and Clara came back down alone.

"What was it?" Clara asked.

"It sounded very much like the sounds we heard earlier. I figured it was whoever Mike and I saw running through the field. I think *that* was a coincidence. Even if it were them that we saw, I don't think they got into the basement. The last two times I heard the sounds, they were from below the floor, and what was that all about with Laura saying, 'he's leaving'" I stated.

"Well, you know as well as anyone, she's tuned in too. Now do you see what we've been talking about with this perfume? It's so overpowering!" Clara said.

"I'll say! There was a woman who bought the glasses at the Fountain and I thought her perfume was strong, sheesh! Clara, I don't know if power of suggestion is at play here with what Laura said, but the powerful negative feeling that was getting stronger is almost gone. There's is still a feeling of something here in this room," I replied.

"It's our diary-sneaking woman who goes into Beth Ann's room. I don't think there's ever been a negative feeling when the smell of perfume has been present," Clara said.

"They're settled down, mom, but Mary wants you to go back upstairs. She asked why we got them up and I just told her that you were worried about a draft with them laying on the floor. Laura didn't say anything different," Beth Ann said as she returned to the living room.

That was quick thinking on Beth Ann's part, I thought.

"Is that it? I mean, are there going to be more disturbances?" I asked.

"Let me consult my crystal ball," Clara said, chuckling. "You never know, Paul. There seems to be a pattern when the most activity occurs. But, even though we believe that to be true, there are still random incidents all the time. And with that, I'm going back to bed, and you both should do the same."

"G'night, mom," Beth Ann said.

I said goodnight to them both and Beth Ann returned to her bedroom. I told her if she hears something and thinks I'm sleeping to wake me no matter what. Was it like this all the time inside, I wondered? Do they ever get a chance to sleep through the night? Since the girls had gone upstairs, I decided to turn off the lamp. There was still a glow coming from Beth Ann's night light and that was enough to see everything on the near side of the living room. I didn't much like the kitchen being at my back, and I didn't want to put my head at the other end of the couch and have the back window behind me. Man, what a chicken, I thought.

"What was going on?" Mike said.

"Jesus Christ, I think I stained your mom's couch….don't do that!" I whispered. I could hear Beth Ann laughing and it sounded as if she were attempting to cover her face hoping no one would hear her, especially me.

"I can hear you, Beth Ann, and it's not funny!" I said.

"I'm sorry, Paul. It was so quiet and you should have heard yourself. It was so sudden, and it was cute the way you said it. You sounded like Tim when he gets frightened," Beth Ann said.

"Oh, the perfume lady was here, Mike, and the same sounds we heard earlier," I said.

"Those assholes came back?" He asked.

"I don't believe the noises we heard were made by them. I think it was a coincidence that we saw them at the same time. The noises seemed to be coming from the basement," I said.

"Oh, all right, goodnight," he said casually.

I guess you get used to it. Mike was by far, the least of the family members to be overcome by what had been happening. When it came to the girls being upset, it angered him immensely but he seemed to take most of what happened with a grain of salt. He was as level-headed as his mom and dealt with things he was faced with logically and with tact. He was a very bright young man. All of the Dandy kids were bright, and there wasn't a doubt, it was Clara they took after. Their father was the bread winner, period. He had never shown any sort of leadership and by no means was any type of role model, especially to his son. When we're kids, we want to be just like our parents, when we're teenagers, we don't want anything to do with them, and when we grow up, we're just like them. Not in Mike's case. He was successful and there was never a doubt in my mind, during those short, trying months I had gotten to know him that he wouldn't be.

I rolled over facing the couch and listened to the quiet. There was an abundance of it and it sounded great. It reminded me of being in the boy scouts and sleeping in cabins or our tents. There was no sound other than the breathing of your tent mate. When the hum of the refrigerator wasn't present it was dead quiet. I drifted in and out several times thinking there had been noises when I knew it was nothing more than my imagination. Eventually, I felt myself falling deeper into the abyss we know as sleep and didn't wake until I realized I had only been pulling the blanket back up because it was being pulled off of me. I sat upright, focused my eyes to the end of the couch and scanned the room still filled by the darkness of night. I remembered the smell of perfume had dissipated as I was falling asleep but now it was strong again, so pungent and gagging. I attempted to "tune in" to what it was but there was no feeling, no sense of not being alone.

"What do you want? I'd really like to get some sleep if you don't mind," I whispered and quietly chuckled when I heard my words. I waited a few minutes before lying down again. There's nothing here, I thought. It was as if we were playing children's games with some of these sprits. They wake you, then run and hide, probably sneaking a peek from a hidden corner of the room giggling because they had gone undetected after disturbing you.

"Goodnight," I said, and rolled facing the couch. I didn't wake again until I heard Mary and Laura talking in the kitchen about perfume.

When I got up from the couch and looked at the clock in the kitchen, it was almost 10. I had no idea what time it was when I woke. All I knew is that it was before 5:30 because it had still been dark. The girls said good morning and I asked them where everyone else was. Mary said Beth Ann and Mike were still in bed and Clara was upstairs cleaning.

"Good morning, sleepy head," Clara said from the top of the stairs.

"Good morning. The perfume lady is a pain in the butt!" The girls let out a hearty laughter at Clara's greeting to me.

"I woke sometime this morning to the smell of perfume and my blanket being pulled," I said.

"Oh, so she left Beth Ann alone and has directed her attention on you, eh?" Clara said descending the stairs. "Our friend in Mary's room tried to get my attention when I walked by this morning. There was a couple of loud bangs on the door after I left my bedroom. Would you like some breakfast?"

"Just something simple, if anything," I replied.

"Cereal?" Clara asked.

"Sure, that sounds fine, thank you."

"I'll get it, I'll get it," Mary exclaimed. "Captain Crunch or Cheerios?" She asked.

"Captain Crunch, please," I said.

Mary set a bowl in front of me and filled it with cereal. Laura got the milk from the refrigerator and brought it to the table.

"Thank you, girls. Gee, I'll take you home with me if I'm going to get this kind of service. Where's Phil?" I asked Clara.

"He called and said he was stopping on the way home. He said he'd be home by 11:00 or so," Clara replied.

I was fairly sure where he would be stopping. Of course, I wouldn't know the name of the tavern but they all served his favorite liquid breakfast, lunch and dinner. Mike entered the kitchen a few minutes after I sat down. Without even asking, Mary poured him a bowl of Cheerios and set it on the table. I slid the milk over so he could reach it.

"Who were you talking to this morning?" Mike asked.

"Me?" I asked. "No one. HA! Get it, *no one*? I woke up when I felt the blanket being yanked, or pulled, or was that you messing around?"

"No! I went to the bathroom and after I got back into bed I thought I heard you say something. I was gonna come back out thinking you might have said something to me, that maybe you heard me get up. I wouldn't do something like that. We have enough troubles without adding to them," Mike said.

"She likes you," Laura said to me.

"Who the perfume lady? Well, I'm spoken for, Laura, and it would be very difficult for me to like her back," I said.

"Maybe you could meet her again, when you…"

296

"Laura!" Clara exclaimed.

Laura got up and quickly went upstairs, obviously upset. Clara started after her and I asked her to wait and let me go. She turned around from the stairs and I went up to Laura's room. She was sitting on the end of her bed, upset and crying. I sat on the bed next to her and cautiously put my arm around her. I told her it was okay. I knew that she meant nothing at all wrong with what she was going to say before her mom interrupted her. Laura was very emotional and she suffered from emotional instability but she had the heart of an angel. She understood the house better than anyone gave her credit for, except her mom. In her way of understanding, she meant nothing more than what the words she was going to say would mean. And, actually, she was correct. Maybe when I die, I possibly could meet this "perfume woman" and get to know her. Clara interrupted her by shouting her name; I interrupted her with the expression on my face. I think I may have upset her more than her mom because I truly believed she felt my shock. I wasn't shocked at what she was about to say, I was only shocked that she put that type of connection to it. And furthermore, she knew I wasn't angry or upset with her in any way as I sat next to her; this I could feel.

"You okay?" I asked.

She looked up at me after a few moments, smiled and said, "Yeah."

"Don't be upset with your mom, she's not mad at you either. I promise, when you go downstairs, she's gonna give you a hug, okay?" I said.

I took her hand and led her to the stairs. She walked down first and when she reached the bottom and entered the kitchen, her mom gave her a hug.

I only knew Laura from the house. I never had contact with her again after 1974. I really and truly liked that kid. We made a connection and sometimes we never had to say a word to one another. If anything, we shared our energy, our psyche's were tuned on the same frequency, if you will.

Clara and Laura went into the living room. Mary was eating her breakfast and I sat down again and joined her to finish my bowl of now soggy cereal. Clara, Laura, and Beth Ann soon joined Mary and me in the kitchen.

"Morning, anything interesting happen after I went to bed?" Beth Ann asked.

"Not really, just a tug of war with the blanket," I replied.

Laura walked up behind me, reached around my neck and gave me a hug. I wish there were words that could describe what it feels like to encounter a psychic connection with someone. I can only give an analogy with that of a blind person. Blind people read by rubbing their fingers over Braille. Each bump represents letters or groups of letters forming words. They can't see them but they can *feel* them. They pass their fingers over the raised paper and feel an 'H' or an 'S.' Two people who connect psychically will share the feeling of 'H'appiness or 'S'adness. In either case, the mind's eye is at work and it can operate in many ways, helping us understand and even communicate. If you walk into a room where two people have been arguing before you entered, there's a sense of tension, of negativity. You can *feel* it, you don't necessarily have to talk to or even look at the people who were involved. When you fight, you create energy—when you die, you create energy—when you make love, you create energy. There's energy all around us and some pick it up with a greater understanding than others. Eventually, if you are subjected to a specific type of energy, over a period of time, you become more and more aware of it, more sensitive to it. Maybe this is where those who make predictions become more accurate because they have learned how to "tune in." They home in on an energy which helps and guides them in their predictions. Before the Dandy house, I had my 'goosies' but they were feelings of something about to happen and, generally, to my dismay, something negative. The energies at the Dandy house were refreshing in some ways and depressing in others. It was somewhat refreshing picking up the energy of the "perfume lady," and very refreshing picking up energy from such a lovely child as Laura. I'm sure I need not explain the depressing side of these energies within the country home. At best, I can describe having the ability to tune into another's psychic energy as exhilarating; at worst, debilitating.

"Well, that was an interesting evening, I must say," I said.

"I'm happy you enjoyed yourself," Clara replied with a smirk.

"Thank you for your hospitality, to you and my new pretty smelling friend. I'm gonna get back to Olean. I have a few things to take care of and I have to work tonight," I said.

"I'm glad it was a fairly quiet night. Some nights you're awake every fifteen minutes from one thing or another. I'm sure we'll see each other soon enough," Clara said.

I said goodbye to everyone and Mary gave me a hug as I was leaving. When I got outside, I walked to the pond and looked over the entire area. We had actually run across that field chasing a *someone*. It was exciting thinking about it yet it gave me a chill thinking about who that *someone* was. Where were the 'fogmen' during the day or even now—sleeping? Or were they connected to our side only at certain times of the night? And what of the dizzy bitch—why hadn't she been dancing, in her circular, swaying movements, along the bank of the pond as I stood there that morning? Walking back toward the driveway, I looked to Mary's window and stopped. It was there, looking out at me; baiting me to come upstairs for another round to drain me of what it needed—energy, so it could recharge and continue tormenting these good, God fearing people.

"I know you're there, you son of a bitch, and your time is coming, you rotten bastard," I said aloud looking at Mary's once-upon-a-time bedroom window. I was sure, there was no mistake; it *heard* me and I *felt* it. There would be a showdown; someday.

CHAPTER XXIII

I had a couple of bills that needed to be paid, I went home to take a shower, change my clothes and get the mail to see what the final utility bills were for the Fountain. Then I stopped by to visit with my mom for a while. I arrived home a little before Debbie and started making some hamburgers for dinner. I was sick to death of submarine sandwiches. Not that hamburgers are any healthier (probably worse actually) but I wanted something home cooked. They were finished cooking a minute after Debbie walked in the door. We talked about last night's visit and she told me her brother never woke her so she could go to bed. She woke with the worst stiff neck. After dinner, I massaged her neck while she talked about work and the problems they'd been having in the data processing room. I got up to do the dishes before leaving for work and she told me not to worry about them. She said her neck felt so much better, she wanted me to massage it until I left. A few minutes later, the phone rang. It was her mother. I knew these conversations could last a while so I decided to do the dishes after all. She frowned, pointing at her neck, and I motioned I only had 5 minutes before I had to leave for work. She offered a more pronounced frown. I gave her a kiss and left to walk to the sub shop and was surprised when I saw Tim's car parked out front. When I walked in he informed me Mary had called off and Jim called him in to work.

"Beth Ann mentioned your name last night, Casanova," I said.

"What'd she say?!" Tim asked, excitedly.

"She said I sounded like you when you get frightened," I said.

"Oh, big deal. She was making fun of me, huh?" Tim said, frowning.

"No, if anything, she noticed your weak spot and thinks it's cute, that's what I think."

The phone rang and Tim answered, "County Morgue, you stab 'em, we slab 'em."

A couple of seconds later, Tim hung up without saying anything else.

"Who was that?" I asked.

"I don't know, they hung up," Tim replied.

"Well gee, I wonder why, Shakespeare."

The phone rang again and I beat him to answering it. It was Clara. She had called the house and Debbie told her I was already at work. She said she called once but must have misdialed because someone answered with another name she didn't quite catch. When I told her it had been Tim, all she could say was, "That dip!"

"Hey, you're a dip, Clara says so!" I yelled to Tim.

He reached under the counter to retrieve his tin, cone hat, and placed it on his head just as a customer walked in. He took the man's order without removing it but the customer paid him no never mind whatsoever. He probably thought it was part of the sub shop's attire. Maybe he thought they were supposed to resemble a torpedo; in a way, it did.

Clara told me that a world-renowned psychic was coming to Saint Bonaventure to give a lecture and asked if I wanted to go.

"What the hell kind of question is that? Of course I wanna go!" I exclaimed.

"Where you going?" Tim asked.

"There's a lecture Wednesday night at Bona's and we're all going!" I exclaimed.

"Yeah, everybody but me, I have to work!"

"See if someone—'okay, bye, Clara'—if someone will work for you," I said to Tim.

"Mary's got some kind of flu bug and I know her, she'll be sick for at least a week; she always is. Everyone else is scheduled either here or at East Side," Tim explained.

"Okay, I'll work for you," I said.

"Bullshit, you need to go more than I do. You're the one with the antenna, you don't need my hat," Tim said.

"You mean, torpedo?" I said.

"Huh?"

"Never mind. We'll figure something out."

I really wanted Tim to be able to go to the lecture and I would have worked for him but I knew when it came down to it, he wouldn't have agreed to the switch. He was a good friend—I never touched his brakes! I didn't know a brake from a muffler when I was 21!

We finished up at our normal time that night. Tim, probably out of sadness, kept his tin torpedo on his head the entire shift. He had three people comment on it and he gave three completely different explanations as to what it represented; from a hair restorer, to a remote antenna that picked up signals from his car radio. The explanation that was given between these two I'll not mention in case any young children read this!

Tim decided he didn't want to go up tonight. He assured me he wasn't upset but I didn't believe him. I told him I couldn't tomorrow, that I had told Debbie I would stay home and Wednesday was the lecture. He said he could go up to the house after the lecture, that maybe everyone would explain what it was all about. I agreed with him yet I felt bad. He had become an integral part of everything surrounding the house and this was probably going to be the only time we would find something out regarding psychic phenomena from an expert. He gave me a lift home and told me he'd give me a call tomorrow. I went in and called Clara to tell her we wouldn't be up and to explain that Tim really appeared upset.

"I think he likes Beth Ann, Clara. I honestly believe that he had hoped to go so he could be in her presence away from the house," I confessed.

"Well, I'll tell you a secret; she likes him. She and Jeff haven't been getting along and all they've done lately is argue. He gets jealous when Tim's around the house and he thinks that Tim and Beth Ann have been spending time together," Clara said.

"They hardly ever talk and rarely see each other," I said.

"Well, I'm not going to say anything either way, Beth Ann can handle herself quite admirably. She knows what's best for her. So, we'll see you Wednesday. We might as well pick you up, it's on the way." Clara said.

"That's fine, Clara. Will there be enough room?" I asked.

302

"We do have a station wagon, Paul. If you don't fit, we'll throw you in the back with the spare tire!" Clara said.

We said goodbye and I went into the bedroom. Debbie asked what time it was and was amazed that I was home. She asked me to come to bed; there was no argument there! We spent time getting to know one another again and were fast asleep shortly after.

When I got up the following morning, I decided I was going to make my own tinfoil hat. I would wear it when I stopped by the sub shop on my way to practice tonight to see if Tim thought I was as nutty as he was. It was an uneventful day. I spent most of the late morning and afternoon with my mother, talking about nothing. The topic of the house didn't even come up. We had lunch together and it was a really nice day. She suggested that Debbie and I come over for dinner and I accepted. Spaghetti! She made the best sauce in the world. She'd better, she's Italian! I went home about the time Debbie arrived and told her we were going out but I didn't tell her where. Of course, when I turned the corner of Eighth Street it was fairly easy to figure out where. I stuffed myself, as always and my father talked about Barbara Stanwyck, the actress. I think he had a thing for her and sometimes it upset my mom. I changed the subject basically to shut him up. We visited for a while until it was time for me to leave for practice. Debbie said not to worry about her, that she would walk home. It was only two blocks so I didn't worry. She said since I stayed home last night, and if I wanted, I could go to the house tonight. I explained that it was nice to stay home, and planned on doing it again. She showed enthusiasm when I asked if she would go to the lecture with us. Of course, she said yes. I drove home real quick to get my hat and went to the sub shop. I put it on and walked in. The first thing Tim did was look under the counter to see if I had taken his.

"How do I look?" I asked.

"Not as good as I do," he said, putting his on.

"I didn't think so. You okay?" I asked.

"I'm fine. Practice tonight?" He asked.

"On my way," I said.

"Then go, I'll talk to you tomorrow," Tim said.

Two things came to mind with Tim's comment: 1. He was upset that we hadn't been able to go to the house as often as we had been, and 2. I think he was really falling for Beth Ann. Number one made me feel bad because we'd been spending a lot of time together, but number two was a great feeling. Tim was a great guy and Beth Ann was a sweetheart. I think they have a lot in common and they seem to get along great—time would tell.

We had a passionate practice. We were all into learning a few new songs and it went great. When I got home, the passion continued, and then I watched a movie with Debbie sleeping alongside me on the couch. It was my turn to wake up with a stiff neck! I woke Debbie up and noticed it was nearly 3 a.m. It took me a few minutes to realize but I had a lingering 'goosie.' It was an indifferent feeling, nothing really positive nor negative, but it was there and it wasn't my imagination. Debbie hadn't fallen into a deep sleep and got up to use the bathroom. When she returned, my guitar that was leaning in the corner on the other side of the room strummed; not once, but twice.

"You gotta be shittin' me," I said.

I got up, turned on the light and expected to see a curtain or something rubbing against the guitar neck. There was nothing near it. The closest thing to it was the dresser and that was two feet away. I thought maybe it slid along the wall a little, then slid again, but it was in the same position it had been since I picked it up two weeks prior.

"What made it do that?" Debbie asked.

"I think it slid against the wall. Let's go to sleep," I said.

I wasn't about to get her worrying, not on your life. I wanted to speak but there was no way I could, not with Debbie here. I couldn't believe it, not for a second. I laid there for at least an hour, eyes wide, listening, feeling; but it had gone. I thought all the proper things, you are not allowed here, go away, you're not wanted, this is my home not yours; GET OUT! I shut everything out and finally fell asleep. There was no tugging of blankets, no smell of extract of lilac, or whatever kind of perfume the "perfume woman" wears at the Dandy house. I woke to an empty bed, it was after 9 a.m. Either Debbie didn't wake me before leaving for work or I didn't remember. I got up, went to the kitchen and sat there. I didn't do anything, I don't believe I even thought of anything for at least half an hour; I just sat. When I did finally begin to think, my mind was assaulted with a million thoughts from psychic phenomena to how many miles was it to the sun. It was as if a valve had been opened and out poured everything I'd read, heard or seen. For a minute I thought I was going mad, or losing control; my cheese had slid off its cracker. I opened the refrigerator and grabbed a Pepsi. I took three gulps, hiccupped, took three more, hiccupped again, and finished the can in the next couple of gulps. I then let out a burp that would have rivaled the sound of Old Faithful. I got up, went to the bathroom and flopped on the couch. I didn't wake up 'til half past 2.

My mind didn't feel as cloudy as it had that morning. I took a shower and grabbed the lone hamburger that was in the refrigerator, left over from the other night's dinner. I didn't heat it or put it on a plate, I just ate it like a cookie. I dropped a few hamburger crumbs on the floor, which I swept up with my hands. It was nearly time for Debbie to get home and I had already decided we were going out to eat. The phone rang as I was getting the mail; it was Clara.

"You will not believe this! Father Al called and said Alex is going to come to the house after the lecture! Can you believe it, he's going to come to the house and give us his impressions!" She exclaimed with delight.

"Oh, My God!" I was awake now! "I'm going to call Tim and let him know. He said he would come up after the lecture so we could tell him all about it. We can tell him, and he can meet the guy who gave it!" I said.

"Okay, you call him and I'll see you about 6:15!" Clara said.

"Debbie wants to go too, Clara. There'll be enough room right?" I asked.

"Sure, Laura and Mary aren't going so there'll be plenty of room," Clara replied.

I called Tim and told him the news. He sounded excited too. I also told him what Clara had told me regarding Beth

305

Ann. He didn't believe me at first but I assured him I wouldn't toy with his feelings.

"So, you are gonna come up after work?" I asked.

"Yeah, I'll be there as soon as I'm done at work," Tim replied.

"Well, don't rush, drive carefully. I have a feeling this guy will be there for a while," I said.

Debbie got home at her usual time and we went to Arthur Treachers to get dinner. We drove home and I was so excited about the lecture, I couldn't sit down to eat. The thought of having a psychic visit the house and possibly tell us what was happening was exhilarating. Even though I wanted to know why I experienced so many feelings at the house, I felt apprehensive and intimidated about meeting him. But I had to know and this was going to be my best chance to get answers.

Clara pulled up just after 6 p.m. and honked. She was early but we were ready and I'm sure we all shared in our eagerness to get answers. Saint Bonaventure was only about eight to ten minutes from our apartment and the lecture started at 7 p.m.. Clara was rattling on a mile a minute, she couldn't contain a single thought. She wasn't actually addressing any of us individually, she was going on about what she thought Mr. Tanous might find when he gets to the house. We parked behind the Reilly Center and hurriedly walked in as if we had been late, yet we were almost 45 minutes early. There weren't too many people seated at the time, and most of those present were students from the university. We chose seats that were fairly close to the stage area that had been set up at one end of the court. The Reilly Center was Saint Bonaventure's basketball court which hosted such famous players as Hall of Famer Bill Murray, Billy Kalbaugh and all-time great, Bob Lanier. Musical concerts of every genre were also hosted at the Center. Moments before the lecture was to begin, I believe I recognized Father Al on the opposite side of the court. I pointed him out to Clara. She thought it was him as well. I had hoped he'd look for us and joined our group.

The lecture was fascinating and Alex held the audience captive with his manipulation of light. When a bright light was placed in front of him, he held his arms out extended, and a few moments later a ball of light appeared in his hands. He showed a slideshow and one picture was that of Beethoven's Castle. In this particular picture, was a ghostly figure that had been described as Beethoven himself. The picture was remarkably clear and the figure in the picture was surrounded by an aura of light. The lecture lasted approximately one hour. At the end, Alex had scores of people come up to him to ask questions. I wanted to join the crowd that had formed around Alex but Clara asked that we return to the house and await for their arrival. Besides, we had to get back before Phil left for work or the girls would be alone. As we were walking out, we passed an elderly gentleman of about 65. I brushed against him as we neared the back door of the Reilly Center and he said with a smile, "Spirits can scare the dickens out of you, can't they?" I simply said, "yes" and continued walking behind Debbie. It didn't even dawn on me until the next day that he had picked up my thoughts. I had been thinking that same thing 10 minutes earlier. I was so angry with myself for not understanding what had happened.

"We're going to have his company all to ourselves very shortly," Clara said, as we all piled into the family wagon. Clara dropped Debbie off at home. She wasn't going to the house but thanked Clara for taking us to the lecture. I went in and said goodnight and told her I would see her when I returned from meeting Alex. She was very excited that I might find answers about my "gift." I gave her a kiss, walked out to the car and began the drive to Hinsdale.

CHAPTER XXIV [A]

ALEX TANOUS—VISITS THE DANDYS

We all sat waiting impatiently for Father Al and Alex to arrive at the house. Over an hour passed before we heard a vehicle pull in. I'm sure we must have looked like a bunch of eager kids, waiting for Santa Claus, as we stood at the back door waiting for the anticipated knock. When it came, Clara turned to all of us and said, "Manners, everyone."

She opened the back door and first to enter was Father Al followed by Alex. His deep set eyes had the look of a shaman, or mystic. They could penetrate your very being and look deep within your soul. Father made the introductions and when he got to me, I looked at Alex, and very hesitantly held out my hand. He said, "I won't tell you if you prefer not to know."

"I'm not sure I want to know anything right now, Mr. Tanous," I said.

Father Al gave his admirable chuckle as Clara asked them to go into the living room. Alex looked like he hadn't had a decent night's sleep in weeks. His color was gray and his posture was weak, as if he hadn't seen a comfortable bed in some time. They weren't in the living room more than a couple of minutes. Alex appeared to be very anxious to walk through the house. Father Al hadn't given Alex any information about the house and he didn't want to hear anyone's opinions or stories. He and Father Al climbed the stairs to the second story first. They were up there for probably 10 to 12 minutes before coming down. As they were descending the stairs, we heard Alex groan. I wasn't in a position where I could see but it sounded as if he were in pain. When they arrived downstairs, they walked through each room, staring with Mike's and ending with Beth Ann's. Alex's gaze appeared to see things that weren't visible to us. He passed by me as he entered the living room and his eyes seemed to be fixed on something out of focus. For the first time, I felt the power of Alex Tanous. I can only describe it as the feeling of static you would feel from a balloon after vigorously rubbing it against your clothing. I hardly felt anything when we shook hands. Perhaps he was capable of subduing his inner self.

As he walked into Beth Ann's room, we all returned to the living room and waited for him to come back from whatever place he traveled. As he entered the living room from Beth Ann's room, his gaze began to clear as he sat down on Phil's ottoman and calmly said, "Did you know you had a mass murder here?" Clara's complexion turned to the color of talc as she desperately attempted to say, "No." We all looked at one another in astonishment and disbelief.

Alex began his explanation of the impressions he had gotten while walking through the house. He said there were seven lost souls, some who were agonizing terribly, but he only gave his impressions of six of them. His descriptions of these spirits are as follows but not in the particular order he gave as I don't remember: Two men, one who had been beaten to death, the other was stabbed. Three women, one he said had bulging eyes, another who had been hanged, and the third was a strawberry blonde girl of about 18 years of age. She had been beaten, tortured and left to die. It was very difficult for Alex to speak of this last victim. The sixth impression he received was that of an elderly woman of about 90. He said he believed the old woman knew of the murders and wanted to tell someone but she hadn't been involved in any way. As he was giving his impressions it was though he had been looking at each one as he described them; his eyes moving over each spirit. Giving his impression of the strawberry blonde was most difficult and he appeared to "feel" what had happened to her. Parts of his body moved as if he were being stung by invisible bees. He said this had all taken place over 100 years ago. He felt that there was a stagecoach run nearby and passengers would be dropped off only to be robbed, tortured and murdered. He said there were hidden and undisturbed graves in the immediate area but, before the murderer or murderers had time to bury them, their bodies were placed in the crawlspace. The opening of the crawlspace door according to Father Al is what caused Alex to groan. He saw the impressions of the bodies as the door swung open. He was emotionally and psychically drained. I believe he was physically drained as well.

We had moved about the downstairs. Alex, Mike, Laura and I were standing in the kitchen. Clara, Father, Beth Ann and Mary were standing just inside the living room. I had to take my opportunity and ask Alex a couple of questions. He had been holding a deck of playing cards and was showing Mike and Laura a trick of some sort. Each time he cut the cards, he would cut at an ace or a jack. Not once did I see another denomination when he cut the deck. As I inched a little closer to Alex a bit of a signal was felt. He looked at me and I asked him if he really could tell when people were going to die. He said he had just recently warned a friend not to drive over a particular set of railroad tracks and his friend had ignored the warning. Alex had been told the following day of his friend's death after his vehicle had been hit by a train.

"Why am I able to feel what it is in this house?" I asked.

"Because you are gifted. It frightens you and you wish you didn't have it?" He asked.

"Yes. It's not just the feelings I get, it's more like I hear the emotions. On Labor Day when the energy was very strong, it physically hurt. I am very fearful of what's in Mary's room."

"The last door on the right, upstairs," Alex stated.

He didn't ask a question, it was as if I had asked him which room was Mary's. That was the way he answered me. After saying it, he looked to the stairway. He had been standing at the side of the kitchen table, his back to the stove. For a moment he looked into the bathroom which was directly across from where he was standing.

"You should be frightened of him. The energy is as powerful as the demon itself, perhaps it is. Your energy is stronger than many I've met who have used it to the good. Embrace it, nurture it, but don't fear it," Alex said.

"I think there are sev…."

Just then, Tim came through the kitchen door almost running into Alex. I looked at Tim questioningly and he said, "I forgot it." With a very disappointed look on his mug.

"Forgot what?" Mike asked.

"The picture we took," Tim said.

Alex looked as if he were going to sway and fall down. He looked at Tim and Tim looked even worse. As I said, Alex's gaze could stare through you right to your core. He never took his hypnotizing gaze from Tim and asked, "You've taken a picture, here?"

"Alex, I didn't want to tell Clara until we had a chance to talk with Father Al and let him see it first. When we heard you were giving a lecture, I asked Tim to bring it when he came up tonight," I said.

"And you forgot to bring it?" Alex said, very disappointed.

"Yes, I'm sorry. I forgot to bring it with me when I left for work and I was worried if I drove home to get it, you'd be gone before I got here," I said.

"Bring it up tomorrow or when you can, Tim and I can send it to Alex," Father Al suggested.

"That will be fine, Father," Alex said.

Father stated that Alex had been traveling extensively and hadn't had a lot of rest. He thought that he should get him back to the University. Clara thanked Father for arranging a visit with Alex and thanked Alex for his concern and coming to the house on such short notice. He said goodbye to everyone and shook our hands. When he shook mine, he shocked the hell out of me when he said, "April 14th, but I can't get the year."

"Okay, no one here knows my birthday, not even Father. How'd you know?" I said.

"Isn't he remarkable?" Father said.

"When am I going to die?" I said as they walked out the back door."

"When you stop living," he said looking back, smiling and added a wink.

"How would he know my birthday, Clara?" I asked.

"How did he know there was a mass murder here? Hell, you got me. He is remarkable though," Clara replied.

Clara asked Mary and Laura to get ready for bed while Mike, Beth Ann, Tim and I joined her in the living room. We talked about Alex's impressions and compared them to the apparitions that had been seen in and out of the house.

"I've spoken of the strawberry blonde haired girl several times and when Alex described her nearly exactly as I had seen her, it sent chills down my spine," Clara said.

"Are you sure Father didn't tell him anything about the house?" Tim asked.

"Absolutely. Father wouldn't think of doing such a thing and Alex had even told him he wanted no information whatsoever before coming up here. The *only* thing Father told him is that we had a troubled house. He didn't even mention haunted," Clara explained.

"Mom, do you think the significance of the letter opener in Mary's picture was a spirit communicating to us that they had been stabbed?" Beth Ann asked.

"There's a chance that could have been something to symbolize that had happened, yes," Clara said.

"Alex didn't really say anything about Mary's room in here when he was telling us what he had felt but why would he tell me I *should* be frightened of *him*, that it could be the demon?" I asked.

"That puzzled me a little too. I don't know, I overheard you tell him about Mary's room and he knew which room that was so I assume he felt the energy there. Why he didn't say anything? I don't know," Clara said.

"I wonder which man was in the picture, the one that was beaten to death or the one who was stabbed?" Mike pondered.

"Probably the one beaten to death. The guy's face looked like it had met with a frying pan," Tim said.

"Alex only gave impression of six people, including the old woman, but he said there was seven. HOLY SHIT! Am I that slow in understanding?! The seventh is in Mary's room! Why would he say that I should be frightened of *him,* he did say *him*? Why did he compare it to a demon? I'll bet you anything, if you called Father Al and he reached Alex, he would tell you the seventh was indeed that piece of shit in Mary's room!" I exclaimed.

"I was standing right next to Paul, mom. Alex did say *him*," Mike said.

"Mom, do you think the strawberry blonde is the one who wears the perfume?" Beth Ann asked.

"I think so, she…"

"No." I interrupted. "Clara, 100 years ago, young girls wouldn't normally wear perfume would they? I somehow connect the perfume to an older woman for a couple of reasons. Every time I smell overpowering perfume, it's usually on an older woman. And the really older ones bathe themselves in it. Like I was telling you about the old lady that bought the glasses, her perfume was so strong, it almost choked me. I didn't mean to interrupt but I think it's gotta be someone else."

"That's okay. Maybe you're right. I thought it might be her because she's been seen in Beth Ann's room by both mum and me. But, I guess that doesn't necessarily mean it's her," Clara said.

"Who's the guy who was stabbed, where does he fit in?" Mike asked.

"The black man—the one who smokes the pipe?" Clara wondered.

"Well, it's not the young boy, I wouldn't think," I said.

"I don't think the young boy, the one with blonde hair who's been seen everywhere, really has anything to do with any of the troubles in the house," Clara said. "He's a random ghost?" Tim asked.

We sat for maybe 10 seconds then all laughed, including Tim. His question wasn't meant to be funny, but it came across that way after we'd all had time to think of an answer.

"That's a good way of putting it, Tim, and he probably *was* a random ghost. He might be the boy who was killed in the buzz saw accident or he may have worked this or another farm in the area. It's food for thought, though. And, I've got a question for you, Paul, before I forget. What was with the shimmy shake when Alex passed you before entering Beth Ann's room?" Clara asked.

"Oh, man! Did you ever take a balloon, rub in on your shirt or some other material, then hold it next to your head?" I asked.

"Are you talking about the static that's created?" Beth Ann asked.

"Yeah. When he walked past me, that's all I could feel! I barely felt anything when I shook his hand, but wow, when he walked by, I felt like I stuck my finger in a socket! I wanted to ask Alex so many questions about the outside crap. You know, what did he think the columns of fog were," I said.

313

"Fogmen," Tim interrupted, with one of his expressions "Yeah, fogmen," I continued. "What's the deal there?"

"Maybe it's like a spirit cocoon, before the apparition materializes completely, they take on the form of something misty," Mike said.

"Spirit cocoon?! That explanation is making *me* misty, Mike!" Beth Ann said.

"My psychic impression? I think the strawberry blonde belonged to the voice we heard outside Tim's car. I do believe the words we heard were, 'I need you to help.' And I believe those words were said after she had been beaten and prior to her murder," I said.

"Holy cow, Paul. That's rather morbid," Beth Ann said.

"Maybe the woman with the bulging eyes said it. Maybe she was running from whoever was after her and she said it before they caught up with her," Mike said.

"And, maybe, since they really are all dumb as stumps, they should all get together, combine their energies and figure a way collectively to have the kid that roams around, all over the place, bring us a psychic note explaining who they are!" Tim said.

We all had a good time that night discussing the outcome of Alex's investigation, short as it was, and trying to identify which of the impressions he extracted psychically from the house and to which apparition we thought they belonged. Tim and I didn't stay late that night as we planned to go up early the next day to drop the picture off. We drove down the road in our own cars slowly and close together. We decided whoever got up first would call the other in the morning. It was an enjoyable evening, spending time with the Dandys. Clara and I both got the feeling there was something brewing on the horizon between Tim and Beth Ann.

CHAPTER XXIV [B]

I will offer you more evidence to dispute the McMahon family's statements saying the farmhouse had been in their family for over a century. Earlier I gave you the second of two letters written by one of the McMahon family members, an Elizabeth McMahon Rowley. The following letter was also sent to and published by The Olean Times Herald, September 6, 1973. This letter was written by Margaret McMahon O'Brien of Bradford, Pa.

And I Quote

"The stories about the haunted house in your paper may sell papers but a great part of it is positively absurd. The McMahon farm had been in my family for over a hundred years. My grandparents immigrated from Ireland, settled there, raised a large family, and my father was born there, remained there until his death. If the Fox sisters trod the ground, it was over a century ago. Your articles have turned this lovely home where love, peace and tranquility abounded for over a century, into a place of horror. My grandparents loved children. My parents not only had their own children and grandchildren there, but friends brought their children, and even friends of friends were always welcome. My many years spent on this lovely farm can never be forgotten. I also wish to take issue with you about the young boy killed by the buzz saw. This unfortunate accident did happen to a fine family, but he is not buried in a nearby pine forest as your article states.

You stated you were careful not to mention the owner. These people are very newcomers to the area, and the name would not have meant anything to most people, but to put a picture on the front page, it is a small wonder that people came in a stampede. Your article speaks of the McMahon Road house spirits,

but with the home's Irish ancestry how could there be any thing there but happy fairies and leprechauns?"

If the McMahon farm had been in the McMahon family for over a hundred years when these letters had been written, in 1973, that would mean the family owned the farm since at the very least, 1873. The records of deeds of this home which I possess go back to March of 1870. At that time the record shows Russell K. and Emily Lafever deeding the home to Elijah Edwards. Upon researching marriage records, there were no records indicating the Lafevers and McMahons, or the Edwards and McMahons married. Also, the first time the deed shows the McMahon family owning the house was in 1904.

I felt the McMahon's should have contacted the Dandys before writing their letters to the newspaper. Better yet, they should have gone to the house for a visit. Chances are, if they had, there wouldn't have been anything for them to rebut.

Clara, Beth Ann and Mike wrote responses to the McMahons' letters and The Olean Times Herald published them.

CHAPTER XXV

When I got up the following morning and hadn't heard from Tim, I called him to see what time he wanted to go to Hinsdale. I explained I had a couple of errands to run and would pick him up around noon time. It was astonishing listening to Alex explain the impressions he had received while touring the house the previous evening. What really shocked everyone was his detailed descriptions of each impression. It really seemed that he was seeing each one as he presented his narrative to us. It must be fascinating and surely mentally exhausting having the ability to psychically visualize the imprints of energy left behind by the departed. He offered these impressions to us from mental images so I assume he wasn't able to actually visually see these people. Father Al assured us he hadn't given Alex the slightest bit of information, no history whatsoever regarding the house. As Alex had given his descriptions, it was apparently very difficult for Clara to keep her feet planted firmly on the floor. He was amazingly and chillingly accurate. His descriptions were uncomfortably similar to those given by others who had seen apparitions.

I pulled in front of Tim's house just about noon, honked the horn and he was out immediately. He hopped in the front seat and we headed for Hinsdale.

"What's up, Mr. Dillon?" He asked.

"Do I smell cologne?" I asked.

"I just shaved, I always slap on aftershave," Tim said.

"Bullshit, you think I just sailed into port today or something? I've been with you almost every night, and the only scent I've ever smelled is oil and vinegar!" I said.

"Why should I put on after shave for you?" Tim asked.

"Gotcha, smart ass! Clara and I have eyes, you know," I replied.

"Well, I thought it would be a change of pace from smelling like oil and vinegar," he said smugly.

On the way to the house, I pulled into Crosby's to get a chocolate shake. I'd been craving one for about a week. Tim went in with me and got a Rocky Road cone.

"Everybody gets Rocky Road," I said as we returned to the car.

"No they don't! The lady in front of me bought a plain nasty vanilla cone; no flavor, no style, no claaaasss. What about you? You and your chocolate shakes," Tim said.

"Hey, chocolate shakes are great—don't be knocking my chocolate shake now, or we're gonna be going to war!" I exclaimed.

"Okay, let's discuss this rationally. Take a look at the magnificence of my choice—I have chosen really great tasting ice cream, excellent flavor and nuts to boot. And when the ice cream is gone I'm not done—see—I still have a cone to eat. And yours, oh what a pitiful, sad choice for a dessert—you simply drink it and then you have to throw the cup away. What a waste!" Tim said.

Tim's description of my shake actually made me feel crappy, he had won the war I claimed we'd be embarking on. I was fumbling for something to say and the only thing I was able to come up with was:

"Yeah, well—at least I still straw I can chew on."

"A waste, I tell ya; you have waste to deal with," Tim replied, holding up the remaining part of his cone in reverence.

"Aw, shut up about your cone already. If it'll make you feel any better, I'll get a cone next time!" I replied

Rather than taking the usual route, I decided to take Main Street, Hinsdale for a change of pace. Either way, we ended up on Flannigan Road to get to Congress Road. Hinsdale's Main Street is about 10 city blocks long. The Central School is on one side of the street followed by residential; the opposite side is all residential except for the fire department. There are no retail or grocery stores in town other than Crosby's just half a mile from Main Street. As we turned onto Congress Road, we noticed a car pulled to the side of the road. There was a girl of about 18 standing at the front of the vehicle looking perplexed. I pulled around her car and parked in front to ask if we could be of any assistance.

"Hi, what's seems to be wrong?" I asked.

"Hi, I don't know. It acted up this morning and stalled. It did it again after I turned the corner but now there's another problem—I can't even get the key to turn," she said.

I opened the hood and asked Tim to try and start the engine. I supposed Tim should have been the one under the hood as I really wouldn't have known what to look for.

"The key won't—never mind," Tim said.

Tim exited the car as I put the hood down. He explained to the young lady the key wouldn't turn because the shifter was still in the drive position.

I asked how far of a drive she had and she said her house was just a little ways up the road.

"Oh my, God, I feel so silly. I can't believe I was trying to start the car when it was still in drive," she said.

"Not a problem, I'm sure we've all done something like that. Well, you pull ahead and we'll follow you to make sure you get home all right," I said.

"Thank you so much for your help. By the way, what is that cologne you're wearing? It smells really good," she asked Tim.

"Oh, I don't know, just my usual aftershave, I guess," Tim said rather shyly.

"He usually smells like oil and vinegar," I said as I opened the door of my car.

"What'd ya say that for?!" Tim asked after we got in the car, followed by a punch in the arm.

"Well, It's true, isn't it? And come on, 'my usual aftershave I guess,' you tell her. You don't know the *name* of your *usual* aftershave? Come one, Hugh, you have another girl on your mind," I said.

"Hugh's my dad's name, BOOOOOB!" Tim said, stretching out the name, Bob.

"I was referring to Hugh Hefner, Cosa Nostra," I said.

"That's Casanova, bud!"

"No, you're gonna meet the Cosa Nostra if you punch me again!" I exclaimed.

We followed the girl until she pulled into a driveway about half a mile up Congress Road. She honked and waved as we drove past.

319

"She was pretty, and she liked my cologne," Tim said.

"Yes she was, very pretty. She liked your cologne, not you, Gilligan," I replied.

When we reached McMahon Road, I picked up something but not the feeling I usually would get when there was energy present. When we found out why I picked up anything it was very perplexing to us both.

"There are people at the house," I said.

"Wha?" Tim asked.

"I don't know, there are people in the house, right now," I restated.

"How the hell would you know that?" Tim asked.

"I didn't, that woman standing at the tree told me," I said.

Tim snapped his heard around to look.

"There's no one back there! I was messin' with ya. I don't know how or why or who but, see, there's a car in the driveway," I said.

"You ass, you called before we came up and Clara told you," Tim insisted.

"I swear to you, I didn't—ask her," I said.

Tim was out of the car and around the house before I had my door closed. I looked at the car in the driveway and wondered, "how the hell would I know someone was here?" My conclusion; a lucky guess. But what of the feeling? Before this was all over, this involvement with the house, I was either going to be insane or I would be solidifying light as Alex Tanous had. I opened the back door and saw that Clara did have visitors, she introduced us as I walked in. They had been friends that wanted to come up for a visit.

"Did I call you today, Clara?" I asked.

"No, Tim already asked me that! Okay, what's going on? The first thing either of you say to me is did you call me," Clara replied.

"See," I said to Tim. "I'm not going to lie to you," I said.

"Then how'd you know there was someone here, what are you psychic or something?" Tim asked.

It was my turn to offer him an expression.

"Will you two stop. Where's the picture?!" Clara said, almost yelling with joy.

"Oh," Tim said, as he took the picture from his shirt pocket.

When handing the picture to Clara, she had been standing at the end of the table near the stairway. She side-stepped past me, never taking her eyes from the photo. She took hold of the only unoccupied chair and sat down hard. You could see the eagerness on the other ladies' faces, her visitors, who were drooling to see what caused the look of shock on Clara's face. Mary and Laura walked in and looked at the picture as their mom held it. You could see by the expression on Mary's face that she had really been frightened, Laura's look was that of indifference. I tried to pick up a "vibe" from her, but there was nothing. She looked at me and I gave her a wink; she returned the innocent flirtation with a smile. I miss her.

"Clara?" One of the women said, hand stretched out, as if asking to pass the picture over.

Clara slowly handed the photo to her, staring at the back of the picture, as if she were still able to see the horror on the subject's face through the back. The woman to whom Clara handed the picture had an expression of sorrow on her face as another looked over her shoulder and turned away saying she couldn't look at it. All in all, there was one, "Oh my God," two gasps and the last, a non participant, other than her brief horrified glance over the other woman's shoulder. Clara looked at the ladies one by one, each looking back at Clara, then all looked first to Tim and then to me. Beth Ann came out of her room, not realizing we had arrived. She could see that one of the ladies was holding something and two of them were still staring at it. When she gazed over the woman's shoulder, she added an additional, "Oh, my God!"

Beth Ann took the picture from the woman who'd been holding it and held her eyes on the man who was obviously terrified and said, "I agree with whoever said it last night, this is the man that was beaten to death." She set the picture on the corner of the kitchen table, and hurriedly walked into the living room; Tim followed.

"Who took this picture?" One of the ladies, Ann I believe, asked.

"Well, Tim and I chased him into the field one night and, when he got out to the tree line, Tim and I shone our lights on him. I raised my camera and took the picture. Right after, Tim sort of lunged at him, but he was gone," I said.

"Gone?" Another of the ladies asked.

"Yeah, he just,…….gone," I replied.

The, "Oh my, God's" won, beating the gasps, when another of the ladies scored after my reply. As the ladies and Clara began talking about the picture and the rest of the trouble at the house, I walked into the living room to check on Beth Ann and Tim. They were sitting on the couch together. I just smiled at them and returned to the kitchen. One of the ladies said she thought they should be going soon. I knew that could have meant within the next five minutes to an hour. I excused myself to the group and walked outside. Clara asked where I was going and I said, "For a short walk."

"Be careful!" She insisted. "But *where* are you going, so we know?"

"Tree line," I replied.

"Paul!" Clara said firmly.

"It's all right, if there's anything, I can handle it. So far, there hasn't been anything outside like what's at the top of the stairs. I'm going to trust Alex and what he said to me last night," I said.

"Please, be careful. At least wait and see if Tim wants to go with you," Clara suggested.

I felt embarrassed having this conversation with the other ladies, whom I didn't know, in the room with us. One of the ladies I found interesting, she was sitting at the edge of her chair, leaning forward, as if watching a sparring match, waiting to see the knockout punch.

"Maybe one or more of the ladies would like to join me?" I asked teasingly. There was a collective, 'NO,' and it made me laugh as I apologized for teasing them.

"See you in a little bit," I said as I walked out the back door.

I was nearly at the end of the pond when Tim yelled from the back yard asking if I wanted him to come along. I told him to stay there and visit, that I'd be back soon. When I was already in the field, about 100 feet or so from the pond, I looked back and Tim was standing at the edge of the pond watching me. I waved at him to go back as I turned around to continue toward the tree line. A couple of minutes later, I turned around again to see that he was gone. He was a good friend and I had a great deal of respect for him. Although he was generally cutting up, the comic of the decade, he did have a serious side; a compassionate side. We had made a pact, including Mike, that if we went anywhere on the property, we wouldn't go solo. I knew that he and Beth Ann were beginning to like one another, and if I had asked him to come with me, he would without hesitation but I wanted him and Beth Ann to get to know one another better. I wouldn't have even considered asking him, besides, I wanted to attempt to let my energy loose while I was alone to see if it was something I could actually connect with. Alex said to embrace and nurture this gift I supposedly had, not to fear it. I didn't fear it, I feared what it might see, or feel—or connect with.

When I reached the tree line, I went to the location we were standing when the picture was taken. I wasn't expecting to see the man in the picture just because I was in the same place, but I really believed there was something about the tree line that somehow was connected with the house. This area, as well as the pond, was significant, and was somehow connected with the troubles the Dandys were having. If Alex had been able to walk the entire property, maybe he would pick up more impressions in these two areas. Here I was, standing in a field, and quite honestly, feeling foolish because I didn't know how to go about opening up, tuning on, or whatever it was that was needed to "see" or "hear" psychically. "Christ, what are you doing?" I asked myself. I tried, tried really hard, but the only thing I heard was a bothersome bee that kept buzzing my head. I walked back and forth from the spot we had taken the picture to 50 feet or more in either direction and never felt anything. "Where are you?" I whispered. Nothing wanted to communicate. I started walking slowly back in the direction of the pond and then returned to the tree line. I must have really looked stupid because that's surely how I felt. Every night, every damned night, something happened. I didn't believe for a minute there wasn't energy present all the time. Labor Day *and* night were more than jumping, the area was teeming with energy. Mary's room was the strongest ever, at least that I had experienced or heard anyone speak of. I honestly didn't believe I'd have survived another three minutes by that door on Labor Day afternoon, at least not mentally. There was something here, I knew it, yet it didn't want to communicate. Why? Try to communicate, that's what it said in one of the books I had read. What did I need to do, place a banner in the field reading, "Departed, with No Place to go? Contact That Silly Man Walking the Tree Line." I was sure no one in the Dandy family would have thought I looked silly out here but I felt a hell of a lot worse than silly. I started walking back to the house; disappointed. I was going to walk straight toward the house but instead turned to return to the pond. Maybe I'd have better luck there. Arriving, I stood at the far end, away from the house. It was such a nice day. Maybe that's why ghosts portrayed in movies usually scare their victims at night or during inclement weather. Hell, standing here, looking at the house, it didn't even look like it could be haunted. It was an average looking farmhouse, small in size really, no massive windows covered in vines, no pillars or steeples, it didn't have long hallways, leading to rooms which had been closed up for years, no furniture covered to keep a decade of dust from settling. Lights didn't flicker on and off, while chains were heard rattling down a dark corridor. It was just an old house on a country road with a pond where you could take a refreshing dip on a Sunday afternoon. Yet, anyone living or visiting here was never sure when a *visitor* might drop in unexpectedly; a *visitor* who didn't need a door to enter. I began walking the bank toward the house when one of the family's dogs began walking toward me and stopped. I saw a ball a few feet ahead of me and I assumed she wanted me to pick it up and give it a toss. I did just that, I tossed the ball high in the air toward the dog, but it didn't pay attention, it just stared at me.

"Whatsa matter? Come on," I said patting my leg.

The dog just stood there. Tim and Beth Ann had walked out the back door looking at Peanuts.

"Come on, boy, come here," I said again.

He didn't make a sound, but lowered his head like dogs do when they growl. I began to worry, I thought maybe he was sick or didn't recognize me. He might attack or something. Beth Ann called to Clara and she came out. She too called Peanuts but he only stood there, continuing to stare in my direction.

"Do you feel anything, Paul?" Tim asked.

"No, Tim, nothing,: I said.

I turned around and walked back toward the pond. Clara asked me to stop and I told her I was only going to walk a few feet. I turned back toward the house and Peanuts was standing as still as a rock. I started walking back toward them and, when I got about 15 feet closer than I had been after tossing the ball, I felt it. Almost the same moment the feeling came, Peanuts barked and ran to stand next to Clara.

"Something," I said.

"Good or bad?" Tim asked.

"I don't know, we haven't learned those interpretations in class yet. Shit, I don't know, Tim, I'm a novice at this. Would you mind walking out to me 'cause I don't think I can move just yet," I asked.

The feeling began to get stronger as Tim started walking toward me; it was a similar feeling to the one I had when I was leaving Mary's room Labor Day.

"Stop! Just hang tight for a second," I yelled to Tim.

I was feeling a lot of different emotions, but the one that wanted to jump out was laughter. When I said, "stop," Tim stopped in such a way, it reminded me of when we used to play a game called, "freeze" when we were kids. When the one who was leading the game yelled, "freeze," everyone had to stop moving. For a few seconds, Tim's right foot was still off the ground, in mid air, when I said freeze.

"You asshole, please don't make me laugh now!" I said.

The energy was almost as strong as it was that afternoon, but damn it, I was prepared to stand my ground. I only wished I had known what I was supposed to do, what thoughts I was supposed to have.

I started walking slowly toward Tim. He was about 50 or 60 feet from me. The closer I got, the more it seemed I was moving slower, *exactly* the same feeling when I was going down the stairs Monday afternoon. There was no possible way I could keep the feeling of fear from overcoming me. I mentally tried to ward off the terrible feeling of dread but I couldn't get it to subside. I was certain, it didn't have to be night to experience such fear, this was my second full blast of the "heat wave" while the sun was high in the sky. Dear, God, I felt as if I were going to faint, and from some unknown place in my mind I yelled, "Get away from me!" I believe Tim had crept a few feet closer to me but I hadn't been aware that he had moved at all. For the next few moments, there was a feeling I'd never experienced before. I have never taken a ride on a roller coaster but I was sure it was similar to the feeling you'd get when you would descend to the bottom of a long hill and suddenly, you are thrust back up quickly. It came very suddenly, and was gone like a feather being blown out of a cannon. The best description I could offer for what I felt next was: revenge. To find an answer in beating the shit out of what had just zapped my very soul from me. I felt like the little kid who just witnessed the biggest bully in school walk up to him and smash every one of his favorite toys, then turn around and laugh and spit in his face. I looked at the three of them, not far from the back door of the house; Clara, Tim and Beth Ann. I motioned for Tim to come to where I was standing. He turned around and looked at Clara and Beth Ann. Then I said, "The boogeyman is gone. It's okay." Tim was walking quickly, and Clara and Beth Ann started walking toward me as well.

"Guys, I just want to talk to Tim for a second, if that's okay," I said.

Tim got to where I was standing, placed his hand on my forearm and asked if I was okay. I let go, just like the little kid would have, after looking at his favorite toys scattered in jagged, twisted pieces of metal and plastic on the school playground. Tim and I walked to the run-off area of the pond as I attempted to explain what had just happened. It was difficult describing what the feeling was but I said it must have been like grabbing onto a high voltage wire only there hadn't been the, 'shake, rattle, and roll' that accompanied the shock.

"What if this happened when you were out in the fuckin' field by yourself? We all agreed that we don't ever go wandering off by ourselves, didn't we? Quit trying to be the heavy weight who thinks because some goddamned psychic says you have a gift that you can take on whatever the hell is in that house by yourself because you can't!" Tim firmly scolded.

"I just wanted to see if I could......"

"I don't give a SHIT what you wanted to see! If you have some great gift that allows you to feel things that most of us can't, that's fine. But you're not a professional in this paranormal bullshit. If ya feel something, great, tell us, *warn* us, whatever you think you have to do, but don't you ever go anywhere alone again!" Tim scolded once again.

"Sorry, Tim. I guess I wasn't thinking of the consequences," I said.

"No, you just weren't thinking. How the hell are we gonna feel if something happens to you? We're partners in the solving of this crap, I can't go solo, I'm too scared. Come on, let's go back to the house," Tim suggested.

As we reached the house, I didn't have the nerve to look at Mary's bedroom window, and Tim sensed that I was very apprehensive about walking past the spot I had stopped to toss the ball, still lying where it landed. We walked into the kitchen and I could hear Beth Ann and Clara talking in the living room. Mary and Laura were at the kitchen table, drawing or coloring. When we walked into the living room, I could feel there was another scolding hanging in the air.

"Well, what the hell was that all about? Would you please explain to me why you felt you had to go to the end of the property line?" Clara asked angrily.

I began to tell her and Beth Ann what had happened but my voice was still shaky. Thankfully, Tim took over and explained what I had told him and also that he had lectured me. I sat in Phil's chair like a rag doll; I was spent.

"So, you wanted to walk to the tree line. You were so sure of yourself, that you could *handle* anything that might come along. You're this big, powerful psychic and you're going to take the spirits on, one by one," Clara began.

"Mom?" Beth Ann asked in a tone of defense for me.

Clara looked to Beth Ann with a, "don't interrupt me" look and continued, "We don't know what we have here and we don't want to see you getting hurt; we don't want anyone getting hurt. Tim's right, Paul, if you feel something, good *or* evil, tell us so we can prepare ourselves accordingly. Don't think you can just march right up and say, 'get the hell out of here' because I don't think you're going to win. Remember how Alex looked after walking through the house. The man almost looked like the man in the photo, he was totally drained! And he wasn't going toe to toe, flinging his energy around like some cowboy trying to lasso the fattened calf. He was here to only pick up impressions, and that drained the very life out of him! What I should do is tell you, here and now, that you are not to visit here again but I can't do that and I won't. You're our friend and we welcome your company but you will never, *never,* attempt anything on your own again, do you understand me?"

"Clara, it happened right here in the yard. When I was in the f....."

"I don't give a damn if it happened while we were all sitting around the kitchen table! Maybe you released energy in some way that antagonized the energy here in the house or out there by the tree line. I don't know, but I just have a feeling if you hadn't gone out there alone, nothing would have happened. So, no more super psychic stuff, right?" Clara said.

"Yes, ma'am," I said, solemnly.

"Oh, God, now I do feel old, calling me ma'am." She chuckled.

I walked over to where Clara sat and hugged her. She gave me what for and I had it coming. I was a damned, arrogant fool and, after that day, I had no intentions of going anywhere alone and I never did. Actually, I didn't visit the house for over a week and wasn't really sure if I was going to go again. I honestly didn't know what to think of my frame of mind regarding the house.

CHAPTER XXVI

I had spoken to Clara a couple of times on the phone during my retreat from the house: once when Father Al picked up the picture, and a couple of day later when she called to tell me that it had been fairly quiet. I caught up on lost time with Debbie, my parents and my music. I had read more about the paranormal, but didn't have the interest I had before that last visit that had torn something from me. Tim and I talked about the house at work and often about Beth Ann; he really liked her but she was still involved with Jeff. We didn't return to the house until Mike called one afternoon to ask if we wanted to go searching for signs of the old stagecoach roads that were possibly nearby. We met up one late afternoon with Mike, Randy, Mike N. and a few others and drove to the Burton Road where Clara had told Mike the old coaches may have passed. Clara had been searching old maps and records hoping to locate information about roads that were used decades ago. We were quite a ways from the Dandy house but even in the area we were searching, strange things happened. We kept seeing lights near the treetops and every time we got nearer to them, they would vanish. As we walked through the woods searching for what might have been an old wagon road we would hear noises and where we walked we experienced several cold spots. I attributed most of them to atmospheric conditions. There were several of us in the woods and we didn't all walk together. It sounded like large objects were hitting the ground and Mike said maybe branches were falling. I don't know who, but someone said it was "giant acorns" falling. Every time we heard something hit the ground, everyone would yell, "giant acorn," It was getting late, and we didn't really like being this far from the house. We walked deep into the woods and were nearly ready to leave when we came across ruts in the ground that appeared to be made from wheels of some sort. The trees in the surrounding area weren't all that big, not that I would have been able to predict how long a tree had been growing, but the trees at the sides of the ruts were much bigger. We may very well have found the lost road where stagecoaches might have traveled. We all decided to go back to the vehicles and leave. Someone said Randy had gone into a trance while we were walking the woods. Neither Tim nor I were present when he supposedly did, and actually, we didn't want to know why he would. Rather than go back to the house, Tim and I drove directly back to Olean.

"I think some of these other guys are coming up with stories just to spice up the problems at the house," Tim said.

"I thought the same thing, Tim. Mike is about the only one I trust to be completely honest with us. Randy seems to be straight up too but I don't understand this trance shit, I replied.

"Are you burnt out with the house?" Tim asked.

I had to think for a few moments to find the right word before answering his question. Burnt out wasn't the right term but I guess I had to be truthful and tell him what I had really been thinking. "When I went to Mary's room Labor Day afternoon, no before that even, when we were sitting outside, I had a sudden urge to walk to the tree line. I didn't know why, but it felt like something I had to do. Clara absolutely would not allow me to leave and Debbie agreed with her. But even before I had the urge, my head was on fire—inside, not as if I had a fever, or I felt hot. When we first arrived, and after walking into the kitchen, I knew there was a storm coming. It was after we all came inside and heard noises coming from upstairs and Debbie said something about noisy people. After being the smart ass, challenging, threatening whatever it is in Mary's room and then trying to walk downstairs…"

"What, you okay?" Tim asked, almost swerving to the edge of the road.

"Tim, I was scared out of my fucking mind! Then, after walking through the field and being disappointed that there was nothing, then walking back to the house, and the um, the dog just, just staring….the power… energy. Alex said maybe it was, maybe it was a demon," I was explaining, but was losing it at the same time.

Tim pulled to the side of the road and stopped the car. He waited until I was ready to finish, jump out, or whatever it was I needed to do. I told him to go ahead; I was okay. I didn't really know if I believed in demons, in the devil. I was raised

Catholic and I believed in Heaven and hell, but I don't think I believed the devil could mingle with us on earth. Perhaps those who committed evil deeds were in some way, influenced by a demon but to be alive and well in Hinsdale, New York? I didn't want to believe that.

Tim dropped me off and I went inside. I don't think I thanked him or even said goodnight. It wasn't very late, maybe midnight. I climbed into bed and wrapped my arms around Debbie. I believed I held onto her all night.

Almost two weeks passed before Tim and I went back to the house. Mike said everyone was probably going to walk up the hill to where the Gregorian chant was heard. We were supposed to meet at Keith's trailer. My mind had cleared and Tim and I were both up to checking it out. We also wanted to see what kind of shenanigans some of the other guys were up to. I had talked to Clara and she told me the kids were having some really strange things happening to them in town as well as other places. I had also talked with Father Al and met with him at the Friary to discuss the two horrible episodes I had experienced. To sum up Father's advice in a nutshell, he told me that sometimes when dealing with the paranormal, we allow ourselves to be overwhelmed by some of our own thoughts, or even energy. He said on Labor Day, after feeling the cold come from Mary's room, I may have used my own energy against me. Pitting that, and the energy from the room, may have been damaging to my own psyche. He didn't doubt that it happened as I said it did, but he stated that I need to exercise extreme caution with the unknown, that forces of evil can, and will weigh heavy on the conscious as well as the subconscious. As far as the second bout, he explained that some animals are very sensitive to psychic energies and obviously the dog sensed it before I had been aware of it. If it frightened me as badly as I explained, it would be wise to firstly, never, under any circumstances be alone, secondly, when there is an onset of such proportions, pray to the Almighty for the strength to deal with it, and third, and the simplest suggestion he offered; stay away. And on a lighter note, when dealing with Randy, he said to put a 'brain warp' on him. I laughed, as did he when he said this. I was sure he was putting a brain warp on me in some humorous way but he had been serious. He told me to put my thumb on one temple, and my pinky finger on the other, and concentrate. "On what?" I asked him. "On what he might have on his mind." He replied.

I think Father was just pulling a funny on me, but I was going to try it if I had the chance.

On our first group get together at Keith's trailer, there were 6 or 7 of us and Randy did indeed put himself into a trance. He was in a chair, leaning back, so I went over and placed my hand on his head, fingers on his temples as described by Father Al, and Randy raised his arm and pulled my hand from his head. He did this so effortlessly I was shocked. At the time, Randy might have weighed 130 pounds—soaking wet, and he apparently didn't work out. I did it again and I didn't have enough power to even slow his arm from removing my hand. The third time, I used my other hand and Keith used both of his to help and we still could not stop Randy!

"No fucking way." Keith said. "This has to be a leverage trick or something."

I asked Keith to sit down, and I tried it with him. He struggled to move my hand from his head and he was a good sized guy. The second time I tried it, it was a draw. Everyone started cracking jokes, calling Randy funny names and even tickled him during one of his trance episodes, but he never flinched. He either had super human strength, and a hell of a will power not to laugh or he was truly in a trance. Over the next few days, we tried this several more times; Randy always won.

With all of this trance business, we never did make it to the clearing where the chant was supposedly coming from. Several others who had only gone up once or twice had fainting spells, or found they weren't able to move certain parts of their bodies. We were sure some of them were faking and with the seriousness of what was happening at the Dandy house, there was no room for such B.S.

CHAPTER XXVII

The following Sunday, I received one of the most shocking phone calls I'd ever had. Mike had been in a terrible automobile accident. It had been several hours since it happened and I was told they were transferring him from Olean General, thank God, to Buffalo Memorial. I called Tim to let him know but he wasn't home. I left word with his dad to call me as soon as he got in. Clara and Phil were going to drive to Buffalo and Beth Ann would stay with the girls. My first concern was Mike, of course, but I was a bit worried about the girls being in the house alone. Later, I found out that Clara was staying with Mike and Phil and Clara's dad would stay with the girls. If Clara needed anything, she would be able to go to her parents who lived in Buffalo. It wasn't until late that night that I got word that Mike was in critical condition. Everyone was sick with worry and I couldn't imagine how Clara was holding up. Her kids were everything to her, second to nothing. Debbie and I wanted to drive to Buffalo but there was nothing we could do and we would probably only add stress to the family. I called the house and told Beth Ann not to hesitate calling if they needed anything at all. We stayed at home and waited to hear word from Clara.

The following evening, Beth Ann called to brief us about what happened. Clara asked that she call since Buffalo was long distance and Mike had so many friends who needed to be kept informed. Supposedly, Mike had lost control of his vehicle coming up Wagner Hill Road and hit a tree which was very near a long drop off. Mike hit the rearview mirror with his face, and with such force, that it snapped the mirror. Beth Ann told me that Clara said his eye was the size of a small lemon and the doctors weren't sure they would be able to save it. There was one puzzling and shocking aspect of the accident—Clara told Beth Ann that the police had been looking for another victim. Mike was insistent that there had been someone in the car with him. All of Mike's friends were accounted for and there had been no report of anyone missing, yet Mike supposedly went on and on in a semi-conscience state that there was *someone* with him. Later that week, we heard that there was an impression in the windshield on the passenger side of the car, as if someone were thrown into it. The police investigative report stated that Mike couldn't have hit that side of the windshield, according to the angle of the crash. I rode in Mike's car twice and I couldn't understand how he could have lost control. That old car barely made the grade of Wagner Hill, sputtering its way around the turns. You never knew if you were going to make it to your destination riding in that old rust bucket. Once, Randy and Mike said they had *someone* in the car with them, the evening of Labor Day; and another time, Mike swore there was *someone* with him that first night after he returned from Burton Road. Other people, not related or friends of the family had stated the same. Even Father Al believed he had brought an unknown guest away from the house. Could Mike have had a passenger and, if it were *someone* he didn't know, was it possible they could be thrown forward, cracking the windshield? And what about the oven in our apartment and the strumming of my guitar? Had we all brought something home with us at one time or another?

School was back in session and the girls' grandfather was staying with them while Clara stayed in Buffalo to be near Mike. I actually found a bit of sympathy for Phil. He had shown great fatherly support to everyone after Mike's accident. A friend of Clara's had also been looking in on the girls during her absence. Mike had been kept in Intensive Care through nearly the entire month of October. He was receiving great care and had the best support possible, his mom. Clara stood vigil day and night as Mike's condition fluctuated. I only visited Mike one time while he was still in Intensive Care and it had been very difficult seeing him in his condition. He was sleeping when Debbie and I arrived and we stayed for only a few minutes, before the nurses asked us to leave so they could attend to another patient. Clara had shown the signs of a distraught mother, but on the outside she remained strong for Mike and the entire family. Her inner-self was falling apart. We said goodbye to Clara and her mom before driving back to Olean.

After inspecting Mike's car, the cause of the accident was apparent. The tired, worn out engine blew a rod, that lodged in the steering column making it impossible to maneuver the turn. Everyone who knew Mike was absolutely sure the accident hadn't been caused by his ability as a driver. I think the second time I rode with him I made reference to his driving, comparing it to a little old lady returning from a Sunday brunch at a church social.

Clara called and told us Mike would be coming home November, 3rd. She sounded so excited and she said Mike was, "ecstatic with delight." She asked that we give him a day or so before coming to visit so he could get accustomed to sleeping in his own bed again and getting the rest he would need after the long drive. It was apparent to us that Mike wasn't that concerned about getting accustomed to anything, he called the next day and asked if we were going to come see him.

"You're damn right, we are! Deb and I will be up after she gets back from her mom's," I told him.

"What about Tim, have you guys been coming to the house?" Mike said.

"No, Mike. We weren't going to be hanging out in the yard, especially with you in the hospital and the girls having school during the week. We weren't helping matters when we were coming up. Actually, I think at times we made things worse. But the hell with all that, you're home and that's what's most important!" I said.

"Thanks. So, see you later today?" Mike asked.

"You can count on it, buddy," I said.

Fact be known, I had missed going to the house with Tim in the evenings but I was too damned petrified of having another incident like the last one. I don't think I could have mentally gone though another episode like that again. Father Al had been very empathetic during our last conversation but his explanation and the advice given didn't leave me feeling all that comforted.

Debbie and I arrived about 6 p.m. and I was very anxious to see Mike. Before we even got out of the car, Debbie reminded me that we needed to leave no later than 7 p.m.. She didn't want to go at such a late hour but she couldn't stay home worrying Mike might think she didn't want to see him. She said after our very first visit, she would never come up anytime close to nightfall. We were involved in a minor argument about coming up when she arrived home. She suggested we waited until another day, earlier in the afternoon, and come up then, but I told her I'd already promised Mike we'd be up that evening. I wasn't thinking I guess. I was so glad he was home and that he had called asking for us to come for a visit. I was sure Mike would understand when we left early.

We knocked on the back door and it was none other than my little Laura who opened the door quickly. "Hi!" she said with that bright smile, walked out and gave us both a hug."

"Who is it, Laura?" I heard Mike ask.

"It's Debbie and Paul!" Laura yelled.

Clara came out of the living room and greeted us. Debbie and I walked into Mike's room. He was sitting on his bed and Debbie walked over to give him a hug. She talked to him for a couple of minutes, telling him that she was glad he was home and feeling better. Clara called Debbie to join her in the kitchen while Mike and I visited. His eye was still swollen and badly bruised and it was obvious he had lost some weight. He showed me the scar on his chest which made me wince. The poor kid had been through a tough time but now he was home and I'm sure Clara would do everything to make him very comfortable.

"Ya feelin' better, Mike?" I asked.

"Yeah, my eye still hurts pretty bad, especially if I lie on that side. Mom has to put in eye drops and they're more of a pain in the ass than in my eye. What's up with you and Tim? Mom says you're not coming up or even talking to each other," Mike asked.

"He thinks I did something to the brakes on his car," I said.

"What, you?!! You know as much about cars as Lassie!" Mike said.

"Yeah well, I'd rather sleep in Mary's room for a week, than to have Tim think something as stupid as that. I wouldn't do something like that to my worst enemy."

"You okay?" Mike asked.

"Fuck no, Mike!" I exclaimed.

"What did I just hear?" Clara said from the kitchen.

"Sorry, Clara," I said, as I moved closer to Mike. "Is he out of fucking mind? No one would do something like that, at least no one that I know. That's sick, and I rode in his car every night. He's my friend, Mike, and I'd do anything for the crazy son of a bitch. I don't know where he would get an idea like that. I'd rather have him shoot me than to think that," I said.

"What is all this language I'm hearing in here?" Clara asked from Mike's doorway.

"Tim, mom. Did you know about this, the brakes thing?" Mike asked.

"Yes, I did. Beth Ann said something to me about it," Clara replied.

"And?" Mike asked.

"And what? Do I believe it? Not a word of it, it's preposterous," Clara said.

"What are you talking about?" Debbie asked.

"Tim's brakes failed going down the road and he thinks Paul had something to do with it," Clara said.

"What?! Are you kidding me? All Paul talks about is Tim this and Tim that. Except for George, I don't think he could care about anybody as much. What a jerk," Debbie said.

"He's not a jerk, Debbie. There must be some explanation why he would think that," I said. I laughed before adding, "Ha, now I sound like Phil, 'there's gotta be a reasonable explanation.' Yeah, reasonable alright."

"When do you work with him again? I want to give...." Debbie started.

"I quit today," I interrupted.

"Quit, why?" She asked.

"Debbie, how the hell can I work with someone, someone I think the world of who thinks I fucked with his car?!" I exclaimed angrily.

"Language again," Clara said.

"I think the two of you ought to sit down and discuss it," Mike said.

"I've called him at home twice and he hasn't called me back. Christ, I sat in the kitchen the other day after calling and his mom told me he was taking a shower and that she'd have him call right back. I waited all day and he didn't call. It's bullshit," I said.

What I couldn't understand about this insinuation was Tim not coming to me and talking to me. I know if I had proof that someone had tampered with my brakes, they'd better find a damned good hiding place, because I'd be beating every bush trying to flush them out. There were others around who couldn't be trusted in their stories, shouldn't be trusted, why didn't he point his finger at them too? Regardless, I was the loser here, because I lost a friend I had come to like very much. He brought an enormous amount of levity to a situation that had nothing to offer but the opposite.

After our talk with Mike and my apologizes for having to discuss something of a negative nature, Debbie informed me that it was beginning to get dark out and she wanted to go NOW. Clara and Mike laughed as Debbie stood at the doorway to Mike's room, her arms crossed, with an insistent look on her face, like some prison matron waiting for everyone to get into their cells.

"I'm already out the door. I'll see ya soon, Mike. Take care of the kid, Clara," I said.

"Yeah, you hold him down while I give him his eye drops," Clara said.

"It's not time yet!" Mike exclaimed.

"Just kidding. I'm just trying to lighten the air a little. You still have an hour before drop time." His mom said.

"You're not out the door yet, and it's getting darker," Debbie sang to me.

"Bye, you guys!" I said, running to the kitchen door.

"Why didn't you tell me about this thing with you and Tim?" Debbie asked as we got in the car.

"Why, what purpose would it serve? The damage is done, now it's time to lick my wounds," I replied.

"You guys were like brothers in your search for ghosts and goblins. I don't understand," She said.

"Neither do I, and I really don't want to talk about Tim, please."

It was chilly out and driving down McMahon almost made me wish Debbie had worked someplace else and never met someone named Dandy. But it was impossible to disregard the feelings we both had for the family. I don't think it was the excitement of the "fogmen," or the voice of unseen women and children, or even the exhilarating chase of a supposed spirit that I missed. What I truly missed was the constant, comical antics, even in the heightened state of near shock, by a friend who had more expressions than Curly of the Three Stooges. Perhaps soon, Tim and I will sit down and talk this over.

As we made the turn in the road and were heading toward the tree, Debbie reached over and held onto my arm. I reached over and rubbed her hand and said, "There's nothing that's going to happen tonight, hon." The tree was just ahead of us and Debbie's hand tightened on my arm; we passed the tree with flying colors. We got home and there was no room for talk of ghosts or hanging trees, psychics or ex-friends with bad brakes. Tonight there was only time for us and none of the negative things that had been happening at the house were mentioned.

CHAPTER XXVIII

The last time I had been at the house was November 4, 1973, the day after Mike arrived home from Buffalo Memorial. Clara and I stayed in contact and she told me that Beth Ann was going to tell Jeff their relationship was over. I assumed I knew why and didn't ask. Over the next couple of weeks, the incidents happening at the house were sporadic and there was an incident involving Clarke and a bunch of Mike's friends. It seems while driving down Wagner Hill Road, Clarke lost control of the car and nearly had an accident in the same area where Mike's accident took place. I was glad to hear no one was injured. Phil had to go down to help them with the car. A few days later, Jeff was in an accident worse than Mike's, well worse in the sense that his car was totaled. Clara told me he had just purchased the car the day before the accident and had brought it up to show everyone. The last bit of news came as a shock; Tim had joined the Air Force. The real shock, disappointment anyhow, is that he hadn't called to say goodbye, be careful, fuck you, I hope the ghost in Mary's room eats your face off; nothing. I guess it wasn't to be expected. He had a thought in his mind and he was entitled to it. He was *dead wrong!*

Clara called about every other day in November keeping me updated on the activity of the house. She said Mike would really like me to visit if I had a chance and I wanted to, I really did, but I felt if I had started going up more often, the activity might begin to build. I had talked to Father Al and he told me not to have feelings of guilt, that the energy was present whether I was or not. I admitted to him that I had been taunting the energy in Mary's room. I believe this little quiet man had become angry when I told him that. Communicating is one thing, but to harass was another, and totally ill-advised. He told me he would be going to the house within the next few days and, if I wanted to join him, he would be more than happy to pick me up on his drive up. I asked him to call me and if I was available I'd take him up on the offer.

Sometime toward late November Clara called and said the boys had a remarkable thing happen. There were several spending the night, and Mike N. experienced a swing in his personality. "What do you mean, a swing in his personality?" I asked.

"Like it wasn't him and he acted drunk and he certainly didn't have any alcohol to drink. It was so strange, Paul, one minute he was absolutely fine and the next, he acted like he'd been on a binge for several days," Clara explained.

"Did Mike ever tell you about the night when he, Tim and I went to the tree line and that same sort of thing happened to Mike?" I asked.

"No! No one said a word to me about it," Clara said.

"At first we dismissed it as playing a prank on us, but when we got back to the house Tim started to confront him about it but we were interrupted by a walking lantern," I said.

"What, a walking lantern?!" Clara exclaimed.

"That's a whole story in itself. Anyhow, later that night, we did talk to Mike about it but he remembered nothing. He was talking very strangely and his personality changed for sure," I said.

"I wish you had been here. Mike N. was having a cigarette and I was worried, with the way he had been acting, that he might have an accident with it. No sooner did I say that than the ashtray slid across the floor. He put his cigarette out in it as if nothing happened! You really need to come up when you can. Things are beginning to take on a whole new meaning," Clara explained.

"I will Clara. I talked to Father and he said he was going up for a visit and he would stop and pick me up on the way," I said.

"Is something wrong with your car?" Clara asked.

"No, there's nothing wrong with the car. I have a morbid fear of something upstairs, in your house," I said.

"I talked with Father Al too. He told me you admitted to him that you'd been quite the agitator with Mary's room guest?" Clara questioned.

"Well, not really agitating, I just voiced my concern and told it to get the hell out, that I was stronger than it and it wasn't welcome there," I said.

"Ah, you challenged it. Have you ever challenged someone to something and they accepted? That may be the case here. That's why you've become the center of attention when it comes to Mary's room. You offered a challenge, now you're not owning up to your end of the deal."

I never looked at it that way—I found that comical in a morbid way. I stand outside Mary's room, pounding my chest announcing I'm king of the Dandy house and this power says, "Oh yeah, come in here and we'll see." Now I've backed down, like a cowering, scared little rabbit and my challenger wants the games to begin. Well, the joke's on me.

"You think now that I challenged it, it wants to rumble?" I asked.

"What do you think? I know if you got my dander up and ticked me off, then turned and ran, I'd be right behind you," Clara said.

"Maybe I can apologize, perhaps there's some way I could let it know that I only said it out of anger or something," I said. "Oh my, God, listen to me, talking about apologizing to a damned ghost!"

We both laughed and that was good. I remember a bully in school who always singled someone out and one day it was my turn. Well, he was big, and all of his former victims would run away until he caught up with them the next day and beat them up. I did the same thing and ran away two days in a row. After talking to my dad, he said face the bully or I'd have to come home and face him. I chose the bully and the third day I didn't run, we fought, he again beat me up, but after, we became friends. There was a problem here at the Dandy house though. I didn't want to get beat up again and I sure as hell didn't want to become friends, not with a demon!

A couple days later, Father Al called before leaving the friary to visit the Dandys, but Debbie informed him I was asleep. He asked her not to disturb me and he would catch me another time. My next opportunity, and mustering up the nerve, was early December. The band was scheduled to play but

Jamie had gotten sick and we had to cancel. Debbie had made plans to spend the night at her mother's and I had nothing to do. I called Mike to see what he was up to and he informed me that some of the guys were going to spend the night and that I was more than welcome to join in. I accepted and told him I'd be up around 7 p.m.. I called Debbie and told her what had happened with Jamie and I told her I would be at the Dandys.

"Are you sure you feel all right going up alone?" She asked.

"Sure, what could happen? Some of the guys are spending the night and I might too. It all depends on what's going on," I said.

"Be careful, call if you need me," Debbie said.

"Thanks, love you," I said.

I changed my clothes and grabbed a pillow to take with me in case I did spend the night. As I turned onto State Street, I looked over at the sub shop and could imagine Tim's tinfoil hat under the counter. I wondered if his commanding officer was going to allow him to wear one at boot camp. I was sure he had the men in his company rolling on the floor every time he opened his mouth or looked at them after one of his quips. I didn't care what he thought. I missed him and his stupid comments. Maybe some day he'll realize he made a mistake in judgment.

I arrived at the house later than I anticipated. The roads coming up to the house were bad. At one point on Wagner Hill, I didn't think I was going to make the grade. Then, as I got to the end, just before the McMahon turn where the wind blows across the road, I nearly got stuck in a drift. It wasn't a good night for traveling McMahon Road wasn't a whole lot better. The open field allowed the snow to pile up and it was tough getting through. I had no doubt, if it kept snowing I wouldn't be leaving tonight.

When I got out of the car, I looked at Mary's window. I don't remember if I said it out loud, maybe I said it to myself, but I remember saying, "I'm sorry." What a buffoon, saying you're sorry to a damned window. I knocked on the door and a little princess named Mary, opened it. "Hi, Paul, long time, no see! Mike, Paul's here!" She announced.

"And how are you tonight?" I asked her.

"Fine, are you spending the night?" Mary asked.

"If the snow keeps coming down, I won't have a choice," I said, turning around to look at the driveway.

"Yay!" She said as she ran into the living room.

"Hey, Paul. I'm glad you could come by," Mike said.

"Thanks, Mike, I missed everyone," I said.

"Miss Tim?" He asked.

I couldn't say anything. I don't think I wanted to. I lost a friend over something, to this day, I don't understand. The kitchen was warm and you could hear the wind tightening its cold hand all around the house. We walked into the living room when I told Mike I left my pillow in the car. I walked back out to the kitchen and couldn't get the back door to open. I fidgeted with the lock both ways and it wouldn't budge. Mike must have heard me and came out of the living room.

"What's wrong?" He asked.

"I can't get the damned door open!" I said.

He turned the knob and it opened, no problem. We looked at one another but didn't say anything until I started to walk out.

"Would you stay here?" I asked.

"Absolutely," Mike replied.

I opened the car door, reached across to the passenger seat and grabbed the pillow. Apprehension was there and I didn't want to back out of the car. There was nothing there but I already got myself keyed up when the door wouldn't open. I stood up, closed the door and turned around to see Mike standing at the door waiting for me. I let out a sigh of relief as I walked into the kitchen. Mike closed the door behind me and I immediately turned around to open it. It opened with no problem. I looked at Mike.

"Maybe it was just stuck," he said.

"Yeah," I said, and I was sure Mike didn't believe that any more than I did.

We walked back into the living room where I saw Mike N. Keith, and Randy. We all said hi to one another and I took a seat on the floor. Mike suggested we go into his room so we could talk without worrying what words might slip out that could possibly get us into trouble. In single file, we walked through the kitchen and into Mike's room. As I explained, Mike's room was small, so we took up refuge where we could, I flopped on the floor.

"How are the roads, Paul?" Randy asked.

"They're getting bad, Randy. I didn't think I was going to make Wagner and then I hit a drift at the bottom. If it keeps up, it'll take the road crews all day to get them cleared in the country," I said.

"I hit a drift in at the bottom of the hill too and the plows were out just a couple hours earlier," Keith said.

"Anything in the house, Paul?" Randy asked.

"Let the house sleep, please, Randy," I said.

Clara came downstairs and stood at Mike's door. "Hi Paul! When did you arrive?" She asked.

"Oh, about 20 minutes ago, I guess," I responded.

"I'm glad you could make it. I thought you had to play tonight?" Clara asked.

"No, Jamie got sick on Thursday so I called and canceled. It's a good thing too, 'cause I don't think many would have made it to the dance. Hell, I don't think we would have made it with this weather," I replied.

"Well, you're probably right, the roads are going to be bad. They're forecasting another 6 to 10 inches," she informed us.

Even though I was in a room, literally packed with people, I found myself wishing I hadn't come. I should have gone out to Debbie's mom's and spent the night. Instead, I was at the house and according to the weather forecast, would be at least until daylight. We hung around in Mike's room until Mary and Laura went to bed. They both came in to say goodnight to us after which, we went into the living room to watch TV. Mike and Clara brought out the cots and a few extra blankets. On the television, was an old western with Gene Autry. No one was really paying attention to. We were sitting around talking about movies, music and, "what would it be like" type questions. Mike N. was the first to fall asleep, he obviously wasn't the night-owl type. Randy and Mike were challenging each other on songs and who performed them when Beth Ann came out of her bedroom and walked into the kitchen. No one paid any attention to her at first until Mike looked into the kitchen and saw her on the floor. He went out to see what she was doing but she didn't respond to him. We heard the concern in Mike's voice so Randy and I went out to the kitchen to see if we could help.

"She must be walking in her sleep," Mike said.

"Has she done this before?" I asked.

"Not that I know of," Mike replied, getting her to her feet and walking her back to her room.

"That was creepy, Keith said."

"Her eyes looked cloudy, like she was on medication or something," Randy said.

"Sometimes people sleep walk—shit, here she comes again," Keith said.

"Hey!" Randy said as she gave him a kick before sitting on the couch.

As she sat there, she said something to the effect that, "Mama gave it to me, and it's all mine." It seemed she was petting something or playing with something. Yet she held nothing in her hands. She got up from the couch and went into the bath off the kitchen. Mike and Keith were close behind her. Randy and I followed.

"What's she doing?" Randy asked, trying to see over Keith's shoulder.

"She's acting like she's making something, cooking, rolling dough, I don't know," Mike said.

Keith and Mike backed up as Beth Ann came out of the bathroom and attempted to open the back door. Mike pushed on the door as it began to open and Beth Ann lashed out at him. Then she went after Keith who had just been standing at Mike's side. Mike calmed her down by talking to her and slowly walked her back to her bedroom. Keith gave a chuckle looking into the living room because Mike N. was sleeping through this whole ordeal. No sooner had Mike gotten Beth Ann to her bed than she got up and attempted to crawl out the window. Randy and Mike brought her out to the living and had her sit on the cot that Keith had been on earlier. Mike N. was startled awake when the cot Beth Ann sat on snapped with a loud thud as Beth Ann landed on the floor very near Mike's head.

"What's going on?" he asked.

"Go get your parents, Mike," I said.

Randy and Keith helped Beth Ann up and walked her back into her bedroom, as Mike ran up the stairs. Moments, later, the three of them, Mike and his parents were in Beth Ann's room as she sat crying on her bed. We all stood and stared in amazement, wondering what had happened to her. Meanwhile, Mike N., still sleepily asking, what was going on. Clara stayed with Beth Ann until she fell asleep. Phil, on his way upstairs, told us to settle down, it was time to get some sleep.

"What the heck is happening?" Randy pondered.

The howling of the wind added to the unsettling noises randomly heard throughout the rest of the evening. I believe everyone slept with one eye open.

Just over a week later, we were getting together again and this time there would be a photographer joining us, a Jim. S., and a mountain of a kid, home on leave, also in the Air Force. Mike M. didn't believe anything whatsoever about the stories surrounding the house. Frankly, I had high hopes the entity in Mary's room would make an appearance when he was present. If it had, it was safe to say, he'd win hands down. He was huge! We all gathered in the living room as usual and Mike M. kept saying things like, "bring on the ghosts," and "nothing's gonna scare me." Altogether, those present were: Mike, Randy, Jim S., Mike N., Keith, Mike M. and me. Beth Ann was in her room and fell asleep early. She'd been having a tough time lately and Clara had taken her to the doctor.

Early on, the house was quiet and I went to the kitchen to get a glass of water When I returned to the living room I sat on one of the remaining cots. The cot was reinforced with springs, allowing for a little give when you tossed and turned. When I sat down on one end, a moment later, I raised up, as if someone sat on the other end. I turned around to see who sat down and there was no one there. Jim S. had been lying on the couch alongside the cot and sat up, staring at the other end of the cot. I turned around again and said, "Would you like a drink?" To *no one.*

347

"I saw that," Randy said.

"Yeah, me too," Jim said, now snapping pictures at nothing.

"Saw what?" Mike M. asked.

"When Paul sat down, it appeared someone sat on the other end of the cot, but no one did. I saw it too," Mike N. said.

"Yeah okay, whatever you say," Mike M. replied.

"I saw it too, Mike," Jim S. agreed.

"Paul, I think there's something by Phil's chair," Randy said.

I had been smoking a cigarette. I walked over, leaned down toward Phil's chair and blew smoke at it. There was an outline, a form, that the smoke had traced around. Everyone seemed to see it and I took my hand and swatted at it. Randy went into a trance immediately after. I still didn't really know what to make of these trances but I had a thought. I asked Mike M., a monster of a guy, to do what Father had told me to do with the "brain warp" idea. He thought that was silly but I wanted to see Randy raise Mike's arm from his head. He had arms the size of tree trunks and there was no way in hell Randy was going to budge him. Mike M. humoring us, went over to Randy and placed his hand on Randy's head. Seconds later, Randy started to raise his arm along with Mike M.'s arm with little, if any effort at all. Everyone gasped, and Mike M. was furious. Keith and I got between him and Randy because it appeared he might punch Randy he seemed so mad. We explained what had happened with Randy and the trance and Mike M. calmed down. Still, there was just no possible way that strength came from Randy alone. A few minutes later, Randy snapped out it and he said, "There's someone here with us," I'd never seen an instance when Randy predicted or felt something but he certainly seemed sincere and more than a little concerned. It was probably half an hour later before I felt anything. What I felt wasn't ominous, although I'd been wrong before. Jim S. had been taking pictures the whole time since the, "rise from the cot trick." We all began settling down, still talking, but quietly. Mike M. was heard several times saying, "No way," or "That's not possible" as we were telling him random incidents pertaining to the house.

"She's sleeping," Clara said as she walked into the living room. "If she has another incident come and get me immediately."

"We will, mom," Mike told his mother.

"All of you settle down and get some rest," Clara said walking toward the kitchen.

Mike M., Mike N., Randy, and Mike Dandy were all on the floor. I was on the cot next to the couch, where Jim S. was lying, and Keith was on the cot next to me. I'd been facing the window toward the back of the house. All the lights were off downstairs except Beth Ann's nightlight and a dim light in the kitchen. The moonlight was bright on the snow and you could make out the yard and lay of the land looking out the window.

Jim S., Keith and I were chatting about photography and my band when I caught movement at the window. I was sure it was the pine tree. It had snow on it and was moving from the wind. I kept my eyes on the window when a few moments later, and very clearly, a woman was standing at the window, her face very close to the glass, looking directly at me. I said nothing, I just stared back. The feeling I had was that I was going to die! That was a great thing to think I thought. Jim said something to me but I didn't pay attention. I raised myself from the cot, still saying nothing, got up and announced that it was time for me to leave. Everyone was asking what was the matter, or why, but I said nothing. No more than 10 seconds later, Beth Ann was screaming in her room, "There's a woman in my room!" I looked at the window and the woman was no longer looking in. Beth Ann came out of her room but there was no smell of perfume following her this time. She sat on the cot I had been lying on as I went to the kitchen to turn on the lights. I went back into the living room to explain what I had seen and Beth Ann's description of the woman in her room was exactly who I had seen. She had black hair, wearing a sort of a high collared dress, and her hair was either wet or very shiny, but her eyes spoke evil. Of course my statement of leaving was out of the question. There was no way I was going outside alone at this time of night. Trying to drive anywhere through a blizzard would be suicidal. Mike M. walked into the kitchen to go into the bathroom. A few moments later he was yelling something indistinct, running back into the living room.

"The goddamn doorknob in the bathroom was jiggling like crazy!" He said.

We all heard a bang and it was Clara coming down the stairs.

"What the hell is going on?" She demanded.

"Paul saw a woman at the window and then there was a woman in Beth Ann's room," Mike said.

"And the door in your bathroom is alive!" Mike M. said.

"All right, everyone settle down. Beth Ann, do you want to come upstairs and have your dad come down?"

"No, mom, I'll be all right," she said.

"Maybe some of you ought to sleep in Mike's room," Clara suggested.

"Mom, I think we should all stay together," Mike said.

"Okay, try and settle down and get some sleep. Call me if anything else happens," she said heading for the stairs.

"Mike, your fly is open." Randy told Mike M. so nonchalantly that everyone began to laugh, including this giant of a kid. We all took our respective places once again and attempted to sleep. I don't think I took my eyes off the window until daylight broke. The feeling of *someone* with us remained throughout the rest of the morning.

CHAPTER XXIX

The house was affecting Beth Ann very strangely lately. Clara kept me informed of all the events happening at the house. She called to tell me that Beth Ann attempted to kill herself twice while at school. That was very difficult to believe. There were several kids around when she attempted this and Dave T., a close friend, kept an eye on her at school. Clara also informed me that Craig suffered from the house's antics when he came home on leave. It seems everyone's personalities were changing when they're at or near the house. Craig was acting very oddly as he, with several in the car heading back to the house, started shouting something about the horses. Clara said Randy and Mike were with him, as well as the little ones, and they had no idea what in the world he was talking about. I talked to Randy on the phone and he recounted the entire story to me. He said when they arrived at the house, Craig got out of the car, but was still acting weird as hell. He was yelling that he had to help 'Pa' with the chores. Then, according to Randy, while standing in the back yard, he asked where the barn was, obviously amazed when he couldn't see it.

"What barn?" I asked.

"You got me. Craig was actually walking toward the pond when he asked. I told him we already went by it and took him into the house," Randy replied.

"You trying to tell me that Craig wasn't Craig?" I asked.

"I guess, he's not one to make things up. He was really acting strange and his eyes looked as if he were in a daze," Randy said.

"That's unbelievable and makes no sense but Tim and I saw something similar happen with Mike in the field. He wasn't acting like himself either—Unbelievable," I said.

"Yeah, it's getting stranger all the time. All right, I'll let you go, it's almost six o'clock and I need to get home for dinner. I'm sure Clara will keep you informed. If you need to talk, you know how to reach me," Randy said.

"Thanks, Randy, bye."

"Who were you talking to?" Debbie asked.

351

"Randy, he was filling me in on the new twists in the house," I said.

"Huh?"

"It seems everyone's personality changes when they're around the house. Yeah, I know, it sounds crazy. Something happened to Mike one night then Beth Ann. Now Craig is also acting weird," I explained.

"Would you live there?" She asked.

"Only if you were with me, and you protected me!" I said, batting my eyes at her.

"Not me, bub! I just thought of something. I couldn't take my clothes off, knowing a ghost was watching me!" Debbie said.

"I could take them off for you!"

"Not now, frisky, we have stuff to do," she said, slapping my hand.

Debbie and I started preparing for Christmas, decorating the apartment. We were going to go with some friends and pick out a tree tomorrow. Christmas was just over a week away and we really hadn't planned anything yet. The one thing we were sure of was that we would be spending time with both families. Debbie's oldest brother, Mike would be home for the holidays. He attended an out of state college and it was always nice to see him when he was able make the trip home. Debbie and I had been going together for nearly a year before either of us was aware that we used to play together when we were children. There was a family in North Olean where she had been a friend of the daughter and I was a friend of the son. One day, her brother Tim reminded her that they used to tease her as a child by saying, "Debra Lynn, skinny as a pin." When he reminded her that day, the rhyme shot from my memory like a cannon ball. We discussed it, and realized we used to catch fireflies together when she was eight and I was ten. I probably thought she was cute then, too!

Debbie came into the kitchen and asked, "Weren't there plans for Alex to return to the house again?"

"I think Father Al and Clara had talked about it. I believe Alex needs to find a sponsor or something to help with the cost of funding the research," I said.

"Oh, he doesn't do it on his own? He doesn't have his own research team?" She asked.

"I'm not sure, hon, I think he just tours the country as a psychic, explaining psychic phenomena at his lectures," I said.

"He had such deep set eyes, spooky looking," she said with a cringe on her face.

"Yeah, he did. I don't know if I would want the ability to see spirits or the residual energy they leave behind as he does, with such magnitude. I think that's what he actually gets: impressions from the energy," I said.

"It's all too creepy for me, I don't understand how you deal with it. Labor Day you looked like you were twenty years older than you are," she said.

"Ah, now I'm a dirty *old* man, is that what you're saying?!" I asked.

I started to chase her around the table and she ran into the bedroom. That wasn't a good idea—unless she planned it!

After we ate dinner we took a drive to K-Mart to look at more baby items. I found it refreshing being away from the house and, with my beautiful wife. Debbie and I were married in a simple ceremony on October 11, 1973. Our parents wanted us to wait but we had a child on the way and felt it was the right thing to do. Looking back, there were so many mistakes made...so many wrong decisions but this hadn't been one of them. It was the mistakes made afterwards that took their toll.

When we got to K-Mart, I had Debbie stand on the front of the cart and I pushed her around the store. We were acting like kids and enjoyed every second of it until I didn't quite negotiate a turn in an aisle and wiped out an entire display of paper towels. There must have been over 50 rolls of paper towels scattered everywhere; rolling down the main aisle, under other peoples carts, one even went straight up and landed in a woman's cart. She thanked us! She was just about to walk over to the display and get a roll. I felt awful and started to pick them up when I got a super hot feeling in my head.

"You're tough?!" Someone asked.

From my knees, as I was picking up rolls of towels, I looked up expecting to see a manager preparing to yell at me.

There was no one around except two ladies looking at laundry soap.

"You okay? You look like you seen a ghost." Debbie asked.

"HA!" The voice came again, very loud, very clear. I looked down both aisles, on either side of us but there was no one there. There was no place else for anyone to be except directly in front of us but the only people anywhere around us were the two ladies arguing about which box of laundry soap was the best deal. I stood up, holding about five rolls of paper towels and walked around the aisles to either side of the display. I was waiting for someone we knew to pop out from somewhere but there was no one else in the immediate area.

"Honey, are you okay, what are you looking for?" Debbie said.

"I heard a voice," I said.

I picked up most of the rolls of towels, attempting to put them back as neatly as possible, but when I was done, the display looked like a huge double set of bowling pins. We finished shopping, Debbie now walking along side of me and went to the checkout. I was trying not to think about the voice I heard and we spoke no more about it. I was sure I knew who it was. Debbie didn't mention it again. I knew it was *someone* and I was almost positive it was Mary's *someone*. Somewhere deep inside, I hoped it was someone in the store who was messing around but I knew I was hoping in vain. The pain I had in my head before I heard it was the same type of pain I had Labor Day while sitting at the picnic table. What the hell was this? I stay away from the house so they come to me? There was no way I was going to tell Debbie my thoughts about the voice. I would tell Father and Clara.

It was still early enough after checking out, so we decided to drive out to Crosby's to get dessert. Debbie has a banana split; it was obvious what my choice was. We were so close to the house and I had the strange feeling of being called to come out. Rather than sit at Crosby's and have our after dinner treats, I started the car and pulled out.

"Hey, I better not spill this!" Debbie said.

"I'm sorry, you want to stay?" I asked.

"No, go ahead. Did you get napkins at least?"

"Oh, yeah, sorry," I said pulling a wad of napkins from my shirt pocket.

"You in a hurry, or something?" She asked.

"No, not really. It's just that, I came out this way every night for so long and we're so close to the house, I just didn't feel like looking at the same scenery," I said.

She didn't respond to my lame excuse for leaving. Was it open season now? Was I a target for something that I pissed off, something that wants to take me up on my threat? No one ever said anything about making threats or antagonizing a spirit. Clara said she gets mad and yells "get out!" when the noises get bad but she never said anything about retaliation. I wondered if there were going to come a day when I had to face whatever it was I pissed off. Who was going to win? Well, this was a bully I didn't want any part of. If it meant I had to go upstairs and apologize to an empty room, so be it. I didn't want to hear random voices floating on the air and I surely didn't want Debbie involved in any way—I will make my peace. I will go to the house, tell Clara everything, from my challenge to the room that afternoon, to the comments I made to the window when I was in the yard. It sounds so ridiculous, insane even, thinking of giving an apology to an empty room but I didn't want any further involvement with the house, on location or wherever I might be.

Debbie and I arrived home and I took the bags from the back seat. It was only about 9 so we decided to watch TV for a while. I threw our empty containers from Crosby's away, (what a waste, I could hear Tim say) while Debbie looked for something to watch—she settled on Gunsmoke.

I brought in our pillows and blankets from the bed and tossed them at her, totally covering her on the couch. "What are you doing?" She asked with a muffled voice.

"We're gonna camp out tonight! We're gonna watch Mr. Dillon shoot the bad guy and then we're gonna fall asleep on the floor!" I said.

"Oh, you think so, huh? The hell with Mr. Dillon, get over here!"

"God, help me!"

I'd forgotten we were in the living room. When I sat up wondering why the bed seemed so hard, I slammed my forehead into the underside of the coffee table. "Shit!" I whispered. I looked over at Debbie; she was fast asleep, she too had her head under the table. I slid it back so she wouldn't suffer from the same forgetfulness I had. I propped myself up on one arm and found myself staring at her while she slept. What the hell was I doing chasing ghosts while I left her at home? I knew she really didn't mind in the least but it wasn't right and I'm glad we stopped going every night. We had a great night tonight and that was so much more important than anything else. I got up to look at the time; it was just past two. I thought about lying back down then decided I'd better wake her so her back wouldn't give her trouble after sleeping on the floor all night.

"Come one, let's go to bed," I whispered.

"What time is it?" She asked.

"A little after 2," I whispered, kissing her cheek.

"I don't have to get up yet, let me sleep." She whined.

"I know but we're on the floor—your back, come on."

She got up and went to the bedroom as I picked up the pillows and blankets. I got her settled and went out to turn the lights and TV off. It really had been a good night, except for the voice.

I woke a few minutes before Debbie and went to the kitchen to scramble some eggs and make some toast. The alarm would be going off in less than 15 minutes so I had just enough time to get it done before she was out of bed. I had everything ready to put on the plates when the alarm went off. I walked into the bedroom and announced, "Madam, breakfast is served," carrying her plate, then returning to the kitchen to get mine.

"That's so sweet" She said when I returned. "But it would be even sweeter if I had something to eat it with."

"I forgot the forks! Dammit!" I exclaimed returning to the kitchen.

We ate our breakfast, then I took the plates to the kitchen while Debbie took a shower. I had planned to join her when the phone rang; it was Susie. She said she woke up sick and wouldn't be able to pick Debbie up for work. I thanked her for calling and told her I'd take her in. She said she would call tonight if she didn't think she was going to make it tomorrow. I went to the sink and was about to rinse the dishes when I remembered our water pressure was horrible. You couldn't turn on the water in the bathroom and the kitchen at the same time, you'd only get a trickle from one or the other. I didn't want the cold water coming on harder in the shower because I'd have been in *hot* water!

"Who called this early in the morning?""She asked walking into the kitchen.

"Susie's sick, she won't be going in today," I told her.

"Oh, that means I have my own personal driver, huh?" She asked.

"Yeah, I guess you're stuck with me," I said.

"I was stuck with you last night, it wasn't all that bad," she said, offering my second morning kiss.

"Be careful, or you'll be stuck again," I said.

"Promises, promises," she said, walking away to get dressed.

We arrived at B.O.C.E.S. about 15 minutes early so we sat in the car and talked. "You don't like Susie do you?" She asked.

"She's got a very dry sense of humor, almost arrogant. No, not really," I said.

"She's okay once you get to know her, although, she does like to talk about people."

"What do you mean?" I asked.

"Come on!" The voice was in my head, but the heat wave didn't accompany it, I jumped when it came.

"Well, if someone ..... you okay? Debbie asked.

"Yeah, I just got a chill is all," I said. I wasn't going to tell her I heard another voice.

"Well, if someone wears something she doesn't like, then it looks terrible. Once one of the girls was wearing the same dress she owns, the pattern's the same but the colors are different. She said it was the most distasteful things she's ever seen anyone wear to work," Debbie explained.

"Yeah, that's interesting. Sounds like she's a nitpicker," I said, hoping no more voices were ready to pop out of the air.

"No it's worse than that! A couple of guys that work here are going bald and she's always going on about how she doesn't understand how a girl could fall for a guy who was losing his hair," she explained.

"Have you ever mentioned that a lot of guys don't like women with fat asses? Tell her that one, see how *she* likes being criticized," I said.

"You're mean!" She said, punching my arm.

"Well! She's got a fat ass, not only that, her hips are wider than her shoulders, if that isn't out of proportion. She'd be better off walking on her hands!" I said.

Laughing, she said, "I'm going in, you're terrible!"

"That's not what you said last night," I shouted, as we waved goodbye.

I guess we were lucky, I wasn't going bald, and she didn't have a fat ass.

I drove back down Genesee Street and, instead of turning left to head back into town, I turned right, toward Hinsdale. It was an impulse, I hadn't planned turning right, I simply did. If I was going to the house, only Clara and Mike would be home. Phil would normally be home about this time but I think today is payday for him, so he would probably make his usual stop. It seems both of my visits during the day were disastrous so what was I doing? *You're tough? Come on!* Who belonged to this voice? Mary's tenant? Maybe a combination of energies, or was my involvement with the house finally taking its toll on me. Maybe the voices were only my own imagination—*Dear, God,* I thought, *please don't let that be the case.* I did swing at something in Phil's chair that night when Randy went into one of his trances but I also offered *whoever* sat on the cot something to drink so that was a nice gesture, wasn't it?

Lately, everyone was becoming someone else at the house and that had absolutely nothing to do with the prior incidents. But why, *why* was I the only one with the gift of "hearing"? Maybe, since the spirits can't accomplish what they want, they're going to take the living as hosts and continue their reign of terror. It really didn't matter what was or wasn't happening up there. It wasn't going to be happening in random retail stores, harassing and making comments, pressing to start a fight. I'll take the fight to them, if need be, because I resigned myself now that I wouldn't allow this to affect me or my life. In the beginning, Tim and I were no different than any of those other people driving up to the house, hoping to catch a spirit in the lens of their camera or to see an apparition roaming the countryside. If there was any difference at all, it was our friendship and the trust we and the family had for each other. Even though I hadn't been visiting as much as I had in the past, there was still something about this damned house that stayed with me. Perhaps, it was like a virus, a germ that I shared with the house. It affected, then infected me after a period of time. I hoped that wasn't the case, but I believe that something had made a connection with me and as long as I continued to visit, it would continue to communicate.

I have never heard of anyone being inoculated with a "psychic shot," There was no doubt, the house needed me for something and I constantly found myself drawn to it, persuaded to be a part of everything. I didn't know what to think of this new development of the house clutching at people's personalities. I didn't know who was totally honest with what they'd seen, heard or felt. If you get a couple dozen of people together and a few of them start shouting, "I see it, I see it!" a few more will endorse that statement with the same exclamatory words whether they see it or not. Not to mention, the ones who "see it" first fraudulently say so to gain attention. Others just don't want to be left out. They want to be included, accepted into the select few who just might be telling the truth. The house had become a narcotic for me. I was like a smoker craving nicotine after quitting cold turkey.

The closer I got to the house, the more I wanted to turn around an get away from there. The more a toothache hurts, the more you want it yanked from your jaw until you sit in the chair. I had planned to call Father Al today to see if we could get together. He might be able to offer something that would make me feel better, safer. I knew I had to try at least one more thing on my own before running to him for cover.

I was nearing the bottom of Wagner Hill and ready to turn on McMahon, when I stopped. I felt as if I were going to make up with someone, to reconcile our differences and let bygones be bygones. To bury the hatchet, so to speak. Would I go in guns blazing or whimper up the stairs asking to please leave me alone, "don't hurt me any more?" Would it take my visit mercifully or would it see me as a weak, sniveling coward after boasting such a huge ego, threatening and telling it to get the fuck out? Would it then proceed to annihilate me, mentally and psychically? I didn't exaggerate when I told Tim that I was scared out of my mind. Sitting at the bottom of McMahon Road, just over a quarter mile from my possible mental executioner, I felt as if I had *lost* my mind. Maybe if I just let sleeping dogs lie, I won't have to worry about getting bitten— again. Possibly, it will forget about me and concentrate on those within reach. Was that fair? Didn't Father suggest that I may have added just a little more fuel to the fire? What was it, go forward and take my chances or turn around and take my chances?

I sat there, dumber than a stump, for over an hour. I thought of what it must be like living here when those who died here might still be present. Was evil *always* evil or did it have a compassionate side?—Always—Is there anything that is, or was, *Always?* I decided to take my chances—I turned around.

I drove down Wagner Hill Road, out to the Hinsdale Highway, past Crosby's, and into Olean, where another impulse struck and I drove to Saint John's Church. I stayed there for as long, if not longer than I sat thinking at the bottom of McMahon Road. I grew up in North Olean, attended Saint John's parochial school and worshiped at Saint John's Church. Rather than battle with the unknown, I thought it might be wiser to go right to the top with this one. I had faith and if my questions couldn't be answered here, they couldn't be answered at all. When I left Saint John's I didn't leave with verbal answers but I left all my questions with the Head Guy. I felt I was in good Hands walking back to the car. Whatever was to happen now, I would accept, because I knew I was playing for the Home Team, and let's face facts, The Home Team was unbeaten.

Now that I was back to reality, I realized I was hungry. I wasted an hour sitting on a dirt road, talked with the Man upstairs another hour creating a game plan, and now it was time to join the living once again and nourish the belly. I went to Pick Ups restaurant and ordered lunch for Debbie and me. They told me it would be about 10 minutes so I took a seat at the counter and asked for a Mountain Dew while I waited. Just to be sure, I called Debbie from the pay phone to let her know I was bringing food. In our playful haste this morning, we both forgot to grab her lunch. She was relieved when I called because she called the house to see if I could bring her something. See, I told you I was psychic! I asked her to get a couple of drinks from the vending machine so I wouldn't have to try and jostle take-out sodas while driving.

I paid for our lunches and the waitress handed me two neatly folded bags. I went outside, hopped in the car, and headed for B.O.C.E.S. Everything was such a short drive in Olean. You could be on one end of town, order something from the other end, and be there within 10 minutes to pick it up. When I pulled into the parking lot, I saw Debbie standing at the side employee door. I got out of the car as she began walking toward me.

"Let's eat inside, so we don't have to worry about holding everything," I said.

"Okay!" She said with that, "light up a room" smile.

We walked to the lunch room and found a table that was empty. I had planned to tell her about my travels today but didn't want a bunch of nosey people eavesdropping. I was glad Susie wasn't here. I had a small hole in my jeans—she'd probably tell someone I looked like a homeless person!

"What'd ya get me?" Debbie asked excitedly, as she looked in the bag. "Ooh, steak… and a baked potato, yummy!"

"Look in the other bag, not as skinny as a pin, D. Lynn," I teased.

"Strawberry shortcake?! I'm in heaven!" She exclaimed.

"No, I am. Start eating so you don't have to hurry," I said.

I didn't know how to start with what I wanted to tell her but she made it easy when she asked what I did that morning. "I went to Hinsdale," I said.

"Why?" She asked, in mid-chew.

"Honestly, I hadn't even thought of going. I went with the thought of making peace with whatever was there. We didn't see anyone when I heard the voice in K-Mart last night because there wasn't anyone there," I said.

"You lost me now," Debbie said.

"I believe the voice I heard was from the house. I had the same exact feeling I had Labor Day afternoon, *exactly the same*," I explained.

"Now you're scaring me. I don't think I want you to be hearing voices when you're away from the house. But why did you go there this morning? You said you wanted to be rid of all of this," she said.

"I stopped at the beginning of the road and thought for about an hour. Either I was going up and confronting this with anger or possibly the opposite or I was leaving with the hopes that, if I didn't go, it would simply stop," I said.

"And?"

"I left and went to church instead. The next time I visit the Dandys, it will be just that, a visit. If I feel anything, I just won't acknowledge it," I said. "At least I will try not to acknowledge it."

"Well, I'm sure you know what it is you feel and only you can decide how to handle it. Have you talked to Father Al about this?" Debbie asked me.

"Last week but I'll be calling him again," I said.

People were starting to leave the lunch room so I assumed it was time for Debbie to go too. I was hoping I didn't upset her and that everything was going to be okay now. Overall, I had a better outlook, believing I had my faith on my side. After all, that's what most of these troubled houses were fought with, faith.

"Picking me up?" She asked.

"Hell, no. Maybe some strange man will give you a ride home," I said teasingly.

362

"Well, if I have to ride with a strange man, I might as well ride with the strangest man I know and that's you," she replied.

She gave me a kiss and I walked her to the end of the room, tossed our trash into a trash can, returned to where she waited for me and stole another kiss, which was *my* dessert.

CHAPTER XXX

The following week Debbie and I spent quite a lot of time together and Christmas was wonderful. We spent time with the families, time alone, and we hadn't been to the house for some time. The weekend before Christmas was insane for our band. One night, we played in one city from 9 p.m. to midnight, took the equipment down, packed it into the milk truck and flew like hell to a post prom 30 miles away. We were to play from 1 am to 4 a.m. but were a few minutes late getting set up. Both gatherings turned out great but we couldn't wait to get home—it had snowed the entire time we were on the road.

I received a call from Clara informing me that Tim had come home on leave and he had been going to the house every night to visit. I didn't hear a word from him the entire time he was home. Beth Ann was having a horrible time. Her personality had changed several times in the past couple of weeks. One evening, she was rushed to the hospital after she told Tim she had taken more medication than she should have. Clara told me Beth Ann's stomach was pumped shortly after arriving at the hospital but nothing was found. There was no trace of drugs in her bloodstream either. Clara and the doctors were puzzled since they had been told she took several pills. Something odd occurred as well, Clara said that Beth Ann seemed to be speaking a foreign tongue! Later that same night, Phil injured his thumb and had to go to the hospital for stitches. Something else unbelievable happened: Tim had slept in Mary's room! Craig spent the night as well and there was an incident involving him which I wished I had observed.

Late that evening, Clara heard a horrible racket downstairs, and Laura called to her because Craig was in some sort of trouble. When they reached Mike's room where Craig had been sleeping, they noticed that everything in Mike's room was doing the "Psychic Samba!" His dresser, bed, as well as other items in his room were jumping all over. Phil was caught in the middle of this "Jaw dropping Jitter Bug" attempting to rescue Craig who was caught between the bed and the dresser. They didn't know if Craig was knocked out or "psyched out," but he wasn't conscious either way. Phil was able to get him out of the room and used household ammonia to bring him out of it. Clara said everything in Mike's room suddenly stopped doing the, "Hokey, Paranormal Pokey" as soon as Craig came to. Seeing that would have been worth going round three with "He who hides behind Mary's door."

Over the next two weeks, I surprised myself and visited with the Dandys twice. In a way, and this may sound silly, I felt as though I hadn't done all that I could have. Actually, when Tim and I were spending the evenings at the house, I don't believe we were really *doing* anything but entertaining ourselves. In the early visits to the house, we may have warded off potential trespassers and maybe we even played interference, keeping the energy from the interior of the house. Mike was finally able to return to school, and Keith moved in with the family in early January. During my first visit in January, Keith, Mike and I took a drive so we could talk. Why I ended up driving Keith's car, I don't remember. We drove around the camp roads and took a road that led into Cuba before turning back. It was the first time driving in the winter that I'd hit a patch of black ice. It scared the living hell out of us! I wasn't driving fast but when you hit ice, it doesn't matter what speed you're traveling. Somehow, and it had to be the good Lord, I kept the car on the road. It was harrowing, because we swerved back and forth across the road many times. The car finally came to a stop, sitting precariously at the top of a ten foot ditch. I put the car in reverse, luckily the rear tires gripped the road and I backed up with no problem— Thank God! Keith was laughing and having a good time saying, "Yeah, what a ride!" No, it wasn't a fun ride at all. One, or all of us could have been injured and that would not have been good. I got out and told Keith he could drive. I've tried to remember why I had been driving; I can't.

"I can't understand Tim, Paul. He said you drove his car once and, the next time he drove it, the brakes went," Mike said.

"My God, Mike, the car was a heap to begin with. I don't mean it was junk but it had its quirks. I wouldn't want to see anyone get hurt and, as I said, I was in the car with him almost every night," I said.

"You don't have to convince us. I think I know you well enough to think differently," Mike said.

"You guys were pretty close, weren't you?" Keith asked, finally turning the car around.

"I thought so. I really enjoyed our nights at the house. We had a ball 'til all this dumb shit started happening with me. I just can't believe he thinks what he does. Everyone else had car trouble, why is it his car was tampered with and for what goddamned reason?!" I said, angrily.

"You guys just need to talk it over, get it out in the open," Mike said.

"Out in the open? It was put out in open to everyone *but* me! Instead of insinuating to everyone else what he thought, why the fuck hadn't he come to me and ask? Screw it, let him think whatever the hell he wants. But I thought he would know me a little better than that," I said.

"I'm really sorry. After hearing you two together, you'd think you'd been friends for years. He's a real nut, that's for sure. Even when he was scared shitless, he always found a way to see the humor in it," Mike said.

"Yeah, Mike, there's no humor now though, is there?" I replied.

Keith drove us back to the house and we all went inside. We sat at the kitchen table and I was asking about Beth Ann, if she was doing better. She had been getting over the past few days but it was touch and go with all the incidents she'd experienced. She and Tim were getting along and that was good. She's such a sweet girl and, in spite of what Tim thinks, I think they would make a great couple—they're both such caring people—well, she is for sure. I just couldn't figure Tim anymore. I asked Mike where his car was and he informed me his dad drove it to work and totaled it.

"Not another accident?! What happened?" I asked.

"He was going to work and a truck squeezed him off the road. He rolled the car, Paul, and walked away to call for help!" Mike said.

"I hope I wasn't near your car any time before the accident. I wasn't, was I?" I asked.

"No, and come on, we know better, forget about it," Mike said.

"Yeah, easy for you to say, Mike. Is you dad okay?"

"Surprisingly, yeah. He's been talking about getting me another car but money is tight right now," Mike told me.

"You guys have had your share of bad luck with vehicles, Keith said."

"It seems like everybody who comes up here has that," Mike said.

"What year is your milk truck, Paul?" Keith asked.

"1953. It's a Divco, made by Ford. It's got over 300,000 miles on it and still runs good too. It had dualies but I was driving through an alley and the truck was just a little too wide. I scraped the rear fenders on the walls of the buildings on either side of the alley and ripped both of them off. We decided it really didn't need dualies and removed one tire from each rear axle," I said.

"That's a neat looking truck, did you guys paint it?" Mike asked.

"We painted the body but we had a sign painter make the signs," I said.

It was nice to talk about something besides the problems with the house. All the while we sat there, the feeling was with me. It bothered me and it may have even scared me a little because I never knew when the "heavy weight" would offer a rematch. Clara was in the living room and I wanted to talk to her about the intentions I had the morning after dropping Debbie off at work. I was afraid if I had followed through, it would have stirred the house, bringing another unwanted confrontation. I so wanted to ascend the stairs to Mary's room but that would have been psychic suicide. I excused myself from the kitchen table and joined Clara in the living room. Laura and Mary were sitting with her. I really didn't want to discuss this with them listening and I asked Clara if we could have a talk alone.

The girls went into the kitchen with Mike and Keith but still within ear shot. I pulled Phil's hassock over and sat in front of her.

"What's on your mind?" She asked.

I scooted a little closer. I could see prying ears at the kitchen doorway.

"The house has really gotten to me, Clara. I guess that's why I haven't been coming up as often. This thing with Tim has me all messed up. I'm hurt and I guess just as angry because he never came directly to me; I had to hear it second hand," I said. "Both Father and Alex told me to nurture this 'gift' I have, not to fear it, but I don't understand how I can do anything but fear what happens every time I come to the house."

"I don't know what to tell you about Tim but, as far as the house goes, have you talked with Father Al? Have you been honest with him about how deeply the house has affected you?" Clara asked.

"Yeah, I have, a couple times now," I said.

"What are his recommendations and what does he believe causes you to experience such disturbing feeling?" She asked.

"He told me to have faith, to be very careful and, if that didn't help, I needed to stay away. He also said that it was possible my energy, supposedly because I have so much, was offering the energy of the house something to feed on. Alex said something almost the same the night he was here. The way Father explained it to me, I assume I feel it stronger because I generate so much of my own power. It just sounds so damned stupid to me," I said. "Now I have to deal with having feelings or hearing random voices outside the area of the house."

"I don't think it sounds the least bit stupid. In fact, it makes perfect sense if his assumption about your energy is correct. The house has severely affected us all, Paul, don't feel alone. Beth Ann would never act this way if we weren't living in this damned house, and I'm sure you can see the difference in each one of us since we've met. Phil, the kids, and I are stuck here for the time being. Our financial outlook is bleak and moving is out of the question. You, on the other hand, can come and go as you please. If you feel you're not able to withstand the stress the house causes you, don't come up. We'll miss you but there's no sense in putting yourself through hell," Clara said.

"I feel as though I've let you down by not coming up and, frankly, as I said, staying away doesn't help that much 'cause I'm connected in some way to the energies." I said.

"Nonsense! You're *not* a professional psychic, Paul. You may be more sensitive to the power or energies of the house but all that means is just that: you're more sensitive. I believe in time, if the energy reaches out, you'll be able to turn it off. I don't believe there's anything you can do to help our circumstance. I don't mean to sound cruel but, really, what can you do? I think I understand what you're saying but I honestly think part of the reason you've continued visiting is because you feel some connection with whatever the hell we have here. Now, according to Father Al, you've opened your psyche wide open." Clara said.

"I'm sure you're right, Clara, but I feel there has to be something I can accomplish to help get the energy out of the house," I said.

"How! Father Al comes to visit often and yet we still have the same apparitions, voices and other disturbances after he leaves. It's going to take something or someone very powerful who has worked in psychic circles for years, someone like Alex. Hopefully, he'll return in the spring and he'll be able to finish this thing for good. I know you *feel* you want to help and maybe that feeling is from the connection you have with the house, I don't know, but let it go. Your friendship and support is all we ask of you," she replied.

"I'm sorry, Clara, I really thought I'd have been able to help," I said.

"You have! You've been our friend and you've been a great support for us. The girls love it when you come to visit and you, along with Tim and all of Mike's other friends, have helped us all to keep our sanity. If you were able to come in and take whatever we're dealing with out of here, it would be great, but you can't. You don't need to feel you've failed because you're not the one able to stop the trouble."

"I still feel there's something I have to accomplish here and, you're right. I'm not the one to cleanse the house, if that's the word I should use, but there's something, something unanswered. I feel the thing in Mary's room is the heart of the house and it seems to really hate me. I thought if I was able to beat it, since it is determined to assault me, the house would be a helluva lot quieter, maybe normal," I said.

"Well, whatever it is, I can't tell you. Maybe you're just obsessed with what has happened with you and those feelings give you the impression that you've not finished what you *think* you have to do. Do you have any idea how many psychics have called me offering their help? Plenty! There's been all sorts, from mediums, to psychometrics, to the amateur exorcist. Remember the guy who wanted to come to the house, gather all the spirits into his body and exorcize them at home! Good God! I'm sure they all mean well and *believe* they can achieve what they think, but I'm just not ready to let everyone who calls come into our home and turn it into a psychic circus!" Clara said.

"What's a psychometric or whatever you called it?"

"Yeah, psychometric—someone that can reveal something about someone by touching an object that they themselves have touched," Clara explained.

"Oh. Well, what can someone like that accomplish here? There isn't anything they can touch that will give information on what's causing the trouble is there?" I asked.

"They might be able to figure out who was responsible for throwing Mary's lamp across the room. They're able to get impressions from spirits that have touched objects."

"They can actually give information about someone dead?" I asked.

"So it seems. Often, the police will employ psychometrics to help them in solving serious crimes....murder, for instance," Clara said.

"Wow, that's interesting! I remember seeing someone on TV who was handed items of random people in the audience and, unless it was a setup, they were really accurate!" I said.

"Mom, Keith and I are going to run to the store, do we need anything?" Mike asked.

"Yeah, Mike—hang on a second, Paul," Clara said.

Clara went into the kitchen with Mike. She certainly gave me something to think about as well as setting me straight on my involvement with the house. As I said, in the beginning, it was curiosity that brought me to the house. But after all of the incidents that Tim and I had experienced, but more importantly, what I had experienced on my own, I began to believe I was to be more instrumental in solving this haunted dilemma. Had I gotten the wrong impression with what I had confronted? Maybe I was even becoming egocentric thinking I could control the energy of the house. Whatever the case, I continued to read, study and attempt to understand.

Clara reentered the living room. "Okay, I had to get some money for Mike to pick up a few things from the store. I have a question for you, now. What do you make of Randy and his trances?"

"Sure, put me on the spot to judge someone's character. I don't know. I don't understand the purpose of trances other than to allow spirits to speak through them and I just don't buy that side of it. I've never seen Randy attempt anything like that. But whatever the hell he does, he's becomes remarkably strong! You know that brain warp thing that Father Al told me about?" I asked.

"Yeah, I don't understand the concept of it, but yeah, you told me about it. Why, what's up?"

"Well, I couldn't bend his damned arm and I think I might be just a little stronger than Randy. Mike M. tried it—he couldn't budge Randy's arm! That guy is a tank; there should have been no way Randy could have removed his hand from his head!" I explained.

"No one told me about that. When did this happen?" Clara asked.

"The evening Jim S. spent the night with us. That reminds me: I haven't talked to him to see if he caught anything on film that night," I said.

"Wow, Randy removed his hand too, huh? He is a big kid! Well, I have some chores to take care of. You're welcome to stay and follow me around the house if you feel you have something else to say," Clara said, getting up from her seat.

371

"No, I think I've said what was on my mind. Thanks for listening to me. I still wish I could resolve these problems, you and the kids don't deserve to be going through this," I said.

"Well, thank you, and you're welcome. Any time you feel you want to talk, I'll listen."

"Thanks again, Clara. I'm sure we'll have plenty of time to talk again," I said as I made my way to the kitchen.

"You going now, Paul?" Mary asked.

"Yup, time to get back to Olean, Mary. You guys be good for mom, okay?"

Mary and Laura both said yes as they gave me a hug goodbye. They were such good kids. I wanted to turn around and talk to Clara again after Laura gave me a hug. I've heard that identical twins were able to feel each other's emotions. If that's really true, I would have to believe that there really is something to extra sensory perception. Not every time I am close to Laura, but more often that not, there are feelings received from her that I can understand. I can't describe them perfectly but I guess I can *feel* her demeanor at that time. Even without looking at her expressions, if I held her hand, I was sure I'd be able to tell her frame of mind. I find that interesting and fulfilling for some reason. That day she was very happy and there was something that had made her that way, something that was going to happen either that day or soon after. No, I didn't know then and never thought to ask at a later date; I wished I had.

I left the house and again stood in the yard looking at Mary's window. There were no threats, no calling of names and no feelings. Perhaps today was the first day of our peace talks; a truce in the making. I turned and walked to my car before this possible cease-fire might *back* fire. I drove very slowly, idling down McMahon Road, taking in the serenity of this country setting. If there was never a word uttered of apparitions, ghosts or disembodied eye or voices, it was the perfect place to live to get away from the hassles of the city. What were the chances of the Dandys finding the only (was it?) haunted house in the area to call home? Why hadn't the disturbances begun as soon as they moved in? Did it take time for energies from the family members, particularly Laura's, to charge the area, the house?

Driving toward the hanging tree, I tried to imagine a group of people standing at the base of the tree, staring up at the bulging, lifeless eyes of their—criminal—victim? I stopped under the tree, got out of the car, and walked to the dilapidated barn. I remembered what Alex had said regarding an elderly woman who knew of the murders at the house. Had she known of the lynching as well and why was someone hanged from this tree. I wanted to know the answers to some of my questions. Maybe it wasn't crucial for all of my questions to be answered but there were some I *had* to have— this was one of them. Alex said bodies were buried nearby and possibly one of the impressions he received from the house may have been that of the person who was hanged. Was it logical to bury the body far away from this barn? But chances are, if someone had indeed been hanged here, the body wasn't far from the scene of the lynching. When the snow of winter is gone, I plan to spend many afternoons looking for that little mound of extra dirt left after a burial. Today it will undoubtedly blend with the rest of the land but there might be that one clue helping to recognize the burial spot. It was nearly the end of January. Spring was just around the corner and there were going to be lots of sunny afternoons to walk the fields in search of the resting places of those who may be lost, searching for their own eternal peace on the Dandys' property.

I returned to my car and drove from McMahon Road back to Olean. I arrived home about 1:30 and decided to gather the laundry up and take it to the Laundromat. Grabbing the laundry soap, I noticed there wasn't much left in the box. I'd need to stop at Richardson's Grocery to get another box. It took me a full two hours to finish the laundry and return home. I beat Debbie there by ten minutes.

We had an enjoyable evening but Debbie had been complaining about pains in her back and stomach. I rubbed her back most of the evening while we sat on the couch watching TV. She suggested we go to bed early because she was very uncomfortable and felt the pain might subside if she were able to lie down. We went to bed before 10 p.m.—earlier than we had in a quite some time. Hopefully, she would feel better in the morning after a good night's rest.

CHAPTER XXXI

About 4 a.m., Debbie woke me and said her pain was much more severe which made me worry that the baby was coming. She said no, it was too soon, that maybe it might have been from sitting at her desk for so many hours at work. She wasn't able to get back to sleep and the pain had worsened. I called the hospital to get some advice and they recommended we come in and have her checked. We arrived at the hospital about 6 a.m. and indeed, after assessing her condition, our baby was ready to join the world. We got her registered and were informed that her doctor, Dr. Cash had been called, and he would be arriving presently. The pains were coming closer together, causing alarm for both of us. I called my parents and Debbie's mom to let them know it was time. All voiced their concern because the baby wasn't due for nearly two months. I was asked to leave Debbie's room so the nurses could check her. I was nervous and scared with the concern of our child being a preemie and the complications that sometimes arise with early births. After about 15 minutes, I found myself in the hospital chapel asking, praying that our child be okay. I was hoping that my mom or Debbie's mom would arrive soon, I didn't want to be alone with my worry; I didn't know what to think or how to handle it.

I walked back to the waiting area near Debbie's room, anticipating the arrival of a nurse with some information. It was probably 20 minutes before anyone came out to tell me something. "Mr. Kenyon?" A nurse asked.

"Yes," I said, standing.

"Dr. Cash is in with your wife. If you'd like, you may come with me and talk with the doctor."

"Yes, please—thank you," I said.

Every possible concern went through my mind during that walk down the hospital hallway, with its sickening, blue painted walls. Someone says the choice of blue is calming to the patients. Yeah, but I think only if the patient is taking the matching, little blue pill—valium!

As we entered Debbie's room, I felt some of my uneasiness lift as I saw she was smiling he usual bright smile. Dr. Cash was also smiling and greeted me as I entered.

"Hi, Paul, how are you?" Dr. Cash said.

"Never mind me, how's she, how's our baby? I nervously asked.

"She's fine and so is the baby. It'll be coming a little early but everything looks good. We've given Deb something to help with the pain; we'll be taking her in soon."

"Thanks, doctor," I said.

Dr. Cash said he'd be back shortly and excused himself to the hallway of nauseatingly painted walls.

"Is he sure, everything is okay?" I asked.

"Everything's fine and I feel a whole lot better. I can still feel the contractions but they don't hurt like they did 15 minutes ago," Debbie explained.

"We still haven't decided on a name!" I said, sitting on the edge of her bed.

"Paul if it's a boy, and Lynn if it's a girl."

"NO! I don't want a junior! I know two people everyone calls junior and they're goofs!" I exclaimed.

"Being a junior doesn't make them a goof. The two juniors you know are just naturally goofy. We'll talk about it after he or she is born," she said.

"Okay, but are you sure you're okay?" I asked again.

"I just told you, I'm fine—quit worrying. You're just like your mom, worrying all the time!"

"Well shit, this is our baby, I have to worry," I said.

Dr. Cash returned with a nurse and checked Debbie. He was only in the room for about three or four minutes and exclaimed, "It's time!"

The nurse went into the hall and waved to someone, an orderly, who came into the room to help get Debbie to the delivery room. We kissed each other before they took her down the hallway. Leaving she said, "I won't be alone when you see me again, so you better have more than one kiss ready!"

"I will, I love you!" I said, blowing her an invisible kiss.

I watched as they pushed her down the hall and she managed a wave before they rounded the corner. I went back to the waiting room where Debbie's mom and brother Tim were already seated. I was disappointed my mother hadn't arrived yet. She lived closer than Debbie's family. Debbie's mom, brother, and I visited while we waited and discussed names for the baby. Of course Tim suggested his name. I think every name possible was suggested during our talk, at least it seemed that way! My mom finally arrived. She explained she had to wait for my father to get to work and take care of his early morning duties before he could return home to pick her up.

"How long as she been in the delivery room?" She asked.

"They just took her in, maybe about 20 minutes ago, mom," I said.

Mom, Debbie's mother and brother greeted each other, then continued the, "name-game." I was too restless sitting there listening to them suggest every name imaginable. I excused myself and walked down the hall, hoping to locate the delivery room. Of course, I was stopped after I turned the corner, when a nurse told me I wasn't allowed past the nurses' station. I asked her how Debbie was doing and got the usual response when asking a question in a hospital, "I'll check for you," but you never see that particular person again. Isn't it strange, you ask a hospital employee a question and they become the lost sock in the dryer! I walked back to the waiting room and had a seat.

"If it's a boy, instead of having a junior, how about turning your name around, call him Joseph Paul," my mom suggested.

"Mom! We haven't decided on any names yet, but we will," I said.

"The day of Paul's confirmation he still hadn't decided on a name and we suggested using his uncle's name because it was his complete name backwards. His uncle's name is Leonard Joseph Paul and Paul's is Paul Joseph Leonard." My mom told everyone.

"That's a nice name," Debbie's mother said.

We continued, reluctantly, coming up with yet more names, until I was certain this time, every name, with the exceptions of Ebenezer and Henrietta, were mentioned. Oh, I don't think Egroeg was suggested either. We were all getting hungry and one of the nurses said we could get something from the hospital cafeteria. After she left, I suggested that hospital food was an aid used to lengthen a patient's stay. Debbie's brother said we should order a pizza.

"In a hospital?" His mother asked.

"Sure, I bet the employees order out all the time." Debbie's brother said.

"I'm not too sure, Tim, I don't see too many walking around. They've probably all become patients after eating the cafeteria food," I said, bringing a chuckle out of everyone.

We were still talking about food, when a nurse approached me.

"Mr. Kenyon?"

Her question at this point made my own question pop into my head. Was I the fist person she asked, or do they randomly ask people who were waiting around hospitals if they were the person they were looking for? If I had answered no, would she have asked Debbie's brother? If he said no, would she walk the halls asking every male she saw? Next time, I thought, I'll try that and then follow the person. It might be quite interesting to see the results.

"Excuse me, Mr. Kenyon?"

"What will you do if I say no?" I asked.

"Sorry?"

"Yes, that's me," I admitted.

"Would you like to follow me and see your new son?"

"Mom, um, both moms…we have a son, I mean I have a son, you have a grandson!" I exclaimed.

We all followed the nurse down the hallway to the nursery. When we arrived, there were four babies in all, and we all were looking at names on the end of the cribs but we didn't see my last name. Just then, the nurse who had come to get us wheeled an incubator into the room and pulled it as close to the window as possible. My two moms started their, "oh, he's adorable," and "look, look, he's looking at me" mom stuff, but the only thing I said was, "He's covered with hair!" I knew he had Italian blood, my mom is of Italian descent, but were we somehow related to primates?!

377

"That's normal, Debbie's mom said. "Preemie's generally have more body hair, it'll disappear after a while."

"Yeah, when I get my razor and shave him!" I exclaimed.

"Stop it!" My mother scolded. "He's adorable!"

A different nurse came out of the nursery and walked toward us; here we go again.

"Mr. Kenyon?"

I'm gonna try it, I thought.

"Actually, they just took him to emergency. The poor guy fainted when he saw how much body hair his baby has!" I said.

"Excuse me?"

"Shame on you!" Debbie's mother said.

"I'm sorry, I couldn't resist. Yes, that's me," I said.

"Would you like to see your wife now?"

I was almost ready to hit her with another one, but instead I said, "Sure would!"

"Follow me." The nurse said, turning around.

What did she think I was going to do, go in the opposite direction? I walked into Debbie's semiprivate room. Here's another misconception surrounding hospitals. How can a room be both private, and not? I walked over to Debbie's bed, looked around, including under her bed, then gave her a huge kiss.

"What are you looking for?" She said, *semi* groggy.

"Well, the nurse said this was a semiprivate room, I wanted to make sure there was no one lurking in one of the corners, or under your bed," I said.

There was a report of resounding laughter from the other side of the curtain, separating Debbie's bed from her semiprivate roommate. I didn't know anyone was in the room and, I must admit, I felt really dumb at that moment.

"That was a good one!" A male voice said, still laughing, which evidently frightened his newborn child awake.

"Thanks," I said to the man behind the curtain—hoping he wasn't from Oz. "So, how do you feel, mom?" I asked my wife.

"Tired," She whispered. "And sore!" She whispered even quieter.

"Sore? He's so small, he could've slipped through the eye of a needle!" I exclaimed..

More laughter and, "Thanks, for that one. We were in labor over 16 hours, we needed a good laugh!" *(We* were in labor?) The voice of the unseen male said.

"Did you see all the hair on his body? Dr. Cash said that's normal for preemie's but it will go away in time."

"You're mom says it'll disappear and Dr. Cash says it'll go away. Where the hell is it going to go? I have to shave mine. What's his hair gonna do, grow inward?" I asked.

The people behind the curtain obviously didn't own a television or get out much because they were still laughing and talking about the "baby through the needle" trick. Now, I would assume, they were rolling on the floor. I was hoping, if Debbie had to stay much longer, the hospital staff could locate a room that wasn't described as "semi" anything. A third nurse came into the room and asked Debbie how she was feeling, only she stopped at the first bed to ask. I thought, "what a coincidence, her name is Debbie too." I was wrong; the woman said, "I'm Lorraine, Debbie is in the bed next to me."

"Oh, I'm sorry, my mistake." The nurse said.

After the nurse found her way to curtain #2 she again asked, "Hi, Debbie, how are you feeling?"

"Fine, pretty tired, but I feel okay."

"You're going to be tired. The medication is going to keep you groggy for a while. Can I get you anything?" The nurse asked.

"My son!" Debbie exclaimed.

"We'll bring him in after a bit. The nurses are checking his vitals and making sure everything is okay," the nurse replied.

"Is anything wrong?" I asked, nervously.

"Oh, no, the little darling is doing wonderfully. He's only been out for an hour, we keep every preemie at least that long. I assure you, he's fine. Oh, and when you go out and the other family members come in, please tell them one at a time," the nurse explained.

"Okay, thanks," Debbie and I said in unison.

The nurse left and I got up on the bed with Debbie.

"Oh, no you don't, this is how I ended up in here!" She said.

The laughter started again. These people were either lonely or really *didn't* own a television. I figured I might as well keep them going.

"Hey Mr. and Mrs. Lorraine, if they happen to bring your baby back later and he resembles a small primate, it's ours," I said.

Debbie gave me a good whack after that one. We could hear shuffling feet and the bathroom door shut. Apparently, Lorraine's husband was averting an accident he wouldn't want to have to explain to the nurse.

"Honey, I'm sure our moms and your brother want to come in and see you. Let me run out and see who wants to come in first," I said.

"Okay, I love you and thank you for our son," Debbie said.

"Don't thank me, I couldn't have done it without you!" I exclaimed.

More laughter, including from the bathroom.

I walked back to the nursery where I found the three of them still gawking at our first born. I told them they could go in but one at a time. It was only right that Deb's mom went first, the others agreed.

"Don't say anything funny when you go in. The people on the other side of the curtain are easily amused," I told Debbie's mother as she walked away.

"Did you two talk about a name while you were in there?" My mom asked.

"No, mom, not yet, but we will. Maybe we'll name him after dad."

"No one name's their babies Harold anymore," she said.

I saw that this was going to be difficult. Everyone was going to give their suggestions and the only ones who'll be happy will be the one that suggest the name. I continued talking with whoever wasn't in with Debbie until it was my turn to go back in. I was thinking about Lorraine's husband and what he had said about his wife being in labor for 16 hours. I couldn't imagine what that would be like for the mom to endure labor for that many hours. One of the nurses came out while Debbie's brother was in visiting to tell us my son's weight. He only weighed 4 pounds, 13 ounces; "a tiny tot" the nurse said. A few minutes later, Dr. Cash arrived, still adorned in his hospital greens. He told us that our baby's lungs were a little weak but not to worry, they would develop in time.

"Don't worry? He's going to be okay, you're sure?" I asked.

"Yes, absolutely, Paul. We've delivered babies that have only weighed 2 pounds, a few even less than that and they grew up to be big and strong. Two of my girls were preemies and they're just fine. You probably know them, they're about your age; healthy as can be," Dr. Cash explained.

Dr. Cash had a large family, nine daughters! Story goes, they kept trying to have at least one son but, after nine, they said that was enough. I don't know if that was a true story and I didn't dare ask, even though I was sure he wouldn't have been the least bit offended presented with that question. He had a great bedside manner and showed honest compassion for his patients.

"I have my rounds to do so I will say congratulations and job well done," Dr. Cash told me.

"Thanks, doctor and thanks for being here so quickly this morning," I said.

He nodded as he walked away and Debbie's brother came back from visiting his sister.

"Debbie said she's really tired and wants you to come back in," he said.

"Okay. Are you guys going to hang around, or what?" I asked.

"No, we're going to get going. I'll get your mom home, so you might want to call your father at work and let him know," Deb's mom said.

"No, I'll call him, you go see Debbie," my mom said.

I thanked Debbie's mom for taking my mother home and thanked them all for coming. We all gave one another hugs and I told them I would call them later this afternoon or early evening. I walked them to the elevator and ran down the hall to the nursery to see my boy. I felt scared, not only because Dr. Cash said his lungs were weak, but also because we, Debbie and I, were so young. I don't have a problem saying she was more mature than I in many ways and she was tough. Thinking back, I would gladly, with no hesitation, join those haunting the Dandy house to have just one month of that first year back again. Hindsight, yeah, it's too bad that we understand something when it's too late. I watched the little guy for about 5 minutes and was surprised it took that long for the waterworks to begin. I felt a little embarrassed because of this and went back to Debbie's room, where I found her sleeping. Poor thing, she was worn out. I don't profess to know what it's like to give birth but, with the experience of observing my last son's birth, Noah's, and the 22 hours of labor his mother went through, it wasn't too pleasant. I didn't dare wake her. Instead, I sat beside her bed, lightly rubbing her cheek and hair. I had no plans of leaving any time soon. I saw a pillow in the chair at the end of the bed so I snagged it and placed it behind my head, sitting there adoring this lovely young wife of mine.

Let me break for a cause here and say to each and every one of you reading this, to set this book down, go to your significant other, and tell them you love them, unconditionally. Not only will it make them feel good, you'll feel like a million too—try it! Well, what are you waiting for, GO!

Watching her, there in her hospital bed, listening to her even breathing, was very soothing. I truly understood at that moment how much I really loved her; adored her. I never doubted it and the circle was now complete; we had begun a family. She woke for a moment, looked at me sitting in the chair beside her bed, smiled and quickly drifted off to sleep again. I wasn't exaggerating about her smile being bright enough to light a room. She had many great attributes, most of which I'll not discuss, thank you, but her smile was certainly in the top three of a very long list. Her tolerance, oh my, her tolerance. It was insurmountable, especially for me but even that eventually had its breaking point. I won't discuss that either.

I had fallen asleep, when the nurse gently woke Debbie and me to announce, "It's feeding time."

My goodness, the way she said it, I expected her to hand us a couple of baby bottles and to see a line of petting zoo animals come marching into the room! No animals, but a little person who was voicing his hunger quite loudly was carried in by another nurse. Debbie sat up and repositioned herself to feed the little tyke and, my God, was he little! It took a little time, patience and manipulating to help the little fellow find the target. Once found, he had no problem filling his tiny belly. One of the nurses stayed with her, probably to be sure he was getting the proper nutrition. I found myself thinking Debbie was a natural but—never mind, there weren't too many steps to feeding your child: you aim, he seeks, the feeding begins.

Mom and son went through their first session of bonding and Deb asked if I wanted to hold him. I surely wasn't going to say no! The nurse took our son and carefully set him in my arms as I sat in the chair. Even when holding him, I couldn't believe how tiny he was. He only covered half of my forearm, and his hands, palm to the tips of his fingers, were only as long as the first knuckle of my index finger. He was a miniature all right! The nurse told me it was time to place him back into the incubator. As she reached to take him from me, he let out a burp that shocked us all. Even Lorraine, on the other side of the curtain said, "Oh My!"

After the nurse left, I went over to Debbie and hugged her for a long time, thanking her for our little boy. We both had a good "happy" cry, full of smiles and kisses. She said she'd really like to take a nap. The nurse said she'll have to feed the little guy every two hours so it was important for her to get her rest. I told her I'd be in early tonight but if there was anything she needed to call the house, her mom or my mom. After another long hug and a few more of her delicious kisses I left. I'd already made my plans for the rest of the afternoon—to buy the furnishings to fill a baby's room!

I went to three stores that afternoon, filling the trunk, back seat, as well as the front seat with everything I could think we would need and some things just because they looked like we would need them. I got a bassinet with two different bumpers, a swing, a walker—no, I put that back, a crib, 6 or 8 blankets with elephants, giraffes and other assorted animals, 3 different mobiles to hang over the crib, a ton of stuffed animals, and bottles, extra nipples, and an alarm clock. I don't know where I heard an alarm clock—suddenly I remembered. Someone had told me they got an alarm clock for a puppy to help pacify and keep him quiet. Ah, what the hell, our son was no bigger than a puppy! After my shopping, I retuned home and took everything into the house. I made numerous calls to friends and family to tell of the new addition to the house, fell on the couch, and collapsed for about an hour.

When I felt I was about to fall asleep, I got up and called Clara to tell her the news. She said we'd have to bring him up so they could all get a look at him. The very thought of taking our son to the house filled me with reluctance, apprehension and fear. I didn't have proof that there was anything to worry about but I wouldn't take him up until I talked to Father Al. I had no idea if the paranormal could have an affect on such a young child but I wasn't going to take the slightest chance. She told me they had tried to contact Alex as things had been getting bad again but they weren't able to contact him by phone. She said she would call me and keep me informed of everything that happens.

I called my parents to see if they were going to the hospital, and my mom said they'd be going about 7 p.m.. I told her I'd see them there, hung up and took a much needed shower. I stood under the head of the shower until it began to run cold, got out, shaved and got dressed. I had a feeling Debbie was hungry for something besides hospital food and stopped at McDonald's before going to the hospital. In my haste to get the things we were going to need for our nursery, I totally forgot to get something for Debbie. "Moron!" I said, and the voice from the drive thru speaker at McDonald's said, "Excuse me?" I told her I wasn't talking to her and pulled up. When I got to the window to pay for my order, the girl had given me a real nasty look. I explained to her why I had said "moron," and she, thankfully, understood. I drove away and headed for the hospital. Now, I had to figure how I was going to smuggle a Quarter Pounder and French fries into Debbie's room. I parked in the parking lot and it dawned on me—they have a gift shop, I'll go in and get her something there and I might even be able to hide the food in whatever I get her! I looked around the shop, carrying my McDonald's bag and found just the right two things; I big stuffed bear and a basket of flowers. I'd set the bag of food on the side of the basket, and held the bear in front to conceal it as I carried it in. I paid for my purchases, picked up a card, wrote a little something inside and went to the elevator. I pressed 2 for Debbie's floor and hoped my plan worked. I was certain I had the only flowers in town that smelled like a burger and fries!

When the door of the elevator opened, there were two nurses standing, waiting to enter. As they stepped aside, I walked out and around them and straight to Debbie's room. So far, so good, I thought. I walked into room 207, passed the closed curtains of her roommates bed, and pulled the curtain that was closed around her bed open. She wasn't there. I hadn't noticed if the bathroom door was closed as I entered the room and assumed she was either in there or perhaps at the nursery. I asked her roommate through the curtain if she knew where she was and she said she had just left to go to the nursery. I took the McDonald's bag out of the basket, placed it on Debbie's bed and covered it with the blanket. Then I picked up the bear and basket and walked to the nursery. On second thought I turned around, took her gifts back and placed them on her table in case she came back before I found her. I left again, only to nearly knock Debbie down when I rushed out the door.

"I didn't know where you were," I said giving her a hug. "I just got here, I started to come look for you once, but then I had to come back," I said.

"For what?" Debbie asked.

"Come into the room and see," I said, grabbing her hand to lead her to the bed.

I received another hug and a very passionate kiss. I couldn't wait to give her the food!

"Lift up your blanket," I said.

"Oh my God, I'm starving! Thank you! Only one?" She said peering into the bag.

"Sheesh, I thought I should get you two but you can't be that hungry, are you?" I asked.

"The stuff they brought in for dinner killed the plant your aunt and uncle sent me when I set it down next to it. The only thing I had was one bite of cherry cobbler and the milk. Cherry cobbler they call it but I call it cherry gaggler!" Debbie exclaimed.

Of course, she was kidding but that didn't make the folks behind the curtain laugh any less hard. Before we left this hospital, we were going to have to meet these people. They were either easily amused or what we were saying was funnier than it sounded to us.

"Sit down and eat before the Gestapo comes in, confiscates it and sends you to the showers," I told her.

"Showers?" We heard Lorraine say from behind the curtain.

"Yeah, that's how the Germans killed over six million Jews." Presumably, her husband said.

"By making them take showers?!" Lorraine asked.

"No, not regular showers—I'll explain later."

Debbie and I subdued our laughter as best we could. I may sound cruel, but I was beginning to believe those on the other side of the curtain, didn't read, watch television or possibly pay attention in class. No matter, by their conversations we've overheard, they seemed very happy. Debbie devoured the burger and fries in record time.

I looked at her in amazement and asked, "How do you keep your gorgeous figure eating like that?"

"I didn't eat much, I just ate it fast. Come on, let's go see our kid," she said.

"You sure you had enough to eat? The flowers and stuffed bear are still available," I said.

She slapped my arm so hard, I was glad I was in a hospital! She said something when she slapped me, but I wasn't able to hear her over the laughter coming from her roommate and her roommate's husband. We walked out of the room and down the hall to the nursery, where we saw my mom and dad standing at the window.

"Well, what do you think, Grandpa, did I do okay?" I asked my dad.

"You did just fine but he sure is a little shit. Is everything okay medically?" My dad asked.

"Yeah, Dr. Cash says he's gonna be fine. He said his lungs are a little weak but he's confident that they'll get stronger with time," I said.

"He sure eats like a pig, I can tell you that!" Debbie exclaimed.

"Have we decided on a name yet?" My mom asked.

"I liked your suggestion, Joseph Paul. I've always liked the name Joe," Debbie said.

"Well, you better give him a name soon, you need to start talking to him and calling him by his name," mom replied.

"Mom, he's not even 24 hours old. We'll decide on something by tomorrow. By the way, when are the two of you coming home?" I asked Debbie.

"I can come home tomorrow but he can't come home for at least a few days." She said.

"Why, what's wrong?" I asked.

"Nothing, worry wart. Dr. Cash wants to keep him in the incubator for a while and let him build his strength." Debbie explained.

"Dr. Cash is a good doctor; he has a very good reputation; he knows what's best," dad said.

"When is he going to eat again?" My mom asked.

"I just fed him before Paul came in about an hour ago so it won't be for about another hour," Debbie said.

My mom seemed disappointed. We knew she wanted to hold her grandson. Generally my father wasn't one for hanging around but, surprisingly, he said, "Well, we'll wait so your mother can see him... well, and me too!"

"Thanks, dad. Come on, let's take a walk," I said.

"Who?" Debbie asked.

"Me and dad," I replied.

My father looked kind of shocked but agreed to go. We walked toward the waiting room, where he stopped and dropped some change into the coffee machine, asking if I wanted anything.

"I'm fine," I said.

"So, is there something on your mind?" He asked.

"I'm scared a little, I guess. I'm not sure exactly what to do with a baby. What happens if he gets sick, do we bring him to the hospital or take care of him at home and hope it's nothing serious?"

"You know what you have? You have the new father fidgets. He's gonna be fine and so are you and Debbie. What do you do when you get sick? You'll do the same thing for your kids when they get sick. And don't worry, Debbie will have that mom's intuition and will know what to do naturally. Make sure he's always warm and fed and keep him away from drafts but I'm sure they'll give you a packet of information on how to take care of your newborn. Jesus, Mary and Joseph, this is a talk you should be having with your mother," dad said.

"Well, I wanted to talk to you for a change. I'm always talking to her. It's about damned time that I talked to you and you listened. I know I haven't done everything right in your eyes and I just wanted to say thanks for being there when I did need you and for taking care of my mother—finally," I said.

That last statement was very hard to say but it needed to be said. He pondered for a minute, playing with the buttons on the vending machine before saying, "You're a good son, you had a tough childhood and for what it's worth, I apologize."

I've never seen my dad cry and, if he had, he would never have allowed me or my brother to see it. If I didn't change the subject, he might not have been able to conceal his emotions.

"Hey, I went out today and bought everything I could think of. A whole nursery full of stuff!" I said.

"Good, if there's anything you need, tell your mother. I'm sure you probably forgot something you're gonna need," dad said.

"Thanks, but I think I got it all, the car was full!" I said.

Debbie's mother and brother arrived. They walked over to us and said hello. I told them not to go to Debbie's room, that she and my mom were at the nursery. They left and walked down the hall toward the nursery. We turned to follow them when I got that sudden blast of heat in my head, and nearly fell against my dad.

"What's the matter?" Dad asked.

It took me a few seconds to come to grips with the strength of it this time. I looked at my dad and said, "Fine, I just got dizzy for a second."

"Well, take it easy, you worry too much," he said.

I thought this was over. I was sure it was. My first thought was, what if this happened again when I was holding my son and I dropped him or something? As we were walking, I turned toward the vending machines and told my dad to go ahead, I wanted a drink after all. When he turned the corner, I quickly went back down the hall to the pay phone and called Clara.

"Is everything okay up there?" I asked.

"Yeah, why, where are you?" Clara asked.

"I'm at the hospital. I just got a blast and it was as bad as Labor Day. So, there's nothing happening tonight?" I asked.

"No, other than a few of our 'bump in the night' sounds, it's relatively quiet. Are you okay?" Clara asked.

"Yeah, I really don't know why this is happening when I'm not at the house. It scares the hell out of me," I said.

"Talk to Father Al the first chance you get. In the meantime, take it easy. How's the little one doing?"

"He's fine and I really should go. I was with my dad when it happened. I told him I was getting a drink and if I don't get back, he's going to coming looking for me," I said.

"All right, be careful, and call Father. I'll say a prayer for you," Clara said.

"Thanks, Clara."

A prayer? I was beginning to believe prayer wasn't the answer. Actually, I didn't have a notion of what was going to help with any of this. I walked down the hall, stopped at the vending machine again and bought a Pepsi. I realized Debbie didn't have anything to drink with her dinner so I got her a can of root beer. No one was at the nursery except a short stocky man with very thick glasses. I said hello and, when he greeted me rather solemnly, I realized he was the unseen voice on the other side of the curtain in Debbie's room. He appeared worried and when I looked through the nursery glass I saw that oxygen had been hooked up to one of the incubators. As I started to walk away, I turned around and stopped a few feet from him. I gazed through the glass at the oxygen-fed incubator. I felt the strangest sensation. I had thought I felt something when I passed the man the first time. I closed my eyes and tried very hard to 'feel' something. I felt that I could feel him praying and the strongest sense of dread or sadness very much like the one I felt that evening when Tim and I were near the pond. I could see his child's face through the incubator. It was a warm feel, a feeling of, "everything is going to be okay," Frankly, that didn't make a damned bit of sense to me. I took a step closer to the man, and said, "You're Lorraine's husband, aren't you?"

"Yes, I am. Do I know you?" He asked.

"We haven't met but I'm Debbie's husband,—the other girl in your wife's room."

He looked at me through his thick glasses, then said, "Oh, yes! Hi, my name is Bernard."

He offered me his hand, and I put the can of root beer under my arm to accept his handshake. The moment our hands touched, I felt his anguish all too clear. I didn't hear words, I didn't see anything, but I *felt* pneumonia and something else but it wasn't about his child. It was something very muddled, as if I had been looking at words that were written backwards or something. I've never, *never* felt anything remotely as strong from anyone before or since. It was much stronger than anything I had shared with Laura. We held hands but a brief few seconds, but in that time, I felt as if I had watched a movie in fast forward speed. When we let go, he asked if I was all right. I was, but what I felt more, was that his *baby* was going to be all right. I've asked myself ever since that day how I knew so positively that his child was going to be all right but I can offer no answers.

He teetered for a second and it was my turn to ask if he was all right. "Yeah, I think so. Just a little woozy I guess," Bernard said.

"Your baby is going to be fine. Lorraine is wondering where you are," I said.

"Oh, is she awake? I'd best go to her."

He rushed past me, as I stood staring at his baby. I'm not a damned psychic! What the hell am I doing telling someone something I shouldn't whether I felt it or not? And what if his baby wasn't going to be all right, then what? I stood there getting angrier at myself when I heard my dad say, "What the hell are you doing? We're all in the room, come on!"

What in God's name was happening to me? I felt like a freak and I remembered telling Alex I wanted to be like him. No, no I don't! I did not want feelings from other people.

I followed my father as he rounded the corner and walked into 207. Debbie's side of the room was full of people, no one was on the side where the curtains were closed. Debbie had just finished feeding our son, Joseph Paul, which I was informed was his chosen name. Who was I to argue? I was proud but wouldn't have suggested it myself and I wouldn't have minded at all if we had chosen another name.

A nurse came into the room and went to Lorraine's side of the curtain. We could hear her ask both of them to sign a release for treatment of their child. It was apparently when Bernard took his turn to sign that Lorraine said, "Nurse, Bernie suffers from severe dyslexia. If you would allow me to sign for him and you be a witness, I would greatly appreciate it."

"Well, I don't know. I'm the bearer of this instrument, this paper, I think I need to get someone else to witness it," the nurse said.

"I'd be happy to be your witness if that's acceptable," I said, without hesitation.

"I suppose that would be okay," the nurse told me, as she came from behind the curtain and motioned for me to come over. Seeing Lorraine for the first time was heart-wrenching. There was a wheel chair beside her bed. She only had one leg and she had long, ugly scars running the full length of both arms. I didn't stare but my initial look evidently said something, because she apologized explaining she had been in a horrible car accident and was thrown through the windshield. I felt so terrible and sad for them both. I told her I was sorry and was glad to have been able to be of some help. They both thanked me and Bernie offered his hand again. I was hesitant but I certainly couldn't be rude so shook his hand once again. I found myself reluctant to let go. There was nothing this time; no feeling. As we broke our handshake, Lorraine offered her hand and, thankfully, the only feeling I got was the feel of her extremely soft skin. I thanked them for allowing me to witness for them and returned to Debbie's side of the curtain.

"That was nice of you," Debbie's mom said.

"They're very nice people." I moved closer to her and whispered in her ear, "Their baby has pneumonia."

"Oh, no." She replied quietly.

"What mom?" Debbie asked.

"I'll tell you later, Debra, or Paul can tell you," Debbie's mom said.

Debbie's mom and brother left a few minutes later. My parents followed shortly thereafter. We thanked them for coming and for the gifts. I sat on Debbie's bed after everyone was gone and told her about Lorraine's accident and their baby's condition. I also explained what I had felt when I shook Bernie's hand. When I heard Lorraine tell the nurse her husband had been dyslexic it blew my mind! I had seen or again, "felt" scrambled words the first time I shook his hand. Dear God, how was I able to feel that from another human being? Had I picked something up at the Dandy house or, as Father Al said, was my 'gift' maturing from being subjected to the energy of the house for such a long period? Debbie and I quietly discussed why I might not have picked anything up the second time I shook Bernie's hand. I suggested it might have been that he wasn't distraught as he was when I met him at the nursery. Still, there should have been something. Whatever the reason, the first handshake was quite shocking.

I left about an half and hour later so Debbie could get what rest she could. She'd have to be up every couple of hours. I wished I could step in to help but I wasn't built that way. I suggested she talk to Lorraine even if they leave the curtain closed. No one has come to visit them since Debbie moved into this room and that made us both feel very sad. She said she would talk to her and maybe offer to go to the nursery with her so they could see our babies together. We hugged and she gave me a kiss that made me want to stay, but after all, she was in a semiprivate room!

When I got home, I flopped on the couch and turned the television on. The house was very empty without Debbie. I sure hoped she felt the same way when I wasn't home. If she did, it made me feel terribly guilty. I had every reason to feel that way. She was very understanding about my going to the house but that didn't make it right for me to be gone so often. I looked at the crib and bassinet in their boxes and thought I should start putting them together. I decided to wait until Deb got home tomorrow. I was sure she'd want to take part in furnishing our son's room together. I flipped through the channels on the television several times and finally decided on an episode of Hogan's Heroes when the phone rang.

"They just rushed little Robert into surgery!" Debbie exclaimed."

"Who?" I asked.

"Lorraine's son, hon."

"There's blockage in one of his lungs, that's what caused the infection. He's going to be okay," I said that as if I were relaying a message I'd just been given and it shocked me.

"How do you know that?! That doesn't make sense. how can you say that? I'm going to keep Lorraine company for a while. Her husband doesn't know because he drove back to Salamanca and they don't have a phone," Debbie explained.

"Fuck that, ask Lorraine for their address, I'll go get him," I said.

This is nuts. When I gave Debbie the explanation about Lorraine and Bernie's child it was if I had been reading it from a piece of paper. I didn't think about what I was saying, I just said it. It made absolutely no sense whatsoever, not to mention, the fear I had felt after saying it. Did Alex perhaps infect my psyche with his when we shook hands? Nonsense and bullshit, this was not happening!

She came back to the phone a minute later and said, "Never mind, she just got off the phone with him, he's on his way back. She said he called from her mom's because he wanted to say goodnight," Debbie said.

"I'm coming back to the hospital, honey," I said.

"You know where to find me," she said.

I put my shoes on and was on my way out the door when I realized my keys were on the arm of the couch. I can't remember my damned keys but I can pick up feelings from other people? Right! I was back at the hospital is less than five minutes. Walking down the hall, a nurse stopped me and told me visiting hours were over. I informed her that they weren't over for me and kept walking. Moments after entering

393

Debbie's room, the nurse and a security guard came in and told me I needed to leave so the patients could get their rest.

"He's my husband, and I have every right to want him here!" Debbie exclaimed.

"And they're my friends. I'd like them both here too, please don't ask him to leave—please?" Lorraine pleaded.

The nurse told the guard it was okay yet he was reluctant to leave. The nurse repeated that it was okay. If there was a problem she would summon him.

"Well, my job is to keep people out after visiting hours, and visiting hours are over. You're going to have to leave, sir." The security guard said to me.

"Please, my son is in surgery. My husband isn't here yet and Debbie and Paul are just about the only friends we have. Please, allow him to stay, PLEASE!" Lorraine said, now crying. Debbie walked over to Lorraine's bed and put her arm around her to offer comfort which made Lorraine sob harder.

"Look, there's no problem, there is not going to be a problem. I returned to be with my wife and our friends in their time of need. I'm staying regardless of what you say and, if you want me to leave, you're going to have to *try* and physically remove me," I said angrily.

"Now listen to me, you're going to ......"

"That's enough." The nurse interrupted. "I'll take the responsibility for this. You're welcome to stay, Mr. Kenyon. Thank you for understanding, John, you can leave now." The nurse told the guard.

"Nurse, I really….."

"I said, you can go, we'll discuss it no further," the nurse told the guard.

Still, the guard stood in the center of the room glaring at me as if I were on the FBI's 10 most wanted list. I decided it best to return the glare but not say anything. He would probably start all again if I had said anything and Lorraine was upset enough. After half a minute, he eventually turned and walked out of the room.

The curtain was pulled open between Debbie's and Lorraine's beds now and I could see there was a pile of spent Kleenex on Lorraine's bed table.

"I'm so worried, Debbie," Lorraine sniffled. "We have tried to have a baby for over a year, then after I had my accident, we weren't passionate for almost two years. I just didn't feel like a woman after what happened. Can you believe it, the first time we did become passionate, I got pregnant! Go figure. Now, our son is in surgery," Lorraine said, sniffing again.

She began to sob uncontrollably and Debbie placed her arm around her once again. Where was the fairness in this, I asked the Man upstairs in my head. From the looks of Lorraine's scars, she must have spent a great deal of time in the hospital after the accident. She lost one leg and we had no idea what other injuries she sustained besides what was apparent. A nurse came in and asked if she would like something to calm her nerves. She refused. Why are staff member always trying to force feed people, "something to calm their nerves," but when you go to the emergency room with an injury, it takes an hour to be seen and then sometimes several more hours before someone comes to *tend* to you? At least have enough staff on duty to be prepared to take care of the sick and injured. Lord knows, you're charged enough for what care you are given!

While Debbie comforted Lorraine, I excused myself and walked to the nursery to take a look at Joe. Hey, he had a name now! When I peered through the glass I could see the little stinker was sucking his thumb! I said a few things he couldn't hear through the glass, then walked to the vending machine and bought three sodas. I chose a Dr. Pepper for Lorraine, got Debbie's and my usual drinks and went back to their room. I offered the Dr. Pepper to Lorraine. She thanked me and said it was her favorite. Hmm. A few minutes passed and Bernie walked in. He sat alongside Lorraine, who leaned forward to reach for him. I had a lot of admiration and respect for this man. A lot of men wouldn't stay with a woman who had gone through what she had. It was very apparent they cared for one another immensely. Debbie motioned to the door, hinting to let them alone to have some privacy. After leaving the room, we slowly walked toward the nursery.

"I feel so sorry for them, honey," Debbie said, reaching for my hand.

"So do I, sweetheart. They're really nice people. They have their problems, and Bernie sure seems to be a great husband," I replied.

"It's almost time for me to feed Joe. I really don't want to take him to the room. I wonder if they would allow me to sit in the waiting room instead?" Debbie said.

"Well, why don't we go and ask," I suggested.

We walked to the nurses station to ask. Two doctors passed along the way, and it appeared they may have just come from a surgical procedure. When Debbie explained that she was Lorraine's roommate and that she wanted to sit in the waiting room to feed her son, the nurse said she didn't see a problem with it. She told us to have a seat in the waiting room and she would bring Joe out in a few minutes. Shortly after, our son was brought to us, bundled up. His little face was all that was visible from beneath his fluffy, blue blanket. Debbie breast fed him and it appeared he was really getting the knack of it.

"A chip off the old block," I said, as he began suckling.

"You're awful!" Debbie replied. "Isn't he perfect?!" She added.

"Yeah, now. You won't be saying that when he's two and he starts throwing his food across the kitchen!" I said.

"That'll be okay, I'll just clean it up and give him more to throw," she said, smiling brightly.

"What the hell did you ever see in me?" I asked.

"I like drummers. You just happened to be available, so I settled for you!" She said.

"Now, *you're* awful!" I exclaimed.

After Joe's feeding and a couple of decent burps, she handed him to me until the nurse came to retrieve him. Oddly, it was pleasant sitting in the waiting room of this hospital with our little boy. It was quiet, relaxing and simple. Maybe there was something to these blue walls after all! A few minutes later, the nurse came back to return Joe to the confines of his protective, in more ways than one, incubator. We walked with her and waited until Joe was tucked in, then went back to the room. When we entered, Lorraine and Bernie were all smiles.

"Robert is going to be okay! The doctors said the operation was much less complex than they first suspected," Lorraine said.

"Our doctor came in and explained that there was a small piece of skin, an extra flap, is that how he explained it, Lorraine?" Bernie said, then asked his wife for confirmation.

"Yes, there was a small flap of skin blocking one of the chambers of his left lung, causing his difficulty in breathing. When the x-rays were taken, they hadn't recognized the skin because there was so much fluid. They said it was a relatively easy procedure to correct the problem and clear his lungs. They had him in and out of surgery in less than an hour and a half!" She said, almost yanking Bernie off his feet when she wrapped her arms around his waist.

For what seemed like a full two minutes, I could feel Debbie's eyes on me. Finally, I turned and said, "What?"

"How did you know, how *could* you know? And why these people, why not everyone you meet...what's happening to you? There is absolutely no way on this earth you knew what we just *now* learned," She asked.

"I don't want to talk about it," I simply said.

"Honey, how could you know? I believed you when you said you felt things at the house but I felt things too. I was probably just feeling scared or apprehensive like everyone else but I guess what you were feeling, you really *felt*!" Debbie exclaimed, still staring at me.

"What are you guys talking about?" Lorraine asked with a nervous chuckle.

"When I called Paul at home and told him they were rushing Robert into surgery, he said he was going to be okay. He said..... "there was a blockage and that he was going to be okay!'" Debbie explained.

"When Bernie shook your hand at the nursery, he told me he felt funny, dizzy afterwards, but not a regular dizzy feeling. He said he thinks you passed your energy to him," Lorraine said.

"Wait a minute, energy?" I asked "What do you mean, energy?" I asked again.

"Bernie's sister is extremely psychic. We've been desperately trying to reach her but she's been out of town working on a case in Maine. We knew she could tell us what might happen," Lorraine said.

"When you said my baby was going to be okay, I really wasn't paying attention, I knew you said it, but I was too deep in my own thoughts. Then, when you said Lorraine was wondering where I was, I had a weird feeling. I'm not in the least bit psychic, Paul, but my sister is very gifted and can pick up on people, especially me. I swear to God, that woman knows what I'm thinking when she walks into the room! When you shook hands with me, I had a feeling similar to what I sometimes get when I hug my sister. It's not always but it sure happens a lot more than not," Bernie said.

"Did you feel anything when you shook my hand?" Lorraine asked.

"No, nothing whatsoever," I said.

"You ought to go to that haunted house that's up near Hinsdale. Maybe there's something you can help them with," Bernie said.

Debbie and I laughed so hard, the nurse came in and told us to keep it down, people are sleeping. I couldn't help myself when I told her they should wake up and attend to their patients. She didn't appreciate the comment and, frankly, I didn't care in the least. When I said it, Bernie agreed, and told her that they would like a big late dinner sent in to celebrate. The nurse left and we all laughed, a little less noisily but we continued for several minutes. We deserved to laugh. Lorraine and Bernie definitely deserved it and it was good. When we calmed enough to talk, Lorraine asked, "Um, may I ask, why are we all laughing?"

"I've been involved with the house since the middle of last August but only as a friend. I'm not a psychic, Lorraine. I don't know what these feelings are but they're very random and aren't always correct. Sometimes it's like getting hit by a semi. Only recently, I've been randomly picking up things before they happen or I hear people's feelings. Honestly, I don't really like the feelings I get. Now I'm scared I'll hear or feel actually, since I don't really hear anything, I'm scared I'll feel something really bad from someone," I explained.

Bernie and Lorraine stopped laughing, Lorraine was welling up, as Bernie turned and said, "Thank God the feelings were correct this time." We all went from hysterical laughter to spilling over. It was a good feeling, and these were good people.

Debbie suggested I go home, and get some rest because that's what she was going to do. I said goodnight to Lorraine and Bernie, giving them both a hug. The only feeling I got from either of them was that of thanks. Debbie jumped up on her bed as I sat on the edge, and held her so tightly I thought she was going to break; she didn't complain. I loved her so much. How in God's name had it all gone so wrong in such a short time? Writing that, and remembering her back in 1974, really made me once again, want just one of those months back.

We finally let go of one another, said goodnight and I walked out, stopping to tell Lorraine and Bernie that I was very happy that everything was going to be okay with Robert. When I got out to the parking lot, the air was so refreshing, I stood there taking in several long, deep breaths. There was no big city smog in Olean. The air was fresh and crisp during the winter. I turned around and looked up at all those windows. How many others in those rooms did I know something about? None I hoped. I really didn't want to know.

When I got home this time, again, I flopped on the couch; I was sleeping within 10 minutes.

The phone woke me; it was just past 9 a.m. It was Debbie calling to ask if I'd like to come get her. I was out the door, *with keys,* before the dial tone had faded into the electronic void. I found her at the nurses' station, picking up some info, placed in a folder by Dr. Cash. She looked vibrant, making even the dull, drab walls illuminate as she passed by. Over the next few days we began setting up house for our little one.

CHAPTER XXXII

Clara called today very upset. She told me Beth Ann was still having serious problems with the house and her personality. She and Keith were in Beth Ann's room and they heard two voices, one of a male, the other a female. The male voice asked what *they* were going to do now that Beth Ann was being taken to a doctor. The female's voice had said she didn't know, that it was easier when Beth Ann was sick.

"What do you think they meant by 'easier,' Clara?" I asked.

"I guess they believed it was easier to manipulate her when she was sick," Clara said.

"Did anyone else hear the voices?" I asked.

"Yes, Keith was with me. When we first heard them, it sounded like they were either coming from the basement stairs. Like they were on the other side of Beth Ann's bedroom wall or from outside. I jumped up and checked both locations but of course there wasn't anyone in either place. When I returned to the room, Keith told me they continued talking."

"Of course there wasn't anyone in either place, Clara. They're haunting everyone's mind in the house not just the house itself. They want you out and they're not going to stop until you are. Have you tried to contact Alex again?" I asked.

"He called two nights ago from Boston. He said he had a sudden impulsive urge to call. He knew something was terribly wrong. He explained that when he flew over the house he had impressions of possession with someone in the house. I told him...."

"Wait a minute, he flew over the house, on his way to Boston?" I interrupted.

"Not *flew*, flew but astral projection," Clara explained.

"He told you he felt a possession of someone in the house?" I asked.

"Yes, and he even said that he was most concerned with our oldest daughter. I think he's the person to release us from these problems, Paul. I really do believe that. He's mentioned again that he's trying to get an investigative team to the house and will really push harder to find someone," Clara said.

"I called Father Al twice yesterday to tell him about our baby, his name is Joseph by the way. The first time he answered, the connection was so bad I hung up and called back. When he answered again, I didn't hear anything after his hello. I thought I could still hear him and I kept asking if he was there but there was nothing but static. I hung up again thinking Ma Bell was having technical problems then the phone rang. I answered it but there was no one there. Debbie suggested calling the phone company, which I did and the call went through. I reported the trouble with the technician and attempted to call Father a third time with no luck," I explained.

"Did the technician say they were having difficulties?" Clara asked.

"No, but listen, it gets better. Now I was curious, so I called the main switchboard at Bona's and asked if they would connect me with Father Al's extension. As soon as his line rang, the line, his or mine went dead so I called my mother next. When she answered I told her we were having trouble with the phone. Yeah, we were having trouble all right, but only connecting to Father's phone," I said.

"That's really weird, Paul. It almost sounds like the energies of the house are succeeding in keeping the two of you from communicating," Clara said.

"Yeah, but I was one persistent SOB. I called the switchboard and told the operator we were having trouble getting to Father Alphonsus and would she please call him and tell him I needed to speak to his as soon as possible. I assumed she was able to pass the message on because almost immediately after hanging up the phone rang again," I said.

"Was it Father?" Clara asked.

"I believe it was Clara, 'cause as soon as I answered the damned thing, I got nothing but static. Doodlie, doodlie, do, do, do!" I sung.

"My God, I guess. Have you tried to call him today?" Clara asked.

"Not yet, actually I'm very hesitant to try. I just hope the forces are on his end, not to be mean, but I think he has more oomph on his end than I do," I said.

"Have you had any more trouble with, well, whatever the hell you're having trouble with?" Clara asked.

"Not since the hospital. Next time I see you though, I want to tell you something extraordinary that happened at the hospital. That's why I was trying to contact Father, to tell him about it. I wanted his opinion and hopefully get an answer to something I don't believe I have any reason to know," I said.

"Well, keep trying, and I'll keep you informed of what's going on here."

"All right, Clara. Take care and please be careful," I said.

Possession? According to nearly everything I've read, possession was generally connected to demonic forces. A new movie had been released recently about possession, "The Exorcist." We hadn't seen it, and I wasn't too sure I'd wanted to. I'd spoken to a couple of people who had seen it. They said it was, by far, the most disturbing and scariest movie they'd ever seen. The story revolves a young girl who becomes possessed by a demon. Her mother takes her to doctors and clinics trying to find the cause of her recent disturbing behavior. Eventually, finding no apparent medical cause for the young lady's alarming change in personality, one doctor suggests seeking out an exorcist. From that point, the movie takes you to a heightened state of "Oh my, God" one friend told me. I couldn't believe for a moment, that was happening to Beth Ann, or anyone else who had a sudden personality change at the house. I could grasp the idea that their house was haunted by your typical spirits but not the atypical demon.

The cases of possession I had read about mostly occurred in third world countries with witch doctors, healers and soothsayers acting the part of the exorcists. There were a couple of cases described in the book that occurred in the United States, but there wasn't much detail to either case to offer a conclusion of being genuine demonic possessions. What's more, most of the case studies I had read about, rarely involved more than two sides of supernatural activity. Some cases spoke of poltergeist activity as well as apparitions, some had a combination of apparitions and disembodied voices. However, there were none that involved the aforementioned activities with possession. In cases of possession, objects would seemingly move on their own or loud noises were heard within the proximity of the supposed possessed subject but these were attributed to demonic forces, ruling out a poltergeist. It seems anything typical of hauntings that manifests within the area of a possessed person were always supposed actions of the demonic power. It was rare that a priest was given permission to perform an exorcism. Those rare occasions were only when there was overwhelming proof that a person was indeed possessed. It was still remarkably difficult to put things into perspective regarding the Dandy house, and I've never totally understood any of it.

"How're things at the house?" Debbie asked.

"The same, although I don't understand why people's personalities seem to change. It hasn't happened to anyone I wouldn't trust to be honest about it though," I said.

"Who besides Beth Ann has been affected?" She asked.

"Well, Craig started acting peculiar. Randy said when he was home on leave, he starting asking where the barn was and said that he needed to help his pa with the chores. He said something about horses, too," I said.

"He had to help his pa?" Debbie asked.

"Yeah, when's the last time you heard anyone call their father pa? And don't forget that Mike was acting really strange when the three of us were in the field that one night?" I said.

"Well, I don't pretend to understand any of the stuff happening up there. But what I really want to know is how in the world did you know anything about Bernie or his baby? That will baffle me for as long as I live. You've told me about the goosies you've gotten most of your life, but this is creepy; really supernatural type of stuff," Debbie said.

"I'm as in the fog about that as you, hon. Why doesn't it happen with everyone? I'd rather not have any feeling and go back to being just plain, simple me. If this continues the way it is, my mind's gonna snap!" I said.

"Well, I know who you are, and that's all that matters to me." She said, giving me a kiss.

"Where would I be without you?" I asked, hugging her.

"*Not* with me." She said.

"I wouldn't like that." I said.

"Come on, let's go see the beast," Debbie said.

"You're kidding me! I make a comment of how much hair Joe has on his body and I get clobbered!" I exclaimed.

"When we get back, we need to get everything put together but I'll have to pick up a couple wrenches from my parents' house," I said.

"Okay, we'll go see our little boy and stop on the way back. I'm gonna help ya put everything together too!" She said.

"Oh, no!" I received a good whack for my comment as we walked out the door.

When we exited the elevator on the second floor, we noticed Bernie, Lorraine and their little boy, Robert, preparing to leave the hospital.

"Wow, you guys going home already?!" Debbie asked.

"Yes, and I am so ready! Robert is recovering nicely from his surgery. We're ready to start our family life, finally!" Lorraine said.

"That's great, you two. We're very glad everything went well and you're feeling better," I said.

"When's your little one going home with you?" Bernie asked.

"He should be going home by the end of the week. We're going to set his little nursery up when we get home today. It's exciting, isn't it?" Debbie asked.

"Yeah, I just wish I could be of more help to Bernie. He's going to have to do just about everything," Lorraine said sadly.

"Well, I can take care of both my babies!" Bernie exclaimed, bending to kiss them both.

"Thanks for all your support, Debbie and Paul. We only had each other and you guys were great to us. Bernie's mom is in bad health and my family; well, that's another story," Lorraine said.

"Yeah, and thanks for all the laughs you gave us. I especially liked the one about the semiprivate room!" Bernie said.

"You take care of little Robert and each other. He's going to be fine now and he's lucky to have you as parents," Debbie said.

Debbie bent over to give Lorraine, who was sitting in her wheelchair with her son on her lap, a hug. She motioned for me to bend down to share one with me too. Bernie offered his hand, which I took. I felt nothing but kindness but I saw a dark circle in my mind's eye, surrounded by spikes of green light. When our hands separated he looked at me through his thick glasses very oddly. He rubbed his right wrist as if it hurt him. Lorraine looked up at him and asked if it had been bothering him again.

"Yeah, I'm sure it will the rest of my life." Bernie said.

"What's wrong with your wrist, Bernie?" Debbie asked.

"I was in gymnastics in school and I shattered my wrist on the rings. Somehow, my wrist slipped into the ring during my dismount and I shattered nearly every bone in my right wrist," Bernie explained.

"No, not again," I said, and walked to Debbie and whispered, "Black rings" in her ear, then bent down and said the same thing to Lorraine. I looked at Bernie and asked what color the rings were.

"I think, yeah, they were black. They were made of a resin compound. Why?" Bernie asked.

"That is amazing!" Lorraine said.

I've had enough of this unless I could see the lottery numbers before they're picked, that is! We talked about it for a minute and Lorraine said I should contact Bernie's sister. They gave me her name and said I would find it in the phonebook as well. We said our goodbyes and good lucks, as Bernie pushed his wife and baby to the elevator.

"Maybe you ought to be his personal advisor," Debbie said.

"No, no more, hon. Don't even joke about it. I really don't like knowing anything. Let's go see Joe," I said.

We went to the nursery and spent the next two hours with our son. We wished he were coming home with us so our family could be complete. There were two more babies in the nursery today than there had been two days earlier. I've heard

405

it said that there are more babies born between the months of January and April than any other time. I think it has something to do with the heat of summer. I'm not sure if the reason was that it was tougher on women to go through labor in the heat of the summer or if the heat of the summer was when the babies were conceived. Well, it makes sense both ways, doesn't it?

After spending our time with Joe, Debbie and I went for lunch and stopped at my parents' to get the wrenches that I needed to put the bassinet and crib together. Debbie visited with my mom while I went though my dad's tools to find the right wrenches and instead, I decided on a crescent wrench; I had everything else I needed. Returning from the basement, I overhead Debbie discussing the strange incident between Bernie and me.

"Hi," I said, coming up the basement steps. I took a seat on the couch next to my mom.

"Hey, mom, remember Caesar?" I asked.

"How could I forget it?" She replied.

"Who was Caesar?" Debbie asked.

"I can't believe I didn't tell you about him! I had a pet boa constrictor; a big sucker, too. I kept him in a aquarium in the basement and he got out once. My dad and I found him wrapped around a hot water pipe. He got sick and I ended up giving him to Dr. Bothner at Saint Bona's," I explained.

"He used to feed it live mice. Once he put a live guinea pig in the aquarium for its lunch, I didn't like that," mom said.

"Yeah, the guinea pig ended up being mom's pet. She even trained the damned thing. After I got rid of the snake, we used the aquarium for the guinea pig. You just called it guinea, didn't you mom?" I asked.

"Yeah." She said with a smile, obviously remembering the enjoyment Guinea gave her.

"Anyhow, she trained it so it wouldn't go to the bathroom anywhere but in a small 'potty bowl' she put in the aquarium. Damnedest thing, she'd have it sitting in her lap for over an hour and it never had an accident!" I said.

"How did the snake get sick?" Debbie asked.

"He had parasites that made him meaner than hell and very aggressive. I'd let him wrap around my body and he was

406

always gentle, never squeezing hard or being aggressive. But later after getting sick, he would hiss, and smack the glass of the aquarium with his mouth whenever I walked toward it. I really felt bad, and worried that he'd injure his jaw hitting the glass as hard as he did," I said.

"How big was he?"

"When I got him, about five and a half feet. When we took him to Bona's, almost eight feet," I said.

"Wow, I wouldn't want a snake that big wrapping around me!" Debbie exclaimed.

"I think we got off the topic we were talking about, Debbie. She was telling me that you were able to, or told somebody anyhow, that their baby was going to be okay?" Mom asked.

"Yeah" I said making a face at Debbie. "I just felt it was going to be okay."

"Even if you feel something like that, you shouldn't tell someone, just in case something were to happen. The doctors could have made a mistake in surgery or something and the father would have really been mad at you for giving him false hope," mom explained.

"I didn't think of that and I said it without thinking. It just popped out," I said.

"Well, be careful with things like that. You never know what could happen," mom said.

"Yeah, I guess you're right, mom."

"What did you eat?" I asked Debbie, noticing a plate on the end table next to her.

"I had a piece of cake, mayonnaise cake!" She replied.

"What, I don't get any?" I asked.

"I had a feeling you were coming by today, so I made a cake. You know where the kitchen is," mom said.

Mom made the best mayonnaise cakes imaginable—they were always so moist. I had to have a piece before we left so I went to the kitchen and cut a slice. I poured a glass of milk too; you've got to have a glass of milk when you're eating cake. I yelled in to ask my mom if she wanted a piece; she didn't. I went back into the living room, and took my seat.

"Did you leave any for your father!" Mom exclaimed.

"It's not that big! There's still more than half a cake. That should be plenty, shouldn't it?" I asked.

"I'm just picking."

We visited for another hour or so. Mom surprised me when she brought out one of the pennies I had found when digging at the Fountain.

"Did you even notice the date on this one?" She asked.

I looked at it—it was a 1922, minted in Philadelphia. Of course I knew that because it had no mint mark. After looking at it, I looked at her, quizzically. Was I missing something?

"Well?" She asked.

"That's what I'm trying to figure out. Oh, you were born in '22!" I said.

"Not just that but the '22 Philadelphia is the most expensive from that year," she said.

How could I have missed that? I knew my coins pretty well I thought. I knew most of the key coins of all denominations. Most of which I didn't have. How this Lincoln hadn't hit me between the eyes when I looked at it surprised me.

"Well, take it with you when you leave," mom said.

"No, you keep it, it's was the year you were born. So no, you keep it. I'll bring over a plastic case to put it in. Put it in your cedar chest," I said.

"No, it's yours, take it home."

"Come on, Deb. I'll drop you off. Grab a holder and bring it back and I'll be home right after," I said.

Debbie got up and gave my mom a hug. I took my plate and glass to the kitchen and told my mom I'd be right back. She tried to give me the penny again but I wouldn't take it. It was hers. Many people get each coin from a certain year, a birth year set, and give them as presents. I hadn't been able to afford coins in good condition from '22 and now we have the most expensive coin from that year. The rest would be easy with what I made from the Fountain fixtures. I drove home, went in to grab a holder, and asked Debbie not to do too much without me.

"I'll be back in 10 minutes tops. I want to put the crib together so don't you start without me!" I said as I darted out the door.

She grabbed my shirt, pulled me around and gave me a kiss and I was out the door again, in the car and back at mom's in less than three minutes. When I walked in the back door, she was cleaning my plate and glass already. She couldn't stand to have even one dirty dish in the sink.

"Here, where's the penny?" I asked.

"It's back on that windowsill," she said, pointing at the sill with the Bermuda info on it. I had asked what the brochure was about a month earlier and my dad said, "I just might take your mom there!" If it had been two, or three years earlier, I would have laughed at him. He didn't do much of anything for my mother in all my years. But as I said, he treated her like a queen after her heart attack. I guess he finally realized what she meant to him, that she was worth her weight in gold; and she was. It's unfortunate when your childhood can sometimes follow you.

I picked up the penny from the windowsill, placed it in the coin holder and set it back on the windowsill.

"Don't forget it's there, put it in your cedar chest," I told mom.

"You should take it with you." She said, as my dad walked in.

"I ate half your cake," I told him.

"Half a cake is better than none!" Dad said.

"I gotta get. I told Deb I'd be right back. I borrowed a crescent wrench, dad. I gotta put the crib together, and I needed a smaller wrench than the ones I have."

"Well, don't lose it, and bring it back when you're done," he said.

Before going out the back door, I gave my mom, who had still been standing at the sink, a hug. Even then, I think she still worried when dad came home because I sensed stress. It could be from anything though. She stressed about every little thing. Things have been too good the past few years for her to be worrying about that any longer—unless there was something I didn't know about—I prayed not. I said goodbye and drove home—thinking, wondering. No, Not a chance, I would have known, somehow I would have *certainly* known.

After I got home, Deb and I took on the task of putting baby furniture together. She told me that Clara had called and I said I would call her back when I was finished. Her mom had called too and asked if she would like to go with her when she went to the hospital to see Joe. It sounded to me like mom wanted to spend time with her daughter and I suggested she go. I said I'd be up a little later. Her mom was going up after work which was only half an hour from now. I told her to go ahead, I'd finish up and be at the hospital when I was done.

"I hope the instructions aren't going to be like the ones you get with kids' toys. You know, put slot A of side 1 into slot D of the back and connect side 2 with 4 nuts and 4 lock washers to the bottom after being sure slot D is secure with the right side of the top," I said.

"So you're the one who writes these directions? That's exactly what these say!" She replied jokingly.

"You gonna go with your mom?" I asked.

"Yeah, I better call her before she leaves," Debbie said, picking up the phone.

I started reading the instructions on assembling the crib. After reading the first three lines, I threw them on the floor, looked at the pieces and figured it would be easier to just put it together without them. If I got stuck, I'd use them as a reference only. Debbie's mom was at the house a few minutes after Debbie had called her. I told her I'd be leaving as soon as I was done. It hadn't taken long at all and I didn't need the instructions at all. There were 2 screws left over. I hoped they were extras and that I hadn't missed something. I looked it over and didn't see any holes I may have missed. Everything appeared to be complete. Of course, when I turned it on its bottom and tried to roll the crib across the floor, it didn't move. Looking down, I realized it didn't roll because the wheels were still in a bag sitting on the kitchen table! "Dummy!" I said, to myself. I flipped the crib back on its side and tapped the self-seating wheels into each of the four holes on the legs.

"There, finished! That was easy," I said to the crib.

I went to the phone to make three calls, one to Clara, one to Father Al and one to my mom. I called my mom first.

"Hello?" She answered.

"Are you okay?" I asked.

"Yeah, why?" She asked.

"Nothing really, I just wanna make sure you're all right," I said.

"Well, you had to call for a reason, is there something wrong with *you*?"

"No, I just want—is dad treating you okay; he's not being that way again is he?" I asked.

"No, everything's fine. I don't think you'll ever have to worry about that again."

"You'd tell me if there was anything going on?" I asked.

"I'd probably tell your brother first but yes, I would," she answered.

"Okay, I believe you. I'm gonna run to the hospital and see Joe. He should be coming home in the next couple of days," I said.

"All right, you'd better believe me. Bring him over when you get him home."

"We will, mom—love you."

"Love you."

There was nothing in her voice and, really, I thought I was worrying for nothing. I don't think she would have been able to tolerate being treated badly again. At least I felt at ease after talking with her. I next attempted to call Father Al. The call went though this time but there was no answer. He was a busy man and I didn't expect him to be in whenever I called. Now it was time to call Clara and see if there have been any new developments with the house.

"Hello?"

"Hi, precious, is your mom available?" I asked Laura.

"Hi Paul! MOM IT'S PAUL! What are you doing?" Laura asked.

"Well, I just put our son's crib together and now I'm talking to you."

Giggling, she said, "Are you gonna bring him up so I can see him?"

411

"Sooner or later, I will. He's still in the hospital 'cause he was so small when he was born. He has to be in an incubator for a while, just until he builds his strength," I said.

"Just like an egg!" She laughed. "I don't think you have to worry about him coming up here. They won't bother a little baby," Laura said very sincerely.

I swear to all that is holy, that's exactly what I was thinking when I told her he had to stay in an incubator. My thoughts were exactly like hers. I worried about taking him to the house.

"Here's mom, bye Paul!"

"Hello, how are things with you?" Clara asked.

"Okay, got the crib together and it has two ends and two sides, so I guess I did something right," I said.

Laughing she said, "Does it have the most important part, the bottom?"

"Yes, Clara, it has a bottom too, smart ass," I said.

Still laughing, "Well, Beth Ann doesn't have an ulcer, thank God. The doctor said she has a nervous stomach and they gave her something for that. But we've had some more problems involving vehicles," Clara explained.

"Oh no, now what the hell happened?" I asked.

"Well, Phil's been having trouble with his car so he borrowed Mike's to go to work. As he drove though Franklinville, he saw a semi coming straight at him, in *his lane*! He swerved off the side of the road, lost control and the car rolled over three times!" Clara explained.

"Jesus, Mike mentioned that but he didn't go into detail. Is Phil he okay?" I inquired.

"Surprisingly, yes. The car ended up on it's roof in a field along the side of the road. Phil said he blew the horn at each vehicle that passed but, either they didn't see the car, or ignored him if they had. He squeezed out of the window and walked quite a ways in one direction but never found a house. He turned around and went the other direction. He finally found one. He called me and Keith and Mike went to pick him up," Clara said.

"Is he home?" I asked.

"Yeah, Mike and Keith insisted he go to the hospital to at least get checked out. The doctor was amazed he hadn't gotten badly injured or killed. They sent him home and told him to rest."

"Holy cow, Clara. There've just been too many accidents lately and none of them have been the driver's fault. I'm not saying the house has anything to do with them all or any of them for that matter, but gee, what a hell of a coincidence, huh? How's Mike doing?" I asked.

"He's having trouble with his memory but he's getting along okay. We plan to brighten the house up—you know, colorful wallpaper and stuff like that. Maybe that'll help take the gloominess out of the house. If nothing else, it'll make the house look alive! Alex sent a lock of his hair for our protection. I thought if anyone needed protection right now, it was Beth Ann. I put some of it in my ID bracelet and asked her to wear it," Clara said.

"Any new information about Alex coming up again?" I asked.

"Nope, didn't we talk about this the other night? He's stepping up his efforts to find someone who will come up. We did talk about this! You're having trouble with your memory now! I talked to Father, he said he had a nice visit with you."

"I've been having so much trouble trying to reach him by phone that I finally decided to go to Bona's and meet with him. I asked if he would bless Joe if we brought him to the University. He said he'd go one better. He came to the house and blessed us all. Clara, he's a remarkable person. We had a really nice chat, and again, he told me not to worry about the feelings I get. That's kinda difficult to do, especially when they nearly knock me out sometimes!" I said.

"Well, apparently they're getting stronger but you seem very reluctant to accept that," she said.

"I can't understand how I'm supposed to embrace this psychic awareness as Alex suggested. Maybe it's easier with his experience, but it scares the hell outta me! I'm getting ready to go to the hospital, Debbie and her mom are waiting for me," I said.

"Okay, well, I'll let you go so you can see your boy. Don't forget, you have to bring him around so we can see him," she said.

"Oh, I will—he's so tiny! All right, Clara, I'll talk to ya soon."

We hung up and I left to take the short drive to the hospital—I had my keys too!

I would not resign myself to taking our newborn to the house before Father Al blessed him and that took place on January 29th. Even after, we stayed away from the house and played family the entire time. I had only one incident with the "heat waves" in my head. Two days after Valentine's Day I was standing in line at the grocery store, waiting for a woman with two small children in front of me to be checked out. Her youngest, a boy of about 3, kept sticking his hand on the conveyer belt that moves the groceries forward. I said something to the mom that he might get his hand pinched and she gave me a "mind your own business" look. A few seconds later, I received the "psychic sign" and at the same moment the boy got his pinkie finger stuck alongside the belt, ripping the entire tip off. "You jinxed him!" His mom blamed me! I said nothing, but thought, "pay attention, next time."

Chapter XXXIII

My band didn't play February 23rd and Debbie agreed to take Joe to the house for a *short* visit. I called Clara to ask if that was a good day to come up. She said that would be absolutely fine. I said we'd probably be up about noontime but wouldn't stay too long. It was only a week away and I still had my concerns. When the day arrived, I felt apprehensive and, if I felt the slightest twinge on the drive up, I would forget the whole thing and turn around.

My friend George called and told me he read another article about the house in the paper today. I'd read the paper but didn't see anything about the house. I was perplexed and called him back to ask. He informed me the story was in the Buffalo Courier Express. I was going to have to wait to get a copy because Debbie was ready to visit the Dandys.

"You're sure you're okay with going up today?" I asked Debbie who was bundling Joe up.

"Yes, but if there's one noise or someone starts talking about what's been going on, I want to leave immediately. I don't want to hear one word about ghosts or voices; nothing about haunted anything. I love Clara but I just don't want to share in this paranormal stuff," Debbie said.

"Okay, I agree, I only want show off this little shit! We won't stay long, honey, I promise."

"All right, grab the bassinet and bag please, I'll take him out," she asked.

"You have an extra bottle?" I asked.

"No, but I have an extra breast!" She said.

"Yay, I don't have to share!"

"You are so lucky I'm carrying your son or, chances are, you might not be able to produce another one!"

"Ouch!" I cringed.

"Exactly. Hurry up!" She demanded.

"Yes, ma'am," I said with a big smile.

Driving up, I could see Debbie stealing a look at me every now and then. I already knew what was on her mind and said nothing. I felt okay. It was a nice sunny day and it wasn't too cold. I was thinking about the little boy who lost the tip of his finger because of his mom's ignorance. Had I picked up a feeling from Bernie all the way down the hall when I got the "heat wave" before talking with him at the nursery? I had attributed it to the house, but then, why would the house, or the resident in Mary's room send something to me? We hadn't been visiting and I hadn't been getting any feelings. I tried putting the feelings together with anything that happened the days I had them but couldn't correlate something particular to each one. Perhaps, that's all it was, getting some random signal from someone in distress or about to be. I liked that idea a whole lot more than thinking the house was going to contact me whenever it had an inkling to do so. Actually, the more I had read and began to fully understand, the surer I was that my goosies were just that, random signals being picked up from the abundance of energy all around us.

"What are you looking at me for?" I asked Debbie.

"I'm just watching your expression to see if there's anything there," she said.

"There's nothing, but we aren't there yet. Believe me, if I suddenly make a quick u-turn, you'll be the first to know there's *something,*" I said.

We traveled the entire distance of Congress and turned up Wagner Hill Road. So far, so good. As I turned onto McMahon Road, Debbie asked me to stop.

"What?" I asked.

"Anything? A standing on end hair, a twinge, a chill, a voice telling you it's show time; anything?" She asked.

"Nothing, Debbie. Do you really think if there was something, I'd continue?" I asked.

"No, I guess not but I know you. You promised to come up and you'll likely to go just 'cause you promised." she said.

"No, not a chance. It's fine right now anyhow. If something comes, we go!" I said.

"All right, thanks," she said, reaching for my hand.

I leaned toward her to give her a kiss. I felt she was going to be a mom like my mom; protective as a hungry lion. I continued driving up McMahon, turned the corner toward the house and said, Shit!"

416

"What, what's wrong? What do you feel? Turn around, NOW!" Debbie demanded.

Laughing, I said, "No, not that, honey, I meant to bring Mike's flashlight back and forgot it."

"Well, did you have to say, shit like that? You scared the hell out of me!" She said.

"I'm sorry, I didn't mean to frighten you."

I pulled into the driveway and parked. I went around to Debbie's door and opened it. I took Joe while she got out. She took him back, I grabbed the bag out of the rear seat and walked around back to get the bassinet from the trunk. Clara, Beth Ann and Mary came out to meet us. "Let me see, let me see!" Exclaimed Mary.

"Mary, be careful, he's very tiny," Clara warned.

Clara took the bag from me and carried it into the house. I followed with the bassinet and observed a few of Mike's friends looking Phil's car over.

"Hey, guys," I said.

"What's up, brought the little one for us to see, huh?" Mike said.

"Yeah, I'll be out in a minute, let me get this inside," I said.

I took the bassinet into the living room and set it up on the floor. Debbie, Clara and the girls came in to get a better look once Joe was out of his blanket. We all heard noise from upstairs and Debbie immediately looked at me.

"It's Laura, honey. Don't start worrying," I said, although I didn't how I knew it had been her.

A moment later Laura came into the living room, gave me a slight hug, passed me in a hurry and rushed to the bassinet to get a look at our new addition. Once the blanket came off, there was a roomful of "oohs" and "awwws."

"I'm gonna go outside for a minute, hon. I'll be right back," I told Debbie.

"Okay," She replied.

Before going outside and as quickly as I could, I stood at the bottom of the stairs, trying to feel something. Then I walked into the bathroom off the kitchen. I liked it; nothing. I walked outside to see how much damage there was on Phil's car.

"How'd this happen?" I asked, while looking at Mary's window.

"Some asshole was on the wrong side of the road, with his lights *off*. He ran right into the car!" Mike said.

"I don't think anyone that lives here should drive anymore," I said.

"Keith was driving," Mike replied.

"He lives here, now, doesn't he?"

"Oh—yeah. But, I don't think that has anything to do with it. You don't do you?" Mike asked.

"Not really, Mike. I was being a smart ass, I guess. There've just been too many problems with vehicles. Gee, even Tim's but we won't talk about that," I said.

"It still bothers you doesn't it?" Mike asked putting his hand on my back.

"Like if I had just learned about it this very second, yeah," I replied.

"Just forget about it, we all know better, man," he said.

"Yeah but I wish he did. Okay, I'm gonna go back inside, I'll talk to you in a bit. Come in and see my kid!" I took one more look at Mary's window before going in.

Mike and I walked through the kitchen and, as we began to walk into the living room, Clara yelled, "STOP!" We both stopped in our tracks. Then I realized why she had yelled; mom was breast feeding. Mike realized it and all but ran back into the kitchen making us all laugh.

"I'll come back in when it's safe. Just let me know," Mike said from somewhere in the kitchen.

"About 20 minutes, Mike," Debbie replied

I sat on the floor like a bump on a log while they all talked baby stuff. The birds were singing and that was a good sign. I found it funny to think that birds might somehow be able to detect paranormal activity. It's been said that all animals are more sensitive than humans to a lot of things. I think it was in school that we learned animals were aware that earthquakes were imminent. But what is it they sense regarding paranormal activity? It's a shame we can't study them scientifically in an attempt at finding the connection. I guess we find them more useful in experimentations to find the results of what chemicals, and soaps are likely to cause us harm. A score for human vanity, a *sore* for our friends, the animals.

"Anyone want something to drink?" Clara asked.

"I do," said Mary.

"Well, you can help yourself!" Clara said, laughing.

"Debbie, Paul?" Clara asked again.

"Yeah, I'll have some Koolaid, if you have some," I said.

"I just made cherry Koolaid, Paul, you want some?" Laura asked.

"Sure, thanks, hon."

"Debbie, you want some too?" Mary asked.

"No, hon, I'm okay, but thank you," Debbie said.

"Can Joey have some, mom?" Mary asked.

Chuckling Clara said, "No, Mary, he's too young for Koolaid."

Laura brought my Koolaid and sat on the floor next to me. She didn't have to say a word, I think I knew what she was thinking. She looked at me with her cute smile. I smiled back and said, "It's quiet, and it's gonna stay that way too." She nodded, stood up, and walked over to her mom who was now holding Joe, patting his back. We'd been there about an hour and Debbie hadn't given me the "it's time to go" look yet. When Laura sat next to me, I felt as though Debbie was feeling us both out, attempting to spot a sign from one or both of us. She looked at me every now and then, checking my body language; my expression. All's fine and well at the Dandys today. At one point while sitting on the floor, I believe I sent out a psychic, "thank you" aimed directly at the heart of the house. I enjoyed the connection I had with Laura, I found it neater than hell. Whatever it was that we had, I would have loved to have it with a bunch of people. Father Al said psychic energy could build, be strengthened within oneself. I think that's how he put it; something very similar to that.

Mike, Keith and Randy came in to take a look at our Joe. They all swarmed around Clara who was still holding him. I could see Clara was enjoying him even though she has four of her own. Clara had a miscarriage and had lost a baby when

Christina Michelle was only one day old. There was no doubt that she loved children not just her own. "Why's he so little?" Mike asked.

"He was a preemie. What did he weigh when he was born, Debbie?" Clara asked.

"Four pounds, thirteen ounces," Debbie said.

"Oh my, that is tiny!" Clara exclaimed.

"What do they normally weigh?" Keith asked.

"Well, I guess it's safe to say that seven and a half pounds is average," Clara said.

"Wow, he was only a little over half that!" Randy said.

"Believe it or not, he was a lot smaller than he is right now, you guys. His hands weren't much longer than the first knuckle of my index finger," I said.

"Can I hold him for a minute?" Beth Ann asked.

"Of course! Clara, do you mind?" Debbie said.

Clara walked over to where Beth Ann was sitting and, ever so carefully, placed Joe in Beth Ann's arms. Beth Ann was all smiles and began cooing as soon as he was settled against her chest. I was a very proud dad at that moment and felt a tear attempting to break through. But I knew if it did, many more would come. Before that could happen with all these people in the room, I got off the floor, picked up the glass Laura had brought me and took it to the kitchen. I walked back into the living room as Keith, Mike and Randy were coming out.

"Nice job, dad!" Mike said.

"Thanks, Mike, I appreciate it," I said.

"Yeah, he's cute. Thank God he doesn't look like you!" Keith exclaimed.

"Piss up a bent rope!" I said jokingly.

The three of them went back outside and, as I sat on the floor next to Debbie, I got an ever so slight hiccup of energy slip into my mind. I pushed back with good thoughts, the thought of our newborn son, the love that his mother and I shared, anything that I could think of the made my life feel full.

"One of you girls get up please and let Paul sit on the couch!" Clara said.

"No, Clara, I'm fine. Let 'em sit, I'm good, really," I said.

I hadn't noticed immediately upon returning to the living room but the birds weren't singing as they had been when we arrived and the air seemed heavy, confining. This, along with the feeling I received when I sat down, made me start the feeling process. I still didn't quite grasp the exact way to "hear" the feeling. I waited a minute, turned around and snuck a quick peek at Laura; she didn't look back with her beautiful smile, which she *always* did when we looked at one another. I was sure Clara noticed something or perhaps she felt it too because she watched Laura and me gazing at one another. The feeling was ever so slightly different. I couldn't understand what it could have been. It somehow seemed to push, subside and push again with more force. I figured the sensation had changed because I had begun to learn how to push my own good feeling from my own psyche. Clara had that look she often did before or during one of her "umbrella nights." Jesus Christ, not now! Suddenly, the feeling was moving about my mind with the speed of a freight train. I had to do something. I got up and started lowering the legs on the bassinet, an act that made Debbie's expression turn from her typical glowing self to mud. Lord, going through those simple steps of taking down a baby's bassinet felt more like digging in, preparing yourself for incoming; wondering how long before the enemy infiltrates your lines. I began sweating and everyone in the room knew what was happening, especially Clara and Laura. Clara's face was drawn and ashen as she hurriedly helped Debbie wrap Joe in the protection of his blue and white blanket, decorated in the most popular Disney characters. Where was the "heat wave"? "Don't you *dare* assault me, or my family without telling me you're coming, you son of a bitch!" I thought. There was no warning and, when it began, it was forceful. It backed off only to become stronger again. I, in turn, attempted to return the push with my own shove, to no avail. I tried several times again but I was losing. My impulse was to run upstairs and have it out. I wanted to take my chances with this lowly bastard once and for all but I had Debbie and our innocent son to worry about. I was so totally fed up with this battle of psyches. What was worse, I had been assured previously I had neither the

421

power nor the energy to stand against the menace that made its presence known so abruptly, so powerfully.

"Come on, come on, get him to the car, I'm right behind you!" Clara exclaimed.

"Laura, honey, will you grab his little -"

I began to ask Laura to grab Joe's stuffed animal and, with no further warning, BAM—the energy of the house—like a baseball bat, driving in the wining run, slammed a psychic club directly across my forehead. I dropped the bassinet in the middle of the floor as I fell against the doorframe to catch my balance. The heat wave was upon me, with all the force of each previous attack combined. I heard Beth Ann yelling to Mike and Randy, who I could hear entering the kitchen. This unseen bastard was beyond angry. His loathsome energy stuck harder than in the past and I imagined myself losing consciousness, falling to the mercy of its force. I reached deep within my psyche, attempting to muster all that I could to block the assault but there was nothing and I all could do was scream, "Stop!"

"Get him outta here!" Beth Ann screamed.

Mike and Randy, each grabbed one of my arms and began to all but carry me through the kitchen. As we passed the stairs, a second wave slammed into my very soul and, this time I dug so deep I found an inner strength that gave me enough fortification to stand on my own and face the onslaught. Mike later told me I asked him to let me go, that I didn't want to retreat. I would face it I insisted. Instead, he and Randy continued getting me out to the car which had already been started. I began to get into the driver's seat by habit when I asked Mike to please drive for me.

"Keith, please follow us down and bring Mike back. I don't want to drive down McMahon; I can't Mike, I won't make it—please?" I said.

"You got it!" Keith said going to his car.

"Mike, drive, please?" I asked.

"Are you going to be okay *after* you get to the end of the road?" Clara asked.

"Mike will be there if I'm not but I'm sure I will be," I said.

Laura was standing next to the car; I looked at her and thought, "thank you," which she returned with a smile. It would be okay, soon. As Mike began backing the car out of the driveway, I glanced up at Mary's window and, for a brief moment, I was sure I saw a dark figure at the side of the window. I turned away and looked out the car window and, once again, to Laura who was also looking toward the same window. Had she seen it? I hoped not, she was too frail, too innocent to have to deal with such hatred. Mike, very slowly and cautiously, drove to the end of McMahon Road and stopped. Keith parked right behind us and, for the first time since we got in the car, I saw that Debbie was in tears. "Son—Of—A—Fucking—Bitch," I muttered quietly, emphasizing each word.

"You okay, Paul?" Keith asked, after walking to the driver's side of the car.

"Yeah, I think so, but I'd like you and Mike to stick around for a bit if you don't mind," I said, my own tears streaming down my cheeks.

"Hell no, man. We'll stay as long as you need us," Keith said.

"Well, this is the last time I will ever bring my son up here and I am going to, once and for all, find a way to drive this fucking house into hell!" I said.

Mike got out of the driver's seat but I remained seated in the rear seat for a minute or two. Mostly now, it was my anger that needed conquering. I felt somewhat better and I didn't break my promise to Debbie. At the first sign, I was up and all but ripping the bassinet apart, attempting to get it collapsed. I felt miserable because we didn't simply get up and leave after a very pleasant visit. We ran out of there as if being chased by a crazed madman. Perhaps we had. We sat there for nearly 10 minutes when we saw Clara and Beth Ann walking down the road toward us. When they arrived at the car, they had concern on their faces. Clara asked, "Would you like Mike to drive you home and have Keith bring him back?"

I didn't say what I thought after her question but rather said, "No, I'll be okay, Clara. I'll probably take an hour to get home as slow as I plan to drive but we'll be fine now."

"If you really think so but I'm sure he wouldn't mind. Would you, Mike?" Clara asked.

"Not at all, mom. You sure you're good, Paul?" Mike asked.

"Yeah, I feel much better, Mike. Thank you all for your concern," I said.

"I'm sorry Father wasn't here, Paul, but even if he had, I have a feeling this may still have happened," Clara said.

"I think you're right Clara. As soon as we get home, I'll call," I said.

"I'd feel better if you'd stop at Crosby's to at least know you'd made it that far."

"Okay, I will—thanks, Clara."

"Debbie, honey, you all right," Clara asked walking to Debbie's side of the car.

"Yeah, I guess I'm more upset at the way we had to leave. I wish this big dummy didn't have to feel this shit. You know what's really weird? Nothing bad happens when he has a feeling. We all just get scared because he *does,*" Debbie said.

"Well, I wouldn't say nothing happens, something's definitely happening to his mind, as well as his physical self."

"I don't think he has a mind!" Debbie exclaimed with a refreshing laugh.

"Hey, don't talk like I'm not here, for Christ's sake!" I said. "Okay, we're going to drive very slowly and head home. I'll call you from Crosby's and then again from home," I said.

"All right, *please* be careful!" Clara said.

Debbie and I thanked them and I began driving down Wagner Hill Road. I felt like a little old man, I never went over 10 miles an hour all the way to the Hinsdale highway and no faster than 30 after reaching it. I called Clara from Crosby's as I said I would and again when we got home. I just simply didn't get it. What was I, on the mental hit list? Everyone involved with the house was either involved in accidents, having their personalities toyed with or experiencing "heat waves" in their heads. That last one was no heat wave, that was a building fallin' on my noggin! I stopped at my parents' house to get yesterday's Buffalo paper before it was thrown away. I wanted to read the article George had told me about. My parents weren't home so I let myself in with the spare key. I was in and out in within one minute.

After calling Clara, I unloaded the car and brought everything inside. Joe, sleeping, was placed in his crib and Debbie asked what we should have for dinner. I told her to choose something and we could make it or I could get take-out. It didn't matter to me. We decided on KFC. I waited about half an hour before going out to get it. It had been a rough one coming home, wondering if the, "Babe Ruth" of the Psychics was going to get in the batter's box again. He didn't and, for that, I was more than thankful. Speaking of giving thanks, I'll never utter those words again at the Dandy house unless it's to the living.

CHAPTER XXXIV

I'd like to offer you the entire story that was published in the Buffalo Evening News (now The Buffalo News) dated February 22, 1974. The story was written by Bob C., and some of what is in this article has already been explained in this writing. There was an error in the article that was corrected in a later edition. Bob C. had written that the psychic that visited the house was Ted Serios when, in fact, it had been Alex Tanous.

Wednesday afternoon, I spent 2½ hours with a demonologist who, I had been told, wouldn't want to talk about an exorcism he performed. Because of that report and the word "demonologist," I expected to meet a grumpy character who would want me to get the devil out of his company as soon as possible. But Father Alphonsus Trabold, an assistant professor of theology at Saint Bonaventure University, turned out to be a charming gent who was happy to talk about Satan and other spirits. And before we got to the exorcism experience the 48 year-old religious man held me spellbound with a story of a mysterious house in a small town near Olean. The troubles in the house, occupied by a couple and their four children, began in July when a lamp sailed across the bedroom of one of the girls. Because she was the only one involved, the reaction was that an overactive imagination was at work.

But then the entire family began hearing strange noises and seeing apparitions. And when Father Alphonsus, a member of the American Society of Psychical Research and the venerable Society of Psychical Research in Britain, was asked to visit the home, he found that some of the neighbors also had seen apparitions near the home.

Father Al: *"One night, two 20-year-old boys volunteered to stay in the house and watch for apparitions. About 2:30 in the morning they heard a noise and ran out into the backyard. They saw a strange figure, cornered him against a tree and took a picture of him with a Polaroid. Before they could seize* him, he moved to the rear of the tree and disappeared. It was a moonlit night and the tree was on a large lot. So they could see for quite a distance. The ground was very rough—they'd had trouble moving on it—and they were sure no human could cover it in the time they got to the other side of the tree. I sent the picture to the American Psychic Society and they advised me the creature in it was a spirit. Another time the family came home and found a small pen knife pinned to a picture of one of the girls. The picture was hanging on the wall and the pen knife had been on the other side of the room when they left the house earlier. Sometimes when they were in the house, they would see apparitions outside. At times when they were in the yard, they would see apparitions inside the house. The word 'apparition' makes most people think of wraithlike objects. The apparitions they and the neighbors saw were solid.

On the top of the second floor of the house is a half-attic that contains a chimney. The attic is never used because it is so small and the floor is so weak. One day some members of the family flashed a light in there and saw that a number of bricks had been removed from the chimney and were piled neatly in a corner.

When *Ted Serios, a well known and respected psychic, visited the house, he got the feeling that seven murders had been committed in the 100 or so years it has been standing. When he looked into the half-attic, he said he got the feeling that many of the murders had been committed there.

When he said one of the victims had been stabbed in the heart, we naturally thought of the pen knife sticking into the picture. When he said that one of the victims had been hanged we thought of the time the lady of the house saw an apparition hanging from a tree. He also said that three of the victims had been burned to death. Some members of the family living in the house have awakened with burns on their bodies.

Lately they have been plagued with an inordinate number of car accidents and car problems. In one 2-week period they had four accidents.

Bob C: *"Why don't they get out of the house?"*

Father Al: *"They are trying to, but here again they have problems. They don't have much money and to date they haven't been able to find a house big enough and in the right price range."*

Has he been able to help them in any way?

Father Al: *"I have given them peace of mind by telling them about psycho kinesis and giving them examples of mind moving matter. Of course they take comfort from the fact that the American Psychic Society is working on the problem."*

"I visit them a couple of times a week and they're always glad to see me because nothing ever happens when I'm there."

Does this ever lead him to wonder if the people are telling the truth?

Father Al: *"No, because the first thing I do in a case like this is interview all the people involved. After I did that this time, I was sure they were telling the truth. My next step was to see if there was a natural cause for the incidents like the lamp flying across the room. Say, a strong gust of wind that could have blown it off the dresser. I found it couldn't have happened that way. After investigating all possibilities in the natural area, I decided that this was a paranormal situation and began looking for the answers in that direction. And as I said, I'm still looking."*

Hey, how about Father Alphonsus the Exorcist? Like they say on the Johnny Carson show, "He will be with us as soon as possible." Like tomorrow.

*Should have read Alex Tanous

Clara called me the following Thursday to tell there was yet *another* car accident. Mike had borrowed Phil's car which had been repaired the prior Friday, the day we had taken our son up for a visit. She told me the road was icy and he lost control on the hill, hitting a tree. I couldn't believe it, they were being plagued with the worst luck when it came to being on the roads. This time, Phil had to buy another car, there was just too much damage to repair this time. He was able to find a fairly decent car for a good price in town. At least he would have transportation to get to and from work until they might get something better. In our conversation, she told me about two mediums her cousin had called to tell her about. She was going to attempt to contact them and see if they could offer their services. "Nothing ventured, nothing gained," she had said. I don't think Clara had much more faith in mediums than I but anything was worth trying at this point. And, again, my opinion regarding mediums may have been harsh. I really didn't understand their talent.

Clara called me again on Saturday afternoon, the 1st of March to tell me Mary's resident may have moved into Mike's room.

"Mike's room, why do you say that?" I asked.

"We were in the living room watching television and suddenly there was a loud crash. At first we thought the sound had come from outside the house, but when Mike walked into his bedroom to look out the window he saw his lamp on the floor," Clara explained.

"Could it have fallen, Clara?" I asked.

"I asked him the same question. Some things that happen around here have to have natural causes but the lamp was on the opposite side of the room and you could see where it had hit the wall. Before I forget, did you see the second article Bob C. wrote in last Saturday's paper?" Clara asked.

"Second article? No, I read the one from Friday's paper but didn't know there was one in Saturday's. Do you still have it?"

"Uh-huh, I'll save it so you can read it. Is there a chance you could come up today?" Clara said.

"No, Deb and I have a bunch of stuff to do and I have to play tonight. Why?"

"Paul and Peggy, the mediums, are going to be stopping by later. I thought maybe if you were here, they might come to some sort of conclusion as to why you are having such difficulty." Clara said.

"Aside from all that's happened and last Friday's home-run hitter, I'd really like to meet them. I'm thinking the same as you, Clara, I'd like something other than text book answers or explanations offered by comparison to other case studies. I honestly don't have a handle on this paranormal stuff," I replied.

"I know what you mean. There doesn't seem to be a definitive answer to anything involving this house. There have been so many different forms of psychic phenomena here, it boggles the mind," Clara said.

"Sure does. Well, give me a call tomorrow if you can, I'd like to know what impressions they get. It will be interesting to see if they arrive at the same conclusion as Alex," I said.

"All right, talk to you later, Paul."

I've read so much regarding the paranormal and there were many stories that, by comparison, sounded very much alike. As in all professions, you have experts, while others are just getting started and are sort of the eyes, ears, nose and throat psychics of the paranormal world and don't particularly specialize in one area. If I really wanted to be a gifted psychic, I believe I would be most interested in astral projection, being able to separate the astral body, or spirit, from the physical body. This is something Father Al has discussed a couple of times with us. He said he's attempted and achieved it several times. Once, he said he feared he wasn't able to get back but somehow the conversation was interrupted and we hadn't gotten a complete explanation as to what he meant. Before my involvement with the Dandy house, I hadn't really given the word, "psychic" a second thought. It's like the word, "sick," and when uttered, leaves one with vague understanding. If someone says, "He's sick," you ask, in what way? It's the same with psychic, as there are many ways one can be psychic. It's a broad subject and covers many areas involving the mind and spirit. A medium can communicate with the dead, a clairvoyant sees things beyond normal human vision, whereas someone who is able to move inanimate object with his mind is a telekinetic. All are psychic and, now when someone tells me of someone who's psychic, I want to know in what regard. And of course, there are those that are gifted in many areas of the psychic field. So then, I suppose these "heat waves" I had been experiencing fall in the category of telepathy. Something I've learned over the years, at least for me, the gift doesn't function when I want it to. It seems, for me, the only times I would experience something of this nature was when someone else was gifted as well. Occasionally, I might try extra hard and pick up something from someone but the results are foggy, muddled. Something else I've discovered, the more stressed or tired I am, the more active or pronounced the "feeling" was. Odd though, I picked up such strong impressions from Bernie that first time I shook his hand, standing at the hospital nursery. And, the insight of his baby's having pneumonia was almost like reviewing a movie clip in my mind's eye. He said he wasn't psychic in the least yet the feelings I'd gotten from him were stronger than any I have ever experienced. I honestly believe that something, some energy from the house, spilled over into me causing the "goosies" I've had as far back as I can remember, to become more heightened. If Alex had been correct about the impressions he'd gotten from the house, why is it he *hadn't* emphasized more clearly to everyone, the ominous strength of Mary's room? I vividly remember his words when he said, "You should be frightened of him," regarding the feelings I got from her room. "The energy is as powerful as the demon himself," he had said. Was Alex truly capable of suppressing his energy from others so that they're not aware of it unless he wanted them to be? Maybe it's part of the id that he is able to control at will. There was so much I wanted to understand, and nearly as much that I wanted to forget.

CHAPTER XXXV

I didn't talk to Clara again until the following Sunday. That Thursday, Paul and Peggy returned to the house and brought a psychometric. I found it humorous when she was telling me. I had forgotten what a psychometric was and, for some reason, I had heard her say, "mechanic." I suppose with all the car accidents that had been happening, that was what I had on my mind. The psychometric, I didn't get her name, asked to see the lamp that had been thrown in Mike's room. When she held it, she told Clara the lamp had been thrown as a message to the family. Here we are again, being given clues, but nothing clearly explaining what it actually meant. She envisioned two people in the living room while holding the lamp, a male and a female. The female's attire was that of a long dress and she felt that the man had been blind, because what she had actually seen was that the man's eyes were dark or covered in some way, giving her the impression that he was blind. Paul had been outside walking the grounds and, when he came in he said there was a woman standing under the pine tree at the beginning of the drive, calling Anna. He said he wasn't certain if she had been calling someone named Anna or was telling him her name. In one of our thousand discussions at the house, Clara had mentioned that people visiting had thought they heard voices saying the name, Anna. Paul and Peggy had been up that Thursday and I was puzzled that Clara hadn't called me to tell me they were returning. I assume she might be thinking that, after my bout with the house three weeks earlier, I wasn't in a hurry to go back regardless of what I might have told her. She said Phil was anxious to find a job closer to home but he hadn't been able to find anything that paid as well as his position with the Ford Motor Company. The whole family was at their wits end worrying about their finances, the problems with the house. They needed peace of mind, hoping to wake from their shared nightmare caused by this paranormal quagmire. Many tried to help, most failed, but there was Alex. He was determined to find someone to sponsor a trip to the house. One still had hope.

It was almost the end of March, 1974. At first, I was at the house nearly every night, usually with Tim, and a few times I had taken the drive alone. Debbie was reluctant to visit often and I think her main reason was that she had feared fear itself. She told me that her apprehension would get the best of her and that it really had been difficult going up after our first visit. I knew she had been frightened that night when the car died under the tree but I hadn't really understood how badly it affected her. Everyone has their own tolerances to a given situation, and hers, she explained, were very low. Labor Day had been her breaking point, she had told me but she agreed to visit again after Joe was born because she was very proud in showing off her firstborn. When we went to bed that night, she told me she had been reluctant to go but agreed because she had strong faith in Father and made herself believe that nothing could penetrate his sacred blessing.

There was an energy not just within the confines of the house as there were numerous reports of apparitions seen all around the property as well as beyond its boundaries. The house had become a topic that seemed to ease its way into conversations for miles around. Fuel was added to the fire with the various articles published in the Buffalo Evening News in March and April of '74. One particular article quoted a letter written by a reader who stated Father Al had been a sucker for falling for the Dandys' story. The writer quoted Barnum's axiom, "A sucker is born every minute," and implied Father had certainly been conned by the family's allegations of spooks. Bob C. responded in defense of psychics who dealt with the mind, about which little is understood and went on to say that psychics are rarely recognized for their achievements. Bob expressed his delight in meeting a man like Father Al and said he believes his contributions in one day would be more than Barnum could have offered in a lifetime. Take that, reader! It seems there were more negative letters and statements reaching the desk of Bob C. than there were positive, unlike those that Bob S. received at the Olean Times Herald when the story first appeared locally. Freedom of speech, freedom of the press, and free to make an ass of oneself. Non believers went on and on, harassing, calling names, and degrading those that did. But those with an open mind, or truly believed, didn't go out of their way to shame or dishonor those that didn't. As with the gentleman who purchased the mirrors from me, he basically degraded me by association alone. My comments to him, which I admit were rather crass, weren't said because he insulted the Dandys by calling them names. My crude reference of what he could do with the mirrors was given because he insulted me personally; I believe he had it coming. Everyone is entitled to his opinion but there is no cause to demean someone for something that they didn't believed was true.

I received a very interesting and exciting phone call from Clara on April Fool's Day. She had received a call from a student attending New York University. She informed Clara that they, a film crew and Alex, would like to come to the house and cover the story. It was to be sponsored by the University and the Institute for Psychical Research. My hope was Alex would be rested when visiting this time. I had the feeling he would need it. As I understood it, they were going to be on location for at least an entire day. When he visited last winter, the house zapped Alex of his energy and he hadn't been at the house much over an hour. I can't imagine what he would be up against or what steps he would take to prepare and protect his psyche from whatever type of paranormal assault he might be faced with. There would be no doubt that Father Al would assist in any way that he could but I still couldn't fathom how Alex could withstand something so powerful as the entity in Mary's room. He was such a gifted psychic, able to open any and all channels of communication with the dead. Alex was not only precognitive but post-cognitive as well, allowing his psyche to pick up the indirect communications of the spirit world's energy; something the average undeveloped psyche of most cannot. The anticipation of his and the film crew's arrival was nerve-racking. His shocking descriptions of the impressions he'd received on his first visit were so true to what the family and many others had experienced over the past year that they were beyond belief. At the time, we all believed it to be far beyond that of coincidence. During Alex's first visit, he had made a statement that psychics sometimes misinterpret first impressions and, besides wanting to help the family with their problems, this was another reason he was returning to the house with a full crew. For myself, I had been fearful of going to the house as often as I had. I truly believed I was experiencing what I now call "heat waves," more often and with such magnitude was because I challenged and threatened the entity in Mary's room. I proved to myself, as well as to everyone else, that, with my weak and untrained psyche and my earlier arrogant attitude, I was no match for something I couldn't begin to understand. But when the time came, with Alex and Father Al on the front lines, I would stay back with everyone else and hope to learn what was keeping the family in such mental torment.

It was April the 11th, 1974. Clara called to tell me that Beth Ann wouldn't be returning when Alex and the crew arrived at the house some time tomorrow. I hadn't even known she was gone! She had gone to Chicago a few days earlier to spend Easter with Tim. Tim called today to ask is she may stay a little longer. He didn't want her to be present when Alex came this time. He was protecting her from what we hoped was going to be the last confrontation with the house's energy. I say energy, because Clara finally convinced me, after many discussions, that energy was a more suitable way to define what had been causing mayhem at the house. Ghosts, spirits or apparitions, whatever you prefer to call them, were certainly seen by scores of people during the Dandys' residency but I had to agree with Clara, that the energy was the source of everything which occurred. None of the "heat wave" bouts I experienced included an apparition. It was pure psychic energy. Clara and Phil agreed to let Beth Ann stay in Chicago. It was probably best as her mental state had deteriorated when she suffered with her personality difficulties. The house had affected nearly everyone who had visited in one way or another. Even campers from nearby retreats had made comments of seeing strangely dressed people walking their properties. The figures seen were usually women. The infamous blonde boy, or someone fitting his description, had been seen over a dozen times at various locations over the past year. Was Clara correct—was there a spiritualist convention taking place encompassing the entire area? Hopefully, when Mr. Tanous arrives, we might get answers.

Debbie, Joe and I went to visit my mom this morning, the 12th of April. Debbie played hooky because Joe had a doctor's appointment and, rather than take an hour off work to go with me when I took him in, she planned to take the entire day off. She felt bad because Fridays were pretty hectic. She figured they could do without her one day.

"So, today is the day the psychic comes back to the house, huh?" Mom asked.

"Yeah, but I don't know what time. That's why I gave Clara your number, in case they arrive early," I said.

"Are you going with them?" Mom asked Debbie.

"Nope. I was thinking about it but I'm not involved with the house. I'm interested in knowing what they finally figure out but Paul can tell me when it's all over. I don't have to be psychic to know that whatever is happening isn't going to stop and they're probably going to end up moving out. That's my gut feeling anyhow," Debbie replied.

"Beth Ann is staying with Tim in Chicago; I'll bet they get married," I said.

"Tim's a nice kid." Mom said.

"He's a jerk, if you ask me. It seems everyone has had car trouble at the house, including us, but when something goes wrong with his car, it's somebody's fault." Debbie replied.

"What do you mean?" Mom asked.

"Oh, his brakes went out and he thinks…."

"What time is Joe's appointment?" I interrupted.

"12:30, but I want to get the prescriptions filled before we go to the doctor," Debbie said.

"Well, we could get them filled on our way to get the blankets you want to buy," I said, making a face at Debbie. "That way I can run the prescriptions in, go get the blankets, and I can pick them up on the way back."

"Either way, whatever is easier," Debbie said, making a face of her own.

"You got any mints, mom?" I asked.

"No, but there's some gum on the kitchen table," she replied.

"Oops, he spit up, Debbie—here, here's a tissue," mom said.

I had hoped my interruption had taken my mother's mind off what Debbie had started to say about Tim's brakes. Or for that matter, the fact that she had said we had car trouble at the house. I hadn't told my mom too much about the house and I certainly didn't utter a word about the "heat waves" I'd been experiencing. I know I broke a promise to her by continuing to go to the house after the first experience but I had been determined to get the answers about the house that I needed. Those answers became less important to me after Labor Day. Regardless of the outcome after Alex arrived, I knew I wasn't going to visit the Dandys as much as I had these past eight months. My questions may never be answered to my satisfaction. Alex may learn more during his investigation but that didn't necessarily mean he would know the reasons the house, or energy, had its interest in my psyche; if that indeed were the case.

Debbie and my mom, who was carrying a half naked baby, announced they were going to give Joe a bath in the kitchen sink. "In the sink?!" I exclaimed.

"Yes, I can't bend over the tub and he made a boom-boom. We want him cleaned up when he goes to see the doctor don't we?" Mom said.

"Yeah, but in the sink? Yuck! And what the hell is a boom-boom?" I asked.

"He's got diarrhea and he needs a bath," Debbie said.

"Well, he'll probably fit in a bowl, give him a bath in one of those," I said.

"He's not that tiny anymore!" Debbie exclaimed, smacking me.

"I can hear dad now, 'Jesus, Mary and Joseph.' He'd go nuts if he saw you giving him a bath in the sink," I said.

"He would do no such thing," mom said.

"I'm gonna call Clara and see if she's heard anything. You better hurry, it's almost noon," I said.

I went into the living room and called Clara. No one from the group coming in had called yet. She said Phil has decided to stay home from work tonight. He has an odd feeling when they start their investigation, they're going to stir up a "hornet's nest," as he put it.

"I thought they were only coming in today, but were going to start fresh in the morning with the investigation?" I asked.

"I'm not entirely sure how or when they're going to conduct this investigation. I believe they're going to be here all weekend. Their plans aren't clear to me but I got the impression they were going to be here for more than one day," Clara said.

"We're going to be taking Joe to the doctor shortly, so if you call, call our house. We probably won't be home for at least a couple of hours. Debbie wants to buy some new blankets today too," I said.

"Doctor, is he okay?" Clara asked.

"Yeah, it's just a checkup. Right now he's bobbing in the kitchen sink," I said laughing.

"I heard that!" Debbie shouted from the kitchen.

"Kitchen sink?!" Clara asked.

"Yup, Debbie and my mom are giving him a bath," I said.

"Oh, you had me confused there for a minute. All right, we'll call if we hear anything," Clara said.

Mom and Debbie came back into the living room and placed Joe on the couch so he could be dressed. The excessive body hair was going away, I don't know where, but he didn't have as much. He was still very tiny but it was obvious his lungs were developing just fine because when he was hungry, you could have heard him a block away!

"There you are, all clean and ready to go see the big bad doctor," mom said in baby talk.

"Don't tell him that, he'll think the doctor will be mean," I said.

"Does he looked worried?" Debbie asked.

No, he didn't look worried but I worry when he has to go to the doctor because I always think they're going to give him a shot and that hurts the little bugger!

"Okay, get his bag and stuff, we're ready to go," Debbie said, walking toward the front door.

"Drive careful," mom said.

"I will," I said, giving her a hug and a kiss on the cheek.

"Thanks, mom," Debbie said. "We'll see you later. I'll call and let you know how he's doing."

We drove to Dr. Cash's office and informed the nurse we were there. I told Debbie I had to go to the bathroom and walked down the hall. I think I ate too much chili the night before because my stomach was acting up. As I walked into the bathroom I noticed there were happy little drawings hanging on the wall, the kind you'd expect to find in a child's bathroom. I guess when you're a pediatrician, the atmosphere of your office extends to the restroom as well. Before sitting down, I inspected the roll to be sure there was paper on it. Too many times, you find yourself in a public restroom taking care of business only to find out too late that there isn't any paper. I was in luck, there was a full roll on the spool. I had been thinking about the film crew that was coming with Alex and wondered what type of equipment they would be bringing. I would imagine, since the Institute for Psychical Research was involved, they would bring state of the art, high technological equipment. I wasn't entirely sure if they used special equipment when filming paranormal cases. One of the stories I'd read talked about infrared because it displays the changes in temperature. I was sure whatever was needed, they would bring.

As I was washing my hands, it hit me—hard, and with a bright flash behind my eyes. My eyes felt like they did hours after looking at the bright light of an arc welder. The last two times I had one of my heat waves, the onset was as hard as this one but it lasted briefly, with a residual feeling lasting a few minutes longer. This one wasn't letting up, it must have been nearly a full minute, and I really began thinking it was a medical issue, not psychic. However, when it did begin to subside, I turned toward the door because I sensed someone had walked in. No one had, I was alone, but the feeling of someone present was heavy in the air. I splashed water on my face, and there was a knock on the door.

"You okay, in there?" Debbie asked.

"Yeah, be right out," I said shakily. She could hear the distress in my voice, because she asked again.

"Yup, it was the chili we had last night—be right there."

She didn't say anything else but, looking in the mirror, I knew she would see something was wrong. My face looked as if I had stayed in the sun too long—my cheeks and forehead were a rosy red. I knew I couldn't stay in here, she would be coming in to check on me. I splashed more water on my face but the redness remained. Either I could bury my face in a magazine or simply tell her what had happened. I was sure it would be the latter.

"Are you sick?" She asked after sitting down next to her.

"Yeah, sick of the house making a house *call!*" I said.

"You're kidding me! Another episode like the one you had when we took Joe up?" She asked.

"Yeah, but it doesn't mean it was the house. Remember, I had one at the hospital before talking to Bernie. It doesn't necessarily have to be connected with the house. It could be connected with someone here. I don't know; it's annoying. This one lasted longer than any of them. Maybe I oughta have Dr. Cash examine my head," I said.

"Someone ought to. You feeling better now?" She asked.

"Yeah, still have the feeling of...... I guess as if someone were here," I said.

"Well, you better let them know there's no room in the car for them. We are NOT taking anything home with us," Debbie exclaimed.

"Debbie, you wanna follow me?" A nurse said from the desk.

We walked back to a waiting room, where the nurse took Joe's temperature, blood pressure, and listened to his heart. I imagined his heart beat like that of a hummingbird but, when I asked the nurse, she assured me that it beat faster than adults, but not that fast. A few minutes later, Dr. Cash came in, cheerful as always, making a comment of my uneven sun burn.

"And how's our little one today?" He asked.

Why is it doctors and nurses too for that matter, take possession of your children when you bring them in for a check up?

"He had a case of diarrhea this morning, but other than that, he's been fine," Debbie said.

Dr. Cash checked him over thoroughly and gave him a clean bill of health. He said his lungs sounded good and he was gaining weight at the rate he had hoped. I didn't particularly like the word 'good' regarding the condition of his lungs but I accepted it.

"Would you like some cream for that sunburn, Paul?" Dr. Cash asked.

"No, it'll pass," I replied.

With that, he chuckled and we left the examining room and returned to the desk. The nurse wrote down our next appointment, which Dr. Cash suggested and handed me the little appointment card to remind us. We drove to the drugstore and I took the prescriptions in. The pharmacist, Larry, told me they would be ready in about half an hour. I saw the manager, Ted, and he wanted to show me a trick before I left. He stuck a dime to his forehead, tapped the back of his head with his hand, and the dime fell into his shirt pocket.

"Hey, that's pretty neat, Ted. I said, but thought he really needed to find something to do with his spare time.

"Yeah, I worked on it all night last night to perfect it, unh, unh," Ted said.

"I'll have to try it and show it to George," I said. "Okay, gotta run, wife's waiting in the car with our new baby!"

What a character he was. George and I both worked at CVS pharmacy when we were seniors in high school and, I'll tell you, there were a lot of characters working there. George and I would mimic every one of them. Pops was my favorite. He didn't actually work there, he was the driver who made deliveries to the store. He sounded like Elmer Fudd, "no weturns, no weturns," he would tell us when we had items to return that weren't ordered and were delivered by mistake on the previous delivery.

I returned to the car and drove to the store where Debbie wanted to purchase the blankets. I told her since Joe was sleeping, there was no reason to wake him, and said we'd wait for her. Besides, I knew her all too well. If we had all gone in, we would be her captives and would have been in the store for at least 2 hours! She was only in the store for about 15 minutes but I could see she was carrying more than blankets. I got out, opened the trunk and helped her place her packages inside.

"These are heavy blankets," I said.

"Well, they had a sale on toasters and other appliances," she replied.

"Ah, I see. If there were midget goats with a sale sign in front of them, would you purchase one, or possibly more?" I asked.

The only response I received was her glowing smile and my usual slap. She said she was hungry, so we stopped at KFC, picked up something for lunch, and spent the rest of the day at home.

After lunch, I called Clara, but there was still no word from Alex. I was going to tell her about the incident at the Doctor's office but decided it wasn't necessary. The redness on my face had all but disappeared. I still didn't know what to make of it unless it had something to do with my blood pressure—that would be something to worry about. Joe was put down for a nap while Debbie and I cleaned the apartment, then settled in to watch a little afternoon television. I told her to turn it to whatever she wanted to watch, it didn't matter to me. And of course, she chose a soap opera. Tell me something, how does an actor playing a particular character leave a soap, only to have someone new take that same character's place? That was just plain dumb! Once, I heard my mom and an aunt talking about a soap they both watched where this had taken place. My aunt had made the statement, "I liked the old so-and-so better than the new so-and-so." That's my whole point, one so-and-so can't be replaced by a new so-and-so! Why not just kill the character off and be done with it? Just plain dumb!

The phone rang, and startled Debbie and me both out of a sleep.

"It's for you," she said sleepily.

"Hello?" I answered.

"Hello, Paul. Have you heard from Clara?"

It was Father Al.

"I spoke to her a while ago but she hadn't heard anything from Alex yet," I replied.

"Oh, good, good. I tried to call when I got in but there was no answer. Maybe they're outside or are away from the phone. I'll try calling a little later," Father replied.

"Okay, Father. She said she would call me if she heard anything—I can call you if she does," I said.

"No, she told me the same, but I was out much of the day and I had no messages from her, so I assume Alex isn't in yet. I should be in the rest of the evening is she tries to call," Father said.

"I'm surprised you got through. I thought the house wasn't going to let us talk after all the calls we've tried to place to one another," I said.

"Ah, yes. I don't know if that was the house or maybe technical problems the phone company may have been having but it was very coincidental since I was able to place other calls that went through without a hitch," Father Al said.

"Same here, Father. Okay, I'm sure we'll be seeing each other soon."

"Yes, well take care and I'll be talking to you soon," he replied.

"All right, Father, bye."

Maybe the crew had arrived and she was outside meeting them all. I have to admit, the anticipation of Alex returning was, for me, like that of a child waiting for Christmas morning. Waiting to rush down the stairs and tackle the multi-colored wrappings concealing all the neat things you asked for. Of course, there was one package that had the shape of something you expected but it was far to light and didn't make any noise when it was shaken. But your name was on the label and it was from Santa—it just had to be something you asked for, but you'd forgotten. Then, when you opened it you discover a new Sunday's best sweater. Your mom frowned as you tossed it aside; pressing forward, looking for the next cool gadget that was written on your list. Along with everyone else, I was hoping Alex wasn't bringing a sweater. I hoped he was *leaving* something that would bring peace to the house, its occupants and visitors from here and beyond.

"No word, huh?" Debbie asked.

"Nope, it's nearly 5, I'm surprised they're not here yet," I replied.

"Are they flying into Buffalo or driving out?" Debbie asked.

"I never asked. I would imagine they would be driving if they're bringing a lot of equipment—yeah, of course, if they were flying in, they'd have told Clara what time their flight arrived," I said.

"That makes sense. You wanna start something for dinner, while I get Joe up; it's his dinner time too," Deb asked.

"Well, since you're gonna feed him, why——"

"Not one more word or you'll get yours!" Debbie interrupted, walking into the bedroom.

"Yeah, promises, promises," I said, opening the fridge door. "Hey, let's have breakfast," I yelled, my head in refrigerator. "I can whip up——"

"You don't have to holler, I'm right here," Debbie replied, standing behind me.

"Oh, I can whip up a nice omelet, with sausages and——"

"How about making egg salad?" She interrupted again. "That's quick and easy, and there won't be any dishes to do," she added.

"Oh…. all right, that sounds good."

Lifting the eggs from their individual slots in the refrigerator door, I noticed the only beverage we had was about half a gallon of milk. Turning around, I saw there was only half a loaf of bread.

"While the eggs are on, I'm gonna run to the store, is there anything you want?" I asked.

"Do we have any pickles?" She asked.

Opening the fridge door, I said, "No."

"Get some pickles and some chips too," Debbie replied.

"What do you want to drink?" I asked.

"Pepsi or Root Beer is fine. Oh, and get some Rice Crispies and marshmallow—not marshmallows in a bag, marshmallow in a jar; I want to make Rice Crispie Treats," she replied.

"I know! Anything else, your majesty?"

"Yeah, better get some bread and milk too," She told me, looking in the fridge.

"That's what I was originally going for," I said, standing at the door.

"Hang on a sec." She said, looking in the cupboard. Chuckling, she added, "Um, would you get a box of Rice Crispies too, please?"

"Ahhh, see, I'm not the only one who's forgetful," I said.

"Get outta here, the water is beginning to boil. Wait!" She said, again looking in the fridge. "You better get some mayonnaise too, sorry."

"Oh, boy. Is that it, are you sure now?" I asked.

"Bye, see you soon! Bet you can't beat the eggs before they're done," she said, with that sunshine smile.

I drove to State and 13th streets, Richardson's Market, for the groceries. I pulled a cart loose and methodically pulled each item on my mental list from the shelves. I've never been one to dawdle in a grocery store. I knew where everything was, threw it in the cart and headed right to the checkout. I had a craving for M&M's and did a quick u-turn, almost running into another shopper's cart. I turned down the candy isle, grabbed a bag of what I had a yen for and back to the checkout.

"Whoa, you in a hurry, Paul?" Max, one of the owners of the store asked.

"Yeah, I'm trying to beat the eggs," I replied.

"Beat the *eggs*?" He asked quizzically.

"I've got some eggs boiling on the stove and I wanna get home before they're done. Debbie said I couldn't beat them," I explained.

"Oh okay, well, let's get you checked out quick." Max said, opening the other checkout for me. "Anything in it for ya?" He asked as I started emptying the cart.

"Well… you know. Hey, that's an idea! Thanks, Max!" I exclaimed.

I was checked out in a hurry, grabbed both bags and sprinted out the door. Debbie usually let the eggs boil about 12 minutes, and I knew I was pushing at least 10 now. There was no traffic to wait for, good! I got the green light at Seventh Street, turned down Sixth and was in the house within 2 and a

445

half minutes of leaving the store. I pulled the bags from the front seat, flew up the steps and opened the door. Debbie was rushing from the couch to the kitchen. "I beat 'em! Don't you dare touch that pan, I won!" I exclaimed.

"No you did not. They're done, I was just about to take them off the stove!" Debbie argued.

"Yeah, but if I hadn't come in, you'd still be sitting on the couch, I won!" I repeated.

"Okay, it was a tie, is that fair?" She asked.

"No, I won, plain and simple—you owe me," I exclaimed victoriously.

"Oh, and what is it I owe you?" She said, with an impish grin, walking toward me.

"Well, we uh, we can....um... stop it, I'm gonna drop the milk!" I said, as she was getting frisky.

"Gimme one of these bags, you can take your eggs off the stove and I'll put things away," she said, taking a bag off my hands.

"M and Mmmmm's? I told you I was gonna make Rice Crispie treats," she whined.

"I know, they're for later. Maybe you can add them to the Rice Crispie Treats," I said.

"Yuck! If you don't want them, I won't make 'em," she whined again.

"Yes, I want them. I'll have the M&M's later; tomorrow—maybe I'll never eat them!"

She smacked me, causing me to drop the egg I had been peeling. We both looked at it on the floor, and burst into laughter. It wasn't really funny, but we were enjoying ourselves in the kitchen together. Joe was in his bassinet, looking up at a mobile of different shapes and colored objects. I guess you had to be a baby to enjoy looking at them, I sure as hell didn't see anything interesting about it. I mixed up the egg salad, while Debbie poured us something to drink, and placed some chips on each of our plates.

"We gonna eat in the living room?" I asked.

"Of course, I wanna watch Hogan's Heroes," she replied.

"Oh, God. Would you like a pickle?" I asked.

"Later I will," she said, with that impish grin again.

The phone rang—"Would you get that, please?" I asked, while spreading the egg salad.

"There's no one there, just static. I heard someone for a second, but I couldn't make out what they were saying," Debbie said.

"They'll call back if it was important. Maybe it was Father Al, we seem to have a problem every time we call each other," I said. "You want two sandwiches, don't you?" I asked.

"Yeah, please. I didn't eat much lunch, I don't think the chicken was thoroughly cooked," Debbie said.

Hogan's Heroes theme was playing, we timed it perfectly; for Debbie anyhow. I didn't mind Hogan's Heroes; my favorite was All in the Family but that was on Sunday night. I was sure that the networks would be playing re-runs of that show during the day soon too.

Again, the phone rang—I answered it this time.

"Hello?" I said.

I could hear someone, but couldn't understand them. "Hello!" I said with force.

Now it sounded like two different people were saying something, but again, the voices sounded like they were far from the receiver. I listened for a few more seconds and I was hanging up there came a loud wailing sound. I brought the receiver close to my ear again and the sound began to subside, but I could hear a voice—it was a female's voice.

"Who is it hon?" Debbie asked.

"Shhhhh!" I said, holding one hand up.

"She's......" (a male voice) *"Must help......can't ....please......"* (female's voice)

Was the house contacting me? I had the receiver pushed so tight to my ear it was beginning to hurt. I didn't dare tell Debbie what I was hearing—I hung up and said -

"I do think the phone company is having trouble. We used to have a similar problem at my parents' house because they had a party line with the Hamiltons who lived next door to them. Every so often we'd hear someone say, 'get off there, click,'" I said, walking back into the living room.

"We should have them check it out. I'll try to remember to call from work tomorrow," Debbie said.

We finished our simple dinner, listening to Shultz say, "I hear nothing, Nothing!"

"Yeah, me too, Shultzy, I hear nothing too," I said to the television, then glancing to the phone.

"You gonna help me make the treats?" Debbie asked, handing me her plate.

"Sure, we can get sticky and gooey together," I said walking to the kitchen with our empty plates.

"I have to feed Joe once more before I start, then I'll put him down," she said.

"Okay, I'll clean up while you're doing that," I replied. "I can't believe they haven't gotten to the house yet. They must have left New York City late."

"How long does it take to drive here?" Debbie asked.

"I think about 6 or 7 hours. It's almost 7:30, so they must not have left 'til this afternoon," I responded.

I picked up the phone to call the time and temperature to check if the phone was working properly. "The time is: 7:27— the temperature is: 61 degrees." The electronic voice said.

"Who'd you call?" Debbie asked.

"I called the time to see if the phone was working, and it is," I said.

I cleaned up the kitchen, did the few dishes and put them away while Debbie fed Joe. I was going to call Father Al to see if it had been him attempting to call, but didn't. The more I thought about having problems only when I tried reaching him the more I was convinced it wasn't a problem with the phone company. I just couldn't believe something supernatural kept us from making contact but there was one brief passage in one of the books where someone had a similar problem. Of course, Phil's statement came to mind, 'There has to be some reasonable explanation,' and in this case, the hope was still there.

"Man, he fell asleep quick," Debbie said, coming out of the bedroom.

"He's gotta get a lot of rest to get those bones growing," I said.

"Well, would you like to help me make the treats or would you rather *have* a treat?" She taunted.

448

I chose the latter.

It was about 8:45 when we started mixing the marshmallow and Rice Crispies for our second treat of the evening. I insisted she throw a few M&M's into the mix, but she wouldn't hear of it. She spread the mixture onto a cookie sheet and told me I had to let it cool for a few minutes, as she walked into the bathroom. Of course, I was digging at it when she returned and was promptly scolded.

"You're like a little kid, you just can't wait," she said.

"Well, they're probably better while they're still warm," I insisted.

"You're eating M&M's with them?" She exclaimed.

"Yeah, they taste good together, try some of both and see if I'm wrong," I said, shaking a few M&Ms into her hand.

"Mmmm, they are good!" She exclaimed.

"See, I told ya you should have put some in the mix, but no, you wouldn't listen to me!" I scolded.

I had challenged her, and we now had I fight on our hands. She took one square of treat and started smearing it in my face, which prompted me to retaliate. Before long, we were covered in Rice Crispies and marshmallow.

"No, don't throw my M&M's at me!" I yelled.

"Well, you wanted them, now you're gonna get them," she said, tossing nearly a handful of colorful chocolate drops at me.

I reached for another treat and forced it down her blouse and she retaliated with a handful of the same, smashed on top of my head.

"Oh, now you're gonna get it!" I said, grabbing the jar of marshmallow.

"You wouldn't dare!" She dared.

I stuck my hand, what I could fit of it, into the jar and pulled out a handful of soft, gooey marshmallow. I had her cornered, I faked for her hair, pulled her blouse up, and smeared the white, sticky goop all over her belly. She opened the refrigerator door and I yelled, "No, nothing cold!" I yelled, laughing hysterically because her blouse was stuck in folds against her stomach.

She reached in and brought out the remaining mashed potatoes from KFC.

"I'm sorry, would you like gravy on these?" She asked, opening the fridge door again.

"No, I'm sorry, no I don't like gravy, please!" I pleaded.

She didn't hesitate, and with such grace, reached in, pulled the top off the gravy container, and with a snap of the wrist, covered me. Neither of us put gravy on our potatoes at lunchtime, so I had been dressed in a full pint, of the Colonel's own brown, cold, now coagulated, gravy.

"God, this is cold! I started walking slowly toward her, when she asked, "Would you like coleslaw with your meal?"

I got to her before she had a chance to open the refrigerator door again and pinned her against the wall, when she started laughing hysterically, because somehow, I had an M&M stuck inside the upper half of my left ear.

"You think that's funny, huh? Well, here's some—BAM!

This time it was even more different from the "heat wave" at the doctor's office. I heard someone, and wasn't sure if it was Debbie talking to me, or if it had come from elsewhere. *"You need to help me!"* I heard it twice and the second time, I had been looking directly at Debbie, but her lips didn't move. Somehow, I knew the feeling I was having wasn't caused or connected to the voice but, rather, it was outside the source of the energy that had assaulted me. The voice was separate, a demanding plea for help to get away from the energy.

"Honey, come on, try to stand up," I heard Debbie saying to me. "Here, sit in the chair," she said, pulling a chair out from under the table.

"Alex is coming, he's almost at the house. They're pulling up to a building with bright lights, lots of bright lights," I said.

"Hey, snap too, come on, honey?" She said, trying to get me to focus on her.

"Yeah, okay. Someone is calling Clara, they're almost here, just a little ways from the house—but they won't find their way, they'll get lost," I said dreamily.

"How do you know?" She asked.

"What?" I asked, lightheaded.

"You okay now? How do you know they're here, or almost here?" She asked again.

"I saw them, babe, I saw them pull up someplace to call—to call Clara. I saw Alex, he was looking out his window of the car and he was looking at me—it looked like he was looking at me! I know I was looking at him and I saw his eyes, they were looking directly at me. HOW? Goddamn this shit!" I exclaimed.

Debbie put her hand to my ear as I lowered my head, she pulled her hand back, and held it out in front of me, and teasingly said, "Do you want this M&M?"

I took it from her and popped it in my mouth. I gazed into her eyes while chewing it, and she couldn't hold it in. She began to laugh, staring at me while I, dripping in gravy, sat eating an M&M she had plucked from my ear. I began picking individual Rice Crispies from her face and held them in my hand. With no warning or feeling of them coming, the tears, like rushing water over floodgates began to stream down my cheeks. She leaned down, hugged me and said very softly, "I love you and this will all end soon, it will, Paul—it has to."

Debbie held me for a good 15 minutes as I let out the hatred, sadness and all the other emotions that have been building in me these past few months. I just couldn't figure out what was happening to me and the more these feelings came, the more I began to believe I had something mentally wrong with me. Maybe it wasn't the house causing all of this. She said all of this would be ending soon, well—soon wasn't soon enough—the phone rang.

"It's Clara, hon." Debbie told me.

"Tell her I'll call her back shortly, I've got to clean this mess up and take a shower!" I said.

As I walked into the kitchen, I heard Debbie saying something about "gravy," and that I really needed to take a shower. Even though we were very aggressive with throwing the food, the only thing that made a mess was the gravy and I had most of it on me. I cleaned up as best I could but every time I bent down to wipe the floor, another plop of gravy fell to a spot I had already cleaned. I decided to get the rest after I showered. Before undressing, I returned to the living room to get some newspapers to keep the food I was wearing from getting all over the bathroom floor. I turned the shower on, stripped down, lay my clothes on the newspapers, then proceeded to wash the leftovers down the drain. A moment later, Debbie followed suit and joined me.

"Don't get too close, we'll get stuck together; this marshmallow is melting again from the heat of the water!" I said.

"Well, I always said I was stuck on you, hadn't I?" She asked. "Clara called to say she was going to meet the crew and have them follow her to the house. Now, would you please tell me how in the hell you could see them? How could you possibly know someone was in the process of calling Clara and, even more, that she was going to lead he way to the house!?" She added, marshmallow dripping from the end of her nose.

"Deb, if I knew that, if I knew any of this crap that was happening with me, I'd be the new, modern age Norstradamus. I'm very frightened from all of this and would really like it to stop. Are they all going to stay at the house?" I asked.

"No, they're going up to learn the way there then they're going to be staying at the motel," she explained.

"Did she want me to call her back?" I asked.

"She didn't say but I'm sure she'd be glad if you did. Are you okay, now?" She asked, washing the gravy off the back of my neck.

"Yeah, I guess I am, I just don't want this happening anymore. It's not good and it's dangerous. I pray to God Alex can rid the house, me, the air in general from all of this shit," I said.

"Me, too. We were having fun, 'til you got; um… what are you doing?" She asked.

"Having more fun!" I replied……….

Deb and I finished cleaning up random pieces of Rice Crispie treats and residual gravy from the floor and walls before I called Clara.

"Did you ever take the wrench you borrowed back to your dad?" Debbie asked.

"What made you think of that now?" I asked.

"I don't know, it just popped into my head."

"Yeah, don't you remember, the day we stopped before going to the doctor's," I said.

"I didn't pay attention, I just thought I'd ask 'cause I was thinking about it," she replied.

I called Clara after removing one of the Colonel's sides from my side, as well as from the rest of my body parts. She told me that Alex and the crew were there but would be leaving soon to get some sleep. They would be returning bright and early if I wanted to come up.

"What time are they coming back in the morning?" I asked Clara.

"They're not exact on the time but sometime after 8:00 she said. They're still unloading everything, then they'll be heading to the motel," she informed me.

"Okay, another jolt tonight, for no reason, and I got something this time, a voice, 'You need to help me,' it demanded. I don't think the voice and the 'heat wave' were the same, I think the voice was on the tail end. Clara, will Alex rid me of this personal haunt?" I asked.

"I'll tell Alex. Father will be here tomorrow too, so we should have quite the show of power!" Clara stated.

"Yeah, let's hope we have more power on our side than the opposing team has," I replied.

"Okay, I'll see you in the morning, Paul—and get some sleep! Oh, Is Debbie coming with you?"

"You going up in the morning with me?" Debbie said nothing but shook her head to the negative.

"No, Clara, she's not coming," I said.

"Okay, see you soon then."

We hung up and Debbie and I went to bed. We both checked on Joe and he was fast asleep, making baby sounds. Looking down, I could see that he was indeed growing rapidly. I didn't understand all of this new paranormal activity, well new since Labor Day really, but I was glad it couldn't affect this little one—at least, I didn't think it could. I was confident after Father Al's blessing, all was going to be okay and it had been for a short while. As I said before, Father was the psychic police of the good guys but that didn't necessarily mean the bad guys were going to run and hide. The real bad guys in the natural world didn't run and hide either, they assaulted the police, showing no fear whatsoever. I hoped that wasn't going to be the case tomorrow morning. The good wasn't always triumphant over the bad in society, what would make me believe it will when dealing with the paranormal? One can only hope; and pray. Debbie set the clock for 7 a.m., and I turned out the lights. We held each other for a long time before finding comfort in sleep.

CHAPTER XXXVI

I woke several times during the night. The anticipation was overwhelming and it took me an additional hour after letting go of my wife to get to sleep. I woke fifteen minutes before the alarm told me it was time to go to battle. I got out of bed quietly, walked around to Debbie's side and turned the alarm off. I thought of waking her but I decided to wait until I was ready to leave. She was up at 3 a.m. feeding Joe and she didn't need me waking her again so soon. I went to the kitchen; I felt hungry but decided to just have a glass of milk. I was very apprehensive. I knew I wasn't going to be instrumental in any way in today's proceedings but I was certainly involved and, in some cases, more than others who had been affected by the house. Something, someone, was reaching out to me psychically, for help, yet I didn't have the slightest idea as to how I could help anyone. Hopefully, Alex and Father would be the "All-Star" team, and take care of any and all requests. If anything, Alex would rid the house and everyone involved of any energy seeking out a connection of communication with the living. It was nearly 7:30 and I wanted to get going. I went to the bedroom, bent and gave Joe a kiss and gently woke Debbie to tell her I was going.

Sitting up, she said, "Please be careful. If anything begins to happen, go to Father Al or Alex, whichever is closer. Don't play the big shot, let the pros take care of whatever there is. I want you to come home in one piece, even your screwed up brain," she said.

"I love you. I'm sorry I became involved to the extent I have but I feel I have to get the answers to a lot of questions. If I really have some sort of psychic gift, I want to know how to use it properly not have it use *me* improperly. I'll be careful, I just want the bad stuff to go away. I'll call you as soon as I get there, unless you are going back to sleep," I said.

"No, call me regardless whether I do or don't. I have to be sure you got there okay. Call, okay?" She asked, rubbing my cheek.

"I will, as soon as I walk in the door. I love you, Debbie. I really wish you were going to be there but I totally understand why you can't," I said.

"I love you too, and I wish I could too, but I can't; I just can't."

We hugged and kissed each other and I bent to give Joe another kiss.

"See you soon," I said.

"I love you, please—please be careful!" She said again.

"You too, don't worry," I said as I left the bedroom.

I walked into the living room, took a handful of M&M's and stuck them in my shirt pocket. "Screw this," I said, turned around, and picked up the bag that was lying on the end table. "I had chips to offer Phil as a peace offering maybe I can use M&M's as a bribe with the energy," I said to myself as I walked out the door.

Driving up State Street, I was watching the cars coming at me, wondering where they were going. Some were undoubtedly going to church, some shopping, but I bet none were going to a haunted house to watch an exorcist at work. The entire trip to Hinsdale, I worried about getting hit again and drove at least 10 mph under the speed limit, my foot poised to hit the brake at a moment's notice. I sure as hell didn't want to end up in a ditch or cause harm to someone else. I was passing Crosby's and the thought crossed my mind, to make a quick u-turn and head back home. And what purpose would that serve? I asked myself. Turning on Flannigan Road, I thought something was coming, then realized I was feeling extremely scared; petrified. Father had said that when a demonic energy is challenged, and especially by a man of the cloth, it becomes much stronger, wiser and will tempt and taunt you with everything it can. Were they really going to be dealing with something that was truly demonic? Alex did say the energy in Mary's room could very well have been the demon, at least as strong as a demon. Either he was assuming this because it may have been something he found to be more powerful than anything he's felt in all his years of experience dealing with the paranormal, or he's actually gone head to head with a demon in the past. Father has performed exorcisms and I'm sure he would know when a demon reared its ugly head.

I was approaching the bottom of Wagner Hill Road, readying myself for whatever lie ahead. A simple turn of the wheel onto McMahon Road was like holding back a pissed off bull. I felt as if I was making one of the biggest mistakes I could have made by not letting things be, but I couldn't do that. I was in too deep. If Alex and Father Al were able to cleanse the house of its unwanted guests and energy, wouldn't it be safe to say that whatever was harassing me would also be beaten? I stopped at the hanging tree as I did the day I stopped before visiting Saint John's Church and took a few minutes to say a silent prayer. Well, I was this far, there was less than half a mile to travel to find out what was going to happen. So be it—I pressed on.

There was no place to park out back, so I maneuvered a three point and backed into the cutout. I noticed a young man walking past the front of the house and toward the back. I walked to the back door and let myself in. Inside, the house was swarming with people, setting up photography equipment and lighting. When I came to the living room doorway, Laura and Mary shouted, "Paul's here!" and ran up to me.

"There are a lot of people here, Paul!" Mary exclaimed.

"I see that," I said, as Mary walked towards Beth Ann's room. "How are you Laura?" I asked.

"I'm fine. Everything in the house is going to be quieter soon, I think," she said.

Strange, with the connection Laura and I had, I think if 5 different people, including her, voiced their predictions about the outcome of the house, I would choose what she would surmise over all of them. She had great insight in the house but I felt she had no idea how to deal with it. If she had, I believe the house would have had a challenge on its hands. Somewhere within this little person's psyche was a great deal of energy.

"I hope you're right, Laura, everyone needs a rest from all of this," I replied.

"Good morning, Paul, how are you?" Clara said.

"Excited, nervous, ah—scared... what else? Worried?"

457

"Worried? That's one of the words bouncing around in my head," Clara said.

"Worried whether or not the one who shoots flaming arrows into my brain is going to have his ah—butt kicked!" I said.

From behind me a voice said, "Well, you can be rest assured, there will be many changes in the psychic energy of the house. After Father Alphonsus and I dispel the spirits and residual energies that are proportionate with the vortex of the house, there will be peace once again," Alex said, walking into the kitchen. "How are you, Paul?" He said offering his hand.

"I'm hesitant, Alex, and nervous," I said, accepting his hand and offering a thought.

"You've been assaulted again today, the struggle of powers in the house and mixed signals can surely confuse one's psyche," he said, still gripping my hand. "Evil has more tricks, not more power, and when both attempt to communicate to one host, the evil will prevail, only because more trickery is used. The pure of heart are subdued by the evil's energy because it uses its strength to hold its prey, as it were, at bay. Do you understand?" He asked, still holding a firm grip on my hand.

"A blow to the head has a greater sensation than a light tap to the head, but both are felt," I said.

"Exactly," He said letting loose of my hand, "And that's why when you were summoned, called to listen, be warned actually, it was exactly that, a blow to the head," Alex said.

"Alex, how do you know what I was feeling—what I was trying to tell you without telling you?" I asked.

"The psyche is like a covering over the conscious mind. If one has the ability to lift the covering using his own energy he can see what's beneath. In your case, you have a message still within your psyche sent by two entities from this house. There is another, deeper yet, that involves a child and a parent with a learning disability, not retarded by any means, but... something to do with language. It has nothing to do with the house but the signals remain because you embrace them," he explained, quite disturbingly.

"If I wasn't standing here listening to you, knowing for a fact that I was physically here, I would think this was a dream. Because, there is no way on earth you could know what you just told me unless I told you or told someone else who passed it on to you and that's not the case. So, do you know what happened at my house last night?" I asked, not really wanting an answer.

"May I just say that there are many starving children in the world; waste not, want not," he said, with the slyest grin.

"Clara, you said something to him about our crazy antics last night!!" I insisted.

"No, no, no. First, that's the last thing on my mind today, and second, of all people, why would I tell Alex?"

"I don't know, casual talk, an ice breaker—something to talk about, trying to relieve stress, I don't know. You didn't talk about what Debbie told you while any of them were here?" I asked.

"No, I promise, I said nothing," she said. I believed her.

"I wanna be like you, Alex. I want to know what other people are thinking, or feeling," I said.

"Paul, you don't. Have you ever found yourself turning a radio or television off because you were weary of listening to it? Or maybe you were trying to tune in a station that you really wanted to listen to and, no matter how hard you attempted to tweak the dial, the signal wasn't strong enough to pick it up clearly. I can't remember the last time I lay down to sleep and was able to turn the receiving knob to the off position. You say you want to be like someone else. Before wishing for such a perverse notion, be yourself. You're young, you have many years to look forward to." Turning and facing the stairs, he continued, "And, the battle you've been faced with here is one where your white flag should be raised, but understand me…. not for you to surrender and be taken captive. But you must relinquish the emission of your psyche's energy. You mustn't allow your energy to nourish the soul of another, especially to such a negative power. Believing you posses enough positive psychic strength, feeling you can move ahead, challenging the power of this house would be a grave mistake. You are gifted, but let me say with all due respect, your psyche is undeveloped, an infant against brute force and it will lose miserably." Alex paused, his deep set eyes, peering, perhaps into the soul of the house. He went on—"At least three times you've threatened, or mocked the energies of the house, am I correct? You need not answer, it is obvious, as it is clear to me, the forces are pleased you're present. Apologies to such energy only states that you are weak, that you've given in. That, in turn, opens the channel fully to absorb or to steal any energy that's available which, at this time, is yours, Clara's and Laura's. Beth Ann was being used for energy and, in her weakened state, her mind began to be attacked. She's absent now. You must attempt to put a cap on your energy—do not allow it to be tapped. Clara, do you have a feeling of something about to occur in the house?" He asked.

"Sometimes. Other times, I feel the heavy atmosphere of the house pressing down on me but surprisingly, nothing happens," Clara replied.

"The energy is moving around, searching for enough added resources to zap. Possibly, when you have the foreboding feeling, you unconsciously have your channel closed. The energy can't draw from you so it moves on. Now in Paul's case, it appears his channel is open all the time and is ready, excuse the pun, to rock and roll. He...."

"Funny you should say that, he plays in a rock and roll band," Clara interrupted, with nervous laughter.

"That's why I said, 'excuse the pun.' He is always wanting to fight, to take the war to the house's soul, and Paul, you *cannot* do that! I wouldn't attempt to display such arrogance and I have been involved in paranormal activity most of my life. I will be arrogant enough to say that you could never be a match for my psychic energy. I say that out of total respect; for your protection, as well as for anyone around you."

Alex turned to Clara, and with a very kind, and smiling face said, "Laura is very gifted. She has a strong gift of second sight but her conscious mind subdues this for many reasons. I believe she and Paul understand one another and it's a psychic connection, a mutual wavelength of psychic channels. Actually, she possesses more energy than Paul. It's like a volcano—the power is there but dormant. When it's time to

460

erupt, it will generate enough energy to light a city. She holds everything inside. She doesn't want to upset mom. Nor does she want to, thank God, know how to open up to what's on the other side of the wall of her bedroom."

"Dr. Tanous, we're finishing up." A young man said from the living room.

"Ah, it's time to begin," Alex said.

We heard a vehicle pull up outside. Mike came in to say Father Al had arrived.

"Perfect timing," Alex said, walking out the back door.

"What do you think?" I asked Clara.

"Am I alone when I say, his uncanny ability to see everything is scary?" Clara replied.

"Heck no. I couldn't imagine being in his presence for any length of time. He can probably see things in your mind that you've forgotten?" I said. "Shit, may I call Debbie? I told her I would as soon as I arrived and she's probably worried!" I asked.

"Of course, you know where the phone is," Clara said.

I called Debbie and, luckily she had fallen back to sleep. She didn't notice how long I'd been gone. I explained that everything was all right and that Father Al had just arrived. I didn't know what was going to happen, as they just finished setting up all the equipment. I told her I'd call her back as soon as I knew something. We said goodbye and I turned to greet Father Al.

"Hey there, Father," I said.

"Hello, how are you this fine morning?" He replied, offering me a brief hug.

"Good, Father. You feel tense; are you feeling okay?" I asked.

"Ah, yes... apprehension comes to all of us, but I arrived with an open mind and a heart full of prayer and faith. We're all going to get through this with our heads held high," he replied.

When Father Alphonsus Trabold walked into a room, it was like seeing the rays of the sun breaking through a bleak, dark overcast of ominous clouds. He was a joy to listen to and it was always an honor to be in his company. Setting aside all the paranormal and psychic jargon, he was a man of great worth and given the highest respect by all those that knew him. If I didn't know better, I would believe he had written the book on Franciscan values. I've never heard him utter a negative word, and even if there were something that required a negative response, he somehow always answered with a positive retort. If the Lord above had any notion of changing the minimum requirements of becoming a saint, Father Al could pass with flying colors—I miss him so.

"Could everyone come into the living room, please." The only female of the investigative group, Jan, asked. "We need everyone, except those from the crew, to leave the property for several hours."

"Yes, I prefer that no one is here that might cause a false reading. The house has to be clear of anyone who is residing here, or has been involved with the family. Not only do I want no false impressions, I prefer that no one involved offer any energies, positive or negative," Alex stated.

We all began walking back to the kitchen when Clara asked, "What are you going to do?"

"I guess I can run back home until later. Do we know what time to come back?" I asked.

"Alex, how long would you like us to be away from the house?" Clara asked.

"Let's say, return about 5 p.m.. Have you some place you can go for that long?" Alex asked.

"I'm sure we'll manage," she laughed. "We'll see you about 5 then. Good luck!" Clara said.

The kids all went to their rooms to get whatever they were going to need for the period away from the house. Clara said I was welcome to stay with them but I decided I should go home in case Debbie needed anything. Clara and I waited in the kitchen while Mary, Laura and Mike went to their rooms.

"We're ready, mom," Mary said.

"You coming back later, Paul?" Laura asked.

"Yes, I'll be back, you gonna be okay 'til you can come back?" I asked.

With a smile, Laura said, "Yeah, but that's when everything will get really weird, when we come back."

"What do you mean, Laura?" Clara asked.

"I don't know. That's just what I think," Laura said.

I looked at Laura after she answered her mom and she offered her usual smile.

"You two, I just don't know!" Clara exclaimed, walking toward the back door.

When we all were in the back yard, I gazed up at Mary's window. It wasn't 10 seconds later, when Clara said, "Now don't you be sending flaming arrows of your own up there, leave it alone!"

"Not a chance of that happening, Clara. I was just trying to feel if the fear they constantly sent out was turned inward, worrying about their own psyches. And even though I said that, I have no idea what the hell it meant!" I said.

"They should have a camera directed at the pond. There's always been a lot of activity around there," Mike said.

"Mom, am I gonna be able to sleep in my room tonight?" Mary asked.

"We'll see, honey. Even if they say the room is clear, you might not feel comfortable sleeping in there. We'll just have to wait and see what happens, and how you feel, lying in your own bed," Clara replied.

I walked to my car as Clara and the kids backed out. We waved, as I looked one more time to the tree line and at the front of the house. It still looked the same, a typical country home, surrounded by what were once hay fields. It was a bright sunny day and the view to the distant mountains was clear, the trees in full foliage. I wished more than anything that I could have stayed and watched Alex and Father Al in their attempts to cleanse the house. Was there going to be resistance, were the energy forces not going to give in to their requests of leaving? Hopefully, we would all get to watch the video after it was filmed. We were told the film crew worked with NYU's educational television station and this undertaking was for Jan's doctoral thesis as well as support for Dr. Tanous.

I was having difficulty driving away but I noticed Clara was still on McMahon Road, at the turn, probably waiting to see if I'd had car trouble or something. I got in the car, turned the key and drove down McMahon Road. No one was going to experience vehicle problems today, I was sure all of the energy was concentrated on the house and the two men who were going to attempt to discharge it. As I got nearer to Clara's car, she began driving further down the road and came to a stop directly under the hanging tree. I pulled up behind her, parked, exited my car and walked up to Clara's window.

"What do you think, is it going to be our house again when we get back?" Clara asked.

"Your guess is as good as mine; I hope so. Ya know, when you think about it, we just left a battle field. Problem is, I believe there are good guys within the enemy's lines as well. Not everything affecting the house is negative. I think the only negative force is upstairs. Did you feel anything in the house, especially when you were talking to Alex?" I asked.

"I did, but I was sure it was mostly Alex's energy. I believe the house is waiting, trying to hold ground. Why?" I replied.

"It was like watching a movie, the atmosphere of it all. When you're at a scene where you know an attack is inevitable and you're waiting for that moment when the first strike takes place," Clara replied.

"Yeah well, the first strike took place when we were still there. I believe when Father Al arrived the house's energy pulled back and dug in." Bending down, and looking in the back seat, I asked, "Laura, anything?"

"I think there's gonna be a big war and we're gonna win," she responded, smiling.

"I think you're right, sweetie," I reached in the passenger window and she took my hand. Alex read this young lady correctly, she had strong psychic energy. I hoped she didn't have her own "heat waves" to contend with. Chances were, being at the house all the time, she might have but she never complained, rarely bothering her mom, even when the energy of the house made her extremely restless.

"Well, I guess I'll drive back to Olean and come back around 5 or so," I said to Clara.

"All right, drive careful; we'll see you soon," she replied.

I walked back to my car and wondered why I hadn't asked them to follow me home. I'm sure Debbie wouldn't have minded but then again, she might once we all got to talking. I was sure the main topic would have been that of the house, offering each other our opinions of what we thought might have been happening. She really wasn't interested in hearing any more about it until this was over and done with. I stopped at Crosby's on the way home, called Debbie to tell her what was going on and asked if she would like something. I told her I'd be home shortly, hung up, and went to the counter to order. She wanted a banana split, extra nuts, and I gave the girl my choice as well. She added so many nuts that you'd hardly notice there was anything else in the container. I paid for the treats and left, again driving cautiously on the way home. I tried to contact Alex while driving back to Olean and I felt really dumb because I knew I didn't have that kind of skill. At least not enough to know how to use it or know if he heard me.

When I got to the four corners in Olean, State and Union Streets, I saw a minor fender bender. It looked as though a woman had turned left before it was safe to proceed and a car heading east clipped the rear of her car. There didn't appear to be any injuries other than the woman's pride. I turned the corner and drove the six short blocks home, pulled up to the curb, and took our desserts into the house. Debbie met me at the door.

Chapter XXXVII

"It's too bad you drove all the way up there only to have to leave right away," she said, taking the carrier from me.

"Naw, see, I was supposed to go so I could stop and get some fun stuff to eat," I replied, walking into the house.

"Oh my God!" Debbie exclaimed. "No chocolate milkshake?" She asked.

"Nope, I thought a change of pace might be nice, I got a hot fudge sundae," I replied.

"Have you eaten anything yet today?" She asked.

"No, I had a glass of milk before leaving but this is brain food. Good tasting too!" I said.

"Let me make you something and you can have this for dessert. It'll only...."

"No, sit down and eat your split or it'll melt. I'll have my sundae. I can eat later before going back to the house," I said.

"Okay, but I still have some pancake batter left over with real maple syrup, and ..."

"Here," I said, taking her banana split. "I'll put our desserts in the freezer so we can eat them together, *after* I have some pancakes!"

"I thought you'd see it my way for a change," she said.

Debbie whipped up 5 hearty pancakes and smothered them in Franklinville's world renowned pure maple syrup, which would send any sensitive tooth running to the dentist! After eating, I declined my sundae when Debbie asked me if I wanted it. If I'd eaten it after all that syrup, I would have been bouncing off the walls.

"Do we have time to go to the store before you return to the house?" Debbie asked, eating her nut smothered banana split.

"Oh, sure. I won't leave 'til about 4:30. Where did you want to go?" I asked.

"I want to pick up a couple of new outfits for Joe and get some groceries," she replied.

"Yeah, that'll be fun. I can push you both in the cart!"

"Oh, no, not the way you drive shopping carts!" She exclaimed.

"I don't drive them, I push them," I corrected.

"Yeah, well you shouldn't even push them. Remember the last time at K-Mart and don't forget the time before that when you ran over the poor old lady's foot!" She reminded me.

"Well, I had the right-of-way; I was in the main aisle. She should have stopped and looked both ways before entering the flow of carts!" I said.

"You're awful, but you'll do—for now. I'll get Joe ready; you wanna get his bag ready for me?" She asked.

"Yup, if I can get up, the pancakes are weighing me down."

We left the house about 12:15 that afternoon. I tried not to let the house enter my thoughts but that was like not paying attention to a hockey game when you were the goalie. We spent all of the next three hours looking at baby items, purchasing a few, including a stroller and loading a cart nearly full of groceries from Richardson's. Not once did we play bumper carts. We arrived home about 3:50 and unloaded the car. The phone rang as I was pulling the stroller from its carton. Debbie answered it and I asked if it was Clara, she shook her head no. I continued making sense of the items we brought into the house, trying to find room for it all. I knew something was up with the conversation Debbie was having, because every time I got near her, she stopped talking in mid sentence. "Who is that?" I asked, and she only waved a dismissing hand at me, giving no answer to my question. I finished putting the groceries away, barely finding room for everything, folded the empty bags and placed them in the closet. When Debbie hung up, I asked again who had called.

"No one special," she replied.

"Well, special or not, who was it?" I insisted.

"Someone who called to ask me something," she replied, with a sheepish grin.

"And what did the someone ask you?" I dug further.

"Something that I don't want to tell you about—not yet, anyhow," she replied, giving the indication that she *did* want to tell me.

"I'm breaking you down... you're gonna tell me. come on, let it out," I prodded.

"I can't tell you but I will tomorrow, I promise," she said, smiling bigger.

"Oh no you don't! Tomorrow is my birthday and I do *not* want you planning something silly."

"I'm not planning anything. If you think I'm planning a surprise party, you're wrong," she said.

"I am?" I said, disappointedly.

"Yes, but I'm sure you'll be happy anyhow. I'm not going to share you on your first birthday together with me," Debbie said.

"It's not my first birthday with you, we were together last year," I said.

"Yeah, but not together, together," she said.

"You're impossible to talk to, I'm gonna eat my sundae," I said, walking to the refrigerator.

"We still have half an hour before you have to leave," she said, with her smile that melted my heart. I put the sundae back in the freezer, and—well, you know. At 4:45 I was looking for my right shoe—I guess it was possible to be late for work due to a missing shoe. I found it and was ready to leave, the sundae would have to wait.

"Well, let's try this again. Call me, be careful and drive slow," Debbie said, wrapping her arms around my neck.

"I will to all three demands. You sure you don't want to take Joe to my parents' and come with me?" I asked.

"No, I really would like to. I'll go when the house is simply called a house, not a haunted house or troubled house—just a house," she replied.

"Okay, I'll call as soon as I get there. I love you, Debbie, thanks for being so understanding," I said, pulling her close to me.

"You're welcome but I *don't* understand, I just accept that this is important to you," she said.

We kissed and I picked Joe up from his crib very carefully so I wouldn't wake him, gave him a kiss, handed him to Debbie to put back in his crib and walked to the front door.

"Love you, insane man," Debbie said from the bedroom door.

"Love you too. I'll see you soon and you better be ready for what I really want for my birthday," I said.

"I think your mom's baking you a cake," she said, smugly.

"I'll cake ya!" I exclaimed.

"I hope so! Go, it's almost 5," she said.

Driving past the building where I managed the Fountain of Youth was tough today. Tomorrow would have been the one year anniversary of my being in business. Now the windows, were boarded up and the sign removed. I wondered what had happened to it. The wrecking crew would soon come to tear the building down. It was a depressing thought. Such a waste, Olean Savings and Loan; such a shame. Business owners within a community should adopt a policy, with the help of the city, to create a contingency fund where businesses could receive financial aid, of course paying a nominal interest fee, by taking out a loan from such a fund. Far too many building have succumbed to years of neglect and the elements. Instead of making the necessary corrections and repairs, the owners allowed them to become a pile of rubble. The building that once stood becomes a short lived memory of the grand part of the community it once was. Olean was founded in 1810 and there weren't a hell of a lot of Olean's old landmarks left standing.

I was approaching the turn onto Congress and I was excited as one could be. Alex, Father and the crew, have been at the house since early morning, hopefully giving it a piece of what-for. When I turned onto McMahon, I had to fight to keep from becoming the next up-and-coming Indy 500 rookie, as it took everything I had to keep from speeding up the dirt road. Rounding the corner, I saw Mary and Laura exiting the car. Had we returned at the same time? The rear of Clara's car was semi blocking the cutout at the end of the road, so I pulled up as far as I could and parked next to her car. I got out and walked to the back yard. I was alone. I stood directly in the center of the yard, staring at Mary's window. Of course, as I stated before, I had no idea how to feel something at will, but I tried; nothing but my own thoughts came to me. I walked in the back door and saw Clara and Father talking near Mike's bedroom door, Mike was seated at the kitchen table. I saw no sign of Laura or Mary and assumed they were upstairs. Clara nodded to me and Father gave a smiling, "hi, Paul" as I entered. I proceeded to the living room doorway after tapping an "hello" to Mike on his back. Alex, listless, his face drawn and looking much more haggard than he had after his first short tour of the house last year, was seated on the hassock He was staring straight ahead toward the front of the house; re-energizing I thought. I excused myself into the room and called Debbie as I'd promised. We talked briefly, as I explained that the crew was still moving equipment and Alex hadn't spoken to us yet. She asked that I call when I leave and we hung up.

I returned to the kitchen and sat with Mike. Father and Clara were still in conversation. Mary and Laura *were* upstairs. They came down moments after I sat down at the table.

"I went in my room, Paul, and it was warm like the rest of the house!" Mary exclaimed.

I looked at Laura and she smiled. "That's good, Mary. Maybe you'll have your own room again!" I replied. "Did you leave the door open so the room could get some fresh air?" I asked.

"Yeah, and I opened my drapes and window too! I'm going to sleep in there tonight and I won't be afraid of anything!" She said.

"I'm glad, it'll be nice to sleep in your own bed again," I replied.

"Come on, Laura, let's go back upstairs!" Mary exclaimed, grabbing onto her sister's arm.

"I'm gonna join the Navy," Mike suddenly said, rather gloomily.

"What brought this on?" I asked.

"Well, mom and dad aren't going to be able to afford to send me to college and I can further my education in the armed services so why not. I'd been thinking about it lately. I'm not going to find many worthwhile opportunities around this area after graduation and I sure as hell don't want to work in a factory!" He explained.

"I'm sorry you can't attend college, Mike. You're right though, you can get the education of your choice in the service. Have you decided on what you want to do?" I asked.

"There are a few things I'm interested in but I think I want to go into nuclear energy," he explained.

"God, don't say energy," I said, kidding. "When you gonna enlist?" I asked.

"As soon as I graduate. Jump in with both feet, right away."

"Alex would like everyone to gather together so he can explain the afternoon's events to you." A young man from the crew said.

Mike and I walked into the living room after Father Al, as Clara called up to the girls. It was very crowded and I took my usual seat on the floor near Mike. The crew members stood on the far side of the living room. Jan was seated in Phil's chair. Clara and Mary sat on the couch. Laura sat beside Mike and me. Alex moved the hassock to the center of the room and sat down. His color was very pallid. He looked physically ill and very withdrawn. I didn't want to be like him after all. He looked at Laura and smiled before speaking.

"There is a lot of energy in the house and I believe some of the force behind it has me somewhat confused. The impressions I received on my first visit are not what I saw today. Mary's room was by far the worse." He gazed at Clara and Mary sitting on the couch and offered a smile. "But I feel confident that the entity there will move on and find peace. I believe a young girl died in that room long ago. It was very difficult to convince her to leave but I believe she finally agreed. She had been in the room for a very long time before passing away yet I wasn't able to discover how she died. There seemed to be a another energy source blocking what I was receiving from her and it appeared as it were a sort of mask surrounding this energy. What's more, I received a burn on my body earlier today when entering the room. I'm sure it's similar to the burns that members of the family received." He looked to Father Al, who then added, "Psychics aren't infallible, and the impressions they receive can easily be misinterpreted. Sometimes, their interpretations come across in several

471

segments, oftentimes, many energy forces crossing paths with one another. Alex and I spoke after leaving Mary's room and I found him to be unresponsive at first but he came around quickly. During his confrontation, he was so weakened by the energy that he had to be helped before he could stand up. I've observed this with other psychics and can only say Alex's encounter with the energy in the upstairs bedroom was one of great proportions."

"I could feel the air around me change, standing just outside the door of the room, prior to Father Alphonsus helping Alex step out of it, and I'm about as psychic as a rock." One of the crew members added.

Looking at Alex, I thought that he had been in the toughest psychical battle of his life and that possibly, there was more here than his gift would allow him to deal with. I wanted to say something but I was too embarrassed to speak up. It wasn't gone, Alex only temporarily tied a psychic rope around the soul of the house. I'm not saying that I knew anything more than he did but I had felt something numerous times, something extremely powerful. As Father Al stated, "the longer you are subjected to an energy, the more sensitive you become to it."

I leaned toward Mike and quietly said, "It's still here, it's only keeping away from his strength."

I would wait and, hopefully get a chance to talk to Alex privately before he left. I didn't want to talk in front of everyone especially what I had to say would be, "Alex, you may be wrong."

Father Al continued, "We know very little about the mind and how it functions. Dealing with psychic phenomena is even a greater puzzle with the experts. We've all experienced little nuances and some believe that is the psyche tuning in for a brief moment, acutely aware of the energies around us. The next time you get the feeling that a phone is about to ring and it does, remember that feeling. When you have a sudden notion that someone is going to say what you were thinking, remember that as well, because it's possibly your psyche tuning in on the same wavelength as the energy occurrence that is about to happen." Father Al looked to Alex.

"Jan, you have something to add?" Alex asked.

"Tomorrow, we'll be filming interviews for any who wants to be involved. I'd like to gather as much as possible from anyone who has had any type of experience in or around the house."

Clara tapped me on the shoulder and Jan smiled. "I want to thank everyone for their cooperation, and for my outstanding crew that's been invaluable during this session today." Jan concluded.

"Does anyone have anything they'd like to add or ask?" Alex asked, then turned toward me and pierced my heart with his deep, soul searching eyes. "Paul?"

"No, I'm fine, I don't have anything to say, I don't think—no, thank you." Well. that was embarrassing, I fell over my words as they tried to come out. After the talk, some moved to the kitchen, while many of us stayed in the living room.

.We all introduced ourselves to each other and talked about the afternoon. Two of the guys said they were "whipped" after following Alex around the house.

"It was amazing, every time Alex was in a sort of conflict, you could feel the atmosphere of the room he was in change. I mean, I've never really experienced anything supernatural except what Father had said. You know, little quirks that seem to happen when you were thinking about it, but, man, we all felt what was going on with Alex." One member said.

"That could have been—- what do they call it? Mass hysteria." Another member said.

"I wasn't hysterical, were you, Jan?" The one who had spoke first said.

"No, I wasn't. Jan said.

"Come on, you know what I mean! Mass something, where a bunch of people all see or hear the same thing." The obvious, skeptic of the crew said.

Jan asked me, "Are you one of the two who took the picture of the supposed ghost?"

"Yeah, I'm guilty, that was me," I admitted.

"Tell me about it, if you don't mind," Jan said.

"Yeah, what happened?" I believe Steve said.

"Well, my friend and I saw someone and thought he was a trespasser. We ended up chasing him through the fields to the

473

end of the property where he stopped and basically threw himself against a tree. I assumed he was giving up, that we had run the breath out of him. I thought if I could get a picture of him, he could be identified later and be prosecuted for trespassing. Phil was tired of everyone coming to the house. Anyhow, I snapped the picture and Tim sort of lunged for the guy. I don't know why, I wasn't about to play police and escort him back to the house at 3 in the morning," I explained.

"So what happened?" Jan asked, hurrying me along, looking toward the kitchen.

"He disappeared...... At first we thought he went around the tree, and that was impossible because we would have seen him move. We were basically right next to him—he just simply disappeared. Tim and I looked at each other and were back at the house faster than any car could have driven us across the field," I said.

"When did you actually look at the picture? And by the way, I've seen it and it scared," whispering now, "the hell out of me!"

"As soon as we got to the front of the house, I pulled it out of the camera. Oh yeah, it scared the hell out of us too, but not as bad as when he disappeared into thin air."

"Jan, do you still have a copy of the list for the settings of the cameras?" One of the members asked.

"Yeah, let me get them for you," She replied rising from her seat.

I excused myself to use the restroom. When I walked into the kitchen, I brushed against Alex's arm. He was fully charged, I could feel that. I felt that he was sending me a signal; sending something. I turned around and looked at him and he was already staring at me. There was something on his mind and I felt he wanted me to open up during the discussion in the living room. Coming back from the bathroom, I had the strangest feeling. I nodded to Alex, he walked over to where I stood and I asked, "You upset about something I said?"

"No, something you *didn't* say, but I understand and I thank you for not pushing the issue," Alex replied. "There's an abundance of energy here, very strong; but it will leave in time."

"What are you two up to?" Clara asked from the other end of the table.

"Oh, Paul asked if he could get a copy of the picture that he and his friend took. I told him I would get it copied when I got back to New York," Alex said.

"Thanks again, Alex," I said, returning to the living room, wondering why he had told Clara an untruth.

I didn't understand what Alex meant by, "not pushing the issue." He seemed to be prodding me for something to say when we all in the living room listening to his and Father's explanations. Mike and I, Steve, two other crew members, and the one who had talked about mass hysteria were in the living room. Mike and I discussed some of the evening's experiences we had when Tim and I would visit. Steve listened intently while the skeptical member, I don't remember his name, rolled his eyes during our explanations. I asked why he had participated if he doubted these things had happened.

"I was chosen to be part of the crew, that doesn't mean I have to believe everything I'm told." He replied, defensively. "I'm here for the credits, not the notoriety," he added.

"What are you guys talking about?" Jan asked, walking into the living room.

"Bill's just offering his opinion about the stories we were told," Steve said.

"That's my theory, they're all stories," the skeptic said.

"Bill, there's no need to be insulting," Jan snapped.

"I'm not attempting to insult anyone, I only offered my opinion, that's all," Bill said.

Laura, Mary and Father Al came into the living room and I expected our current conversation to cease. Instead, Jan asked another question. "On the way up, Alex mentioned that voices were heard in and around the house. Was anything distinct, could you make out what had been said?" She asked, directing her question toward Mike and me.

"Mike?" I said, suggesting he could go first.

"I heard a voice a few times. The only word I remember hearing clear enough was the word, 'help,' but I didn't understand the rest. It was something like, 'you need to help, or, 'need you to help,' something along those lines. At first, I thought it was someone outside. People were always coming up hoping to see something but when Tim and Paul told me they heard a female voice outside the car they were sitting in later that evening, I dismissed the idea that it was people walking around," Mike explained.

"So, Paul, you and your friend heard a voice that same night? Had Mike told you about it before you explained to him that you had heard it too?" Jan asked.

"No, I had called Clara to tell her we, Tim and I were coming up. It was Tim's first visit and, like everyone else, he was curious. When we heard the voice, it scared the hell out of both of us. We were sitting in the car, parked in the back yard and there was no way anyone could be outside the car, at least from where the voice was heard, not without us seeing them," I explained.

"You had flashlights? Well, I guess you'd need them. I couldn't believe how completely dark it was when we arrived last night," Jan stated.

"Tim had a mini spotlight!" Mike said. "It was bright enough that you could see all the way to the tree line, at the end of our property."

"Yeah, we had lights and we both shone them in the direction of the voice after I was able to get Tim off my lap!" I said, with a nervous laugh. "As I said, we were so scared, I wanted to walk to Mike's window and let him know we were here but Tim didn't think it was a good idea to go alone. He didn't want to get out of the car and go with me. We compromised, and I drove to Mike's window and tapped on it."

"Drove from where, the back yard?" Bill asked.

"Yeah, and when Mike came to the window, we explained what we had heard. Tim and I both thought there was something in the words about help and Tim said it was more of a demanding tone than just making a statement. The voice was on his side of the car."

"What do you think was said?" Jan asked, sitting forward.

"'I need you to help me,' and it *was* a demanding tone." Thinking of the first time I head it clearly, away from the house, I continued, "And besides demanding, she sounded desperate."

"But, you said you weren't *sure* what was said, how...."

"I've heard it twice since and it was as clear as you talking to me now," I said interrupting.

"You heard it again? Inside or outside the house?" Jan asked.

"At home," I said, rather quietly.

"At home?! The ghost followed you home?" Bill exclaimed, laughing.

"Bill *please!*" Alex said.

"Energy of a spirit has a way of moving, relocating," Father Al said. "If there is a message that they feel needs to be communicated and they feel there is a strong enough receiver, Paul for instance, is available, they will reach out to attempt communication to convey that message," he added.

"Father, what are you saying, that a spirit can travel from one location to another... at will?" Steve asked.

"I'm not sure I agree with the word, 'travel,' but in a sense, yes. Alex has the gift of 'astral projection,' and if I may, I have experienced the same, 'out of body' phenomena as well, although," Father offered his wonderful chuckle before continuing, "I believe Alex has the gift in better control than I. Spirits are energy, pure and simple and energy can be dispersed; can move about. I prefer the term to 'pass through' for movement within the spirit world, thus my dislike of the word, 'travel,' even though I believe the definition is the same," Father explained.

Alex and Clara, who had been talking in the kitchen with others, had entered the living room to join us.

"Well, is this a round table, can anyone join?" Clara asked.

"We've been listening to some fascinating stories about the house. I hope you'll repeat them tomorrow for the filming," Jan said. I nodded my head in affirmation.

"Alex, is it a mixing of energies that confuses the psyche?" I asked.

"It can be. Very likely at times. An example, slowly turn the AM dial on your radio in the evening hours, and randomly stop several times. If you're not tuned in to a strong station, you will be able to hear 3, 4 or more stations all crossing over one another's signals. That's a very close analogy of the energy and communications in the spirit world," Alex explained.

"So, if I think, *feel* two different energies coming at me at the same time, they're crossing over one another's signal but, if one suddenly becomes stronger, the weaker one basically disappears, correct?" I asked.

"Yes, again, you can hear the same results with the radio. If you slowly turn the dial and approach a station that has a much stronger signal or is a station that is *closer* to your location, the weaker signals are quieted; squelched, if you will. They're still there but the station with more power, or that's closer, causes them to be fainter or altogether unheard," he explained.

"That day in the yard," I said, to myself, quietly.

"I'm sorry?" Alex asked.

"Oh, nothing, I was just thinking of another incident that happened the day we brought the picture up to the house," I said.

"Ah, the day you got a verbal spanking, not only from Tim, but I really let you have it after him, didn't I?" Clara said. "You learned your lesson, you never went wandering again. As a matter of fact, you didn't even come to the house for what, over a week?" She added.

"Why, what happened?" Jan asked enthusiastically.

I asked Clara to take the floor on this one. Not only did I not want to answer any more questions, I didn't want to re-experience the feeling I had that afternoon. Just thinking about it, brought it to the surface. Nearly the entire time Clara was explaining that afternoon's incident, Alex was looking at me and, quite frankly, it disturbed me immensely. Why is it, I could connect with Laura, a 13 year old, yet I couldn't with Alex? Can a psychic have a force field around them? Hmm, maybe that's what a person's aura is, a force field. Clara finished her explanation of that day and she explained it perfectly, not leaving out the slightest detail, except when Tim and I walked to the pond after he'd walked out to rescue me. But I believe Tim had kept that between he and I.

"Alex, Father, are you ready to proceed?" Jan asked.

CHAPTER XXXVIII

"I'd like all of the family members to remain in the living room with Father Al and me. Also, Jan, Steve and Marty to operate the equipment, if you would?" Alex suggested that everyone move to their appropriate places. Two of the crew members went into Beth Ann's room and two joined me in the kitchen. I had no doubt that energy was still active because the familiar feelings began and they also began to intensify. It was probably obvious to the house's energy that the time had come to see who was strongest.

"I am going to perform a simple ritual of exorcism, in further hopes of cleansing the house of ill and misguided spirits. We will begin shortly," Father Al announced.

"Hi, I'm Brian and this is Connor," Brian, one of the two crew member said.

"Hi, nice to meet you both," I said.

"Wow, this is really cool. It was fascinating listening to you tell about what's been going on up here. What do you really make of it?" Connor asked.

"Ha, I wish I had a good enough answer, Connor. There is something here that can't be explained easily, and I'm not one that could sum it up properly," I replied.

"Alex was totally wiped out today. I mean, you could really see whatever is in this house was draining him. His entire body was shaking, like he'd been standing in sub-zero temperatures for hours," Brian said.

"Yeah, and that room upstairs, when we opened the door, it was like a freakin' icebox! How the hell do you explain something like that?" Connor asked. "When I looked over the priest's shoulder, I was expecting to see an air conditioner in the room somewhere. It had to be 20 degrees colder in there than the rest of the house," he added.

"Oh much colder, Connor, at least 30 or more," Brian said, giving his opinion of the temperature difference.

I glanced into the living room and waited for Clara to look toward the kitchen. Then, in an attempt to let her know I was getting the heebie jeebies, I pointed to the ceiling. She nodded her head that she understood. I'll offer an analogy as to what the feeling felt like. If you've ever burned the tip of a finger, and rushed to run cold water on the burn, the pain would go away almost instantaneously. But a few seconds after removing your finger from the flow of the water, the pain returns and generally, the pain seemed to intensify. Well, the feeling was very similar but I couldn't understand why the sensation would stop. Father Al was talking to the crew member who went to Beth Ann's bedroom and, after a few moments, he came to the kitchen to talk with us.

"Okay, yes, I only ask that you remain quiet during the rite. If at all possible, please don't speak to one another and be perfectly still. It won't be too awful long, so if you would, have a seat and we'll begin," Father explained, and returned to the living room.

The three of us pulled chairs toward the doorway of the living room and sat as if we were taking seats at a movie theater. We watched Father as he placed a small recorder on the couch. Father, Alex and the family knelt in a circle in the living room, holding hands. Father turned his back to us and said something to Alex but, even though we were no more than 15 feet from the "circle of faith," we couldn't make out what he said.

At the most two minutes passed before Father began the exorcism rite. Connor tapped both me and Brian on the arm and pointed at one of the bird cages in the corner of the room; the birds, singing and chirping only minutes ago, were as silent as the night. Shortly after Father began, the birds started fluttering violently around their cages. Eerie, bone chilling wails and screams could be heard throughout the entire house. This was by far, the most spine tingling experience anyone had ever heard at the house. The origin of the sounds wasn't clear, but it sounded as though the entire house was screaming. The three of us heard several odd noises seemingly coming from the shadows of the stairway as well as the from the bathroom just a few feet from us. I was expecting something dark and evil to enter the kitchen at any time. I prepared for something malevolent to single me out since everyone else was in a circle of protection in the living room. We were especially concerned with the stairway, as the noises seemed to move closer to the bottom of the stairs but thankfully, never made it to the bottom. The intensity of energy was felt by everyone. I found out later when we talked, that Connor was sure he saw someone at the window in the living room, the one facing the pond. Connor, Brian and I were so closely huddled, sitting on our chairs just feet from the group in the living room, we could have been mistaken as a three-headed being. As the wails became progressively more intense, the familiar feeling came over me. I felt sick to my stomach, and my head was light. Brian broke the silence Father had asked for and quietly asked if I was okay; I nodded affirmatively. The sensation was different somehow, it didn't have the explosive heat that accompanied it each and every time. Instead, the feeling was like watching water flow from a faucet slowing to an annoying drip. Looking into the living room and seeing the crew members' faces told us they were hearing the same moans of desperation that we were. You could also see that the entire kneeling circle of people was reeling. One loud thud came from upstairs at the exact same time we saw Alex nearly fall to one side. The birds had stopped thrashing about and the wails were gradually subsiding. If it weren't for Father's quick reflexes, Alex would have certainly hit the floor. We weren't able to hear everything Father was saying but the ceremony was obviously over, as the family members were rising from their knees as best they could. Father and Clara both assisted Alex to Phil's chair; he was totally and completely spent. His eyes were closed, his face was the color of alabaster. The wailing was nearly inaudible, but one of the crew members asked all to please remain still and silent as the recording equipment was continuing to roll. Brian, Connor, and I stood at the living room door; everyone else was still in the living room. We all shared the same expression: total disbelief. Alex was still seated. His eyes remained closed, his shoulders hunched up, arms pulled close to his chest. His posture made it appear as though he were trying to stave off any further assaults on his body, his mind. Father Al, kneeling next to his chair, was talking to Alex; calming him. Oddly, the only sound now, was that of the two small birds in their tiny cell-like cages, once again chirping a song of friendly cheer. The crew member who had been operating the audio recording equipment said it was all right to move about. Brian and Conner joined the rest of the crew in the living room, as I walked to Clara.

"Did you hear it?!" Clara whispered, eyes as big as saucers.

"Heard it, felt it, feared it!" I replied softly.

"Come on," she said, gently pulling me by my arm toward the kitchen.

"Mom, is my room going to be okay, now?" Mary asked as Clara and I were walking into the kitchen.

"Shhhhh! Just a minute, Mary."

"What is God's name were those sounds and could you tell where they were coming from?" She asked excitedly.

"I don't know and I wouldn't want to be near the source of the sounds. They came from everywhere, Clara, and from nowhere. There were other noises coming from upstairs, as well as from the bathroom. Is Alex all right?" I asked.

"If I had to answer that with a gut hunch, I'd have to ask my own question; how in the hell could he be all right?" Clara responded.

We looked into the living room and observed Alex still seated. But he was now talking with Father Al. One of the crew members came to the kitchen and asked for a glass of water. Clara got it for him and he took it to Alex.

"The poor man," Clara said quietly.

"We got it, it came through very clearly! The wailing, the moans—whatever it was we got it!" Jan announced, with glee from the living room.

Clara and I walked back into the living room and Alex rose from his seated position, still needing assistance from Father. His color was still ashen and he looked like someone who had been rescued after a week with no food. Father didn't offer his usual grin which he always did when looking someone in the eye, he only nodded. He too looked haggard and weakened and was visibly shaking.

"Quite the evening, hmm?" He asked.

"Are you all right, Alex?" Clara asked, placing a hand on his arm.

"Yes, thank you. I'll will be much better after a bit of rest," he replied.

Alex began walking toward the crew members with the equipment as Clara started a conversation with Father. Watching Alex, it was very apparent he was extremely zapped, physically, mentally; psychically. What he had previously explained to Clara, who related what he had said to me, was he would take the energy into himself as Father performed the exorcism. This puzzled me because I thought I understood the Roman Ritual to be the power that would dispel all spirits, both good and bad from a location or person. Alex was initially an assistant as a psychic to offer the information from his impressions regarding the cause of the haunting.

There was one fairly loud noise heard directly above the living room which made everyone jump and look to Alex. He looked around the room, then to the ceiling and said. "Residual leftovers, nothing to be concerned with," Alex stated.

I looked at my little friend, Laura, and had but one wish; to see a smile—I got it, and, even though we were to trust the two men who were experts in the field of the paranormal, I felt her smile added, for me anyhow, more relief. Mary who was very insistent about her room, asked again if it would be okay to go up now. Clara looked to Alex and Father Al, who both nodded their approval. Mary was very excited and begged mom to go upstairs with her.

"Okay, but just for a minute, honey; we have guests!" Clara said, chuckling.

Mary, all but pulling her mom's arm from its socket, led her to the kitchen, around the corner, then we could hear them ascending the stairs. Alex walked over to me and simply asked, "So, my friend, do you still want to be like me?"

"What's it like, Alex, what kind of inner strength does it take to deal with such power?" I asked.

"It's debilitating to the mind, heart and soul. It's really a strain on your entire being, Paul. It's not something I would suggest as a profession," he said, and finally offered a bit of laughter.

"It's getting late and we have a lot to accomplish tomorrow. Let's say we all meet here about 1 p.m., does that sound okay with everyone?" Jan asked.

There were no objections and I was ready to go home. Bill apologized to Mike and me for his curt statements earlier. He said he never really believed in psychic phenomena like this and couldn't figure out why the other guys were so distraught during the afternoon. Now he understood the way they'd acted and said he would have an open mind in the future. We all said our goodbyes and Alex walked up to me and said, "Happy birthday, tomorrow."

"Thanks, Alex, I wish I could see yours so I could wish you the same," I said.

"Tomorrow's your birthday?" Clara asked, coming down the stairs, obviously overhearing Alex.

"Yeah, but I've had them before, they're nothing spectacular," I said and everyone within earshot chuckled. I walked back to the living room and called Debbie to tell her I would be leaving the house shortly.

When I returned to the kitchen, Laura was standing next to the stove, looking toward the stairway. She wasn't smiling but that didn't mean anything. She wasn't making eye contact with anyone. When she did look toward me and Father Al as we passed the stairs, she was still sort of stone-faced. I winked at her and she gave me one of those "force the creases of your mouth and create a smile," smiles. Not good, I thought, but tomorrow she may look at things differently. Maybe she was confused with all that had happened tonight. As I walked past her, I reached out and touched her cheek and, this time; I received a smile. But it wasn't as bright as usual.

"It's going to be okay," I said, feeling that she didn't totally agree with me. I didn't believe those words myself but we had to be optimists at this point. In single file, we walked out the back door and wished Clara and the kids a peaceful evening. Twilight had taken over the evening sky and I paused in the back yard. This habit had become ingrained lately as I left the house. I looked toward the pond. Jan and Bill were walking out the door and Jan asked what it was I was looking at.

"Nothing really. Just curious about the, um, the 'fogmen.' I was wondering where they were, *who* they were and where, in the scheme of things, they fit it," I said.

"How often did you see them and was it always around the pond area?" She asked, as Bill moved closer, either from total interest or possible fear, as he kept looking at Mary's window too.

"Twice, but the second time there were two separate columns. Both times, Tim and Mike were out here too. I know what you may be thinking, and we thought the same, but the columns *weren't* part of the overall fog cover. The second time, one drifted up there," I pointing at the ridge, at the back of the yard. "And it was totally clear of the fog that had descended over the yard and pond," I concluded, now gazing at Mary's window.

"Yeah, it was the strangest thing I'd ever seen," Mike said from behind us.

"I was watching you while Alex was talking, Paul. You don't agree with him do you, not totally?" Jan asked.

"It's not my place to agree or disagree and I don't have an opinion on what he felt because everyone feels things differently. Jan, I don't know anything about paranormal or psychic activity, other than what I've read and that's only been since I started coming to the house. And of course, what I've experienced here. Alex said he feels I have a gift but gift is not the word I'd choose for whatever this is," I turned around and continued, while looking at Mary's window again, "I'm just an aver....."

"What would you call it?" Jan interrupted.

"Huh?" I asked, turning to face her.

"If you wouldn't call it a gift, what would you call it?" She clarified.

"A curse," Bill answered for me.

"Yeah. See, you are psychic too, Bill," I said with a chuckle.

"Tell her what you think, Paul; what you told me," Mike suggested.

Jan and Bill stood facing me, waiting for a reply to Mike's comment.

485

"No, I don't believe the exorcism was a success and I can't offer you a specific reason why I say this. A gut feeling …..a hunch, maybe a psychic understanding of the energy I have come to know and hate so much. No, this will only be a temporary blow to the energies surrounding the house. Imagination or apprehension isn't part of my saying this. I believe the energy was weakened but I also believe the *source* of the energy is still very much present," I said.

"Why wouldn't you say this to Alex, especially when he specifically asked you during the talks?" Jan asked.

"Jan, Bill—look at Alex, his reputation, his knowledge of psychic phenomena. How could I, some 21 years old, who only one year ago didn't know psychic from psycho, suggest what he's attempted to accomplish here might very well have been a failure? And please, don't say anything to Alex. Give me some time to think this over and talk with Father Al," I said.

"Of course, I wouldn't think of saying anything. I sort of think I experienced a little nuance of my own when Alex asked you if you had anything to say. There were several discussions throughout the day today, and yours and Laura's names were briefly mentioned. I've studied the paranormal and it's one subject that leaves you with a lot of questions. I'm sure, in time, we'll all understand what's been happening here. We'll say nothing to Alex. And with that, I'll say goodnight; we all need our rest. See you tomorrow, Paul?" Jan asked, placing her hand on my forearm.

"I'll be here—I wouldn't miss it," I replied.

"Goodnight, goodnight, Mike."

We both said goodnight to Bill and Jan. Bill had been really sarcastic when we first starting discussing the evenings that Mike, Tim and I spent outside but he seems to have set his arrogance aside and was at least listening with an open mind. I can't blame someone for not believing in such things; hauntings don't happen to everyone.

"Are you two still out here?" Clara asked, opening the back door.

"Yeah, I'll be in a sec, mom," Mike said.

"All right, Paul, you're welcome to stay if you don't want to drive," Clara told me.

486

"Thanks, Clara, but I already called Debbie and told her I was leaving soon, but thanks, really," I said.

"Not too long, Mike, we're going to have a busy day tomorrow," She said, closing the door.

"I think Jan was getting kinda fresh with you," Mike said.

"Get the hell outta here! What makes you think that?" I asked.

"The way she was talking to you and she kept moving closer as you guys were talking. And that, 'see you tomorrow, Paul?' question wasn't said the way someone asks like they were asking if they'd see them at school or work," Mike explained. "And she's cute too, isn't she?" He added.

"I suppose she is but that doesn't matter. I think you're wrong anyhow. She was being nice and she was interested in what I was saying," I said.

"Okay, whatever you say," he said, chuckling. "I'll see you tomorrow, Paul," he said, mocking the flirtatious way Jan had asked if she would see me.

"Mike?" I questioned.

"Yeah?" He said, turning around.

"Kiss my ass!" I exclaimed, and turned to walk to the car with a smirk on my face.

The sky was trying so desperately to secure the last bit of twilight. It was inevitable, soon the countryside would be blanketed in total darkness and all the creatures of the night would travel their familiar paths in search of their next meal. I pulled the car into the driveway and backed into the cutout to turn around. Once facing down McMahon Road, I remembered the night the three of us, Tim, Mike, and I were standing here when we saw the dim light, swaying back and forth, moving in the direction of the hanging tree. Was that the specter of the girl who died in Mary's room? No. I slowly began driving forward, gazing at both sides of the road, and when I reached the first turn, I pondered again for a moment. Was the one who smoked pipe tobacco the girl that died in Mary's room? No. Moving forward, I could barely make out the hanging tree. It was all but swallowed up by the night sky. Now, alongside the tree, I stopped. Was the one who'd been seen hanging in this tree by many people the girl who died in Mary's room? No.

Neither the car nor I hesitated when leaving and had no trouble maneuvering the turn onto Wagner Hill Road. The entire trip home, I asked myself question after question but was unable to answer them adequately. Initially, during the first visit, Alex said there was a mass murder at the house. Seven victims, yet only six descriptions were given and the sixth was that of an old woman who had died recently. That ruled her out and left us with only five descriptions. An old woman *had* died shortly before his first visit. A McMahon family member had died. She had been driven up to take a look at the old homestead shortly before her death and just after the first story had appeared in the Olean Times Herald. As Father explained, psychics are not infallible, they can often make the wrong interpretations. During this visit, we were told of one death in the house, a girl in Mary's room. I honestly felt something was keeping Alex's psyche from tuning in, or possibly, he had misinterpreted today's impressions. I believe in my heart of hearts, he wanted to discuss this but who the hell was I to question a world renowned psychic?

It was just extremely odd that during his first visit, Alex's descriptions of the apparitions he'd received impressions of were what had truly been seen at the house during the months prior to that visit and this visit he only picked up one. I honestly believed the force, the energy in Mary's room *was* the heart of the house and deliberately deceived Alex during this visit.

I stopped at Crosby's on the way home and recognized one of the vehicles the crew had driven to the Dandy house parked out front. Approaching, I saw Jan and Steve inside. After what Mike had said, I thought maybe I should turn around, get it my car and leave. "Nonsense." I said, and walked to the entrance.

"Hey, look who's here!" Steve said.

"Hi, guys, having a late night snack?" I asked.

"Hi, Paul, yeah, we were chosen to come out and get everyone in the crew something for dessert. What do you recommend?" She asked, with just enough lilt in her voice which made me think she was being flirtatious.

"Everything's good here, I'm a sucker for their milkshakes." I said.

"Really, that's what I usually have but sometimes I'll get a rocky road cone," Jan said.

"Banana split for me," Steve said. "Jan, give me the list and I'll put the order in, what do you want?" He then asked..

"Oh, I guess a chocolate shake, with vanilla ice cream…um, medium will be good."

Turning back toward me, Jan said, "So, if you don't have anything to do, why not drop by and visit the crew. I'm sure they'd all love to hear more details about what you and your friends have experienced."

"I already promised my wife I'd be home soon but it's awfully nice of you to ask," I said, sort of nervously.

"Oh, I didn't notice, sorry. Um— well, okay… We'll get a chance to go over more stories tomorrow during the interviews, right?" She stuttered.

"Yeah, we'll have time to talk tomorrow. Enjoy your shake, I'm sure you'll find it quite refreshing, and really, thanks for the invite," I said.

"Yeah, see you tomorrow then," she said walking to the counter to join Steve.

I was very embarrassed and it was an awkward moment but flattering as well. I was sure it was an innocent invitation but I don't believe I would have accepted even if I hadn't called home. I stood behind Steve and Jan when Steve asked, "Why not stop by, everyone's going to be awake for a while."

"Thanks, but I already told Jan I was expected at home," I said.

"Ah, the little missus, eh?" He asked.

"Yeah, we just had our first kid in January, things get kinda hectic," I said.

"My girl and I have talked about getting married as soon as I get my masters. I'm not sure I want to tie the knot that soon after graduating but I've already got a good job lined up, so it's not like we'd be struggling right off the bat," Steve explained.

"I'm still thinking of going to Mansfield College to major in music but it's a little tougher going back *after* you're married. We'll see; ya never know," I said.

"Okay, and that should be it." The clerk said to Steve, handing him his last item of their order. I gave her my order as Steve and Jan walked to the cashier to pay their bill.

"Hey, see you tomorrow, right?" Steve asked, cheerfully.

"Yeah, I'll be up around noon or so. Have a good night, guys," I said.

"G'nite, Paul," Jan said, smiling, and walked out the door after Steve.

I paid for my order and drove home. It might have been fun to sit around with the crew and talk about some of the experiences Tim and I had at the house, but we would probably have time to do that tomorrow.

The exorcism tonight had me a bit confused. I'd read extensively about the Roman Ritual and found it very interesting. In some cases, the exorcist had been injured and mental fatigue had been mentioned in nearly every instance. There was one case involving several priests where one had died after suffering a massive heart attack. Of the 10 or so cases I'd read, all involved possession of a person and no case cited exorcising spirits from a location. In my search for paranormal information, I still hadn't found a complete copy of the Roman ritual. I wanted it to help me understand how the ritual was performed and the connection between it, and say, a psychologist's treatment of the subject. Or maybe just to understand if the ritual was performed using techniques a psychologist might practice and vice versa.

I couldn't believe how closely I had become involved with the house. I'd never have thought I' be sitting with a world-renowned psychic and an extraordinary priest such as Father Alphonsus, discussing exorcism. I should have been topping someone's sundae with nuts, instead, I was beginning to think I *was* nuts.

I arrived home about 9:50. Debbie pulled the curtain of the living room window back after I shut the car door. She met me at the door with a kiss and a promise. 'Oh, oh.' I thought.

"Don't you want to hear about what happened?" I asked.

"You can tell me later," She replied, reaching for the buttons on my shirt.

Chapter XXXIX

It was nearly midnight when I retrieved our ice cream from the freezer and I realized I still had my ice cream from this morning. Debbie grabbed a pillow from the couch, settled in with her banana split and was ready to listen to my recounting of the night's events.

"How's your split?" I asked?"

"They didn't put many nuts on mine. Do we have any in the cupboard?" She asked.

"I think we do, lemme check," I said, getting up and going to the kitchen. "Yup, and they haven't even been opened yet," I told her, taking a spoon from the drawer.

"You can blame me for that, I didn't tell her extra nuts," I explained, handing her the spoon, while I opened the can of nuts.

"That's okay, I wasn't expecting it but it would have been just as yummy without extra nuts on it. Since we have some, I might as well indulge," she said. She looked at me. "What happened?"

"Father performed the exorcism and we all came home," I replied.

She reached over and smacked me as I took a sip of milkshake, nearly shoving the straw through the roof of my mouth.

"Hey!" I exclaimed.

"Well, don't be a smartass! Was it scary?" She asked.

"I don't know if scary is the word to describe it; intense maybe. There really isn't that much to tell. Alex and Father explained all they had done this afternoon, and shortly after, the family gathered together in the living room. That's when Father performed the exorcism. Tomorrow we return for interviews to tell of what experiences we've had while at the house."

"Anything strange happen after you returned?" Debbie asked.

"Well, during the explanations, Alex asked if anyone had any questions or wanted to add anything. He asked me specifically, but I told him, and quite nervously, no there was nothing I wanted to say. Just before Father began to perform the rite, the birds became completely silent but suddenly went nuts in their cages when he starting praying. There were wails and what sounded like muffled screams coming from..... I don't know where—from the entire house. You couldn't actually pinpoint a specific location. Two crew members and I were in the kitchen, sitting near in the doorway to the living room when the sounds began. We also heard noise coming from the upstairs. It sounded as though it were coming *downstairs* and we heard something in the bathroom too," I explained.

"Did you feel anything like you did been?" She asked.

"Anything that was substantial was just before the exorcism but much stronger during. The feeling was very similar but it didn't have the pizzazz it usually does. Meaning it didn't hit me like a semi. Oh, after the discussion, we broke into basically two groups, 'cause there wasn't enough room for everyone in one room. Alex had been in the kitchen and when I went to use the bathroom, I had a feeling he wanted to say something. On my way back to the living room, I asked if I had said something that upset him. He said it was something I *hadn't* said and then thanked me for not pushing the issue," I explained.

I thought again. What, exactly, had he meant? Then I continued with, "I think by, 'pushing the issue,' he meant, talking about the energies I had felt and wanting them to be explained more clearly. I believe his thoughts were that if we got into a long discussion, it might leave doubts about the success of the exorcism," I said.

"What do you mean success?" Debbie asked.

"Remember, when Alex first visited, he said there was a mass murder; 7 people had been killed? Well this time, there was only one entity he received impressions from: a girl who had died in Mary's room. Supposedly, she had been in the room for some time before passing on and he said she had been distraught because the man she was to marry had drowned. Alex received a small burn on his back while in the room

492

during the afternoon's session and blamed it on the entity in Mary's room. When the...."

"What has that got to do with how successful the exorcism would be?" Debbie interrupted.

"Alex said there was an energy that was somehow blocking the energy he felt from the girl. When he and Father were explaining how signals were picked up from the spirit world, they said they sometimes cross one another and that if one signal was stronger than another it would cover it. I believe the energy that burned Alex was not the girl but came from the same source that has been snapping my mind in half when I get my 'heat waves.'"

"Well, wouldn't he know that? He's been doing this for years, hon." Debbie asked.

"Yeah, but Father also explained to me weeks ago that an evil or demonic source will lie and do anything it can to persuade you to believe what it wants. I feel very strongly that the communication Alex had with this girl was being manipulated by the stronger energy; the evil energy."

"You don't think it's over, that the house is clear of whatever has taken control? Also, Alex could be entirely wrong this time and not the first time. He saw 7 spirits or whatever the first time. Wasn't that how many who were seen by so people before he came the *first* time? She asked.

I sat thinking of everything that had been explained in the afternoon, of how Alex looked after the exorcism, of all the different apparitions, voices, sightings, and other countless reports of paranormal activity by family, friends and total strangers. My answer to Debbie's question was, "Yes, there were at least 7 separate apparitions seen."

"Maybe Alex and Father only took the brute out and gave it a good thrashing, but as soon as it gathers enough energy from whatever the hell source is available, it will begin all over again. No, I think if anything, the evil will lick its wounds only to come back for another round. The heart of the house was just that, the heart, and I believed it had control of all the energies in the house."

Debbie didn't say anything for some time. She sat with a concerned look on her face as if she were waiting for dreaded news to come at any moment.

"Did you say anything to Alex or Father about your feelings, *anything*?" Debbie asked.

"No, Debbie, how could I? It would be like going to the president of the United States and telling him that every decision he's made was wrong. There's no way I could say something that would dismiss what Alex says," I said.

"But, if you just gave your opinion. If you at least told him what you felt I believe he'd listen, if just for the safety of the family," she said.

"Well, I can't say anything to Alex, there's no way I could basically tell him I think he's wrong about anything he had said," I said. "But, something is out of whack. I could talk to Father and see what he thinks. But I believe he would rationalize my feelings somehow with my experience. He'd attribute it to the fact that I picked up signals randomly at the house," I said.

"Yeah, but I think Father would consider how much more time you, Tim, and the family spent at the house. That's maybe enough to show you have a deeper understanding of what's really happening," Debbie replied.

"Understanding?! Honey, I don't understand a *thing* that's gone on up there! So I'm sensitive to one particular entity and maybe others as well but that doesn't mean a damned thing. Damn, I honestly wish I'd never gone to that goddamned house. Everyone is going to be happy as a lark—for a while, only to realize it's going to come back to haunt them," I said.

About 10 seconds later a bit of levity lightened the conversation when we both realized what I had said at the end of my reply.

"You know, you really are making some pretty bold statements, right or wrong. And I'm not saying you're wrong, I'm only saying Alex and Father have been involved with this stuff longer than you've been alive. If you...."

I interrupted, "Exactly! That's my entire point; how the hell could I tell someone with their reputations and experience, they're wrong, just because I think something different. There are times when you need to know when to shut the heck up, but then if you find later than you were right about your assumptions, you feel like crap. I'll tell Clara what I think when I see her tomorrow but I won't say anything to Alex or Father Al. There's no point now. Maybe I should have said something when he asked if anyone had anything to add but, again, it's not going to change what he felt. Christ, he might feel exactly as I do but is trusting his experience in the matter to have faith that he has cleansed the house. The bright side is this, if I am 100% wrong with my assumptions, the house is once again going to be a quiet home in the county, Clara doing her gardening, Phil driving back and forth to work and the kids playing in their *own* rooms without a care in the world. I believe that's how I want to see this nightmare end. It's not going to end that way; I know that, yet I have no one I felt I could convince. When I heard the words, 'I need you to help me,' it was the cry of someone who truly needed help and they were *not* words conjured by my imagination, not that anyone ever said it was," I said.

"If you want my honest opinion, you should just see what happens over a short period of time and go from there. If you're concerned about the success of the exorcism, you might as well stop because it's totally out of your hands. I believe you're all correct in some way regarding what has happened at their house and I have no doubt in what you say. You've proven to me, and especially to yourself, that what Alex and Father told you about being gifted is a fact. There is no way in hell anyone who *didn't* have some sort of psychic gift could have known what Bernie was thinking or feeling when you met him, not to mention all the other feelings you've had. Those aren't normal things that happen between people unless there is something special about their, what do you call it, psyche?" Debbie said.

"Yeah, psyche, but I'm not looking to prove anything, I'd just like to see Clara and the kids free of not only anything that's evil in the house, but *everything* that's unnatural. As I said before when we first started going to the house, Tim and I or anyone else could walk away and be done with it, but that's not the case anymore, not for me. And let's completely forget about the problems of the house for a second. Why was I able to understand Bernie's concern over his son's health problem? What really and truly has no logical sense is: how did I see that he had trouble with words or receive a mental picture of 'black rings,' only to learn that he broke his wrist while doing gymnastics on the rings? Come on, help me understand all of this!" I exclaimed, agitated.

"Okay, okay, it's all right. Didn't you tell me Father said something about once your psyche, I hate that word, was opened, it would be open even away from the house and those particular problems. That you don't necessarily have to be dealing with ghosts to receive feelings?" Debbie asked.

"He said something like that, but what, I get involved in a haunted house and suddenly I become a psychic? I just want to say bullshit to that explanation, but I'm tired of trying to understand what's happened to me and that seems to be the only answer anyone can offer," I said.

I felt like a lost little kid, wandering the woods as it was beginning to get dark; I didn't know in which direction to turn to find safety. Father told me it wasn't my position to ask, "why me,' but that surely didn't help to assess or understand either my conscious or subconscious. My thinking processes were totally altered in every day life experiences by this new connection between *their* world and ours. I mean, was I really to believe that my psyche was suddenly "awakened" simply because I visited a haunted house? I needed proof, scientific proof, to convince me that this was a logical possibility. Many year later, many, I was enlightened in a clear, concise conversation with a man who was more involved with the Dandy house than anyone ever had been in the past. His credentials are impeccable, his knowledge of the paranormal, both from the psychic view as well as the scientific, far more than impressive. His name, Dr. Michael Rambacher, who, in all the years of my talks with those in psychic circles, left me feeling with the same admiration and unblemished respect as I had for Father Alphonsus Trabold. Father had also been a very dear friend of Mike's. Mike's knowledge and understanding in the fields of the paranormal as well as science, is mind boggling. His clarification to my "why" questions were answered with clarity, although he did drive the ball a little over my head a time or two. His explanations weren't just opinion, or only those that been derived from similar psychic accounts, but oftentimes were backed up by science. I wish I had known Mike in '73; things would have been a lot easier to swallow.

After our talk, Debbie told me Clara called and said they moved the time for meeting tomorrow to 2 p.m..

"I wonder why they changed the time to 2 tomorrow, it's odd that Clara would call to tell me they moved it up one hour. Are you sure you don't want to go tomorrow? I'd really like you to be there," I asked.

"She said Father Al had some business to take care of at the University. I would like to go if I didn't have to work in the morning," She asked.

"Yeah, but I wouldn't imagine it would be very late. Guess what? The only girl of the group was kinda flirty," I said.

"Flirty? And were you *flirty* back?" She asked.

"What do you think? She—her name's Jan, and one of the guys from the crew, asked me to stop by and explain some of the things that we saw at the house. I told them, *Jan*, that my *wife* was expecting me home, and that's where I am, with my wife. That word still gets me, wife, ha-ha, you're my *wife*; I like it," I said.

"You're a very strange person," she said, going into the kitchen. "You want a glass of milk?" She asked.

"Sure, please," I said.

"Big, small or your Brave's cup full?"

"Small is fine," I answered. "What time does Joe eat again?" I asked.

"About another half hour," She said, handing me the glass. "I'll feed him, 'k?"

"Sure, that's fine, and Happy birthday again!" She said, with a kiss.

"Thank you very much! Does my mom know I'm going to the house tomorrow?" I asked.

"Yeah, but don't get mad that I told her. I figured she wasn't going to stress about you going," Debbie replied.

"Why do you say that?" I asked.

"We talked for about half an hour and she understands you're nosy and crazy. She figures no matter what she tells you, you're going to go anyhow," She said.

"No really, what did she say?" I asked again.

"Really, that's what she said. So, I am supposed to give you your parent's birthday present to you tonight," she said, going into the bedroom.

"Awww, no, not now! We can take it back to their house in the morning and they can give it to me!" I whined.

"They're going somewhere in the morning and they knew you were gonna be gone most of the day, so your dad brought it over and I'm supposed to give it to you," she explained, from the bedroom, while making a terrible racket.

"Aw, shit, that's not right!" I said, whining still. "What the hell are you doing in there?" I asked.

"Oh, damn, you just get your ass in here and look at their gift, I can't bring them all out," she said, grunting.

"Bring them *all* out?—what the hell are…" I stopped asking as I walked into the bedroom, and stopped in my tracks when I seen what all the noise was. My parents had gotten me new hard shell cases for all of my drums. "Holy shit!" I exclaimed. "These things aren't cheap!"

"Well, your dad asked what you needed and the only thing I could think was how you complained that your vinyl cases were tearing and the zippers weren't zipping anymore. Actually, I went in with them so I could help with the cost. But there's more; look under the bed!" She exclaimed.

I got on my knees and pulled the bedspread out of the way. There were two flat boxes which I pulled out and saw something I've wanted for the past few months; new cymbals.

"Are these all Zillians?!" I asked.

"Your dad said they're the brand you prefer. I kinda thought that too, 'cause I looked at the cymbals you have now. That was the phone call I got last night. George called to tell me he'd bring them over when I called to tell him the coast was clear. Isn't the name of the cymbals pronounced, Zil-gen?" Debbie asked, pronouncing both syllables.

"Yeah, but not in mine and George's world. Awww, you guys are the greatest! Well, I've got new covers and new cymbals, I'll have to get new drums now!" I said.

"Ohhhhhhhh no, you just bought that set less than a year ago. And these are not covers, they're *cases*. Those nasty old vinyl things are covers," she said.

"Come here, you smart ass!" I said.

"What? You gonna try and talk me into letting you have new drums, not on your life," she said.

"No, I want to thank you, that's all," I said.

"You can thank me after you feed your son, how's that?" She said.

"I already thanked you … well, that way …..is that what you meant?" I asked.

"It never hurts to thank someone twice," she said.

"That's easy for you to say!" I exclaimed.

"Oh, no it's not!" She said, scoffing. "Get your son up and I'll get his bottle ready," She said, going to the kitchen.

I fed our son, while Debbie sat on the couch with us, thumbing through one of my many books on the paranormal. The entire time she would say, "what?," or "oh, come on," or "that would be scary; some exclamatory remark"

"What are you finding so interesting that's making you talk to yourself so much?" I finally asked.

"I just don't understand how so many people have the nerve to deal with this stuff. It's gotta be scary as hell according to some of the things I've read in here," she said.

"There's a lot there I can't comprehend and some of it sounds dumber than hell. The mind is a strange thing," I said.

"Huh, yours is, we all know that," she replied, matter of factly.

I finished feeding and burping Joe and changed his diaper. He fell fast asleep while he was draped over my shoulder. Eat and sleep, that's about all he'd been doing, but Dr. Cash says he would for a while. He has continued to gain weight but Dr. Cash thought there was a possibility he may develop bronchitis or asthma as he grew older. But he also said if he did, chances were, he would outgrow it. Another word I had no use for when it was used from a medical standpoint. But, he was growing and his check ups had been good. No sign of his excess body hair and I didn't know whose theory had been right, Dr. Cash's, or Debbie's mom's.

Debbie put the book down and I could see she was nodding off. I put Joe back in his crib, bundled him up, walked over and tapped Debbie lightly telling her it was time for bed. I told her to go on in and I'd get the lights and door. It was nearly 2 a.m. and instead of a second thank you, we called it a night. I really wished she'd have gone to the house with me in the morning but I totally understood her apprehension as well as her disinterest in the problems of the house. I missed Tim but I didn't talk about him very often after his allegation. It was difficult to accept but I wasn't going to be the one to make the first move in attempts to clear the air. I would have, had he come to me and said something but I guess sometimes you don't know someone as well as you think you do. I wasn't feeling the anticipation I had felt last night, and tomorrow everyone might see things differently. Maybe the house was cleansed. I believed Father Al's contribution to the conversation last evening was his and Alex's way of letting us know that possibly, neither visit offered a definitive resolution to the questions of why there was such an abundance of paranormal activity surrounding the house. What we, as well as others not directly related to the house experienced, was a great deal of activity caused by, in my opinion, more than the residual energy of one dead girl. Several other psychics have had totally different interpretations of the disturbances of the Dandy house. There was more paranormal activity Labor Day, 1973, than any day prior or after. Numerous apparitions were seen at different times, in different locations, by different people. Alex's first impressions of the house were very close to the number of apparitions and incidents that happened on Labor Day. I don't believe the spirit of a dead girl caused the "heat waves" I felt at the house and I don't presume to know what did. But, I do *feel* that the energy that did cause them had something to do with the demise of the girl.

Debbie woke me when she got up to feed Joe. It was almost 4:30. I got up and offered to feed him but instead, she asked if I would sit with her while she fed him; I obliged. We

500

didn't talk really, and I stroked her hair while Joe was drinking his bottle.

"You keep that up and I'll be sleeping in no time," She whispered.

"Go back to bed, let me finish," I said quietly.

"No, he's almost done and then we can all go back to bed," She said, yawning.

She was a very good mom and a wonderful wife. I was an immature drummer who should have been more careful when we were passionate. We weren't together very long before she was expecting. Her mother had been the hardest to convince that everything would be all right. Her father lived in Arizona and had remarried. Debbie and I didn't think of the consequences on the many occasions we were romantic. We made a mistake, but hindsight is always 20/20.

"You ready?" She asked, very sleepily.

"Give him to me, honey, go climb into bed," I said.

I placed Joe back into his crib and asked God to allow his lungs to be healthy and strong so he wouldn't grow up to have respiratory problems. I crawled back into bed with my wife and held her tightly. I didn't get back to sleep until shortly after daybreak.

The clock dial showed 10:05; it was actually 9:55, as Debbie kept the clock 10 minutes fast. I smelled bacon and it smelled wonderful! I climbed out of bed and peeked around the corner to see Debbie at the stove and Joe in his bassinet in the doorway to the kitchen.

"What are you two up to?" I asked.

"Well, I'm making you a birthday breakfast and Joe is making sounds like a small lizard," She said, smiling.

"Lizard?!" I said, walking to the bassinet. "Did you hear that, mommy said you sound like a lizard?" I asked Joe, who offered a big grin in response.

"Sunny side up, scrambled, which?" She asked.

"Wha?" I asked, turning around.

"How do you want your eggs, sunny side up or...."

"Ohhhhhhhh," I interrupted, "however you're going to have yours, hon," I replied.

"Do you want toast, too?" She asked.

501

I nodded. "And I will start it, thank you. Would you like some as well, my dear?" I asked.

"That would be splendid but just one slice, kind sir. I'm watching my figure," She replied, attempting a British accent and doing so quite well.

"I'm watchin' your figyuh too!" I said, attempting a Groucho Marx impersonation.

We played around, acting the kids that we were, attempting several different accents, only to ask each other what we were supposed to be. Of course, when we sat down to eat, I became Frankenstein from the movie, "Bride of Frankenstein." But I played two parts, that of the monster and also the blind villager who took him in. I picked up a piece of toast and said, as the blind man, "This is bread, to eat." And then, I would rip a bite of toast and say, "Bread, GOOD!" and added a little Frankenstein laugh. But the part that always made Debbie laugh hysterically was the next lesson in life the blind man had taught the monster. "This is wine, to drink."

And the monster's response, "Wine, DRINK!" And of course, in the processing of drinking the wine (milk today), most of it would drool down the front of my shirt. Even though she begged, "please don't," I had to finish properly. So, if you happen to bump into me on the street someday and you notice long stains on the front of my shirt, chances are, I've been impersonating Frankenstein.

We finished our breakfast, played with Joe a while until he fell asleep and then Debbie and I gave thanks to one another one more time. After getting dressed, she asked if I would run to the store and grab a Sunday paper. She and her mom were going to go shopping about 3 and she wanted to see what was on sale. If there's a sale sign on something, even if we were never to find a use for it, she was apt to purchase the item. But, 99% of the time, she was a very wise shopper and always found what we needed at the best price. I think that was a trait that rubbed off from her dad.

I got dressed, reluctantly, and walked up to Sturdy's Newsstand at the corners of Sixth and State Streets to buy an Olean Times Herald. It was going to be a nice day.

I was back at the house in just a few minutes and sat reading while Debbie scanned the flyers in the paper. It was a little after 1 p.m., and I decided I was going to go up to the house a little early.

"Call me when you get there and if you can't, teleport me and I'll try and hear you," Debbie said.

"Teleport you?! You want me to send you from one place to another?" I asked, puzzled.

"Send me.... what? What do you mean, *send* me some place?" She asked, equally puzzled.

I burst into laughter, finally catching on to what she was telling me.

"Do you mean mental *telepathy*?" I asked.

"Yeah, what did I say?" She asked.

"You said to teleport you, that's how they travel in Star Trek; using the teleporter."

"Well, ass, you know what I meant. You don't have to laugh about it!" She snapped playfully, hitting and tickling me several times.

"Okay, okay... I'm sorry, stop, stop it, I'm sorry! I'll call when I get there. Have a good day with your mom and don't buy any Buddha statues just because they're on sale!" I said.

"Hey!" She said walking to the door, where I was standing. "Happy birthday, jerk!" She said, kissing me goodbye.

After last night, the one thing that I was going to do as soon as possible, was watch the new movie, "The Exorcist." It was supposedly based on fact and from the reviews and what Father had said about it, it was going to be something that would give me true insight into demonic possession. I'd heard that it was extremely graphic and the few scenes people had told me about sounded very disturbing. I heard that some people became physically ill at the theater and others walked out during the actual exorcism. I would make it a point to see the movie.

I arrived at the house about 1:45. Three of the crew members, including Jan, were already setting up the camera equipment from different angles in the living room.

"Hi, Paul, Conner and Jan said in unison. Steve was unable to speak. He had a cable in each hand as well as one clenched in his teeth; instead he offered a nod.

"Did you sleep well?" Conner asked.

"Yeah, not bad, thanks. I've been thinking about a lot of things since last night. I'm finding it hard to believe this is over," I said.

"What do you mean?" Conner asked.

I wondered if Jan or Steve had said anything about our conversation last evening but I felt confident they were true to their word. I would assume, if they didn't say anything to Alex, they wouldn't say anything to other members of the crew.

"Some days it was pretty bad in and outside the house. I guess after coming every night for so long and seeing so much activity, it's difficult to be certain all of these problems are going to vanish," I explained.

"Hi there," Laura said, Mary and Clara in tow.

"Hi, ladies, how'd everyone sleep? Did you sleep in your room, Mary?" I asked.

"No, I slept with my mom," Mary said, sounding disappointed. "I wanted to wait at least one night to make sure it was gonna be quiet,""She added.

"Clara, how was it?" I asked.

"Well, I'm so used to sleeping lightly, I didn't sleep all that much. The times I did wake, it seemed calm..... I might even throw in peaceful," Clara said.

"Laura, your turn," I said.

"I didn't hear anything, and I guess I slept like I normally do," She said, offering a shy smile.

One of the first signs of certain, impending activity was the actions of the birds, who were chirping their little hearts out. If I may be so bold to say, they sounded as if they were singing more jubilantly, rejoicing in their aviary tongue.

"What's up, Paul?" Mike asked entering the living room, appearing to be wearing a new bandana.

"Hi, Mike. All quiet last night?" I asked.

"Yeah, as far as I know. I zonked out with no trouble; I was beat," he replied.

"Okay, what's with all the, 'how did you sleep' questions?" Clara asked.

"I dunno, I was just wondering if everything was finally quiet around here," I replied.

Clara looked at me for several seconds, then looked at the birds, as if she wasn't hearing their chirps before asking, "Is there something wrong, is there something you feel? And please, say no, because come hell or high water, this is *our* house again!" Clara said with a chuckle.

"No Clara, I feel nothing but happiness thinking the house has been given back."

"Thinking or *knowing*?" She asked.

I wasn't able to respond immediately and thought quickly of how to answer her question. I wanted to tell her my feelings about the exorcism and Alex's gratitude for not "pushing the issue," but simply said, "I can't *know*. I'm not the psychic here, but I meant it as a positive statement. Just thinking the house is yours again does make me happy."

"Okay, you. But if there's something you want to tell me, you'd better not sit on it too long," she replied.

I looked at Jan who was running a cable behind Clara, she looked as though she was expecting me to tell Clara what we talked about last night. Instead, I decided to follow Debbie's suggestion wait a while to see what might happen.

"I won't Clara. If there's something I think I need to say, I promise, I will let you know," I responded.

"Come on in!" Clara shouted toward the kitchen, after a knock at the back door.

The rest of the crew and Alex arrived to carry on with the interviews. I hadn't noticed Randy had been here, as well as Mike N. They, and Mike entered the living room shortly after Alex and his support group.

"It'll be a few more minutes before we're completely ready. If you would sort of back toward the kitchen area and give us a little room, we'll give a shout when everything's good to go," Bill said.

I moved from the end of the couch closest to Beth Ann's room and maneuvered my way through the crowded living room toward the kitchen. As I reached the doorway, Jan tapped me on the shoulder. She gave me a slight nudge toward the kitchen saying, "I need to talk to you."

Entering the kitchen, I said, "What's up?"

"Are you going to say anything regarding your feelings about the exorcism?" She questioned, quite seriously.

"Probably not, not while Alex is here. There isn't much to….."

"Listen," She interrupted, "if I lead Alex into an interview, asking him questions about the house and any particular members of the family or friends that he feels are particularly psychic, I could then go to you. Then you'd be able to explain your experiences and give an explanation of your beliefs about the exorcism. I already have a set…."

It was my turn to interrupt, "Jan, this is almost a mutiny you're asking me to be involved in. If I can talk to Father before we get started, I might get up the nerve…."

"Father's not coming," she said.

"He's not coming, why?" I asked, disappointed; angry.

"I'm not sure but he called Alex this morning and told him he wouldn't be able to attend the interviews," Jan replied.

"You gotta be shittin' me! I hate to admit it but he's my crutch. I can't explain to Alex what I believed about last evening without Father being here for moral support," I said.

"So, then you do want to talk about it?" She asked, excitedly.

"No, Jan, I can't! If I had decided to say anything at all, I would have found a quite place to talk with Alex and Father privately. I know how important this is to you, but please, please don't ask me to disagree with what this family needs right now," I said.

"Jan, we're ready." A voice said from the living room.

"Paul, it would only be an opinion and I don't believe Alex would be upset in any way if you stated your opinion!" She said quickly.

I stood, looking into her eyes, attempting to justify what she was asking of me. Was this for the making of a controversial film regarding exorcism or did she only want the feelings of someone besides an expert who was able to experience extraordinary things? I felt I was damned if I do and damned if I don't. If I do say I didn't believe the exorcism was a success, opinion or not, I felt it would damage the reputation of a very successful psychic. If I said I do believe it was successful, it would be a outright lie, but I'd rather lie than possibly hurt the image of someone so brilliant and successful in his field.

"Jan!" It sounded like Alex this time.

"Yes, coming—be right there," she turned and yelled into the living room.

"Come on, what are you doing?" Bill said entering the kitchen.

"Paul?" Jan questioned.

"Dammit, Jan… play it by ear, you do your thing, and I'll attempt to answer as I see fit," I said.

We walked back into the living room where Mike gave me a sly grin. I looked at him, and embarrassed about what my expression might be, I stuck my tongue out at him. Lord, did I feel foolish but it was involuntary and I had to do something. I knew what he was implying and, of course, he was wrong.

"Everyone, Jan and Steve have several questions, basically general questions that may pertain to all of you. I believe she also has some that she will ask certain individuals based on the talks we had last evening. So, um…. if some of you will take a seat on the floor beside the couch, Alex, if you would sit in this chair, Clara, please, if you would have a seat on the couch with your daughters we'll get started."

When Clara sat down I asked her where Father was; she only offered a shrug.

Jan was first to take the floor. She stood in front of the camera and explained what the documentary would cover and went through the case step by step, finishing with an explanation of those that would be interviewed. Man, I had a sudden urge to get up, run out the back door, and high tail it back to Olean to the safety of my home as quick as possible. Jan began with Alex, who stood to tell the story of his findings which ultimately finished with the explanation of the exorcism. Not only was Alex a world renowned psychic, he was a very eloquent speaker as well. He told the story stemming from his first visit to yesterday's findings and ending with the exorcism. Oddly he didn't mention the impressions he received the first night. He did however, explain what he believed to be the cause of the problems resulting in the haunting of the house. Most of which had a direct connection with the energy in Mary's room. During his explanation, he looked away from the camera several times while putting his thoughts together and looked directly at me when he spoke of the energy in Mary's room. I took that as a sort of request to let sleeping dogs lie.

Jan, who had been standing beside Steve, who was operating the camera, also looked in my direction when Alex had. Lord above, I felt like I was being led to the gallows no matter what I might say.

Next to offer their experiences was Mike and he did a superb job. He began with the experiences of the family long before I met them, talking of the boy who passed through the yard, around the house, and performing a disappearing act. His account of the fallen Battleship game and chess set, as well as many other incidents he had experienced, including those with Tim and me. Mike appeared cool as a cucumber and addressed each and every question as if he were a seasoned debater. "Excellent job," I thought.

I had been sitting Indian style, hands together in my lap. My palms were sweating profusely, waiting for Jan to drop a bomb on me. Why wasn't Father Al here? It was, in my opinion, more imperative that he be here; even more so than Alex, for his explanation of the ancient exorcism rite. I wondered if Father had been assaulted more violently than Alex or with different psychic weapons. It didn't make sense that he hadn't come. He generally came as quickly as possible when the family was in need of his presence and he'd been here last night to pound the last nails into the lid of the house's coffin. What possible reason would he have to stay away today? Nothing could have been more arduous for him than being pitted against the evils of the house, yet why was he not here?

Jan was announcing that it would be my turn to talk. Believe it or not, I was trying everything I could to get the son-of-a-bitch in Mary's room to come out and play! I thought if anything could get me off the hook of what Jan might be preparing me for, that would certainly do the trick. I looked to Clara as Jan was introducing me, and she offered a smile and a nod. The smile I understood, how was I to translate the nod, say what I want? I couldn't help but think Jan was setting me up to dispute Alex's findings and, even though I firmly believed the troubles were only on hold, I couldn't make that statement.

Jan's first question to me was, "How did I become involved with the family?" And as I began to describe how I'd read about the house in the paper and later found that Debbie worked with Clara, one of the lights nearest me that the crew has set up tipped over barely missing me. I jumped out of the way as it fell to the couch behind me.

"Holy shit!" Steve said.

"Are you okay, Paul? Clara asked walking over to my side of the room.

"Yeah, I didn't get hit," I said.

Connor and Bill picked up the light and reset it in the position it was before it fell (was pushed?) over. The light was on a sturdy stand and it was difficult to understand how it fell over. I looked to Alex who returned the look then he turned his gaze to Beth Ann's doorway, exactly where the light had been set up. After they finished, Jan asked three other questions pertaining to what Tim and I had been experienced when we and sometimes Mike were outside in the evenings. They were easily answered, offering a different experience for each question.

"Do you feel you are in touch with the energy of this house?" Was Jan's next question.

"Well, what exactly do you mean when you say, 'in touch'?" I asked.

"Are you able to communicate with the energy, or spirits if you prefer?" She clarified.

"No, Jan, I'm not a medium. I can sometimes sense when something is going to happen. I suppose you can say that I am able to feel the energy of the house but communicate with it, no," I replied.

"Do you believe the exorcism that Father Al performed has solved the problems with the house, that the spirits will be solace and an eternal resting place?" She did put me on the spot, and I was prepared to answer with my sincerest beliefs.

"I believe the energy has met with a great power in Alex and Father Al. I believe if the house is troubled with spirits that are earthbound and Father is a representative of God, who is above us all, living and deceased, then yes, I believe the spirits will be released from this world," I said.

I looked at Alex after answering and he offered a wink. Actually, my answer was what I really believed. I honestly didn't think the energy IN Mary's room was that of a spirit. To this day, I believe the energy was that of a demon and demons are dealt with on a one to one. A simple exorcism performed on the house itself might be sufficient to convince spirits to move on but whatever was upstairs wasn't going anywhere; not just now. It was wounded, not beaten, and incidents will begin to happen once the energy has had time to rejuvenate itself.

Jan went on, continuing to interview Randy, Keith, and Mike N. After, we took a break, while the crew gathered their equipment to film out of doors on the front lawn. After which, we would walk down to the hanging tree. Alex wanted to see what impressions he might receive on different areas of the property. Along the walk down McMahon Road Alex would stop and gaze across the fields and hillside seemingly seeing things the rest of us couldn't. He would occasionally stare at a location for 1–2 minutes, observing—or maybe communicating with his power. Alex was solemn during the quiet times of his investigating and often times appeared saddened or upset with what he may have been experiencing. His laughter was hearty, his eyes, even though deeply set and piercing, were kind. Yet on this walk, he was disturbed. I wanted so badly to ask what was he seeing but we were told prior to leaving the house, not to speak to him unless spoken to. We continued on to the bend in the road when Alex stopped again, looking deep into the psychic energy that is around us all at all times. Every now and then he'd utter a few words that were not intelligible. Words that probably weren't meant for us but comments or statements to those that may have joined us on our journey to the hanging tree. The tone of his voice was that of a considerate and compassionate man. It sounded as though he were expressing sorrow or consolation to those with whom he communicated. When we reached the hanging tree, Alex stood just feet from its base, looked up shaking his head. Moments later, he dropped his head to his chest slowly nodding side to side.

"Such a pretty young girl," he said silently facing the ground.

"What is it, Alex?" Jan asked softly.

"A young girl, pregnant—hanged from this tree but not by those that lived at the house. By others. Horrible, horrible people who lived nearby. Later the husband asked, pleaded for information about his wife, yet no one offered him any hope of finding her," Alex explained.

"What limb did you see a person hanging from, Clara?" Alex asked, head still tilted down.

"Actually, it's not there anymore. Age and weight along with wind and snow have broken it from the tree," Clara said.

Alex looked at the few branches, large and small lying around the ground and pointed to one of the larger ones and said, "It was that one there."

"Yes, that was the one. It wasn't the largest, but it is definitely the one the person was seen hanging from," Clara said.

"There are unmarked graves, two of them; and you will find patches of flowers growing where two souls attempt to rest peacefully. They do not," Alex said.

I was going to walk over to Clara to speak with her when I saw that she was standing on the small rise where one could overlook the area of the hanging tree. She had a very puzzled look on her face, a kind of frightened expression and I didn't want to disturb her thoughts. Mike had noticed it too and glanced at me; I could only offer him a shrug of the shoulders. I heard Alex say the name Claris or Clarissa and found it odd it was a name similar to Clara. What he said next I found strange and frankly, unbelievable. He said if you listen very carefully you will hear the stream calling the name Claris. The film crew continued rolling as we combed the immediate area looking for anything that might be a grave. Alex had walked over to Clara and they were discussing something and it appeared Alex was trying to soothe Clara; she appeared upset. There was nothing that we could identify as a grave close by but maybe later we could spend more time walking through the brush and check the property. As I said before, maybe someone is buried under the floor of the barn that stands very near the tree. There is a lot of vacant land all along McMahon and Wagner Hill Roads and it's possible, almost probable that there are unmarked graves in the area. The history books also tell us there was a massacre of over 1400 Native Americans in the immediate area. A massacre that was carried out in one single evening. It's no wonder there is so much paranormal activity throughout the area above Haskell Flats.

Alex and the crew had a long drive ahead of them and it was decided to return to the house and get packed up for their trip. It had been a very interesting weekend for all. Everyone hoped their efforts at cleansing the house were successful. At that moment, it didn't matter what my beliefs were, what was most important was having faith and helping the family move forward.

Those who took part in the interviews, Alex, the crew and the family spent a bit of time talking and saying goodbye to each other. A few exchanged phone numbers and addresses to keep in touch. It's too bad the only two numbers I received were misplaced or lost over the years.

CHAPTER XXXXI

I continued to visit every so often after that weekend in April of 1974 but not with the frequency I had in 1973. It appeared through the months of May and June of '74 the exorcism had been successful. Tim and Beth Ann had announced their wedding, planned for May. Instead, the ceremony was pushed up to August. Mike left for his tour in the Navy in late June just as he said he would; shortly after graduation. It was cute, no sooner did Mike walk out the door than Laura began carrying her belongings from her bedroom to Mike's. Mary said she was going to move into Beth Ann's room after the wedding. A lot of changes took place those two months but more were soon to come. It was comical watching Laura carrying down an armful of stuff, throwing it into Mike's room and running up the stairs to grab another load. I thought it wasn't very nice of me to watch and decided I'd better help her with anything that was heavy or bulky. When I entered her room I had a very strange sense of dread and immediately attempted to dismiss it to past feelings being so near to Mary's room. The feeling didn't go away and that disturbed me. I wanted to ask Laura something, anything, but she had a smile on her face so I allowed the feeling to fade. I assumed it was my imagination and nothing more. When I returned upstairs to carry the table down for her, I walked into Mary's room. It was sunny and bright but not welcoming. The feeling was like that of hearing a motor revving up very, very slowly. I quickly walked out of the room, grabbed the table and returned downstairs. Laura was standing at the doorway of her new bedroom; she wasn't smiling.

"It's okay. It's not what you think, sweetheart," I said, as I walked to her.

"I wanted Mike's room 'cause it's bigger but I wanted to be downstairs too 'cause I think we're not alone again," She said.

"Did you tell mom you felt something?" I asked. She only shook her head, gazing at the bottom of the stairway.

I honestly thought the activity was going to begin again long before this and possibly it might have; I'd only been up three times since April 14th. I gave Laura a light sweep across her cheek and told her again that it was going to be okay. It wasn't and she knew I didn't believe what I said. I walked into the living room where Clara was and had a seat on the edge of the couch. The birds were chirping and for that, I was glad. Today was Beth Ann's shower and I knew I needed to leave before everyone started arriving. I had to say something to Clara but didn't know how to start. She helped by asking, "Is there something you want to share?"

I turned to look at her and she gave me the Clara, "I know" stare when I said, "It's getting stronger. It won't be long before there's enough energy to start the chain of events that brought Alex here in the first place."

"Well, we're going to continue sprucing up the place and add lots of cheerful colors. We're not going to let it take over again. I won't let it, I just won't let it," She said, becoming upset. "This is our home and come hell or high water, we'll going to keep it," She added.

"I'm sorry, Clara, I really am. I guess whatever this is, it thinks this is its home too. Alex was wrong. He was wrong on this trip, and whether the powers of the house were manipulating his impressions, or he wasn't able to beat it, it doesn't matter; he was wrong," I said.

"I talked to Father last week and told him I had begun to get the uneasy feelings again. He said it might be due to the extended peacefulness we've had and it was possible that I was expecting something to happen, making me feel apprehensive. I know it's not gone and, deep down I think I believed that about a week after they'd left. We have a lot to do. I'm not going to sit idly by and see our home taken from us again. Now with Mike gone and Beth Ann soon to leave, it'll be the girls, Phil and I to deal with another onslaught of BS. Phil, ha! What help is he going to be? I can't do that again, Paul, I just can't," Clara said, her voice breaking.

Clara was deeply distraught and there was really nothing anyone could do. It wasn't that Father's exorcism was a failure, the energy, the forces were just too strong to be pushed out with a single blow.

"What if Father performed the ritual again, would it have a stronger effect?" I asked.

"Paul, we've talked of the exorcism several times and I believe you're misunderstanding something. Father performed a simple exorcism opposed to a full blown exorcism of a demon from a possessed person. The church would not give Father Al permission for a full exorcism because there was no case of a person being possessed. The Roman Ritual itself is to rid a person of a demon and what Father read was a simple prayer of exorcism to help guide any earthbound spirits to their final resting place. You don't need Church permission for a simple exorcism but he would for a full-blown version." Clara said.

"Well, I guess I had misunderstood. The only information I had regarding exorcisms was from the what I'd read in the books I purchased. I guess this is more complex than I had imagined when it came to receiving help. Still, it wouldn't hurt to ask and it's certainly a good idea to contact Alex again and let him know of the situation," I said.

"Oh, I'm sure I will but right now, I have other things that are just a bit more important. People are going to be arriving soon and I still have so much to do," she said.

"Yeah, and I don't want to be around a bunch of giggling and squealing girls. I'll get out of your hair, and please call me if anything happens, okay, please?" I said.

"I will," she said, as I stood waiting for a better confirmation. "I will, I promise! All right, off with you so you don't end up trapped with a roomful of tittering young ladies."

I couldn't leave without giving Clara a hug, something we don only twice during this whole ordeal. I reached for her, but she was reluctant and I knew why. The hug was a support hug, not one of goodbye 'til later or that of simple friendship. It was one that showed sorrow and right now, Clara wasn't ready to have a hug of support against being beaten again. Instead, I gently rubbed her arm.

I walked into the kitchen and could hear Laura obviously setting up her new room as she liked. I walked to the doorway and saw that she was already turned toward the door waiting for me.

"You okay, little one?" I asked.

"I don't like this house—I don't want to live here anymore," she said in a monotone, very soft voice. My heart went out to her and if it was truly capable of breaking, it did at that moment. I knew, I could *feel* what Laura was feeling and she wasn't mentally capable of handling an assault on her psyche again. She looked so fragile as she turned to sit on the bed, her face drawn. An expression of surrender filled her blank eyes as she stared at a stuffed animal lying on the floor. I could somewhat understand earthbound spirits being trapped, having no guiding hand to lead them to eternal peace, but now that I understood the ritual was offered for the more ominous energy, I knew this was *not* delivered to eternal peace. It was only a matter of time before this presence would once again make itself known, and I believed time was short.

I said another goodbye to Beth Ann and Clara as I walked to the back door. Laura had entered the kitchen from the bedroom as I opened the door and said, "Beth Ann is leaving, do you think they want me now?"

I was thankful Clara hadn't heard her and walked in to talk to her.

"Honey, I don't think they want anybody. They're lost and don't know how to find their way to a better place. If something tries to contact you, it's because they aren't sure who else they can reach out to. You'll be fine and if something comes across, tell it you don't know how to help and you're sorry, then go to your mom. I'm as confused as you are, Laura, and I don't really know much about what's going on, only what I've had to deal with. Anytime you want me to come visit, you ask your mom to call me and I'll come up, 'k?" I said.

"Even if it's real late at night?" She asked.

"I don't care what time it is, if you need me to come I will. There probably isn't much I could do, but I'll be here for you, your sister and mom," I said.

"I thought you left?" Clara said, as she entered the kitchen.

"Yeah, I did, but I had to say goodbye to Laura again. Please, if Phil isn't around, call, all right? I really don't mind, Clara," I said.

"I'm sure things are going to be fine," She said with a chuckle. "How many times have I said that in the past?" She added.

"Mike's not here and when Phil's at work and if there's an emergency of any kind, what would you do?" I asked.

"Okay, I'll call, now get so I can finish what I have to do!" She exclaimed.

I gave Laura an assuring pat on the head and walked out the back door. I didn't want to but I had to know for sure, I walked to the center of the back yard and looked to Mary's window—there was no sensation—no feeling. Was it there—a game of hide and wait? Was it residual energy still in the atmosphere of the house or was it still in a phase of recharging, searching for hosts with enough psychic energy to manifest itself into the overpowering, diabolical force it had been prior to the exorcism? I hoped it was our imagination as Father said to Clara, fear feeding our own apprehension. Whatever was going to happen would inevitably happen and there was nothing to do but wait. Until then, I had decided to stay clear of the house unless Clara needed something. I was going to make an appointment to meet with Father. I had to know his beliefs regarding the exorcism; did *he* think it was a success? We would know soon enough.

Clara called me the first week of July and offered some very startling news. Phil had come home and, upon entering their bedroom he froze in his tracks. A book was floating in the air over the chest of drawers as if unseen hands were holding it open. She said he told her it was only a matter of seconds before it slowly returned and settled on top of the chest. Only three months had passed since the evening Father and Alex performed the ritual. It was obvious it wasn't necessary to ask whether it had been successful or not.

A few days later I received another call from Clara, this time it concerned Laura. One of the family's dogs had acted strangely and begun growling at something under Laura's bed. Upon checking, instead of seeing one of their other animals

517

under the bed, she told her mom it looked like a small, furry creature with sharp teeth. When Laura jumped off the bed to leave the room, she said it felt as if something grabbed at her leg. Of course, Laura, instead of interrupting her mother's sleep, cried herself to sleep on the couch. Any other child would have gone screaming, looking for someone's protection but she wasn't like other kids her age and the house had been whittling away at her little by little since the day the problems began. Again, hindsight, if I had totally understood how severely the house affected my sweet young friend, I would have done everything I could to convince Clara and Phil she needed to leave the house permanently. No one knew, no one could have known because Laura was introverted and communicating with her about the house and what she experienced was very difficult. She was a victim of man's inability to fully understand the psychic and psychological effects a haunt such as this could have on a young person of her mental status. Make no mistake, the house was merely taking a nap; building strength and no outside influence was going to interfere.

Over the next few months, the family tried, in earnest, to cope with the same sort of activity which began shortly after moving in.

Tim and Beth Ann were married in August. It was a wonderful affair aside from a few disturbances that was so commonplace when there was a large number of people in the house. Father had called and asked if I felt like a visit. Clara asked if he would stop by and he called to see if I'd like to accompany him. I accepted his invitation with a little hesitation and was relieved to know that he would do the driving. It was late August, I would only visit the family one more time prior to their leaving. Our visit was brief and somewhat comical. Someone interested in purchasing the house drove down from Buffalo and was startled when he observed one of the house's less ominous occupants—A woman in a flowing dress was standing in the front yard but did the usual vanishing act as did the prospective buyer. Even Father, trying to remain serious and concerned, offered his little chuckle as the people quickly left. The Dandys didn't conceal the history of the house. Yet people, some from quite a distance, showed interest in purchasing the property. Either their offers were ridiculously low or they had second thoughts after walking the grounds. Father and I visited for a short spell. The mood was very solemn and the conversation was choppy, attempting to talk about something other than the damned house. It felt strange: Mike in the service, Beth Ann and Tim married and out of the state. Now it was Clara, Phil, Laura and Mary. I only thought of disaster thinking about the four of them alone in the house. Mary had still not gotten over the problems of her room, how it had taken charge, forcing her out for months and there were times when she didn't feel comfortable being in a room alone. Laura, oh dear Laura, here was a victim with no voice. I was aghast when she told me she didn't like the house and didn't want to live there anymore. Laura didn't share emotions very well and knowing, or as I stated before, feeling what she was dealing with was unthinkable. Clara was a fighter and she was a rock during this battle of paranormal activity but she was alone. Phil didn't offer the support she needed and Clara stressed 24/7 about Mary and Laura. I didn't believe she had a fighting chance against the house, and Father and I both agreed that her mental condition would deteriorate swiftly with a second onslaught of energy. Phil and Clara had no options left, they were looking for the light at the end of the tunnel but it wasn't going to shine, not from the location in Hinsdale, N.Y. In late September of 1974, Phil and Clara decided their only option was to file for bankruptcy.

Clara was, and is an animal lover and activist for the cause, and watching, as she adopted out some of her furry family members, was very sad.

It was early October, Phil and Clara sent the girls to Buffalo to stay with Clara's parents until they finished packing. My last visit was two days before they left. I wanted Father to come but he had a previous engagement he couldn't get out of. When I pulled in a new feeling came over me—a feeling of defeat. Of course, it wasn't a "feeling" feeling, but knowing the house was the victor disgusted me in every sense of the word. When I got out of the car I walked directly to the door and opened it. There was going to be no contact initiated by me this time. *Let sleeping dogs lie*—why did this statement come to mind? It was extremely difficult saying goodbye to Clara and I was only able to talk to Mary and Laura on the phone. I'd known the family for just over a year and a half, and no cliché intended, it felt as if I'd known them half my life. It was time for them to leave, Clara was spent and had nothing left. Phil was an emotional wreck but I was sure the drinking had taken more out of him than the house had.

"Not only am I losing a 'house guard,' I'm losing someone I've grown fond of, a part of our extended family," Clara said, eyes filling up, ready to overflow.

I was a such a wimp when it came to goodbyes and just let it go. "I'm gonna miss you so much, Clara. I only wish we could have done more, but what? We had a couple of the best and that didn't work. I'm sorry you're leaving." I said.

A minute or so passed before either of us made the move to hug the other. We both knew it was going to be a long spell before we saw one another again, if ever. When we did finally hug, Phil got up from his chair and joined us by wrapping one arm around Clara, the other around my shoulders. It had to be very difficult for Phil. He had to worry about the family through this whole ordeal and much of the time he was at work, 70 miles away. I believed at that moment it wasn't that Phil didn't offer the support his family needed, he hadn't had the inner strength to deal with what was assaulting the family. There was a loud bang heard from above but not one of us moved; there was no point. Clara was trembling slightly and Phil held her tighter, his hand brushing my shirt. He pulled me tighter to both of them. It was obvious, we were pooling *our* energy together in hopes there would be one last night for them in their home. Clara loosened her grip and we stepped back from one another, no one said a word. I turned to walk toward the kitchen, when Phil called out.

"Paul?" Phil said.

I turned back to answer Phil, not wanting to stay any longer as there was the slightest twinge of another "heat wave,' and in my emotional state there would be little chance of staving it off. I was no one, a friend of the family, someone who only wanted to help in any way I could, yet this monstrous, unseen force was relentless in assaulting my mind.

"Yeah, Phil," I said.

"Thank you for supporting my kids and Clara. If you and Tim weren't here when I was at work I would have been much worse off than I was. This whole goddamn….."

"There's no need to say anything, Phil. I judged you harshly and for that I apologize. I believe if I had a family I was worried about under circumstances as these and always away, I wouldn't have known how to deal with it either. Tim and I didn't do anything, but for what you think we may have done, you're welcome. I have to go—call me when you get settled, please," I said.

I turned and walked toward the back door and felt a very cold pocket of air as I walked past the stairway. "Just let me get out and I won't return," I thought to myself. I opened the door and walked to my car without hesitation or even so much as looking up from the ground. I had no intention of looking at Mary's bedroom window, the pond or at any other area of the property. Backing out, my eyes never left the dash and I used my peripheral vision to watch the road, praying not to see the least bit of movement from the corners of my eyes. The oddest feeling came over me, I expected to SEE the energy of Mary's room because I was sure it knew I wouldn't be returning. I saw nothing. I backed into the cutout and shifted into drive before coming to a complete stop, literally grinding the gears. The feeling was passing before I made it to the turn in McMahon road and I believe I had been given a reminder as to who was in charge when the "heat wave" began. I didn't understand but the urge to stop at the hanging tree was overwhelming. I began to slow, and without a thought, I slammed my foot down and turned onto Wagner Hill Road, giving no heed to the stop sign. Once away from McMahon, I drove slowly and cautiously down the winding, washboard road.

Clara and Phil would spend one more night at the house as there was still more packing to do. Hopefully, their last evening would be tolerable and a new life would begin soon. I wanted the chance to say goodbye to Laura and Mary but the decision to leave with their grandparents was best. Phil went to stay with his family in Ohio while Clara and the girls stayed in Buffalo with her parents. I was certain I would see them again once they settled, but the chance never arose before they moved from the area. I only spoke to Clara a few times after they moved to Buffalo. I lost contact with her for many, many years after she moved to California. Long after the family moved, Bob C. continued to write bits and pieces about the house in his column for the Buffalo Evening News. I was saddened, my new friends were gone and the house, masquerading as a quaint, inviting farm house, looming over the Hinsdale countryside, sat waiting for the next occupants.

Epilogue

It has been almost thirty-six years to the month since I walked into the Hinsdale farm house, and met the Dandy family; Clara, Phil, Mike, Beth Ann, Mary and my little psyche connected friend, Laura. There have been several people who took up residence since the Dandys. Most moved out after a short stay without so much as looking back. One of the first places I visited when I returned to New York was McMahon Road and the memories of the 70s came flooding back so vividly it felt like the time I had spent there was nothing more than a dream, a nightmare. Standing at the end of the road, staring at the house, brought forth a feeling that I'd never left.

The house, once with its eye-appealing, bright white exterior, is now a dull, faded, tan. Its siding is rotting as if the energies of past years have eaten away at its very core. It sits waiting for the cumulative energy to offer it renewed life of malevolent chaos. After my solo tour of McMahon Road, the pond and the tree line, I returned to the house to chat up its current residents and ask the questions I had prepared on my cross-country drive from Arizona. In summation; the energies remain, but not with the force or frequency of that experienced during the Dandys' occupancy. The house's energies demand a catalyst of which the current occupants do not possess. Yet, they have experienced minor paranormal disturbances since moving in but are not afraid of the apparitions they've seen. One has been privy to more of the activity than the other and that is understandable. The energy of the house is alive and well, but quiet, until there is enough energy for it to feed from, such as our investigative group, or the tours of the house which had been conducted by Dr. Michael Rambacher the past few summers.

Since 1975, there have been many investigations led by professionals and amateurs alike surrounding the Dandy House. So much has come to surface, old and new, adding more proof to this genuine haunt of the Hinsdale, N.Y. farmhouse. One puzzling new development, very puzzling for myself, which has been experienced by many is that of strange ground lights that appear. They are extremely bright and either fade out slowly or are gone in the blink of an eye. The lights mainly appear on the ground with no apparent source and are totally baffling. We experienced one recently only 15 feet from us at the edge of the road. Two of us ran directly toward it as it began to fade out. There was absolutely no source whatsoever for this strange light and we stood in the exact spot it had appeared. Dr. Rambacher's tours of the house and vicinity, including the hanging tree, have yielded an abundance of startling digital photos, films and Electronic Voice Phenomena recordings.

Two new exciting finds have come to light in recent years, one being that of a Shaman's burial site located directly above the Dandy House and the stage coach Way Station foundation consisting of three rooms. The Way Station is located on a short rise just 30 yards from the hanging tree, which by the way, met its fate in 2007 when it was toppled by high winds in excess of 70 mph. Several fascinating EVPs were recorded near the hanging tree this past year, as well as many others within the vicinity of the house.

Our small group of serious, amateur paranormal investigators will continue to search out the reasons for the activity surrounding this out of the way farmhouse, either until we arrive at a definitive conclusion or are unable to continue due to forces beyond our comprehension.

Let me tell you about the family members. In 1975, Phil and Clara as well as the girls, Laura and Mary moved to San Jose, California. Just five years later, Phil and Clara divorced. Phil remarried; one daughter was realized from this new union. Clara took her maiden name back shortly after the dissolution of their marriage. She worked for the city of Santa Clara until 1990 when it was advised by her doctor that she retire. Clara had been diagnosed with Chronic Fatigue Syndrome. Shortly after taking her disability retirement, she, her brother Gordon and her Mom moved to Oregon.

Mike was married to a lovely lady, Katie and subsequently, they too divorced. Mike now lives close to his mom and grandmother in northern Oregon with his three children. He works for Lab Performance Specialists as a medical equipment repairman.

Mary married in '89 to a man Clara tells me is a gem; his name is George. He and Mary have two boys.

Very sadly, Laura passed away September 1, 1992, leaving her husband and two sons. Perhaps, when I die, I will get to know *her* a little better as I wished I had when she was still with us.

Tim and Beth Ann are still happily married and now live in Virginia. Tim is retired from the Air Force and was the Director of Engineering for Spaceports Systems International. I wonder if he had need for an aluminum cone hat in his position? Beth Ann also kept busy as the Armed Forces Emergency Services Director for Vandenberg Air Force Base. She was also the District Operations Director of the Santa Barbara County Chapter of the Red Cross. Tim and Beth Ann are the proud parents of two children. Tim and I have not spoken since his wedding which saddens me to this day.

Clara's dad passed in 1979 of a pulmonary embolism. Shortly after his passing Clara's mom and brother Gordon joined her in California. You remember Gordon? He was the brother standing vigil at the tree when I pulled into the driveway, August of '73. He moved to Oregon with Clara and their mom and sadly passed away from Myotonic Dystrophy in 1996

Alex mentions his visit to the Dandy house in his book, "Beyond Coincidence." Alex passed in 1990 yet the Alex Tanous Foundation lives on.

I've already mentioned Laura and of all the children, I miss her the most. I've not spoken to Mary since 1974 but occasionally hear great stories when Clara and I communicate. I've talked to Mike a few times since the '70s but wish we could communicate more often. Prior to Clara's published work on the house, "Echoes of a Haunting," in 2000, I hadn't spoke with her since 1976 when I was passing through California. We don't talk as often on the phone as I'd like but we email frequently. She probably gets annoyed as I am slow at responding even if the email is only a forward of something we both find dear to our hearts.

Regarding the rest of the gang you've come to be acquainted with, I'll begin with Randy who still lives in Hinsdale with his wife. I've talked with Randy a few times since returning to Olean and I sometimes get the impression he doesn't want to discuss the past. He, as well as Mike and Clara were interviewed for the production of The Discovery Channel's, *A Haunting,* **"Dark Forest."** Frankly, I was puzzled as to why I hadn't been contacted by Clara prior to the airing of the show. I surely had much to contribute to the story as I believe Tim C. and I spent more time at the house than any other non-family member.

The only information I have about Dave is that he moved from the area and is now an established Christian recording artist. I have no information on Mike N., Mike M. or Jim S. Keith moved to Canada and married into a prominent family. I have attempted to locate Keith by any and all means at my disposal with no positive results. Even with the 'World Wide Web' at one's disposal, it can be very difficult locating people. There is also no clue to what happened to the picture taken at the tree line nor of the documentary filmed on April 14, 1974. The key people who were involved have all passed on, and in the past several weeks I have made an uncountable number of phone calls to NYU and The New York Institute for Psychical Research in hopes of retrieving information about the crew that accompanied Alex. I have made two acquaintances, both grad students who are going to dig through the archives at NYU in their attempts to find something about the house or video. I only have the first names of 4 of the crew members, and I have scheduled a trip to NYU this fall to search alumni records with the help of these two gracious students. It's been like looking for the proverbial needle in a haystack. I feel confident that we will find someone who can shed light on either the location of the documentary or someone who was involved with setting up Alex's return trip. Alex had also done everything he could to locate the film and picture for Clara. If anyone has information regarding someone who was with the crew from NYU during the filming of this documentary, please email me at the address provided.

One of the more difficult entries I have to write about is the passing of Father Al. I was very happy that I was able to sit and talk with him on numerous occasions after returning to New York. We did talk about the house often but the majority of our discussions were of other topics. I was the co-founder of a taxi service in Olean which I am no longer associated with and we served the students of Saint Bonaventure with their transportation needs. I have a large extended family of over 2000 students that I have come to know personally over the past 4 years and Father always thought that was amusing. Oftentimes he would ask how many students names I could remember. His response to my answer would be his wonderful chuckle when I told him I knew more faces than names. "It became that way for me as well my last couple years of teaching," he would tell me. I was only 21 when I met Father and I understood little about the paranormal and only slightly more than little when the family moved out. He offered an abundance of information for me to read and suggested several writings available at the University library. Today, in the year 2009, my comprehension of psychic phenomena is much greater than that of 1974 and much of this understanding was offered by my patient friend Al, but my knowledge only skims the surface of information available. My dearly beloved friend, Father Alphonsus Trabold, passed away April 5, 2005, due to kidney failure. Father Al touched so many lives in his teachings, his compassion toward others, and his unshakable friendship he offered to all that he met. I miss him deeply.

There was a recent rumor circulating that the University had supposedly considered purchasing the house as a paranormal research center. I do not have any further information on this, and it may have been just that, a rumor. I have heard about this possibly transaction from three, what I would consider without hesitation, reliable sources, but I can offer nothing more than the mention of this consideration. Recently, many people have asked if any of the many paranormal television shows had been contacted, asking if they would be interested in doing a study on the house. The answer to that is yes, and hopefully, in the future, there can be a professional ongoing investigation of, not just the house, but the entire area.

Until recently, Dr. Michael Rambacher had offered tours of the house to those who were genuinely interested in hearing and learning of its history, but due to many factors, including time constraints, and the lack of a central meeting place, the tours have been canceled. I and a group of 5 other individuals who have continued with the outside investigations of the area, gathering information by way of EVP, EMF detectors and photography in hopes of tying everything together to form a conclusion of the paranormal activity. It's a time consuming process, and there are nights when our group will be barraged by phenomena from every angle. Other nights, we sit and stare at the darkness that surrounds and engulfs our existence—hearing, seeing or sensing nothing. And if anyone is curious if I have experienced a "heat wave" during these investigations, the answer is yes, once, and I think it scared me more because there was hardly any forewarning of its coming.

From my experiences with the house in the past and the understanding I have of psychic energies today, I must come to this conclusion: Not only are there strong energies apparent at the house, but the entire area, much of the Haskell Flats is affected. Some of them have probably always been present. There is one energy that concerns me, frightens me beyond reason. I dealt with it in 1974 and it waits. It has made its presence known to me twice during visits and investigations since returning to New York. It waits for the correct time, a time when the proper paranormal conditions are perfect for that one assault, one that will make the earlier assaults of the 70s feel like a slap on the back. Am I ready? I've been ready for over 35 years, and what I believe in my heart of hearts is it isn't me that needs answers to why the energy is still very much present, but rather, the energy, possibly a particular energy is hoping I will to be able to answer its questions. At the present, I am writing of my experiences with the house as well as the general area since returning to New York. As mentioned before, the new age of electronics and gadgets used in paranormal research has opened a new way of compiling and understanding information. There has been rumors of the house being sold to a university for paranormal research which I am not at liberty to discuss at this time. Possibly, by the time the writing of my next book is published it will be common knowledge as to the future of the House near Hinsdale.

Thanks to:
The Olean Times Herald
The Buffalo News
Saint Bonaventure University's Friedman Library and Dennis
Frank—archivist

Special thanks to Clara M. Miller for her patience and support.

Lightning Source UK Ltd.
Milton Keynes UK
UKHW010655220420
361997UK00002B/757